Multinomial Probit

The Theory and Its Application to Demand Forecasting

This is a Volume in
ECONOMIC THEORY, ECONOMETRICS, AND MATHEMATICAL ECONOMICS

A series of Monographs and Textbooks

Consulting Editor: KARL SHELL

A complete list of titles in this series appears at the end of this volume.

MULTINOMIAL PROBIT

The Theory and Its Application to Demand Forecasting

Carlos Daganzo
DEPARTMENT OF CIVIL ENGINEERING
UNIVERSITY OF CALIFORNIA
BERKELEY, CALIFORNIA

1979

ACADEMIC PRESS
A Subsidiary of Harcourt Brace Jovanovich, Publishers
New York London Toronto Sydney San Francisco

ACADEMIC PRESS, INC.
111 Fifth Avenue, New York, New York 10003

United Kingdom Edition published by
ACADEMIC PRESS, INC. (LONDON) LTD.
24/28 Oval Road, London NW1 7DX

Library of Congress Cataloging in Publication Data

Daganzo, Carlos F
Multinomial probit.

(Economic theory, econometrics, and mathematical economics)
Bibliography: p.
Includes index.
1. Probits. 2. Econometrics. 3. Demand functions (Economic theory) 4. Choice of transportation--Mathematical models. I. Title.
HB139.D33 338.5'212 79-51674
ISBN 0-12-201150-3

PRINTED IN THE UNITED STATES OF AMERICA

79 80 81 82 9 8 7 6 5 4 3 2 1

To Dana

Contents

Preface

The object of many economic analyses is to find a cause-and-effect relationship between a group of independent variables that describe a situation and a dependent variable that is to be predicted for various situations. The tools of these economic analyses, in particular those required to make statistical inferences from data, are the subject of econometrics.

When the dependent variable is categorical, traditional continuous variable econometric techniques, such as multiple regression, cannot be used. Unfortunately, existing statistical classification techniques, which can handle dependent categorical variables, are not particularly helpful either, because these techniques were not developed with econometric prediction problems in mind. It would thus seem desirable to have counterparts of multiple regression able to handle dependent categorical variables while avoiding some of the shortcomings of classification methods.

Discrete choice models are these counterparts; they have been recently studied and even applied to some forecasting problems, the latter mainly in the transportation field.

About the Book

This book is devoted to what is, perhaps, the most general discrete choice model—the multinominal probit (MNP) model—covering both its theoretical and practical aspects, and relating these to other discrete choice models. The main purpose of the book is to compile in a single publication the state of the art in this branch of econometrics, which in the past few years has seen an explosion of developments. The material in the book should not, however, be regarded as final, since research in this area is still proceeding at a healthy pace (e.g., during the year this book was in production, J. Horowitz has reported further work on confidence intervals, M. Soheily and the author have provided evidence on the concavity properties of trinomial probit models, and several encouraging results on optimal sampling strategies have been derived by S. Cosslett, C. Manski, D. McFadden, and the author).

Since many of these developments still remain unpublished, their dissemination to people not actively involved in research has been slow. In order to overcome this, the book is self-contained and the subject matter is presented at a level requiring only a reasonably good background in basic calculus, probability, and linear algebra. The required specialized results in these disciplines have been summarized in the appendices; these include properties of symmetric matrices and quadratic forms, of the multivariate normal distribution, and of convex and concave functions. To improve readability further, the book contains several numerical examples that illustrate especially difficult and/or important passages. In addition, a serious attempt was made to eliminate repetitious or not largely relevant references from the bibliography, while at the same time providing as large a fraction of published or readily accessible material as possible. Although as a consequence of this policy the bibliography may not be exhaustive, the contents of the book (which were often based on well-known "grapevine" concepts and on "fresh" research results obtained by the author while work on the book proceeded) have been made as comprehensive as possible.

Although designed primarily as a reference book–research monograph, the book may be used for teaching in the following two ways: as a basic source of readings for an advanced seminar in econometrics emphasizing the theoretical aspects of MNP, or as background for an applications course on demand forecasting.

The following subjects could be included in the theoretical seminar: MNP choice probability calculation methods, analysis of estimability and unimodality problems in the calibration of MNP models, shortcut prediction and equilibrium methods, and statistical aspects of predicting with MNP models. Of course, the material in the book could be complemented with selected readings from the reference list. In this mode of operation, the book was successfully class tested by the author in the fall of 1978 at the University of California, Berkeley, with a course entitled Advanced Topics in Transportation Theory. The students were Ph.D. candidates from the departments of civil engineering, economics, industrial engineering and operations research, and mathematics.

If on the other hand the book is used as background for a course on demand forecasting, less emphasis should be put on reading and more on "hands-on" learning with one of the available MNP calibration–prediction computer programs. Ideally, such a course would include a laboratory section in which the students would perform the essential tasks of a real-life prediction, starting by specifying a MNP model, designing an appropriate questionnaire, gathering some data, calibrating the MNP model, and finally carrying out the prediction. A three-week intensive course along these lines was devised and taught fairly successfully by the author at the Universidad del los Andes (Mérida, Venezuela) in the summer of 1978. The course was taken by about thirty postgraduate transportation engineering students from several South and Central American countries. The size of the class made it possible to gather a realistic data set with very little effort, which illustrated very well how discrete choice models can be used in developing countries, where data are often lacking.

Acknowledgments

Several individuals and institutions have at one point or another helped me either with the research leading to the preparation of this book or in the preparation of the book itself. To all I extend my sincere gratitude.

Professor Yosef Sheffi of the Massachusetts Institute of Technology, my former student and closest research associate, gave me many comments on the draft of the book and, at an earlier stage, joined me on several research efforts related to MNP. Dr. Fernando Bouthelier, also at the Massachusetts Institute of Technology, has cooperated with me on MNP research as well. His work culminated in a Ph.D. thesis that contains the first computer calibration code that uses Clark's approximation formulas. Subsequently, Mr. Larry Schoenfeld modified this computer code; this led to CHOMP, the research-oriented choice modeling program mentioned in the text. The students of my Advanced Topics in Transportation Theory seminar had to put up with a first draft, which included many mistakes and several handwritten portions. Ms. Mahboubeh Soheily, Mr. Jürg Sparmann, and Mr. Louis Feldman were particularly helpful in identifying errors. Ms. Bonnie Berch and Ms. Phyllis DeFabio, with much patience and even more expertise, typed the manuscript from my almost unintelligible draft and the ensuing, seemingly never-ending corrections. Although several of the above-mentioned individuals have read the text and identified many errors, both large and small, sole responsibility for the remaining mistakes is mine. In particular, I should like to apologize to any authors whose work I may have overlooked.

I also wish to thank the National Science Foundation and the University of California, Berkeley, for providing the financial support and pleasant environment that enabled me to conduct much of the research on which this book is based.

On a different level, but not less emphatically, I thank my parents, Francisco and Isabel, for showing me the importance of learning and for their many sacrifices which sent me through school in my native Spain. Last, but not less intensely, I thank the four women in my life—my wife, Valery, and my daughters, Jenifer, Dana, and Sally—for their love, patience, and understanding.

Chapter 1 An Introduction to Disaggregate Demand Modeling in the Transportation Field

Many different approaches have been used in the transportation field to forecast the usage of a transportation facility or service. In the early days, the techniques were very rudimentary since they were developed by practitioners with a very specific application or problem in mind. An example of such a stage is provided by the simple curve-fitting attempts to model route diversion [see Beilner and Jacobs (1972), for a review]. This stage was followed by another in which transportation engineers and planners borrowed techniques from econometrics and applied them methodically to a variety of problems. Trip-generation regression studies [McCarthy (1969); U.S. Dept. of Transportation (1975)] and application of discriminant analysis to modal split [Beesley (1965); Quarmby (1967)] are examples of the activity of this second stage. As researchers looked for more efficient and reliable ways of predicting how transportation facilities and services are used, it became clear to them that some of the "off-the-shelf" techniques could be improved and new econometric techniques began to emerge. The multinomial logit (MNL) model is, perhaps, the most noticeable such technique. It has been popularized by econometricians and researchers with interest in transportation problems [see, for example, Theil (1969); Rassam *et al.* (1971); McFadden, (1973, 1974)] and has been used in many transportation studies. This book continues the trend and presents a technique, multinomial probit (MNP), which, although developed by transportation-oriented econometricians, engineers, and applied mathematicians, may eventually outgrow the application area in which it originated.

1.1 Demand Forecasting

The objective of transportation demand forecasting[1] is to relate, by means of a mathematical function (called a *demand function*), the amount of traffic on a transportation facility (henceforth called the *usage*) to the characteristics of a population of potential users and the transportation system so that when any of these characteristics is changed, one can predict the change in usage.[2] The characteristics of the population (age, income, population size, etc.) and the transportation system (travel time, cost, etc.) will be called *attributes of the system* or, simply, *attributes* in this book. The attributes of the transportation system will sometimes be referred to as *level-of-service* attributes and the characteristics of the population as *socioeconomic* attributes. It should be noted that these attributes will, in general, vary from individual to individual, and, therefore, their relative frequencies of appearance for individuals sampled at random from the population may be described by probability density functions. To derive a demand function, one specifies, on a priori grounds, a family of functions that relate usage to the distribution of the attributes across the population depending on the value of some unknown parameters. This process is called *specification* and is perhaps the most crucial step in carrying out a forecast.

If we have r unknown parameters $\theta_1, \ldots, \theta_r$, and we denote by $F(a_1, a_2, \ldots, a_s)$ the joint probability density function of the s attributes $A_1, \ldots, A_s$ that appear in the specification of the problem, the demand function could be written as a set function[3]:

$$y = D(\theta_1, \theta_2, \ldots, \theta_r, \mathscr{F}), \tag{1.1}$$

where y is the predicted usage of the facility and $\mathscr{F}$ is a set containing the values of $F(\mathbf{a})$ for each and every value of the attribute vector, $\mathbf{a} = (a_1, \ldots, a_s)$.

In many instances, one specifies that only certain aspects of $F(\mathbf{a})$ (such as the mean values of the attributes) influence the value of y. For instance, to study the number of persons who travel yearly by highway between towns 1 and 2, one can use a "gravity model" with an exponential decay function of travel time:

$$y = \theta_1 a_1 a_2 \exp(-\theta_2 a_3), \tag{1.2}$$

[1] The terms "forecasting" and "prediction" will be used interchangeably throughout this book.

[2] Note that this definition is a generalization of the economic concept of a demand function that relates usage to price. In our case usage may be related to price, but also to other characteristics.

[3] In most cases throughout this book, and as is customary in the probability literature, random variables are denoted by capital letters and the values they take by lower-case letters. We sometimes depart from this rule, as with variables that are customarily represented as capital letters, but the distinction can always be made from the context.

where a_1 and a_2 are the population sizes of towns 1 and 2, respectively, a_3 is the average driving time between the towns, and θ_1 and θ_2 are some unknown parameters. Note that although attributes A_1 and A_2 are fixed, the driving time A_3 could vary across individuals depending on the specific locations of the origin and destination points within the towns. Because of this, a_3 was defined to represent the *average* driving time. That is, the demand function has been specified in terms of the averages of the relevant attributes across the population. In general, a model that is specified *only* in terms of statistical summaries (means, variances, etc.) of the attributes will be called an *aggregate demand model*, i.e., a demand model that is specified in terms of some aggregate characteristics of the system. *Disaggregate demand models*, or models that do not use attribute averages, are surveyed in the next section.

Once a model has been specified, the parameters $\theta_1, \ldots, \theta_r$ are determined from data by means of a *calibration* process. This is done by selecting the parameter values that best fit the data. The technique used depends on the problem at hand. For example, if the number of yearly highway trips, population sizes, and the average driving time between cities are known for several city pairs, it may be possible to obtain estimates of θ_1 and θ_2 in Eq. (1.2) with nonlinear regression. Disaggregate demand models require special calibration procedures.

Once a model has been calibrated, and before it is used for the forecast, it should be validated. This can be done by verifying the accuracy of the model prediction with a "holdout" subsample (that is, a part of the data set that was not used in the calibration process). In the case of the gravity model, one could set aside a set of city pairs (with known populations, travel time, and number of trip interchanges) and would develop forecasts for each one of the city pairs by entering in Eq. (1.2) after calibration. The forecasts could then be plotted versus the observed number of trip interchanges in a scatter diagram. If the dots on the diagram are closely grouped around a 45° line going through the origin, the model could be considered successfully validated. For well-defined problems, statistical tests can be used to verify a demand model.

If a model does not pass a validation test, a different specification must be tried; in doing this one must be careful because, if in changing the specification, one either intentionally or subconsciously uses the patterns observed in the holdout sample, the holdout sample can no longer be properly used for validation purposes.

The final step in a forecast, *prediction*, consists in exercising the properly calibrated and validated model on scenarios characterized by different distributions of the attributes. These scenarios usually represent the different options open to the decision makers. In the gravity model, for example, prediction questions might be: What is the amount of travel between towns

1 and 2 if the average driving time between them, a_3, were reduced by 20%? Or, what if the population of both towns were to increase by 10%?

Forecasting the amount of traffic on a transportation system (i.e. the usage) is sometimes made difficult by the existence of congestion. Because of congestion, some of the level-of-service attributes of a system (travel time, primarily) depend on the usage of the transportation facility, and these attributes cannot be determined prior to the forecast with the demand function. They should instead be obtained simultaneously by solving a set of equations. If for the gravity-model example one observes that travel time is an increasing function of usage, $a_3 = a_3(y)$, forecasting would involve the simultaneous solution of Eq. (1.2) and $a_3 = a_3(y)$. By analogy with economics, these equations are often called the supply–demand equilibrium equations, or, simply, the *equilibrium equations*. The rest of this chapter contains a more detailed discussion of all of these issues and illustrates how multinomial probit fits into the demand-forecasting field.

1.2 Disaggregate Demand Models

Let us imagine that we have gathered a homogeneous population group (i.e., a group of people or entities with the same attribute vector $\mathbf{A} = \mathbf{a}$) and that by empirical observation it is determined that a fraction p of the people in that group opt for using the transportation facility or service under consideration. If one now repeats the same experiment for all possible population groups (all possible values of $\mathbf{a}$) and records the results, one would have developed an empirical relationship between $\mathbf{a}$ and p,

$$p = P(\boldsymbol{\theta}, \mathbf{a}), \tag{1.3}$$

which will be called the *choice probability function* or, simply, the *choice function*. This terminology is used because p can be interpreted as the probability that a choice maker randomly selected from a population group with attribute vector $\mathbf{a}$ becomes a user of the transportation facility or service under consideration. The shape of the choice probability function is what distinguishes disaggregate demand models from one another.

The particular form of the choice function depends on the nature of the choices. In many cases, users are observed to select from a discrete and finite set of alternatives, i, which are numbered from 1 to I. In such instances, one can specify a choice function for each one of the alternatives, which we denote by $P_i(\boldsymbol{\theta}, \mathbf{a})$, $i = 1, \ldots I$, depending on the alternative under consideration. The subscript i will be omitted when the alternative is unambiguously defined. When the set of alternatives considered in the model spans the range of alternatives opened to the choicemaker, $\sum_{i=1}^{I} P_i(\boldsymbol{\theta}, \mathbf{a}) = 1$, and we say that we have a *discrete choice model.* In such cases the choice functions give, for a given value of **A**, the probability mass function of the set of alternatives.

If the observed choice is a continuous variable X, as would happen if we were trying to investigate the relationship among household income, household size, and the vehicle-miles of travel per year per household (the choice X), the set of choice functions $P_x(\boldsymbol{\theta}, \mathbf{a})$, could be interpreted as a probability density function in x, and standard econometric methods could be used. For instance, if the choice function is such that the expected choice (e.g., the average vehicle-miles by families with attribute vector **a**) is a linear function of $\boldsymbol{\theta}$

$$E(X \mid \mathbf{a}, \boldsymbol{\theta}) = \int_{x=-\infty}^{\infty} x P_x(\boldsymbol{\theta}, \mathbf{a})\, dx = \boldsymbol{\theta}\mathbf{a},$$

we have a linear model that may be fitted by linear regression.

The rest of this book is concerned with discrete choice problems since these are the problems for which special econometric tools have to be developed. Thus, unless otherwise stated, it will be understood that the choice set is discrete and finite.

For a discrete choice model, the total usage of the transportation facility y can be obtained from the choice probability function and the probability density function of the attribute vector $F(\mathbf{a})$. If M is the population size, the total density of choice makers with attribute vector **a** becoming users is

$$P(\boldsymbol{\theta}, \mathbf{a})F(\mathbf{a})M,$$

and the total usage is given by integrating this density over the range of **a**:

$$y = M \int_{a_1} \cdots \int_{a_s} P(\boldsymbol{\theta}, \mathbf{a})F(\mathbf{a})\, d\mathbf{a}. \tag{1.4a}$$

This is the demand function, which can, of course, be written in terms of statistical expectations as

$$y = ME_A[P(\boldsymbol{\theta}, \mathbf{A})], \tag{1.4b}$$

where $E_A(\cdot)$ represents the expectation of the quantity in parenthesis with respect to the distribution of **A**. Note that since $E_A[P(\boldsymbol{\theta}, \mathbf{A})]$ gives the fraction of individuals in the population selecting the alternative under consideration, (y/M), it can be visualized as the probability that an individual sampled at random from the population selects the alternative. Because of this probabilistic interpretation, it will be often written as $P(\boldsymbol{\theta})$.

With continuous choices, it is usually desired to obtain the average choice of the population (e.g., the average vehicle-miles of travel per year by a typical household), which is given by $E_A[E(X \mid \mathbf{A}, \boldsymbol{\theta})]$. In cases where the usage is given by the sum of the average choices of all individuals (as in the case of vehicle-miles), the usage is obtained by multiplying $E_A[E(X \mid \mathbf{A}, \boldsymbol{\theta})]$ by M.

1.2.1 Properties of Disaggregate Demand Models

If the specification of a disaggregate demand model is correct, i.e., if the choice probability function closely reproduces reality, it can be argued that the model captures the ongoing human decision-making mechanisms more accurately than an aggregate model, since it deals with individual decision-making units—or with groups of identical units—rather than with heterogeneous groups. Consequently, a model may be transferred to an entirely different scenario (characterized by a different distribution of the vector of attributes) without recalibration. This would be done by substituting in Eq. (1.4a) or (1.4b) $P(\boldsymbol{\theta}, \mathbf{a})$ and the values of M and $F(\cdot)$ corresponding to the scenario under consideration. It must be borne in mind, however, that this *transferrability property* can only be attained if the choice probability function is properly selected and calibrated, and that, unfortunately, proper validation of the choice probability function is a very difficult task requiring enormous data-gathering efforts. Because of this and because in practical instances the selection of $P(\boldsymbol{\theta}, \mathbf{a})$ is an educated guess, the success rate with disaggregate demand modeling must necessarily vary from analyst to analyst and will probably increase in the future when enough experience is accumulated by researchers and practitioners in the field. In any case, since a properly specified and calibrated choice probability function can be used to forecast the choices of any group of people, disaggregate demand models are ideally suited to study the impact of different transportation systems on different segments of the population.

1.2.2 Disaggregate versus Aggregate Data

It is convenient to differentiate between two types of data that are commonly used in transportation studies. If each observation in our data set consists of a value of the attribute vector $\mathbf{a}$ (representing an individual who has been interviewed), and an observed choice, we say that we have *disaggregate data.* If, on the other hand, the data include only information on groups of people, we call it *aggregate or grouped data.* The data set for the gravity model, which consisted of the average value of $\mathbf{A}$ for each city pair and the number of people from each city pair making the choice under consideration (deciding to travel), is an example of an aggregate data set.

Disaggregate data contain more information than aggregate data and are therefore more valuable for calibration purposes. This can be seen by means of the following illustrative argument: If we want to study the behavior of wealthy people, it is not sufficient to study the average reaction of a town with high average income because even in a very rich town there will be a significant fraction of poor and middle-income people, which will filter the results. Some transportation studies have indicated that much of the dispersion in some attributes, such as income and age, is lost when one uses aggregate data [see, for example, Fleet and Robertson (1968) and McCarthy (1969)]. Since the choice probability function of a disaggregate demand model is perfectly suited for calibration with high-quality disaggregate data (a review of calibration methods for disaggregate demand models is provided in Section 1.4), it is possible to use just a few hundred data points in order to obtain accurate estimates of $\boldsymbol{\theta}$. The *efficiency* with which the information in the data is handled with disaggregate demand models is perhaps their most desirable feature, since it greatly simplifies the data-collection process.

1.2.3 Difficulties with Disaggregate Demand Models

The efficiency and transferrability properties of a disaggregate demand model are partially offset by the result of the estimation process being a choice function and not a demand function. In order to obtain a demand prediction, one must enter with the choice function $P(\boldsymbol{\theta}, \mathbf{a})$ into Eq. (1.4). This poses a twofold problem because it may be difficult to obtain the joint distribution function of the vector of attributes $F(\mathbf{a})$, and it may also be hard to evaluate the integral in Eq. (1.4a).

This book will address some of these problems since, as is shown in Chapter 4, proper use of the multinomial probit model can reduce the difficulties.

Another problem connected with discrete choice problems lies in the specification step, because the choice function cannot be selected arbitrarily. Indeed, for a choice model to be properly specified, the choice function must satisfy

$$0 \leq P_i(\boldsymbol{\theta}, \mathbf{a}) \leq 1, \qquad i = 1, \ldots, I, \tag{1.5a}$$

and

$$\sum_{i=1}^{I} P_i(\boldsymbol{\theta}, \mathbf{a}) = 1 \tag{1.5b}$$

for all the relevant range of $\boldsymbol{\theta}$ and $\mathbf{a}$. This, of course, poses some problems because specifications of $P_i(\boldsymbol{\theta}, \mathbf{a})$ linear in the parameters and the attributes are not feasible. Continuous choice models do not present this problem because with them it is more convenient to work with $E(X \mid \boldsymbol{\theta}\, \mathbf{a})$ directly, and $E(X \mid \boldsymbol{\theta}, \mathbf{a})$ is not as severely restricted as $P_i(\boldsymbol{\theta}, \mathbf{a})$.

In order to obtain reasonable specifications of discrete choice models satisfying Eqs. (1.5), one can introduce the so-called *random utility models* [Manski (1973) has provided an excellent discussion of these models].

Assume that instead of defining the choice function for each alternative, we define a function $V_i(\boldsymbol{\theta}, \mathbf{a})$ that is intended to capture how attractive the alternative is to a choice maker with attribute vector **a**. These functions will be termed in this book the *measured attractiveness* functions[4]; they may take on any finite real values and they need not be related in any way. If it were possible to define these functions perfectly, it would be possible to predict unequivocally the choice of an individual with a known attribute vector. However, since according to observation, users with identical attribute vectors do not always make the same decision, we define for each decision maker in the population a set of unobservable *perceived attractivenesses* U_i upon which choice makers base their decisions.[5] Since the perceived attractiveness vector will obviously vary across the population, even within groups of people with the same attribute vector, it is conveniently modeled as a random variable; we shall denote by $U_i(\boldsymbol{\theta}, \mathbf{a})$ the random variable that would be obtained by sampling from a group of individuals with attribute vector **a**. If the measured attractiveness functions are properly selected, they will tend to be close to the U_is for each individual in the population; of course, a perfect match will never be achieved for large populations. One can then introduce some unobservable *disturbances* $\xi_i(\boldsymbol{\theta}, \mathbf{a})$, or *error terms*, which represent the difference between $U_i(\boldsymbol{\theta}, \mathbf{a})$ and $V_i(\boldsymbol{\theta}, \mathbf{a})$, and should, one hopes, be of small magnitude. These random disturbances can be interpreted as capturing different things, among them, errors in the measurement of the attributes in the data and the contribution of *neglected attributes* [attributes that cannot be observed plus attributes that, although observed, are not included in $V_i(\boldsymbol{\theta}, \mathbf{a})$] toward U_i.

If the distribution of $\xi_i(\boldsymbol{\theta}, \mathbf{a})$ [or that of $U_i(\boldsymbol{\theta}, \mathbf{a})$] is known, it is possible to obtain the choice function by calculating the probability that alternative i is the most attractive:

$$\begin{aligned} P_i(\boldsymbol{\theta}, \mathbf{a}) = \Pr\{ & V_i(\boldsymbol{\theta}, \mathbf{a}) + \xi_i(\boldsymbol{\theta}, \mathbf{a}) > V_j(\boldsymbol{\theta}, \mathbf{a}) \\ & + \xi_j(\boldsymbol{\theta}, \mathbf{a}); \forall j \neq i\}, \qquad i \neq 1, \dots, I. \end{aligned} \tag{1.6}$$

Equation (1.6) is the fundamental equation of *random utility models* and satisfies the requirements of a choice function. Note that $P_i(\boldsymbol{\theta}, \mathbf{a})$ is always between zero and one and that the events in brackets (for $i = 1, \dots, I$)

[4] The term "attractiveness" is used instead of the term "utility," which is commonly used in the literature, to emphasize that $V_i(\boldsymbol{\theta}, \mathbf{a})$ need not meet any specific properties of utility for many demand forecasting (and other) applications. The term "random utility model" will, however, be preserved.

[5] At this point we note that it is always possible to find a vector **U** consistent with a given choice. Although such a vector is, obviously, not unique, it always exists. It is then mathematically sound to assume that each and every individual of the population is associated with a perceived-attractiveness vector consistent with his choice.

are exclusive and mutually exhaustive (we assume in this book that ξ and $\mathbf{U}$ are continuous random variables), and consequently $\sum_{i=1}^{I} P_i(\boldsymbol{\theta}, \mathbf{a}) = 1$. It is thus possible to obtain choice functions by specifying attractiveness functions $V_i(\boldsymbol{\theta}, \mathbf{a})$ and a joint distribution for the error terms $\xi_i(\boldsymbol{\theta}, \mathbf{a})$.

The reader may wonder at this point whether this attractiveness framework greatly restricts the form of the choice function. This can be answered by stating that any set of choice functions $P_i(\boldsymbol{\theta}, \mathbf{a}) \neq 0$ satisfying Eqs. (1.5) can be visualized as arising from a random utility model with

$$V_i(\boldsymbol{\theta}, \mathbf{a}) = \log P_i(\boldsymbol{\theta}, \mathbf{a}), \qquad i = 1, \ldots, I,$$

and independent, identically distributed error terms with a cumulative distribution function that is independent of $\boldsymbol{\theta}$ and $\mathbf{a}$, and is given by

$$\Pr\{\xi(\boldsymbol{\theta}, \mathbf{a}) \leq x\} = \exp[-e^{-(x+0.577)}], \qquad -\infty < x < \infty.$$

The reader can verify this statement when the *logit* model in the next section is presented. The next section introduces some of the random utility models that have been proposed and discusses their properties.

1.3 Random Utility Model Forms

The functional form of a random utility model depends on the distribution of the error term vector $\boldsymbol{\xi}(\boldsymbol{\theta}, \mathbf{a})$. In order to present different models in a coherent way, the less general models will be presented first, and then they will be gradually generalized.

1.3.1 Models with Independent Identically Distributed Error Terms

The first model of this type that comes to mind is one in which the error terms are all equal to zero. Such a model [called the *rational* model by Manheim (1979)] can be useful in instances where the variability of ξ is small compared to the differences in V_i across alternatives for the vast majority of the population. Route choice has been traditionally modeled in this way with measured attractiveness given by the negative of the travel time. One problem with the rational model is that if the specification of V_i in terms of $\boldsymbol{\theta}$ and $\mathbf{a}$ is incorrect, the prediction errors may be sizable. In addition, and even if the specification is very good, if $\mathbf{a}$ does not vary much, most of the population will be assigned to the same alternative and a small change in the attributes of one of the alternatives (e.g., travel time on one route) could result in a major shift in the predicted number of people selecting each one of the alternatives. This instability phenomenon has been observed in route-choice models but not in route-choice data. Models without error terms should therefore be used very carefully and with strong a priori grounds.

If instead of zero error terms we model $\xi(\boldsymbol{\theta}, \mathbf{a})$ by a set of independent identically distributed Gumbel variates, with zero mean and independent of $\boldsymbol{\theta}$ and $\mathbf{a}$,

$$\Pr\{\xi(\boldsymbol{\theta}, \mathbf{a}) \leq x\} = \exp[-e^{-(x+\gamma)}], \qquad -\infty < x < \infty \tag{1.7a}$$

(in this expression γ is Euler's constant, $\gamma \approx 0.577$), it is not difficult to show that Eq. (1.6) reduces to the *multinomial logit* formula

$$P_i(\boldsymbol{\theta}, \mathbf{a}) = \exp[V_i(\boldsymbol{\theta}, \mathbf{a})] \Big/ \sum_{j=1}^{I} \exp[V_j(\boldsymbol{\theta}, \mathbf{a})]. \tag{1.7b}$$

According to McFadden (1973), Marschak (1960) seems to have been the first to write explicitly the relationship between (1.7a) and (1.7b). The mathematical derivation involves obtaining the distribution of $\max(U_1, \ldots, U_{i-1}, U_{i+1}, \ldots, U_I)$, by multiplying the cumulative distribution functions of each one of the U_j's and convolving such distribution with the distribution of U_i to find

$$\Pr\{U_i(\boldsymbol{\theta}, \mathbf{a}) > \max[U_1(\boldsymbol{\theta}, \mathbf{a}), \ldots, U_{i-1}(\boldsymbol{\theta}, \mathbf{a}), U_{i+1}(\boldsymbol{\theta}, \mathbf{a}), \ldots, U_I(\boldsymbol{\theta}, \mathbf{a})]\}.$$

Equation (1.7b) is without question the most widely used disaggregate demand model form in the transportation field; it has been applied to different problems [see for example, Dial (1971) for a route-choice problem; Lerman and Ben-Akiva (1975) for an auto ownership model; and Nicolaidis and Murawski (1977) for a modal split study], and its properties are well understood. Some of the most important properties of this model are explored now, but for a more detailed treatment the reader is referred to Domencich and McFadden (1975). A case study is reported in Richards and Ben-Akiva (1975).

The logit formula has the so-called *independence of the irrelevant alternatives* (IIA) property. That is:

The relative probability of choice of two alternatives depends only on their measured attractiveness.

This is true because, as the reader can check,

$$P_i(\boldsymbol{\theta}, \mathbf{a})/P_j(\boldsymbol{\theta}, \mathbf{a}) = \exp[V_i(\boldsymbol{\theta}, \mathbf{a})]/\exp[V_j(\boldsymbol{\theta}, \mathbf{a})].$$

In problems where the unobserved components of the perceived attractiveness (the error terms) are correlated (i.e., the alternatives share some neglected attributes in the view of the choice makers), introduction of a new alternative that is highly correlated with another one but is slightly inferior to it, has a negligible effect on the choice probability of all other alternatives, since the new alternative is a very unlikely choice. In such cases, the IIA property of the logit formula originates obvious problems unless the interdependencies of the error terms are somehow captured by the specification of the functions $V_i(\boldsymbol{\theta}, \mathbf{a})$. This is, however, difficult to do in most cases. Transportation mode and route-choice problems are typical examples in which the logit model can fail to produce reasonable results (McFadden, 1973; Schneider, 1973; Florian and Fox, 1976; Daganzo and Sheffi, 1977). In route-choice problems, for example, it is commonly specified that $V_i = -\boldsymbol{\theta} T_i$, where T_i is the observed travel time on route i (Von Falkenhausen, 1966; Dial, 1971). According to the logit formula, traffic will split itself equally among routes with equal length, regardless of whether they overlap or not. This is, of course, unreasonable, because addition of a minor bypass along one of two routes with equal length adds one alternative to the choice set, and this results in a shift of one-third of the users to the route with the bypass. This phenomenon is explained if one notes that a user is not likely to have several different perceptions for a section of road shared by different routes and that therefore the error terms of the two alternatives defined by the bypass should logically be very highly correlated. Daganzo and Sheffi (1977) discuss this at length and provide a comprehensive treatment of stochastic route-choice models.

In other problems, the use of the logit formula seems more reasonable. The gravity model of destination choice, introduced in the opening pages of this chapter, is perhaps the most widely used trip-distribution model and can be derived from a logit model of destination choice. This is explained below.

We let a_1 be the population in a given zone (zone 1) and a_2, the population of zone $j, j = 1, 2, \ldots, I$. Using the notation in previous pages of this chapter, we let a_{3j} be the average driving time from zone 1 to zone j. In order to avoid problems with the definition of a_{3j}, we assume that the zones are so small that travel times between all possible pairs of points for a given zonal pair $(1, j)$ are reasonably approximated by a_{3j}. Under those conditions, there will be many zones, I will be large, and the number of trips to each zone will be small compared with the total number of trips.

If we specify the measured attractiveness of a trip to zone j by

$$V_j(\boldsymbol{\theta}, \mathbf{a}) = \log(a_{2j}) - \theta_2 a_{3j},$$

i.e., the attractiveness is proportional to the negative of the travel time and to the natural logarithm of the population [as cogently argued by Lerman (1975) and Kostiniuk and Kitamura (1978)], the choice function given by Eq. (1.7b) becomes

$$P_j(\boldsymbol{\theta}, \mathbf{a}) = a_{2j} \exp(-\theta_2 a_{3j}) \Big/ \sum_{i=1}^{I} a_{2i} \exp(-\theta_2 a_{3i})$$

and the total number of trips from zone 1 to zone j is

$$y = \left[\theta'_1 a_1 \Big/ \sum_{i=1}^{I} a_{2i} \exp(-\theta_2 a_{3i})\right] a_{2j} \exp(-\theta_2 a_{3j}), \tag{1.8}$$

where θ'_1 is the fraction of people in zone 1 who take a trip. This expression is obtained from Eq. (1.4b) taking into account that, with the above assumptions on the definition of zones, a_{2j} and a_{3j} are the same for all the choice makers, and $M = \theta'_1 a_1$. Equation (1.8) is approximately equivalent to Eq. (1.2) since for small changes in a_{3j} and a_{2j} the denominator in Eq. (1.8) is approximately constant. Furthermore, in many applications of the gravity model, the generation of trips in all zones is exogenously determined, and in such "production-constrained" cases [see Wilson (1973, p. 64)], the gravity model assumes the exact form given by Eq. (1.8).

An important property of Eq. (1.7), which, as pointed out by McFadden (1973), can be exploited for calibration, is that for measured attractivenesses linear in the parameters [$V_i(\boldsymbol{\theta}, \mathbf{a}) = \boldsymbol{\theta}(i) \cdot \mathbf{a}^{\mathrm{T}}(i)$, where T is the vector transposition operation and $\boldsymbol{\theta}(i)$ and $\mathbf{a}(i)$ are row vectors containing the parameters and attributes appearing in the specification of V_i], $\log P_i(\boldsymbol{\theta}, \mathbf{a})$ is a concave function of $\boldsymbol{\theta}$.[6] A proof that

$$\log P_i(\boldsymbol{\theta}, \mathbf{a}) = \boldsymbol{\theta}(i) \cdot \mathbf{a}^{\mathrm{T}}(i) - \log \sum_{j=1}^{I} \exp[\boldsymbol{\theta}(j) \cdot \mathbf{a}^{\mathrm{T}}(j)] \tag{1.9}$$

is a concave function of $\boldsymbol{\theta}$ can be built around Hölder's inequality, parallelling the geometric programming proof of the (log, log) convexity of posynomials [see Avriel (1976, p. 194) for instance].

An interesting figure of merit of a random utility model is the expected level of satisfaction derived by a randomly selected choice maker from making a choice out of the set of alternatives. According to the definition of the perceived-attractiveness vector $\mathbf{U} = (U_1, \ldots, U_I)$ given in the previous section, it is reasonable to assume that the satisfaction of a choice maker, S, equals the perceived attractiveness of the chosen alternative. But since, by definition, the chosen alternative exhibits the largest perceived attractiveness

$$S = \max_{i=1,\ldots,I} (U_i).$$

Since the U_is are not observable, S cannot be observed. We can, however, derive the distribution of the satisfaction across all the choice makers with $\mathbf{A} = \mathbf{a}$. This is done below:

$$\Pr\{S \le x \mid \boldsymbol{\theta}, \mathbf{a}\} = \Pr\{V_i(\boldsymbol{\theta}, \mathbf{a}) + \xi_i(\boldsymbol{\theta}, \mathbf{a}) \le x;\ \forall i\},$$

[6] Appendix D provides a summary of important properties of convex and concave functions.

and since the ξ_is are mutually independent,

$$\Pr\{S \le x \mid \boldsymbol{\theta}, \mathbf{a}\} = \prod_{i=1}^{I} \Pr\{V_i(\boldsymbol{\theta}, \mathbf{a}) + \xi_i(\boldsymbol{\theta}, \mathbf{a}) \le x\}$$

$$= \prod_{i=1}^{I} \Pr\{\xi_i(\boldsymbol{\theta}, \mathbf{a}) \le x - V_i(\boldsymbol{\theta}, \mathbf{a})\}.$$

Entering with the Gumbel distribution function yields

$$\Pr\{S \le x \mid \boldsymbol{\theta}, \mathbf{a}\} = \prod_{i=1}^{I} \exp(-\exp\{-[x - V_i(\boldsymbol{\theta}, \mathbf{a}) + \gamma]\})$$

$$= \exp\left(-\sum_{i=1}^{I} \exp\{-[x - V_i(\boldsymbol{\theta}, \mathbf{a}) + \gamma]\}\right),$$

$$= \exp\left\{-\exp\left[-\left(x + \gamma - \log \sum_{i=1}^{I} \exp[V_i(\boldsymbol{\theta}, \mathbf{a})]\right)\right]\right\},$$

which also belongs to the Gumbel family. Therefore, its mean is

$$S(\boldsymbol{\theta}, \mathbf{a}) = \log \sum_{i=1}^{I} \exp[V_i(\boldsymbol{\theta}, \mathbf{a})], \tag{1.10}$$

which is the logarithm of the denominator in Eq. (1.7b), and its variance is $\frac{1}{6}\pi^2$. A different derivation of this expression is given by Sheffi and Daganzo (1978a). Several authors have suggested the use of the average satisfaction as a measure of system performance since $S(\boldsymbol{\theta}, \mathbf{a})$ can be interpreted in a way similar to consumers' surplus (Williams, 1977; Ben–Akiva and Lerman, 1978; Sheffi and Daganzo, 1978a).

The logit model, as mentioned above, is by far the most widely used random utility model in travel demand analysis. In addition, binary logit models (and/or binary probit models—see next section) have been applied to traffic flow, safety, toxicology, economics, sociology, and other disciplines [see, for instance, Miller (1972), Versace (1971), Finney (1971), Theil (1967), Warner (1962), and Berkson (1944)]. In the binary case, it is convenient to express Eq. (1.7) as

$$\log[P_1(\boldsymbol{\theta}, \mathbf{a})/P_2(\boldsymbol{\theta}, \mathbf{a})] = V_1(\boldsymbol{\theta}, \mathbf{a}) - V_2(\boldsymbol{\theta}, \mathbf{a})$$

or, letting $V_1(\boldsymbol{\theta}, \mathbf{a}) - V_2(\boldsymbol{\theta}, \mathbf{a}) = V(\boldsymbol{\theta}, \mathbf{a})$, as

$$\log\left(\frac{P_1(\boldsymbol{\theta}, \mathbf{a})}{1 - P_1(\boldsymbol{\theta}, \mathbf{a})}\right) = V(\boldsymbol{\theta}, \mathbf{a}), \tag{1.11}$$

which is the traditional way of writing the binary logit model.

Despite the attractiveness of the logit model for many applications, there are practical situations (such as in stochastic models of route choice) where it fails to produce reasonable results. Because for such problems it is difficult to come up with a priori specifications of V_i that do not behave illogically, some authors have developed ad hoc corrections to the logit formula that apply to specific problems (Sheffi, 1978b, Domencich and McFadden, 1975) and others have developed models with interdependent error terms and error terms with different variances. These latter ones are reviewed in the next section.

1.3.2 Closed-Form Models without Independent Identically Distributed Error Terms

The two models about to be introduced have been recently developed and their properties are not yet fully understood. To my knowledge, neither one has yet been used but both of them may eventually find appropriate application areas.

If the error terms are given by the following independent exponential distribution with mean zero and standard deviation $\sigma_i(\boldsymbol{\theta}, \mathbf{a})$ (see Fig. 1.1):

$$\Pr\{\xi_i(\boldsymbol{\theta}, \mathbf{a}) \le x\} = \begin{cases} \exp\{[x - \sigma_i(\boldsymbol{\theta}, \mathbf{a})]/\sigma_i(\boldsymbol{\theta}, \mathbf{a})\} & x \le \sigma_i(\boldsymbol{\theta}, \mathbf{a}), \\ 1 & x > \sigma_i(\boldsymbol{\theta}, \mathbf{a}), \end{cases} \tag{1.12}$$

the probability of choice can be obtained after a few algebraic manipulations (Daganzo, 1978a). We note that for this model, the perceived attractiveness of any alternative cannot exceed an upper bound, $W_i(\boldsymbol{\theta}, \mathbf{a}) = V_i(\boldsymbol{\theta}, \mathbf{a}) + \sigma_i(\boldsymbol{\theta}, \mathbf{a})$. In writing the choice function of this negative exponential distribution (NED) model, we omit the variables $\boldsymbol{\theta}$ and $\mathbf{a}$ associated with σ_i, V_i, and W_i and we

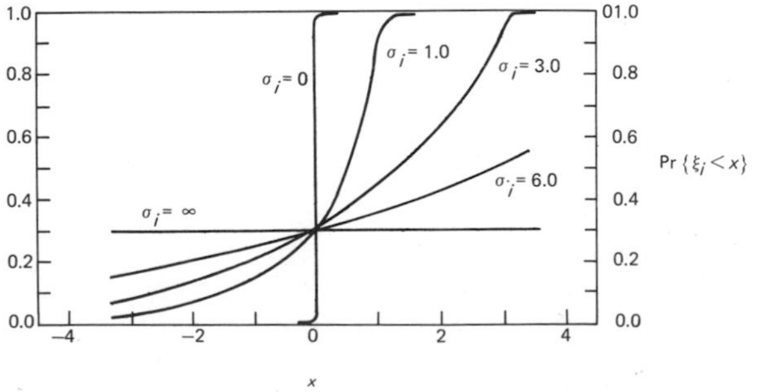

Fig. 1.1 Cumulative distribution function of the error terms of the NED model.

write (i) for the alternative with the ith largest upper bound on the perceived attractiveness $\mathbf{W}$. We also adopt the convention that $W_{(0)} = \infty$ and $W_{(I+1)} = -\infty$. The choice function is

$$P_{(i)}(\boldsymbol{\theta}, \mathbf{a}) = \sum_{k=i}^{I} \left\{ \frac{\sigma_{(i)}^{-1}}{\sum_{j=1}^{k} \sigma_{(j)}^{-1}} \left[\exp\left(-\sum_{j=1}^{k} \frac{W_{(j)} - W_{(k)}}{\sigma_{(j)}} \right) - \exp\left(-\sum_{j=1}^{k} \frac{W_{(j)} - W_{(k+1)}}{\sigma_{(j)}} \right) \right] \right\}. \tag{1.13}$$

If we let $A_{(k)}$ be equal to the difference of exponentials in the above expression divided by $\sum_{j=1}^{k} \sigma_{(j)}^{-1}$, the choice functions for each one of the alternatives can be calculated recursively by

$$P_{(i)}(\boldsymbol{\theta}, \mathbf{a}) = \sigma_{(i)}^{-1} [A_{(i)} + P_{(i+1)}(\boldsymbol{\theta}, \mathbf{a}) \sigma_{(i+1)}], \qquad i = 1, \ldots, I, \tag{1.14}$$

with $P_{(I+1)}(\boldsymbol{\theta}, \mathbf{a}) = 0$.

As an example, the reader can check that if $V_1 = 0.0$, $V_2 = 1.7$, and $V_3 = 0.5$, and $\sigma_1 = 3$, $\sigma_2 = 1$, and $\sigma_3 = 2$, the choice probabilities are

$$p_1 = 0.061$$
$$p_2 = 0.086$$
$$p_3 = 0.853$$
$$\sum_{i=1}^{3} p_i = 1.000.$$

As is expected of a model with different variances, increasing the variance of an error term in Eq. (1.13) in a problem with three or more alternatives with the same measured attractiveness tends to increase the choice probability of the alternative with the enlarged variance. Table 1.1 illustrates the fact for a three-alternative problem.

Table 1.1

Variation of the Probability of Choice of a NED Choice Model with the Variance of the Error Term of an Alternative[a]

θ	Variance $= \theta^2$	$p_1 = p_2$	p_3	θ	Variance $= \theta^2$	$p_1 = p_2$	p_3
0	0	0.4324	0.1353	1.0	1.0	0.3333	0.3333
0.2	0.04	0.4279	0.1442	1.2	1.44	0.2988	0.4025
0.4	0.16	0.4164	0.1673	1.5	2.25	0.2687	0.4626
0.6	0.36	0.3979	0.2042	2.0	4.00	0.2427	0.5147
0.8	0.64	0.3711	0.2578	∞	∞	0.1840	0.6321

[a] Data: $V_1 = V_2 = V_3 = 0$; $\sigma_1 = \sigma_2 = 1$; $\sigma_3 = \theta$.

The NED model could probably be generalized by a model with Weibull error terms. In such a case

$$\Pr\{\xi_i(\boldsymbol{\theta}, \mathbf{a}) \leq x\} = \begin{cases} \exp(-\{[-x + \sigma_i(\boldsymbol{\theta}, \mathbf{a})]/\sigma_i(\boldsymbol{\theta}, \mathbf{a})\}^n), & x \leq \sigma_i(\boldsymbol{\theta}, \mathbf{a}), \\ 1, & x > \sigma_i(\boldsymbol{\theta}, \mathbf{a}), \end{cases}$$

and a more complicated expression would be obtained instead of Eq. (1.13). Beilner and Jacobs (1971) give a simple formula for the probability of choice of a Weibull model in which all the perceived attractivenesses have the same upper bound. Distributions without a full range, such as the Weibull, gamma, or negative exponential, can be useful in instances where there is a clear bound to the perceived attractiveness of an alternative. In route-choice problems where travel time is the main determinant of attractiveness, for example, it is not unreasonable to assume that the perceived attractiveness of a route cannot be positive, since perceived travel time cannot reasonably be expected to be negative.

If instead of different variances one is interested in developing interdependent error terms, as would be the case in many modal split problems, it may also be possible to do so. McFadden (1977) has been recently investigating a generalized extreme value (GEV) model that admits positive correlations among error terms but uses error terms with the same variance.

Although there still seems to be some unresolved questions regarding the GEV model, the following three-alternative special case seems to work well when two of the error terms (without loss of generality we assume they are ξ_1 and ξ_2) are positively correlated and independent of the third one,

$$p_i = \begin{cases} \dfrac{[e^{V_1/(1-\rho)} + e^{V_2/(1-\rho)}]^{-\rho} e^{V_i/(1-\rho)}}{[e^{V_1/(1-\rho)} + e^{V_2/(1-\rho)}]^{1-\rho} + e^{V_3}}, & i = 1, 2;\ 0 \leq \rho < 1 \quad \text{(1.15a)} \\[2ex] \dfrac{e^{V_3}}{[e^{V_1/(1-\rho)} + e^{V_2/(1-\rho)}]^{1-\rho} + e^{V_3}}, & i = 3;\ 0 \leq \rho < 1. \quad \text{(1.15b)} \end{cases}$$

In the above choice functions, V_i is short for $V_i(\boldsymbol{\theta}, \mathbf{a})$ (the attractiveness of the ith alternative), and the parameter ρ indicates the extent to which the error terms of alternatives 1 and 2 are correlated. Note that if $\rho = 0$, Eqs. (1.15) reduce to the MNL model.

For this model, and as is shown in Chapter 4, the expected satisfaction is

$$S = \log\{[e^{V_1/(1-\rho)} + e^{V_2/(1-\rho)}]^{1-\rho} + e^{V_3}\}. \tag{1.16}$$

Since the satisfaction function of a random utility model is always convex (also shown in Chapter 4) it is not difficult to show that the logarithm of the choice probability is a concave function of $\mathbf{V}$ for any given ρ. Therefore, as happens with the MNL model, if the measured attractiveness functions are linear in $\boldsymbol{\theta}$, $\log P_i(\boldsymbol{\theta}, \mathbf{a})$ is concave in $\boldsymbol{\theta}$ for any given ρ.

Table 1.2

Variation of the Probability of Choice of a GEV Model with the Correlation of Two Alternatives

ρ	$p_1 = p_2$	p_3	ρ	$p_1 = p_2$	p_3
0	0.3333	0.3333	0.6	0.2845	0.4311
0.1	0.3256	0.3489	0.7	0.2759	0.4482
0.2	0.3176	0.3648	0.8	0.2673	0.4654
0.3	0.3095	0.3810	0.9	0.2587	0.4827
0.4	0.3013	0.3975	1.0	0.2500	0.5000
0.5	0.2929	0.4142			

[a] Data: $V_1 = V_2 = V_3 = 0$

The existence of positive correlations between two alternatives with the same expected perceived attractiveness tends to decrease their chances of being chosen (see Table 1.2), which is the desired model behavior.

The usefulness of the NED and GEV models, however, remains to be shown, since both of them are generalized by the multinomial probit (MNP) model, which is introduced in the next section.

1.3.3 The Multinomial Probit Model

The multinomial probit (MNP) model is a random utility model in which the error terms have a joint multivariate normal (MVN) distribution with zero mean and an arbitrary variance–covariance matrix.[7] Thus in an MNP model, the variances of the error terms can be different and the error terms may be correlated. Appendix C discusses the properties of the MVN distribution that will be used in this book.

Unfortunately, the choice function of a MNP model cannot be easily written in closed form, except for the case of two alternatives, and thus must be evaluated numerically. A significant part of Chapter 2 is devoted to evaluation procedures of the choice function.

A binary probit random utility model is defined by

$$\begin{aligned} U_1(\boldsymbol{\theta}, \mathbf{a}) &= V_1(\boldsymbol{\theta}, \mathbf{a}) + \xi_1(\boldsymbol{\theta}, \mathbf{a}), \\ U_2(\boldsymbol{\theta}, \mathbf{a}) &= V_2(\boldsymbol{\theta}, \mathbf{a}) + \xi_2(\boldsymbol{\theta}, \mathbf{a}), \end{aligned} \tag{1.17}$$

where the error vector $\boldsymbol{\xi}(\boldsymbol{\theta}, \mathbf{a})$ is bivariate normal with mean $(0, 0)$ and covariance matrix $\boldsymbol{\Sigma}_{\xi}(\boldsymbol{\theta}, \mathbf{a})$.

[7] The error terms are assumed to have zero mean because otherwise it is always possible to add their mean $\bar{\boldsymbol{\xi}}(\boldsymbol{\theta}, \mathbf{a})$ to the measured-attractiveness vector and subtract it from the error-term vector to yield an equivalent MNP model with zero-mean error terms.

The probability of choice for alternative 1 is

$$\begin{aligned} P_1(\boldsymbol{\theta}, \mathbf{a}) &= \Pr\{V_1(\boldsymbol{\theta}, \mathbf{a}) + \xi_1(\boldsymbol{\theta}, \mathbf{a}) > V_2(\boldsymbol{\theta}, \mathbf{a}) + \xi_2(\boldsymbol{\theta}, \mathbf{a})\} \\ &= \Pr\{\xi_2(\boldsymbol{\theta}, \mathbf{a}) - \xi_1(\boldsymbol{\theta}, \mathbf{a}) < V_1(\boldsymbol{\theta}, \mathbf{a}) - V_2(\boldsymbol{\theta}, \mathbf{a})\}. \end{aligned}$$

Since, as shown in Appendix C, $\xi_2(\boldsymbol{\theta}, \mathbf{a}) - \xi_1(\boldsymbol{\theta}, \mathbf{a})$ is normal with zero mean and variance $\sigma^2(\boldsymbol{\theta}, \mathbf{a})$ given by the sum of the variances of ξ_1 and ξ_2 minus twice the covariance of ξ_1 and ξ_2, one can write

$$P_1(\boldsymbol{\theta}, \mathbf{a}) = \Phi\left(\frac{V_1(\boldsymbol{\theta}, \mathbf{a}) - V_2(\boldsymbol{\theta}, \mathbf{a})}{\sigma(\boldsymbol{\theta}, \mathbf{a})}\right),$$

where $\Phi(\cdot)$ represents the standard normal cumulative distribution function.

Letting $V(\boldsymbol{\theta}, \mathbf{a}) = [V_1(\boldsymbol{\theta}, \mathbf{a}) - V_2(\boldsymbol{\theta}, \mathbf{a})]/\sigma(\boldsymbol{\theta}, \mathbf{a})$ and using the probit transformation $\Phi^{-1}(\cdot)$ on both sides, we have

$$\Phi^{-1}[P_1(\boldsymbol{\theta}, \mathbf{a})] = V(\boldsymbol{\theta}, \mathbf{a}), \tag{1.18}$$

which is the form of the binary probit model commonly used by econometricians, toxicologists, etc. [Note the difference between the definitions of $V(\boldsymbol{\theta}, \mathbf{a})$ for logit and probit models.] The book by Finney (1971) is devoted to the theory and application of the binary probit model. The binary probit model has been applied to similar problems as the binary logit model [see Lisco (1967) for one of the first applications in the transportation field].

To demonstrate the effect of covariance terms in $\boldsymbol{\Sigma}_\xi(\boldsymbol{\theta}, \mathbf{a})$, Fig. 1.2 displays the probability of choice of alternative 3 for the following model with different

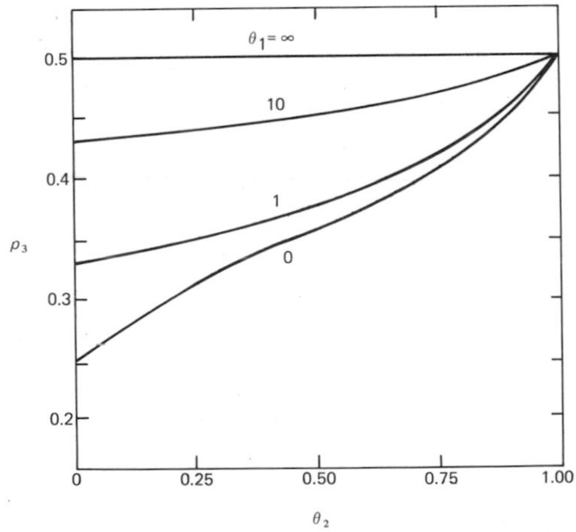

Fig. 1.2 Choice probability of alternative 3 for a MNP model in which the error terms of alternatives 1 and 2 are correlated [$\text{corr}(\xi_1, \xi_2) = \theta_2$] and have a common variance, different from alternative 3's [$\text{var}(\xi_1) = \text{var}(\xi_2) = 1$, $\text{var}(\xi_3) = \theta_1$]. [Adapted from Daganzo *et al.* (1977b).]

values of θ_1 and θ_2 (Daganzo *et al.*, 1977a,b):

$$V_1(\boldsymbol{\theta}, \mathbf{a}) = V_2(\boldsymbol{\theta}, \mathbf{a}) = V_3(\boldsymbol{\theta}, \mathbf{a}) = 0,$$

$$\boldsymbol{\Sigma}_\xi(\boldsymbol{\theta}, \mathbf{a}) = \begin{bmatrix} 1 & \theta_2 & 0 \\ \theta_2 & 1 & 0 \\ 0 & 0 & \theta_1 \end{bmatrix}.$$

Comparing the MNP model with the NED and GEV models (see Tables 1.1 and 1.2 and Fig. 1.2), it can be seen that the MNP model can capture the same phenomena as the other models. One notices that for $\theta_2 = 0$, p_3 increases with θ_1 in a similar way as p_3 increased with σ_3 for the NED model, and also notices that for $\theta_1 = 1$, p_3 increases with θ_2 as p_3 increased with ρ for the GEV model. Although the numerical value of p_3 does not change with θ_1 and θ_2 in the same fashion as it changes with the parameters σ_i of the NED model, and ρ of the GEV model (the models are different after all), it is clear that the MNP model can behave similarly to the other two if the parameters θ_1 and θ_2 are properly chosen. In addition, the MNP model generalizes the NED and GEV models by capturing phenomena these models cannot.

1.4 Calibration of Discrete Choice Models

Several statistical techniques can be used to calibrate the parameter vector $\boldsymbol{\theta}$ of a random utility model. The most widely used ones are discriminant analysis, data grouping, and maximum likelihood. All these techniques are applicable to disaggregate data sets, i.e., data sets in which each observation consists of an observed choice and an attribute vector for an individual from the population.

1.4.1 Discriminant Analysis

The output of discriminant analysis is a set of functions of the attributes **a**, which are used to classify the population into groups of individuals that are likely to select the same alternative [see Anderson (1958), for example]. Such functions are called discriminant functions; they may be linear or quadratic (depending on the assumptions of the model) and are defined for each pair of alternatives $D_{jk}(\mathbf{a})$. According to the theory, alternative j is predicted for all the persons with attribute vector **a** if

$$D_{jk}(\mathbf{a}) > \log(p_j/p_k) \qquad \forall k \neq j. \tag{1.19}$$

In Eq. (1.19) and in the rest of this subsection, p_j and p_k are the fractions of the population (estimated from the data or other sources) selecting alternatives j and k.

Since discriminant analysis associates a unique alternative with each attribute combination, it seems reasonable to conjecture that it may be related to the rational model. We now explore this relationship.

Since the discriminant functions have the two properties [see Anderson (1958)]

$$D_{jk}(\mathbf{a}) = -D_{kj}(\mathbf{a}) \qquad \text{and} \qquad D_{ij}(\mathbf{a}) + D_{jk}(\mathbf{a}) = D_{ik}(\mathbf{a}),$$

the functions

$$D'_{jk}(\mathbf{a}) = D_{jk}(\mathbf{a}) - \log(p_j/p_k) \qquad \forall j, k$$

also have the above properties. If we now define the functions of $\mathbf{a}$

$$V_1(\mathbf{a}) = 0 \qquad \text{and} \qquad V_i(\mathbf{a}) = D'_{i1}(\mathbf{a}). \qquad i = 2, 3, \ldots, I,$$

the aforementioned properties ensure that $V_i(\mathbf{a}) - V_j(\mathbf{a}) = D'_{ij}(\mathbf{a})$. Thus, since Eq. (1.19) is satisfied if and only if

$$D'_{jk}(\mathbf{a}) > 0 \qquad \forall k \neq j,$$

it is also satisfied if and only if

$$V_j(\mathbf{a}) > V_k(\mathbf{a}) \qquad \forall k \neq j, \tag{1.20}$$

which is the attractiveness maximization principle for a rational model with measured attractiveness vector $\mathbf{V}(\mathbf{a})$. Consequently, discriminant analysis can be used as a way of calibrating the rational model whose objective is to minimize the probability of misprediction for a randomly selected individual. Discriminant analysis was one of the first techniques to be applied to a binary discrete choice model in transportation (Beesley, 1965; Quarmby, 1967). Its use should, however, be limited to the rational model since for other models there is not a clear and convenient relationship between the discriminant functions and the choice function.

1.4.2 Grouping of the Data

Another possible calibration method that has been applied to binary models (logit, probit, and others) consists in dividing the data into groups with similar attribute vector $\mathbf{a}$, and recording the observed fraction of choice makers in each group who select each alternative.

Letting $p_{(i)}$ denote the observed fraction of choice makers selecting alternative 1 in class i, it is possible to convert these fractions into equivalent "probits" or "logits" by the transformations $\Phi^{-1}(p_{(i)})$ and $\log[p_{(i)}/(1 - p_{(i)})]$

[see Eqs. (1.18) and (1.11)]. One can then use generalized least squares on Eqs. (1.18) and (1.11) to estimate $\boldsymbol{\theta}$. This technique was introduced by Berkson (1953) and is discussed by Finney (1971) and Domencich and McFadden (1975). The problem with it is that the data must be grouped in such a way as to preclude and $P_{(i)}$ from being equal to 1 or 0, and such tampering with the grouping will tend to bias the results. Grouping has the further disadvantages of giving away much of the information inherent in disaggregate data (as discussed in Section 1.2) and becoming infeasible with more than two or three attributes (because of the large number of groups needed).

1.4.3 Maximum Likelihood

The maximum-likelihood approach seems to be the most efficient way of calibrating random utility models (except the rational model) and is discussed next. Some of the details and special problems with it will be highlighted in Chapters 2 and 3.

The maximum-likelihood method consists of selecting the value of the parameter vector $\hat{\boldsymbol{\theta}}$ that makes the data look most reasonable. This is done by writing the probability density of the data for a given parameter value $\boldsymbol{\theta}$ [the result is $L(\boldsymbol{\theta})$, a function of $\boldsymbol{\theta}$, which is called the likelihood function] and finding the value of $\boldsymbol{\theta}$, $\hat{\boldsymbol{\theta}}$, that maximizes the likelihood function. Maximum-likelihood estimators are statistically well behaved. Their statistical properties for the MNP model are explored in Chapter 3.

If, as is commonly the case, one can assume that the different individuals of the population act independently, the likelihood function is

$$L(\boldsymbol{\theta}) = \prod_{n=1}^{N} P_{c_{(n)}}(\boldsymbol{\theta}, \mathbf{a}_{(n)}) \cdot F(\mathbf{a}_{(n)}), \tag{1.21}$$

where $\mathbf{a}_{(n)}$ is the attribute vector of the nth observation, $c_{(n)}$ the choice of the nth observation, and N the number of observations in the data set. This equation is based on the probability of the nth observation being given by the probability of drawing an observation with attribute vector $\mathbf{A} = \mathbf{a}_{(n)}$, times the conditional probability of observing choice $c_{(n)}$, given that $\mathbf{A} = \mathbf{a}_{(n)}$. Since the terms $F(\mathbf{a}_{(n)})$ are not a function of $\boldsymbol{\theta}$, their values do not affect the maximum-likelihood estimate and they can be omitted from $L(\boldsymbol{\theta})$.

It is usually more convenient to find $\hat{\boldsymbol{\theta}}$ by maximizing the logarithm of the likelihood function, *the log-likelihood function*,

$$\log L(\boldsymbol{\theta}) = \sum_{n=1}^{N} \log P_{c_{(n)}}(\boldsymbol{\theta}, \mathbf{a}_{(n)}) \tag{1.22}$$

because $\log L(\boldsymbol{\theta})$ is a sum (rather than a product) of small numbers and its maximum coincides with the maximum of $L(\boldsymbol{\theta})$.[8]

Numerical techniques must generally be used to find $\hat{\boldsymbol{\theta}}$. When the log-likelihood function is well behaved, the task is tremendously simplified. In particular, note that since the log-likelihood function of linear-in-the parameters MNL and GEV models is a sum of concave functions [$\log P_i(\boldsymbol{\theta}, \mathbf{a})$ is concave in $\boldsymbol{\theta}$ for these models], $\log L(\boldsymbol{\theta})$ is a concave function, and if it has a stationary point (i.e., a point where the partial first derivatives vanish), that point is a unique local–global maximum. This property facilitates the search for $\boldsymbol{\theta}$ and is used in existing MNL calibration codes such as the one of Berkman *et al.* (1977). Ways of finding $\hat{\boldsymbol{\theta}}$ for the MNP model are discussed in detail in Chapter 2.

1.5 Prediction with Discrete Choice Models

This section reviews how choice models are used after calibration. As was mentioned in Section 1.2, the output of the calibration process is not the demand function, but a choice function. It is thus necessary to perform some additional calculations if the total number of decision makers selecting an alternative is to be found [see Eqs. (1.4)].

Similarly, if one wants to calculate the average satisfaction in a large heterogeneous group, $S(\boldsymbol{\theta})$, we would have to average the individual satisfaction measure $S = \max_{i=1,\ldots,I}(U_i)$, across the group. The expectation of $\max_{i=1,\ldots,I}(U_i)$ is taken with respect to both $\boldsymbol{\xi}$ and $\mathbf{A}$ since both of them change across the group

$$S(\boldsymbol{\theta}) = E_{\xi,A}\left[\max_{i=1,\ldots,I}(U_i)\right].$$

Alternatively, we can rewrite the above expression as

$$S(\boldsymbol{\theta}) = E_A\left\{E_\xi\left[\max_{i=1,\ldots,I}(U_i)\,|\,\mathbf{A}\right]\right\}$$

or, since the quantity in braces is the average satisfaction for a heterogeneous group, as

$$S(\boldsymbol{\theta}) = E_A[S(\boldsymbol{\theta}, \mathbf{A})] = \int_{\mathbf{a}} S(\boldsymbol{\theta}, \mathbf{a})F(\mathbf{a})\,d\mathbf{a} \tag{1.23}$$

where $F(\mathbf{a})$ is the probability density function of $\mathbf{A}$ across the group.

[8] The maximum of $L(\boldsymbol{\theta})$ and $\log L(\boldsymbol{\theta})$ coincide because $\log(\cdot)$ is a monotonically increasing function of its argument and, consequently, $L(\hat{\boldsymbol{\theta}}) > L(\boldsymbol{\theta})$ if and only if $\log L(\hat{\boldsymbol{\theta}}) > \log L(\theta)$.

The same technique can be applied to any other *individual figure of merit*, $\tau(\mathbf{U})$, whose average over a large heterogeneous group $T(\boldsymbol{\theta})$ is sought. First, one derives an expression for the average of $\tau(\mathbf{U})$ across a homogeneous group $T(\boldsymbol{\theta}, \mathbf{a})$ and then one expresses $T(\boldsymbol{\theta})$ as

$$T(\boldsymbol{\theta}) = E_A[T(\boldsymbol{\theta}, \mathbf{A})]. \tag{1.24}$$

For instance, in automobile-ownership models, the alternatives of consumers, which we label from zero to an arbitrary large number, are the number of cars owned. A car-manufacturing company would typically be interested, among other things, in the average number of cars owned by a family unit $T(\boldsymbol{\theta})$. To calculate $T(\boldsymbol{\theta})$ we first define $\tau(\mathbf{U})$ as the number of cars owned by a family with attribute vector $\mathbf{U}$. This is indeed a function of $\mathbf{U}$ that can be defined as

$$\tau(\mathbf{U}) = i \qquad \text{if and only if} \quad U_i > U_j, \qquad \forall j \neq i.$$

The expression for the average number of automobiles per family across a homogeneous group, $T(\boldsymbol{\theta}, \mathbf{a})$, is easily derived:

$$\begin{aligned} T(\boldsymbol{\theta}, \mathbf{a}) &= E_{\xi}[\tau(\mathbf{U}) | \mathbf{A} = \mathbf{a}] = \sum_{i=0}^{I} i \Pr\{\tau(\mathbf{U}) = i | \mathbf{A} = \mathbf{a}\} \\ &= \sum_{i=0}^{I} i \Pr\{U_i > U_j, \forall j \neq i | \mathbf{A} = \mathbf{a}\} = \sum_{i=0}^{I} i P_i(\boldsymbol{\theta}, \mathbf{a}). \end{aligned}$$

One could now enter with this expression in Eq. (1.24) to obtain $T(\boldsymbol{\theta})$. The problem is that Eqs. (1.4), (1.23), and (1.24) are difficult to evaluate since they cannot be reduced to a closed form.

A widely used prediction method consists of dividing the population into a few groups of decision makers with similar attribute vector, performing the prediction for each one of the groups, and adding the predictions of each group to yield a total prediction. If one lets $\mathbf{a}^{(k)}$ and $m^{(k)}$ be the representative attribute vector and the total number of choice makers, respectively, in group k, one can write for the prediction from group k, $T^{(k)}(\boldsymbol{\theta})$:

$$T^{(k)}(\boldsymbol{\theta}) \approx T(\boldsymbol{\theta}, \mathbf{a}^{(k)}) \tag{1.25a}$$

since within group k, $\mathbf{A} \approx \mathbf{a}^{(k)}$ and $E_A[T(\boldsymbol{\theta}, \mathbf{A})] \approx T(\boldsymbol{\theta}, \mathbf{a}^{(k)})$.

Of course, the total prediction is

$$T(\boldsymbol{\theta}) = \sum_{k=1}^{K} T^{(k)}(\boldsymbol{\theta}) \frac{m^{(k)}}{M}, \tag{1.25b}$$

where K is the total number of classes.

For Eq. (1.25b) to be accurate, however, the number of classes must be substantially large, especially when the specification of the choice function includes several attributes, and calculating $T(\boldsymbol{\theta})$ may be cumbersome. In order to circumvent these problems, more-efficient prediction techniques have been explored by different researchers. Chapter 4 is devoted to this subject.

In some instances, when the population of choice makers for which the prediction is being made is very homogeneous, it may be possible to use the average attribute values of the population, $\bar{\mathbf{A}}$, as representative of all the individuals,

$$T(\boldsymbol{\theta}) \approx T(\boldsymbol{\theta}, \bar{\mathbf{A}}), \tag{1.26}$$

which greatly simplifies the prediction process. This approach, however, will give incorrect results when, as is often the case, the attribute vector varies significantly. Since the errors that can be committed with this approach can be very large, one should use it only after careful consideration.

In addition to obtaining $T(\boldsymbol{\theta})$, the demand forecaster will usually be interested in obtaining confidence levels on the predictions. This is needed because, as in regression analysis, the value of $\boldsymbol{\theta}$ calibrated from the data varies with the data set and, consequently, so does $T(\boldsymbol{\theta})$. If one regards the maximum-likelihood estimate $\hat{\boldsymbol{\theta}}$ as an outcome (corresponding to a certain, random, data set) of a random variable $\hat{\boldsymbol{\Theta}}$, one can also regard the prediction $T(\hat{\boldsymbol{\theta}})$ as an outcome from a random variable $T(\hat{\boldsymbol{\Theta}})$. One hopes that the mean of $T(\hat{\boldsymbol{\theta}})$ will be close to $T(\boldsymbol{\theta}_o)$ ($\boldsymbol{\theta}_o$ is assumed to be the true value[9] of $\boldsymbol{\theta}$) and its variance will be close to zero. Under those conditions one can build short confidence intervals for $T(\boldsymbol{\theta}_o)$.

Continuing the analogy with regression analysis, we note that even if the maximum-likelihood estimate coincides with the true value of the parameter, the average value of $\tau(\mathbf{U})$ cannot be predicted deterministically for small population groups because different groups (of the same size and with the same distribution of $\mathbf{A}$) will in general exhibit different averages. The average of $\tau(\mathbf{U})$ across a group of individuals, $\sum_{m=1}^{M} \tau(\mathbf{U}_{(m)})/M$ ($\mathbf{U}_{(m)}$ represents the perceived attractiveness vector of the mth individual), must therefore be regarded as a random variable that converges in probability to $T(\boldsymbol{\theta}_o)$ as M increases. If the distribution of $\sum_{m=1}^{M} \tau(\mathbf{U}_{(m)})/M$ is known, one can use it to construct prediction intervals. Chapter 5 explores the statistical aspects of predicting with disaggregate demand models.

To illustrate how one can develop information on the distribution of $\sum_{m=1}^{M} \tau(\mathbf{U}_{(m)})/M$ we derive the variance of this quantity for the automobile-ownership example.

[9] As is customary in econometrics, we assume there is such a thing as a true specification and a true parameter value.

The second moment about the origin of $\tau(\mathbf{U})$ for a randomly selected individual from a homogeneous group, $\bar{\bar{T}}(\boldsymbol{\theta}_o, \mathbf{a})$, is

$$\bar{\bar{T}}(\boldsymbol{\theta}_o, \mathbf{a}) = E_\xi[\tau^2(\mathbf{U}) | \mathbf{A} = \mathbf{a}] = \sum_{i=0}^{I} i^2 P_i(\boldsymbol{\theta}_o, \mathbf{a}), \tag{1.27}$$

and since the second moment about the origin for a randomly selected individual from the population, $\bar{\bar{T}}(\boldsymbol{\theta}_o)$, satisfies

$$\bar{\bar{T}}(\boldsymbol{\theta}_o) = E_{\xi,A}[\tau^2(\mathbf{U})] = E_A\{E_\xi[\tau^2(\mathbf{U}) | \mathbf{A} = \mathbf{a}]\} = E_A[\bar{\bar{T}}(\boldsymbol{\theta}_o, \mathbf{a})]$$

we can calculate $\bar{\bar{T}}(\boldsymbol{\theta}_o)$ with the classification method

$$\bar{\bar{T}}(\boldsymbol{\theta}_o) \approx \sum_{k=1}^{K} \bar{\bar{T}}(\boldsymbol{\theta}_o, \mathbf{a}^{(k)}) \frac{m^{(k)}}{M}.$$

Assuming that the M individuals of the group act independently and that they have been sampled at random, the variance of the average value of $\tau(\mathbf{U})$ for the group is M^{-1} times the variance of $\tau(\mathbf{U})$:

$$\operatorname{var}\left[\sum_{m=1}^{M} \frac{\tau(\mathbf{U}_{(m)})}{M}\right] = \frac{\bar{\bar{T}}(\boldsymbol{\theta}_o) - T(\boldsymbol{\theta}_o)^2}{M}. \tag{1.28}$$

The variance of the total number of automobiles owned by the group is, of course, $M[\bar{\bar{T}}(\boldsymbol{\theta}_o) - T(\boldsymbol{\theta}_o)^2]$. Note also that if M is moderately large (in the tens or more) the central-limit theorem guarantees that the quantities of interest are normally distributed.

An unrelated prediction problem arises when some of the attributes faced by a choice maker depend on the choices made by other choice makers. In some of these cases, the distribution of the attribute vector $\mathbf{A}$ depends on the numbers of choice makers selecting each alternative and cannot be obtained a priori. In the car-purchasing example mentioned at the beginning of this section, it would be reasonable to postulate that if M is large, the price of automobiles would increase with the number of cars purchased by the population according to the standard principle of economic supply. Since the price of automobiles is an attribute of any reasonable car-purchasing model and the price is not known beforehand, one cannot obtain a prediction directly. However, one could obtain, at least conceptually, a function relating the figures of merit previously discussed (y, S, T) to price π [we write $y(\pi)$, $S(\pi)$, etc. to denote such functions]. Since we postulate that the price π depends on $T(\boldsymbol{\theta})$, we write $\pi(T)$ to denote the supplier's price function. The car market is said to be in equilibrium if its values of π_o and T_o simultaneously satisfy $\pi(T_o) = \pi_o$ and $T(\pi_o) = T_o$. In general problems, the variables π and T may be vector valued and need not have an economic interpretation. For instance, in transportation studies an attribute that typically depends on the usage y of a transportation facility is travel time. If travel time t is one of the attributes in the choice function, one has a similar situation in which an equilibrium solution may be formed by solving

$$y_o = y(t_o),$$
$$t_o = t(y_o);$$

in these equations the function $t(\cdot)$ depicts how the transportation facility becomes congested with increased use.

Equilibration problems become complicated when several markets specializing in different commodities and competing for the same customers must be equilibrated simultaneously. This happens, for instance, in transportation-network problems, where the number of people using a road depends on the travel times on all other roads. Chapter 4 contains a description of techniques that can be used to analyze equilibration problems and shows how the MNP model is extremely useful for solving some of these.

1.6 Practical Considerations in Demand Modeling

This section is not included as an introduction to an aspect of MNP, but rather as a closure on the subjects that have been discussed so far in this chapter. The section provides a brief summary of accumulated conventional wisdom in the specification and application of demand models so that, in addition to being an introduction to the MNP model, Chapter 1 will also serve as a concise introduction to demand modeling with disaggregate demand models. Domencich and McFadden (1975) and Stopher and Meyburg (1975, Chapter 16, in particular) provide a more comprehensive treatment of practical issues.

In specifying a model one must decide the attributes that are going to be used, the number of parameters that one is to estimate, and the functional way in which attributes and parameters are combined in the choice function.

The following four features (in approximate order of importance) should be carefully considered when selecting attributes:

availability,	statistical fit,
reasonableness,	relevance.

An attribute should be *available* as part of the data in both the calibration and the prediction stage since otherwise such stages cannot be carried out. It should be noted, though, that an attribute that is not forecastable for certain problems may be forecastable in other instances. For example, although automobile ownership is a good explanatory attribute for trip-generation and modal-split models, it is typically difficult to forecast and its use for a long-term prediction is not recommended. On the other hand, since the automobile ownership characteristics of the population do not vary very much from year to year its use may be perfectly justified for a short-term forecast. Poor availability is one of the main stumbling blocks in trying to incorporate some marketing ideas (such as attitudinal variables) into demand models.

The next item on the list is *reasonableness*; that is, a variable should be considered for inclusion in the model only if there is some strong *a priori* feeling that there is some cause-and-effect relationship between such variable and the choice probability.

The *statistical fit* feature includes the standard statistical properties that one likes to see after the model is calibrated. Namley, the variable should preferably not be highly correlated with other attributes that appear in the specification of the model and should improve significantly the fit of the model to the data. The statistical fit can be checked by the statistical significance of parameters associated with the attribute under consideration or by the improvement in goodness of fit before and after including the attribute. Goodness-of-fit measures for choice models have been developed in the literature and are discussed in Chapter 3.

In contrast to the previous three criteria for variable selection, the last one, *relevance*, suggests a reason for including (rather than excluding) an attribute in the model. Since the purpose of demand modeling is to assess the consequences (effects) of certain actions (causes), it seems desirable to include in the model variables that describe the actions. Such variables are usually called *policy variables* in the demand-forecasting jargon. If one is interested in finding out how the fare of a transit system affects ridership, one should consider the fare as a possible attribute in the specification of the model (the fare would typically enter with a negative coefficient in the measured attractiveness of the considered transit alternative). One rarely has availability problems with policy variables since by definition they are forecastable. However, inclusion of a policy variable in a model should always be subject to the tests of reasonableness and statistical fit.

The selection of parameters to be calibrated cannot be done independently of the attribute-selection stage since the number of parameters is intimately related to the number of attributes; however, as a general rule, one should be careful not to include so many parameters in a model that the resulting goodness of fit is due to the large number of parameters rather than to the causality of the specified model. It is my opinion that this is a mistake often made by practitioners, and which is made all the more tempting by the ever-expanding capacity and speed of computers. The emphasis in model building should instead be on parsimonious models (with few parameters) that can be properly tested and verified.

The specification of a random utility model involves selecting the measured attractiveness functions and, for MNP models, the relationship between the covariances of the error terms and some parameters and attributes. In the comments that follow only the logit model will be discussed. The discussion of specification of error term covariances is left for Chapter 3.

For MNL analysis the specifications used in practice are almost always linear in the parameters since this is the way in which most computer programs work and is also a way of ensuring the concavity of the log-likelihood function. Thus

$$V_i(\boldsymbol{\theta}, \mathbf{a}) = \boldsymbol{\theta}(i) \cdot \mathbf{a}^{\mathrm{T}}(i)$$

where "·" represents the vector dot product, the superscript T denotes the vector transposition operation, and $\boldsymbol{\theta}(i)$ and $\mathbf{a}(i)$ are row vectors including, respectively, the set of parameters and attributes that appear in $V_i(\boldsymbol{\theta}, \mathbf{a})$. By setting the first element of the $\mathbf{a}(i)$ vector equal to 1, one can include constants in the specification of the attractiveness of the alternative.

If desired, the elements of $\mathbf{a}(i)$ can be functions of attributes, rather than the attributes themselves, since for concavity of $\log L(\boldsymbol{\theta})$ it is only required that $\mathbf{V}(\boldsymbol{\theta}, \mathbf{a})$ be linear in $\boldsymbol{\theta}$.

A parameter θ_j can appear in one or more alternatives. Parameters that appear in more than one alternative are called *generic*. An example is provided by a modal-split model in which the travel time by each one of the modes (these are different attributes) appears only in the measured attractiveness of the corresponding mode but all are multiplied by the same parameter θ_i. Such a parameter can be interpreted as the intrinsic contribution of travel time toward any attractiveness of any mode. If, on the other hand, a different parameter were used with the travel time by each mode, the value of travel time would be tied to an alternative and the parameters would be called *alternative specific*.

It is tempting to use alternative-specific parameters in model specification because they usually improve goodness of fit; however, one should bear in mind that by doing that one may be capturing spurious correlations rather than causes and effects.

Some guidance can also be given regarding the appearance of attributes on different attractivenesses. In most models, level-of-service attributes should logically appear only in the attractiveness of the alternative that they describe (socioeconomic attributes may appear in several alternatives simultaneously). Of course, there are cases where this rule produces unreasonable results (as in the route-choice example that was used to illustrate the problems with the IIA property of the logit formula) and in such cases it may be wise to depart from it. It seems, however, even more reasonable to use a model that will enable the model builder to stick with the rule since it is not clear how one should depart from it.

In the transportation field there are already countless examples of the application of the logit model and a growing professional wisdom seems to be emerging.

Chapter 2 Maximum-Likelihood Estimation: Computational Aspects

2.1 The Maximum-Likelihood Method

This chapter discusses the problems associated with finding the maximum-likelihood estimates of the multinomial probit model from disaggregate data. It also presents the techniques that have been proposed to address the problems and analyzes their relative merits.

The maximum-likelihood-estimation procedure is a standard statistical estimation technique that sets the parameters of a model equal to numbers $\hat{\theta}$, called *estimates*, that make the data look most reasonable. The technique is used in many econometric and statistical-inference problems, including multiple regression, discriminant analysis, and contingency tables. Maximum likelihood also seems to be the best estimation method for discrete choice models (see Chapter 1). Before entering the subject in more depth, however, a small numerical example that can be solved by hand is provided to illustrate the approach in a MNP context.

2.1.1 *A Driver Behavior Analysis Example*

At any intersection controlled by a stop sign, the drivers on the low-priority approach are continuously deciding whether the gaps on the high-priority traffic stream are safe for crossing. Normally, drivers accept long gaps and reject short gaps, but gaps of intermediate length may either be accepted or rejected, depending on the aggressiveness and the mood of the

Table 2.1

Gap Acceptance Data Set

Driver	Rejected gaps (sec)	Accepted gap (sec)
1	9, 11	10
2	—	20
3	1, 5, 3, 3, 6	9
4	15, 10	12
5	—	25
6	7	10
7	—	12
8	—	6

driver at the head of the queue. In a "*gap-acceptance*" study, one is interested in inferring the characteristics of the driver population so that unsignalized intersections can be adequately designed. A field study could yield the information in Table 2.1.

One can then formulate the hypothesis that the nth driver in the sample has a *critical time* value such that gaps longer than it are accepted and smaller gaps are rejected. The values of the critical time for an individual may change from gap to gap, so that for the nth driver and any given gap j, the critical time $t_{(nj)}$ can be expressed as

$$t_{(nj)} = T_{(n)} + \xi_{(nj)}. \tag{2.1}$$

In this formula $T_{(n)}$ is the value around which $t_{(nj)}$ fluctuates for the nth driver and $\xi_{(nj)}$ is the amount of the fluctuation. Neither $T_{(n)}$ nor $\xi_{(nj)}$ can be observed, but by definition $E(\xi_{(nj)}) = 0$. It can be hypothesized, however, that $T_{(n)}$ varies approximately across the population according to a normal distribution with mean T and variance σ_T^2. If, in addition, and for simplicity, one hypothesizes that the fluctuations $\xi_{(nj)}$ are mutually independent normal variables with $\mathrm{var}(\xi_{(nj)}) = \sigma_\xi^2$, independent of the individual and the gap, one can write the joint distribution function of $\mathbf{t}_{(n)} = (t_{(n1)}, t_{(n2)}, \ldots)$ for the nth individual. The aim of a gap-acceptance study is to estimate T, σ_T^2, and σ_ξ^2 since as is known in the highway traffic literature [see Blumenfeld and Weiss (1970), for instance] the capacity and level of service of an unsignalized intersection depends on all of these parameters. For a randomly selected driver, $\mathbf{t}_{(n)}$ is multivariate normal since, as seen from Eq. (2.1), it can be expressed as a linear combination of normal variables. Its mean vector is

$$E(\mathbf{t}_{(n)}) = (T, T, T, \ldots)$$

and its covariance matrix is

$$\operatorname{cov}(\mathbf{t}_{(n)}) = \begin{bmatrix} \sigma_T^2 + \sigma_\xi^2 & \sigma_T^2 & \sigma_T^2 & \cdots \\ \sigma_T^2 & \sigma_T^2 + \sigma_\xi^2 & \sigma_T^2 & \cdots \\ \vdots & \vdots & \vdots & \end{bmatrix}.$$

To derive the covariance matrix, we have used the following property of covariances:

$$\begin{aligned}\operatorname{cov}(T_{(n)} + \xi_{(nj)}, T_{(n)} + \xi_{(nj')}) = {} & \operatorname{cov}(T_{(n)}, T_{(n)}) + \operatorname{cov}(\xi_{(nj)}, T_{(n)}) \\ & + \operatorname{cov}(T_{(n)}, \xi_{(nj')}) + \operatorname{cov}(\xi_{(nj)}, \xi_{(nj')})\end{aligned}$$

and the fact that $\operatorname{cov}(T_{(n)}, T_{(n)}) = \sigma_T^2$, $\operatorname{cov}(\xi_{(nj)}, \xi_{(nj')}) = 0$ if $j \neq j'$ and σ_ξ^2 if $j = j'$, and $\operatorname{cov}(\xi_{(nj)}, T_{(n)}) = 0$.

The probability of the observed gap-acceptance pattern for the nth driver conditional on the gap sequence received by the driver, $\Pr\{\mathbf{R}_{(n)}, A_{(n)}\}$, depends on the critical times of the driver, $t_{(n1)}, t_{(n2)}$, etc., as follows:

$$\begin{aligned}\Pr\{\mathbf{R}_{(n)}, A_{(n)}\} = {} & \Pr\{t_{(n1)} > R_{(n1)}, t_{(n2)} > R_{(n2)}, \ldots, t_{(nJ_n)} > R_{(nJ_n)}, \\ & \text{and} \quad t_{(nJ_n+1)} < A_{(n)} \,|\, \mathbf{R}_{(n)}, A_{(n)}\},\end{aligned} \tag{2.2}$$

where J_n is the number of gaps rejected by the nth driver, $\mathbf{R}_{(n)} = (R_{(n1)}, \ldots, R_{(nJ_n)})$ is the vector of rejected gaps by the nth driver, and, in this example only, $A_{(n)}$ is the accepted gap.

This is, however, equivalent to the choice probability of the first alternative of a random utility model with perceived attractiveness vector

$$\mathbf{U}_{(n)} = (0, R_{(n1)} - t_{(n1)}, \ldots, R_{(nJ_n)} - t_{(nJ_n)}, t_{(nJ_n+1)} - A_{(n)})$$

since Eq. (2.2) states that the first element of $\mathbf{U}_{(n)}$ is the largest.

Since $\mathbf{t}_{(n)}$ is MVN distributed, $\mathbf{U}_{(n)}$ is also MVN distributed, and Eq. (2.2) corresponds to a MNP model with

$$\mathbf{V}_{(n)} = (0, R_{(n1)} - \theta_1, \ldots, R_{(nJ_n)} - \theta_1, \theta_1 - A_{(n)})$$

and

$$\mathbf{\Sigma}_{\xi(n)} = \begin{bmatrix} 0 & 0 & 0 & 0 & \cdots & 0 \\ 0 & \theta_2 + \theta_3 & \theta_2 & \theta_2 & \cdots & -\theta_2 \\ 0 & \theta_2 & \theta_2 + \theta_3 & \theta_2 & \cdots & -\theta_2 \\ \vdots & \vdots & \vdots & \vdots & & \vdots \\ 0 & -\theta_2 & -\theta_2 & -\theta_2 & \cdots & \theta_2 + \theta_3 \end{bmatrix},$$

where $\theta_1 = T$, $\theta_2 = \sigma_T^2$, and $\theta_3 = \sigma_\xi^2$. The dimension of $\mathbf{V}_{(n)}$ (and $\mathbf{\Sigma}_{\xi(n)}$) varies with n and equals the number of rejected gaps for the driver plus 2.

A similar model of driver behavior has been estimated by Daganzo (1978b) and values of $\hat{\theta}_1 = 6.3$ sec, $\hat{\theta}_2 = 4.8\ \text{sec}^2$, $\hat{\theta}_3 = 3.2\ \text{sec}^2$ were obtained.

For the example discussed here, it will be assumed that all drivers have the same average critical time $T_{(n)}$, i.e., $\theta_2 = \sigma_T^2 = 0$, since in that case the components of $\mathbf{U}_{(n)}$ are independent and the probability of choice is greatly simplified. For the nth driver Eq. (2.2) yields

$$\Pr\{\mathbf{R}_{(n)}, A_{(n)}\} = \Phi\left(\frac{A_{(n)} - T}{\sigma_\xi}\right) \prod_{j=1}^{J_n} \Phi\left(\frac{T - R_{(nj)}}{\sigma_\xi}\right), \qquad n = 1, 2, \ldots. \tag{2.3a}$$

The likelihood function of the unknown parameters (T and σ_ξ) is given by the probability of the observed gaps on the main road times the conditional probability that they are accepted or rejected as shown in the data set:

$$L(T, \sigma_\xi) = \Pr\{\text{observed gap sequence}\} \cdot \Pr\{\text{given rejection pattern}|\text{observed gap sequence}\}.$$

Since the observed gap sequence on the main road is independent of how drivers on the minor road accept and reject the gaps, the first term of the right-hand side is not a function of T or σ_ξ and can be dropped for maximum-likelihood-estimation purposes. The likelihood function can thus be written as the product of Eqs. (2.3a):

$$L(T, \sigma_\xi) = \prod_{n=1}^{N_\mathrm{D}} \Pr\{\mathbf{R}_{(n)}, A_{(n)}\},$$

where N_D is the number of drivers in the sample. After taking logarithms, it reduces to

$$\log L(T, \sigma_\xi) = \sum_{n=1}^{N_\mathrm{A}} \log \Phi\left(\frac{A_{(n)} - T}{\sigma_\xi}\right) + \sum_{j=1}^{N_\mathrm{R}} \log \Phi\left(\frac{T - R_j}{\sigma_\xi}\right), \tag{2.3b}$$

where the subscript j denotes the rejected gap number within the data set (irrespective of the driver) and N_A and N_R are the numbers of accepted and rejected gaps, respectively.

In order to simplify the hand calculations it is assumed that $\sigma_\xi^2 = 1$ and that only the data for the two first drivers in Table 2.1 are available. Equation (2.3b) becomes

$$\log L(T) = \log \Phi(10 - T) + \log \Phi(20 - T) + \log \Phi(T - 9) + \log \Phi(T - 11). \tag{2.3c}$$

The maximum of Eq. (2.3c) can be found by trial and error or by using a systematic search procedure. By inspection one notes that

$$\log L(T) \ll 0 \qquad \text{if} \quad T < 5 \quad \text{or} \quad T > 14$$

because in these cases either the first or third term of (2.3c) is a large negative number. Therefore, we confine our attention to values of T between 5 and 14.

The interval to which T belongs is successively reduced by evaluating $\log L(T)$ at two interior points and retaining for further consideration only a part of the interval that must necessarily contain a maximum.

The two points selected will be symmetrically located, 38.2% and 61.8% within the interval. The first two points are

$$T = 5 + (14 - 5) \times 0.382 = 8.44$$

and

$$T = 5 + (14 - 5) \times 0.618 = 10.56.$$

The log-likelihood values obtained from Eq. (2.3c) are $\log L(5) = -31.09$, $\log L(14) = -10.36$, $\log L(8.44) = -6.56$, and $\log L(10.56) = -2.41$.

As can be seen from Fig. 2.1, the log-likelihood function must necessarily reach a maximum between $T = 8.44$ and $T = 14$ and, consequently, the left-hand end of the interval can be dropped from further consideration. In future iterations, one will reject the end of the interval that lies to the outside of the lowest of the two middle points.

The next two middle points are obtained from the interval (8.44, 14) in the same way:

$$T = 10.56 \qquad \text{yields} \quad \log L(10.56) = -2.415601$$

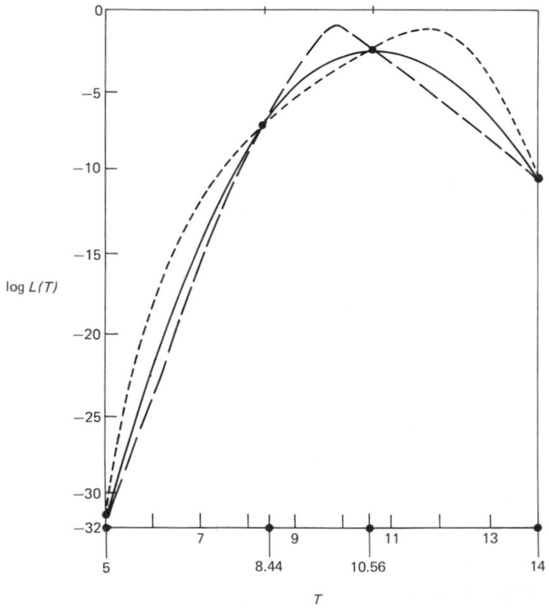

Fig. 2.1 Possible log-likelihood patterns.

and

$$T = 11.88 \qquad \text{yields} \quad \log L(11.88) = -3.707149.$$

The reader should notice that one of these points ($T = 10.56$) coincides with a previous point and that, consequently, $\log L(T)$ did not have to be recalculated at that point. The seemingly awkward numbers 0.382 and 0.618 were selected because they always divide the interval in such a very convenient way. Because of this property, the method is called the *golden section* method [see Avriel (1976) for a more detailed description]. The golden section reduces the length of the interval 61.8% with each function evaluation; this means that after, say, eight more evaluations, the interval will be reduced to 1/48 of its original size. Table 2.2 displays the intermediate results and the maximum-likelihood estimate $\hat{T} \approx 10.58$.

Table 2.2

Summary of Golden Section Method Calculations

Iteration number	Left-end point		Left-middle point		Right-middle point		Right-end point	
	T	$\log L(T)$	T	$\log L(T)$	T	$\log L(T)$	T	$\log L(T)$
1	5	−31.09	8.44	−6.56	10.56	−2.41	14	−10.36
2	8.44	—	10.56	−2.41	11.88	−3.71	14	—
3	8.44	—	9.75	−3.01	10.56	−2.41	11.88	—
4	9.75	—	10.56	−2.41	11.06	−2.60	11.88	—
5	9.75	—	10.25	−2.51	10.56	−2.41	11.06	—
6	10.25	—	10.56	−2.41	10.75	−2.44	11.06	—
7	10.25	—	10.44	−2.43	10.56	−2.41	11.06	—
8	10.44	—	10.56	−2.41	10.63	−2.42	10.75	—
9	10.44	—	10.51	−2.42	10.56	−2.41	10.63	—
10	10.51	—	10.56	−2.4156	10.584	−2.4152	10.63	—

2.1.2 *Data Structures and Corresponding Likelihood Functions*

The previous example illustrated how a problem seemingly unrelated to multiple choice (even the alternatives were hard to identify) could be cast as a random utility model. Thus the reader should not be misled by the terminology used in this book since sometimes problems that at first glance do not seem related to discrete choice have the mathematical structure of a MNP model.

In writing the likelihood function of a MNP problem, one needs to know the procedure that was followed to gather the data *since the likelihood function is the probability density of the data.* In this section, three different data-gathering procedures are discussed: attribute-based sampling; choice-based sampling; and random sampling with alternative ranking.

In the two first cases, the data consist of an observed choice and a vector of attributes for each one of the data points. The data for the third case also consist of a vector of attributes, but instead of an observed choice, one has a ranking of the alternatives in order of attractiveness. This type of data is sometimes gathered by means of consumer surveys in marketing studies.

An *attribute-based data set* is defined as a set of observations that are gathered by stratified sampling of choice makers from predetermined subgroups of the population with one or more similar attributes. The sampling process within each stratum is completely random and is carried out without knowing the choice of the sampled individuals beforehand. In the simplest sampling method one does not divide the population into groups, and observations are directly obtained from the population as a whole. A set of observations generated in such a way will be called a *random sample.* A commonly used random-sampling process in many studies consists of selecting telephone numbers from a telephone directory and/or mailing questionnaire forms to randomly selected individuals. The fundamental characteristic, however, is that the choice of an individual must not affect his belonging or not belonging to the sample.

For estimation purposes, the likelihood function of an attribute-based data set and a random-sampled data set is the same. With the notation introduced in Chapter 1, we have

$$L(\boldsymbol{\theta}) = \prod_{n=1}^{N} \Pr\{\mathbf{A}_{(n)} = \mathbf{a}_{(n)} \text{ and choice} = c_{(n)} \,|\, \boldsymbol{\theta}\}, \tag{2.4}$$

which is the general likelihood function for all sampling processes. For attribute-based and/or random samples, it is convenient to write Eq. (2.4) as

$$L(\boldsymbol{\theta}) = \prod_{n=1}^{N} P_{c_{(n)}}(\boldsymbol{\theta}, \mathbf{a}_{(n)}) \cdot F_{A_n}(\mathbf{a}_{(n)}),$$

where $P(\cdot,\cdot)$ is the choice function and $F_{A_n}(\cdot)$ represents the density function of $\mathbf{A}_{(n)}$ for the sampling mechanism used (random or stratified). Since $F_{A_n}(\cdot)$ is not a function of $\boldsymbol{\theta}$, we can instead use for estimation purposes

$$\log L(\boldsymbol{\theta}) = \sum_{n=1}^{N} \log P_{c_{(n)}}(\boldsymbol{\theta}, \mathbf{a}_{(n)}), \tag{2.5}$$

which coincides with the log-likelihood function introduced in Chapter 1 [see Eq. (1.22)].

A *choice-based* sample is a sample that is gathered by sampling from strata of persons with the same choice. The choice of a choice-based observation is thus known beforehand. A choice-based sample for a modal-split problem can be obtained by "on-board" interview of transit riders and "road-side" questioning of motorists. Interviewing people in the showroom after car purchases could generate a choice-based sample for a car-brand-selection model.

The likelihood equation (2.4) is conveniently written in this case as

$$L(\boldsymbol{\theta}) = \prod_{n=1}^{N} \Pr\{n\text{th choice in sample} = c_{(n)} \mid \boldsymbol{\theta}\}$$

$$\cdot \Pr\{\mathbf{A} = \mathbf{a}_{(n)} \mid n\text{th choice in sample} = c_{(n)}, \boldsymbol{\theta}\}$$

or

$$L(\boldsymbol{\theta}) = \prod_{n=1}^{N} \Pr\{\mathbf{A} = \mathbf{a}_{(n)} \mid n\text{th choice in sample} = c_{(n)}, \boldsymbol{\theta}\}, \tag{2.6}$$

since by definition of choice-based sampling the nth choice in the sample is $c_{(n)}$.

Equation (2.6) can be written in terms of the choice function by using the conditional probability formula

$$L(\boldsymbol{\theta}) = \prod_{n=1}^{N} P_{c_{(n)}}(\boldsymbol{\theta}, \mathbf{a}_{(n)}) \frac{F_{A_n}(\mathbf{a}_{(n)})}{P_{c_{(n)}}(\boldsymbol{\theta})},$$

where (as in Chapter 1) $P_{c_{(n)}}(\boldsymbol{\theta})$ represents the marginal probability that an individual sampled at random from the population selects alternative $c_{(n)}$ *if* $\boldsymbol{\theta}$ *was the true parameter value*. Since the marginal distribution of $\mathbf{A}$ is fixed (independent of $\boldsymbol{\theta}$) it can be omitted from the likelihood equation and one can instead maximize

$$\log L(\boldsymbol{\theta}) = \sum_{n=1}^{N} \log P_{c_{(n)}}(\boldsymbol{\theta}, \mathbf{a}_{(n)}) - \sum_{n=1}^{N} \log P_{c_{(n)}}(\boldsymbol{\theta}). \tag{2.7a}$$

In most cases, calculating $P_{c_{(n)}}(\boldsymbol{\theta})$ is a cumbersome task ($P_{c_{(n)}}(\boldsymbol{\theta}) = E_A[P_{c_{(n)}}(\boldsymbol{\theta}, \mathbf{A})]$ as was discussed in Section 1.2) requiring knowledge of the distribution of the attribute vector across the population, $F(\mathbf{a})$, and the calculation of a multiple integral; thus the maximum-likelihood-estimation method seems difficult to use. Manski and Lerman have developed a non-maximum-likelihood-estimation method that has good statistical properties and only involves calculation of the choice function [Manski and Lerman (1977)]. They propose to select $\boldsymbol{\theta}$ by maximizing the following pseudo-likelihood function:

$$\log L_p(\boldsymbol{\theta}) = \sum_{n=1}^{N} \frac{p_{c_{(n)}}}{f_{c_{(n)}}} \log P_{c_{(n)}}(\boldsymbol{\theta}, \mathbf{a}_{(n)}), \tag{2.7b}$$

where $p_{c_{(n)}}$ and $f_{c_{(n)}}$ are constants representing, respectively, the fractions of the population and sample selecting alternative $c_{(n)}$.

With the multinomial probit model, however, calculation of $P_{c_{(n)}}(\boldsymbol{\theta})$ is sometimes as easy as evaluating a choice function and the maximum likelihood method may still be used (Chapter 4 discusses the efficient prediction methods that can be used with MNP). Furthermore, since the second term on the right-hand side of Eq. (2.7a) can be calculated as

$$\sum_{n=1}^{N} \log P_{c_{(n)}}(\boldsymbol{\theta}) = \sum_{i=1}^{I} N_i P_i(\boldsymbol{\theta}), \tag{2.7c}$$

where I is the number of alternatives and N_i is the number of sample observations choosing alternative i, the extra computational effort involved in calculating it may become negligible if, as is usually the case, N is much larger than I.

In a *random sample with ranked alternatives* observations are sampled independently of their choices and the data corresponding to an observation n consist of an attribute vector $\mathbf{a}_{(n)}$ and a ranking of the alternatives by order of attractiveness. We shall write $j(n)$ for the jth most attractive alternative to the nth observation in the sample and $r_{(n)}$ to the particular ordering corresponding to the nth observation. In this case we can write, instead of Eq. (2.5),

$$\log L(\boldsymbol{\theta}) = \sum_{n=1}^{N} \log \Pr\{R = r_{(n)} | \boldsymbol{\theta}, \mathbf{a}_{(n)}\},$$

where R is a random variable denoting the $I!$ possible orderings.

It is now shown that, for MNP models, $\Pr\{R = r_{(n)} | \boldsymbol{\theta}, \mathbf{a}_{(n)}\}$ reduces to a choice function for an equivalent MNP model. It can be written

$$\Pr\{U_{1(n)} > U_{2(n)} > \cdots > U_{I(n)} | \boldsymbol{\theta}, \mathbf{a}_{(n)}\}, \tag{2.8a}$$

where, for brevity, the dependence of the Us on $\boldsymbol{\theta}$ and $\mathbf{a}_{(n)}$ is not explicitly represented, and $U_{j(n)}$ represents the $j(n)$ component of the utility vector for the nth individual in the sample.

Letting, $\mathbf{Z}_{(n)}$ be a vector with the following $I + 1$ components,

$$Z_{(n)1} = 0, \tag{2.9a}$$

and

$$Z_{(n)j} = U_{j(n)} - U_{j-1(n)}, \qquad j = 2, 3, \ldots, I, \tag{2.9b}$$

Eq. (2.8a) can be written

$$\Pr\{Z_{(n)1} > Z_{(n)j} \; \forall j \neq 1 | \boldsymbol{\theta}, \mathbf{a}_{(n)}\}, \tag{2.8b}$$

which is the choice function for alternative 1 of a random utility model with perceived attractiveness vector given by $\mathbf{Z}_{(n)} = (Z_{(n)1}, Z_{(n)2}, \ldots, Z_{(n)I})$.

Since for an MNP model $\mathbf{U}$ is MVN distributed with mean $\mathbf{V}$ and covariance matrix $\mathbf{\Sigma}_\xi$, and Eqs. (2.9) define $\mathbf{Z}_{(n)}$ as a linear transformation of $\mathbf{U}$, $\mathbf{Z}_{(n)}$ will also be MVN distributed and Eq. (2.8b) defines a MNP model too.

Equations (2.9) can be written in matrix form

$$\mathbf{Z}_{(n)} = \mathbf{U} \cdot \mathbf{\Delta}_{(n)},$$

where $\mathbf{Z}_{(n)}$ and $\mathbf{U}$ are row vectors and $\mathbf{\Delta}_{(n)}$ is a square $I \times I$ matrix with elements $\delta_{(n)kl}$ defined as

$$\begin{aligned}
\delta_{(n)kl} &= 0, & & k = 1, \ldots, I, \\
\delta_{(n)kl} &= 1, & & \text{if} \quad k = l(n), \\
\delta_{(n)kl} &= -1, & & \text{if} \quad k = l - 1(n), \\
\delta_{(n)kl} &= 0, & & \text{otherwise.}
\end{aligned}$$

If, for instance, observation n ranks alternative 1 over 2, 2 over 3, and so on, $l(n) = l$, and for that observation

$$\mathbf{\Delta}_{(n)} = \begin{bmatrix} 0 & -1 & 0 & 0 & \cdots & 0 & 0 \\ 0 & 1 & -1 & 0 & \cdots & 0 & 0 \\ 0 & 0 & 1 & -1 & \cdots & 0 & 0 \\ 0 & 0 & 0 & 1 & \cdots & 0 & 0 \\ \vdots & \vdots & \vdots & \vdots & & \vdots & \vdots \\ 0 & 0 & 0 & 0 & \cdots & 1 & -1 \\ 0 & 0 & 0 & 0 & \cdots & 0 & 1 \end{bmatrix}.$$

As discussed in Appendix A, the mean vector and covariance matrix of $\mathbf{Z}_{(n)}$ are given by

$$E(\mathbf{Z}_{(n)}) = \mathbf{V}(\boldsymbol{\theta}, \mathbf{a}_{(n)}) \cdot \mathbf{\Delta}_{(n)} \tag{2.10a}$$

and

$$\operatorname{cov}(\mathbf{Z}_{(n)}) = \mathbf{\Delta}_{(n)}^{\mathrm{T}} \cdot \mathbf{\Sigma}_\xi(\boldsymbol{\theta}, \mathbf{a}_{(n)}) \cdot \mathbf{\Delta}_{(n)}, \tag{2.10b}$$

where the superscript T denotes the vector transposition operation.

The log-likelihood function can thus be written

$$\log L(\boldsymbol{\theta}) = \sum_{n=1}^{N} \log P_1(\boldsymbol{\theta}, \mathbf{a}_{(n)}, n), \tag{2.11}$$

where $P_1(\boldsymbol{\theta}, \mathbf{a}, n)$ is the choice function for the first alternative of a MNP model with a specification varying with n according to Eqs. (2.10).

These three examples illustrate two related facts:

(1) The MNP model is robust since, even for different data-gathering procedures, the likelihood function basically reduces to a sum of logarithms of MNP choice functions.

(2) If an efficient way of evaluating MNP choice functions is found the three problems discussed in this section and probably others will be tractable.

Before presenting evaluation methods of $P_i(\boldsymbol{\theta}, \mathbf{a})$ for MNP models, we briefly review the components of a maximum-likelihood-estimation program.

2.1.3 Components of a Calibration Program

Since the calculations involved in finding maximum-likelihood estimates are very involved, as can be gathered from the very simple example in Section 2.1.1, they should be programmed for automatic computation. Reference to the example indicates that in order to calibrate the MNP model, we should have the capability to calculate the choice probability function $P_i(\boldsymbol{\theta}, \mathbf{a})$,

$$P_i(\boldsymbol{\theta}, \mathbf{a}) = \Pr\{U_i(\boldsymbol{\theta}, \mathbf{a}) > \max_{j \neq i} [U_j(\boldsymbol{\theta}, \mathbf{a})] \,|\, \boldsymbol{\theta}, \mathbf{a}\}. \tag{2.12}$$

Since for the MNP model the joint distribution of $\mathbf{U}$ is entirely characterized by its mean $\mathbf{V}(\boldsymbol{\theta}, \mathbf{a})$ and covariance matrix $\boldsymbol{\Sigma}_\xi(\boldsymbol{\theta}, \mathbf{a})$ (it is MVN), one can calculate Eq. (2.12) in two steps:

(a) calculate $\mathbf{V}(\boldsymbol{\theta}, \mathbf{a})$ and $\boldsymbol{\Sigma}_\xi(\boldsymbol{\theta}, \mathbf{a})$;
(b) calculate

$$p_i(\mathbf{V}, \boldsymbol{\Sigma}_\xi) = \Pr\{U_i > \max_{j \neq i} (U_j) \,|\, E(\mathbf{U}) = \mathbf{V}, \operatorname{cov}(\mathbf{U}) = \boldsymbol{\Sigma}_\xi\}. \tag{2.13}$$

The function $p_i(\mathbf{V}, \boldsymbol{\Sigma}_\xi)$ denotes the probability that the ith component of a MVN variate with mean $\mathbf{V}$ and covariance matrix $\boldsymbol{\Sigma}_\xi$ is the largest. It will be called the *MNP function* and will be used often from now on. It should perhaps be noted that $p_i(\mathbf{V}, \boldsymbol{\Sigma})$ and $P_i(\boldsymbol{\theta}, \mathbf{a})$ are related by a change of variable,

$$p_i(\mathbf{V}(\boldsymbol{\theta}, \mathbf{a}), \boldsymbol{\Sigma}_\xi(\boldsymbol{\theta}, \mathbf{a})) = P_i(\boldsymbol{\theta}, \mathbf{a}),$$

and that therefore MNP choice functions can be calculated if MNP functions can be calculated. For the binary example in Section 2.1.1, choice probabilities can be easily found because, as was shown in Chapter 1, the MNP function $p_i(\mathbf{V}, \boldsymbol{\Sigma}_\xi)$ reduces to a cumulative normal distribution function; however, for three and more alternatives, evaluating $p_i(\mathbf{V}, \boldsymbol{\Sigma}_\xi)$ is difficult.

The speed with which a computer can calculate $p_i(\mathbf{V}, \boldsymbol{\Sigma}_\xi)$ is crucial for the feasibility of MNP estimation. Modern computers, together with the fast numerical methods described in Section 2.2, have made MNP estimation feasible for problems of moderate size. With the capability of calculating choice probabilities, the structure of a MNP estimation program is straightforward. It is convenient to use a subroutine to calculate the log-likelihood function [as given by anyone of Eqs. (2.5), (2.7), or (2.11)]. The inputs to it are a parameter vector value $\boldsymbol{\theta}$ and the data set, i.e., $\mathbf{a}_{(n)}$ and $c_{(n)}$ or $r_{(n)}$ for $n = 1, \ldots, N$. For instance, to obtain the log-likelihood of a random sample, one calculates $\mathbf{V}_{(n)}$ and $\boldsymbol{\Sigma}_{\xi(n)}$ for each data point with the known specification of the model [$\mathbf{V}_{(n)} = \mathbf{V}(\boldsymbol{\theta}, \mathbf{a}_{(n)})$ and $\boldsymbol{\Sigma}_{\xi(n)} = \boldsymbol{\Sigma}_\xi(\boldsymbol{\theta}, \mathbf{a}_{(n)})$], calls another subroutine that calculates the MNP function to derive the choice probability, takes logarithms, and adds the result for every data point to yield $\log L(\boldsymbol{\theta})$.

As was seen in the example, for a particular estimation problem with a given data set, the log-likelihood function can be evaluated at different values of $\boldsymbol{\theta}$ (the data are fixed and known) until the value of $\boldsymbol{\theta}$ that maximizes it is found. It is thus convenient to have another subroutine level which will evaluate $\log L(\boldsymbol{\theta})$ as many times as needed to search for the maximum of $\log L(\boldsymbol{\theta})$ in a systematic way. Such a subroutine will usually require an initial value for $\boldsymbol{\theta}$ and some definition of the boundaries of the search domain.

For a problem with just one parameter a golden section search (see Section 2.1.1) could be used. In such a case the initial interval—$(5, 14)$ in the example—is the search domain that is provided as an input. Problems with more unknown parameters require more-sophisticated search techniques but the basic structure of the estimation program is the same.

Figure 2.2 contains a simplified block diagram of a hypothetical, random sample, estimation program. The rest of this chapter discusses the technical aspects of choice probability calculations, likelihood function evaluation, model specification, and search for the maximum of the likelihood function.

2.2 Choice Probability Calculation Methods

As discussed by Daganzo *et al.* (1977a,b) and Bouthelier (1978), the number of times the choice probability must be calculated in an estimation problem is quite large. It ranges from 1000 times for a small problem with 100 data points, one unknown parameter, and converging rapidly to 100,000 for a moderate size problem with 1000 data points, five unknown parameters, and converging less easily. This section discusses in some detail ways of evaluating the MNP function since the speed and accuracy of the calculations are very important.

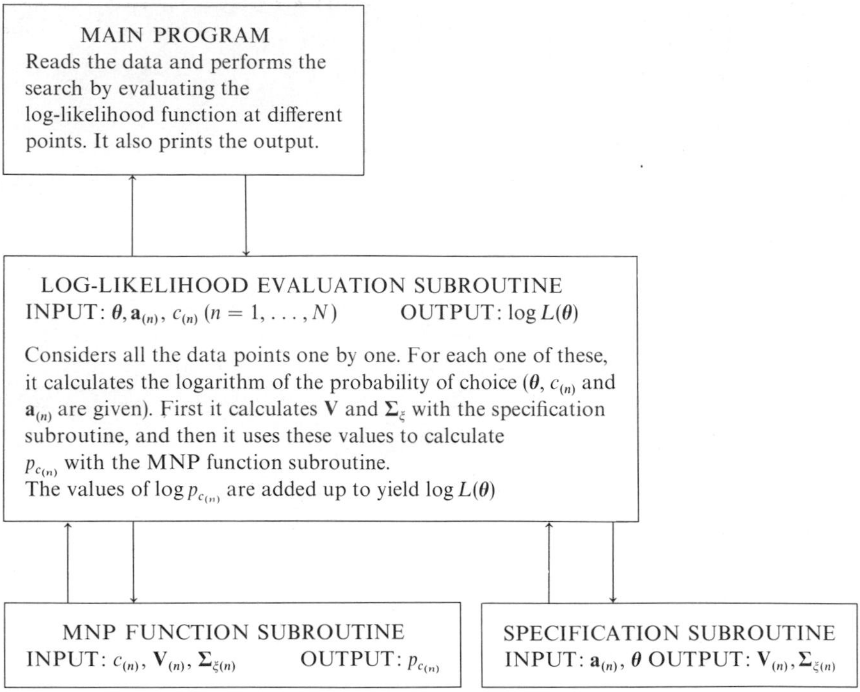

Fig. 2.2 Block diagram of a MNP calibration program.

Three different approaches have been proposed in the literature to calculate $p_i(\mathbf{V}, \boldsymbol{\Sigma})$. In approximate chronological order, they are

(1) numerical integration [Hausman and Wise (1978), Andrews and Langdon (1976)];

(2) Monte Carlo simulation [Lerman and Manski (1977)]; and

(3) numerical approximation [Daganzo *et al.* (1977a,b), and Bouthelier (1978)].

Each one of these methods has advantages and disadvantages, which are reviewed below.

2.2.1 *Numerical Integration*

For the multinomial probit model, Eq. (2.13) can be expressed as

$$p_i(\mathbf{V}, \boldsymbol{\Sigma}) = \int_{\mathbf{u} \in \mathscr{U}(i)} \phi(\mathbf{u} \mid \mathbf{V}, \boldsymbol{\Sigma})\, d\mathbf{u}, \tag{2.14}$$

where $\phi(\cdot \mid \mathbf{V}, \boldsymbol{\Sigma})$ represents the probability density function of a MVN random variable ($\mathbf{U}$) with mean $\mathbf{V}$ and covariance matrix $\mathbf{\Sigma}$; and $\mathscr{U}(i)$ represents the set of values of $\mathbf{U}$ for which $U_i > \max_{j \neq i}(U_j)$.

In an expanded notation, one has

$$p_i(\mathbf{V}, \mathbf{\Sigma}_\xi) = \int_{u_1 < u_i} \int_{u_2 < u_i} \cdots \int_{u_i = -\infty}^{u_i = +\infty} \cdots \int_{u_I < u_i} [(2\pi)^I |\mathbf{\Sigma}_\xi|]^{-1/2} \cdot \exp[-\tfrac{1}{2}(\mathbf{u} - \mathbf{V})\mathbf{\Sigma}_\xi^{-1}(\mathbf{u} - \mathbf{V})^T]\, du_1 \cdots du_I, \qquad (2.15)$$

which indicates that to obtain the choice probability one must solve a multiple integral of dimension I. Since the computational effort increases exponentially with the dimensionality of the integral, it is more convenient to express the choice probability as a function of the difference in utilities, which as is shown below reduces the dimensionality of the integral by one.

Let $\mathbf{Z}$ be a vector of $I - 1$ components, defined as the difference between the components of $\mathbf{U}$ (other than U_i) and U_i,

$$Z_j = U_{j'} - U_i \qquad \text{with} \quad j' = j \quad \text{if} \quad j < i, \qquad j' = j + 1 \quad \text{if} \quad j \geq i.$$

These equations can be alternatively written in matrix form as

$$\mathbf{Z} = \mathbf{U} \cdot \mathbf{\Delta}$$

with

$$\mathbf{\Delta} = \begin{array}{r|ccccccccc|}
 & 1 & 2 & 3 & \cdots & i-1 & i & \cdots & I-2 & I-1 \\
\hline
1 & 1 & 0 & 0 & \cdots & 0 & 0 & \cdots & 0 & 0 \\
2 & 0 & 1 & 0 & \cdots & 0 & 0 & \cdots & 0 & 0 \\
3 & 0 & 0 & 1 & & 0 & 0 & & 0 & 0 \\
 & \vdots & \vdots & \vdots & & \vdots & \vdots & & \vdots & \vdots \\
i-1 & 0 & 0 & 0 & & 1 & 0 & & 0 & 0 \\
i & -1 & -1 & -1 & & -1 & -1 & & -1 & -1 \\
 & \vdots & \vdots & \vdots & & \vdots & \vdots & & \vdots & \vdots \\
I-1 & 0 & 0 & 0 & \cdots & 0 & 0 & \cdots & 1 & 0 \\
I & 0 & 0 & 0 & \cdots & 0 & 0 & \cdots & 0 & 1 \\
\hline
\end{array}.$$

This linear transformation defines $\mathbf{Z}$ as another MVN random variable with mean and covariance given by

$$\bar{\mathbf{Z}} = \mathbf{V}\mathbf{\Delta} \qquad \text{and} \qquad \mathbf{\Sigma}_Z = \mathbf{\Delta}^T \mathbf{\Sigma}_\xi \mathbf{\Delta},$$

or in expanded form

$$E(Z_j) = V_{j'} - V_i, \qquad j = 1, \ldots, I - 1, \qquad (2.16a)$$

and

$$\operatorname{cov}(Z_j, Z_k) = \operatorname{cov}(U_{j'} - U_i, U_{k'} - U_i) = \sigma_{j'k'}^2 - \sigma_{ik'}^2 - \sigma_{ij'}^2 + \sigma_{ii}^2, \qquad (2.16b)$$

where V_j is the jth element of $\mathbf{V}$ and σ_{jk}^2 is the (j, k)th element of $\mathbf{\Sigma}_\xi$. The choice probability can be found by calculating

$$p_i(\mathbf{V}, \mathbf{\Sigma}_\xi) = \Pr(U_i > U_j; \forall j \neq i | \mathbf{V}, \mathbf{\Sigma}_\xi\} = \Pr\{Z_j < 0; \forall j | \bar{\mathbf{Z}}, \mathbf{\Sigma}_Z\},$$

which, if $\mathbf{\Sigma}_Z$ has full rank, can be expressed as[1]

$$\int_{z_1=-\infty}^{0} \cdots \int_{z_{I-1}=-\infty}^{0} [(2\pi)^{I-1}|\mathbf{\Sigma}_Z|]^{-1/2} \exp[-\tfrac{1}{2}(\mathbf{z} - \bar{\mathbf{Z}})\mathbf{\Sigma}_Z^{-1}(\mathbf{z} - \bar{\mathbf{Z}})^{\mathrm{T}}]\, d\mathbf{z}, \tag{2.17}$$

which is an $I - 1$ dimensional integral giving the value of the cumulative distribution function of $\mathbf{Z}$, at $\mathbf{z} = \mathbf{0}$. We, thus, write it

$$p_i(\mathbf{V}, \mathbf{\Sigma}_\xi) = \Phi(\mathbf{0} | \bar{\mathbf{Z}}, \mathbf{\Sigma}_Z), \tag{2.18}$$

where $\bar{\mathbf{Z}}$ and $\mathbf{\Sigma}_Z$ are obtained from Eqs. (2.16) and $\mathbf{0}$ is an $(I - 1)$-dimensional vector of zeros.

Calculating Eq. (2.18) is still difficult for problems with three or more alternatives and further simplifications are desired. A change of variable in Eq. (2.17) can reduce the dimensionality of the multiple integral by yet another unit. Consider the *Cholesky factorization*[2] of $\mathbf{\Sigma}_Z^{-1}$:

$$\mathbf{\Sigma}_Z^{-1} = \mathbf{LDL}^{\mathrm{T}},$$

where $\mathbf{L}$ is a lower triangular square matrix of dimension $(I - 1) \times (I - 1)$ with unit elements on the main diagonal and $\mathbf{D}$ is a positive diagonal matrix.

It immediately follows that $\mathbf{\Sigma}_Z^{-1}$ can also be expressed as

$$\mathbf{\Sigma}_Z^{-1} = \mathbf{L}\sqrt{\mathbf{D}}\sqrt{\mathbf{D}}\mathbf{L}^{\mathrm{T}} = (\mathbf{L}\sqrt{\mathbf{D}})(\sqrt{\mathbf{D}}\mathbf{L})^{\mathrm{T}},$$

where $\sqrt{\mathbf{D}}$ denotes a diagonal matrix with diagonal entries given by the positive square roots of the elements of $\mathbf{D}$; and letting $\mathbf{C} = \mathbf{L}\sqrt{\mathbf{D}}$:

$$\mathbf{\Sigma}_Z^{-1} = \mathbf{CC}^{\mathrm{T}}, \tag{2.19}$$

where $\mathbf{C}$ is (by construction) lower triangular with positive diagonal entries.

We now perform the following change of variable in Eq. (2.17):

$$\mathbf{w} = (\mathbf{z} - \bar{\mathbf{Z}})\mathbf{C}, \tag{2.20}$$

[1] For matrices without a full rank, one reduces the dimensionality of $\bar{\mathbf{Z}}$ and $\mathbf{\Sigma}_Z$ according to some simple rules [see Rao (1965), for instance] until the resulting covariance matrix is nonsingular. The choice probability calculations are thus greatly simplified.

[2] As discussed in Appendix B, a covariance matrix with full rank is positive definite and symmetric; accordingly, its inverse can be expressed as a product of three matrices:

$$\mathbf{\Sigma}_Z^{-1} = \mathbf{LDL}^{\mathrm{T}},$$

where $\mathbf{D}$ is a diagonal matrix with positive diagonal elements and $\mathbf{L}$ a lower triangular matrix with ones on the main diagonal; $\mathbf{L}^{\mathrm{T}}$ is the transpose of $\mathbf{L}$.

which enables us to write the domain of integration of Eq. (2.17) in terms of $\mathbf{w}$ as

$$\mathbf{z} = \bar{\mathbf{Z}} + \mathbf{w}\mathbf{C}^{-1} \leq \mathbf{0}. \tag{2.21}$$

Since $\mathbf{C}^{-1}$ is the inverse of a lower triangular matrix with positive diagonal entries, it is also lower triangular with positive diagonal entries. Denoting the elements of $\mathbf{C}^{-1}$ by c_{ij}^{-1} one can write Eq. (2.21) as

$$\bar{Z}_j + \sum_{i=j}^{I-1} w_i c_{ij}^{-1} \leq 0, \qquad j = 1, \ldots, I-1,$$

or as

$$w_j c_{jj}^{-1} \leq -\left(\bar{Z}_j + \sum_{i=j+1}^{I-1} w_i c_{ij}^{-1}\right), \qquad j = 1, \ldots, I-1;$$

and since $c_{jj}^{-1} > 0$, the domain of integration becomes

$$w_j \leq -\left(\bar{Z}_j + \sum_{i=j+1}^{I-1} w_i c_{ij}^{-1}\right) \Big/ c_{jj}^{-1}.$$

This can be written in expanded form as

$$\begin{aligned} w_{I-1} &\leq -\bar{Z}_{I-1}/c_{I-1,I-1}^{-1} = W_{I-1}, \\ w_{I-2} &\leq -(\bar{Z}_{I-2} + w_{I-1}c_{I-1,I-2}^{-1})/c_{I-2,I-2}^{-1} = W_{I-2}(w_{I-1}), \\ &\vdots \\ w_1 &\leq -(\bar{Z}_1 + w_{I-1}c_{I-1,1}^{-1} + \cdots + w_2 c_{21}^{-1})/c_{11}^{-1} = W_1(w_{I-1} \cdots w_2). \end{aligned} \tag{2.22}$$

The integrand of Eq. (2.17) becomes

$$(2\pi)^{-(I-1)/2} \exp\{-\tfrac{1}{2}\mathbf{w}\mathbf{w}^{\mathrm{T}}\}\, d\mathbf{w} = \prod_{i=1}^{I-1} \phi(w_i)\, dw_i.$$

To see this, replace $\mathbf{\Sigma}_Z^{-1}$ by $\mathbf{C}\mathbf{C}^{\mathrm{T}}$ in Eq. (2.17). The exponent on the left-hand side of this expression follows immediately from Eq. (2.20). The coefficient $|\mathbf{\Sigma}_Z|^{-1/2}$ equals $|\mathbf{C}|$, which is the determinant of the Jacobian of the transformation defined by Eq. (2.20):

$$\left|\frac{\partial(w_1 \cdots w_{I-1})}{\partial(z_1 \cdots z_{I-1})}\right| = |\mathbf{C}| = |\mathbf{\Sigma}_Z|^{-1/2}.$$

Since

$$d\mathbf{z} = d\mathbf{w}\left|\frac{\partial(w_1 \cdots w_{I-1})}{\partial(z_1 \cdots z_{I-1})}\right|^{-1},$$

the determinant of $\boldsymbol{\Sigma}_Z$ drops out of the integrand of Eq. (2.17), which then reduces to the abovementioned form.[3]

The MNP function can, thus, be expressed as

$$p_i(\mathbf{V}, \boldsymbol{\Sigma}_\xi) = \int_{w_{I-1}=-\infty}^{W_{I-1}} \phi(w_{I-1}) \int_{w_{I-2}=-\infty}^{W_{I-2}(w_{I-1})} \phi(w_{I-2})$$

$$\cdots \int_{W_1=-\infty}^{W_1(w_{I-1}\ldots w_2)} \phi(w_1)\, dw_1 \cdots dw_{I-1},$$

or, after integrating the last integral,

$$p_i(\mathbf{V}, \boldsymbol{\Sigma}_\xi) = \int_{w_{I-1}=-\infty}^{W_{I-1}} \cdots \int_{w_2=-\infty}^{W_2(w_{I-1}\ldots w_3)} \Phi(W_1(w_{I-1}\cdots w_2))$$

$$\cdot \prod_{i=2}^{I-1} \phi(w_i)\, dw_2 \cdots dw_{I-1}, \tag{2.23}$$

where the functions $W(\cdots)$ are given by Eqs. (2.22) and the multiple integral is of dimension $I - 2$.

To evaluate Eq. (2.23) one must calculate $\bar{\mathbf{Z}}$ and $\boldsymbol{\Sigma}_Z$ with Eqs. (2.16), $\mathbf{C}^{-1}$ with standard numerical techniques, the functions $W(\cdots)$ with Eqs. (2.22) and the integral with numerical techniques.

This approach is particularly useful for problems with three alternatives, since in that case Eq. (2.23) is a line integral that can be solved with just a few evaluations of the integrand by using, say, Simpson's rule. Andrews and Langdon (1976) suggested this approach for modal-split problems involving three transportation modes but did not develop a calibration method. Hausman and Wise (1978) seem to have been the first researchers to calibrate a MNP model; they used a numerical-integration technique similar to this one.

For a three-alternative problem an evaluation of the integrand necessitates one calculation of $\phi(\cdot)$ and one calculation of $\Phi(\cdot)$. This can be done numerically with [see Abramowitz and Stegun (1965)]

$$\phi(x) = \frac{1}{\sqrt{2\pi}} \exp(-x^2/2)$$

[3] The reduced form of the integrand can also be derived by interpreting Eq. (2.20) as a linear transformation of MVN random variables. As a result of the transformation, the random variable corresponding to $\mathbf{w}$ is a set of $(I - 1)$ independent and identically distributed standard normal variables with joint density function given by $\prod_{i=1}^{I-1} \phi(w_i)$.

and

$$\Phi(x) \approx \begin{cases} 1 - (\{[(a_1 t + a_2)t + a_3]t + a_4\}t + a_5)\phi(x) & \text{if} \quad x \geq 0 \\ 1 - \Phi(x|) & \text{if} \quad x < 0, \end{cases}$$

where

$$t = (1 + 0.2316419x)^{-1}, \qquad a_3 = 1.781477937,$$
$$a_1 = 1.330274429, \qquad a_4 = -0.356563782,$$
$$a_2 = -1.821255978, \qquad a_5 = 0.319381530.$$

Example Calculate the probabilities of choice for the following data:

$$\mathbf{V} = (2, 2, 3) \quad \text{and} \quad \mathbf{\Sigma}_\xi = \begin{bmatrix} 2 & 0 & 1 \\ 0 & 2 & 1 \\ 1 & 1 & 3 \end{bmatrix}.$$

We start with p_1. Substituting these values into Eq. (2.16), we have $\bar{\mathbf{Z}} = (0, 1)$ and $\mathbf{\Sigma}_Z = \left[\begin{smallmatrix} 4 & 2 \\ 2 & 3 \end{smallmatrix}\right]$.

The inverse of $\mathbf{\Sigma}_Z$ is

$$\mathbf{\Sigma}_Z^{-1} = \frac{1}{8}\begin{bmatrix} 3 & -2 \\ -2 & 4 \end{bmatrix},$$

which can be factored as

$$\mathbf{\Sigma}_Z^{-1} = \frac{1}{8}\begin{bmatrix} 3 & -2 \\ -2 & 4 \end{bmatrix} = \begin{bmatrix} 0.612 & 0 \\ -0.407 & 0.576 \end{bmatrix}\begin{bmatrix} 0.612 & -0.407 \\ 0 & 0.576 \end{bmatrix}$$

and, consequently, yields

$$\mathbf{C} = \begin{bmatrix} 0.612 & 0 \\ -0.407 & 0.576 \end{bmatrix} \quad \text{and} \quad \mathbf{C}^{-1} = \begin{bmatrix} 1.63 & 0 \\ 1.15 & 1.74 \end{bmatrix}.$$

Note at this point that

$$(\mathbf{C}^{\mathrm{T}})^{-1}\mathbf{C}^{-1} = \mathbf{\Sigma}_Z$$

and that $\mathbf{C}^{-1}$ can be directly obtained from $\mathbf{\Sigma}_Z$.

The limits of integration are obtained from Eq. (2.22):

$$W_2 = -1/1.74 = -0.575,$$
$$W_1(w_2) = -w_2 1.15/1.63 = -0.706 w_2,$$

and Eq. (2.23) becomes

$$p_1(\mathbf{V}, \mathbf{\Sigma}_\xi) = \int_{-\infty}^{-0.575} \phi(w)\Phi(-0.706w)\, dw.$$

This equation can be solved numerically by using Simpson's rule. We evaluate the integrand, between $w = -3.575$ and $w = -0.575$ [$\phi(w)$ is negligible for $w \leq -3.5$], 11 times at points equally spaced:

$$w_i = -3.575 + 0.3i.$$

The approximate value of the integral is given by

$$p_1 = (0.3/3)(f_0 + 4f_1 + 2f_2 + 4f_3 + \cdots + 4f_9 + f_{10}),$$

where f_i is the value of the integrand for $w = w_i$.

The calculations are summarized in Table 2.3 and the result is $p_1 = 0.2204$. The reader can check that repeating the process for p_2 and p_3 one gets

$$p_2 = 0.22 \qquad \text{and} \qquad p_3 = 0.56;$$

and that, indeed

$$p_1 + p_2 + p_3 = 1. \quad \blacksquare$$

Table 2.3

Numerical Integration Example Calculations

i	w_i	$\phi(w_i)$	$\Phi(-0.706w_i)$	f_i
0	−3.575	0.001	0.994	—
1	−3.275	0.002	0.990	0.002
2	−2.975	0.004	0.982	0.004
3	−2.675	0.011	0.971	0.011
4	−2.375	0.024	0.953	0.023
5	−2.075	0.046	0.929	0.043
6	−1.775	0.083	0.895	0.074
7	−1.475	0.134	0.851	0.114
8	−1.175	0.200	0.797	0.159
9	−0.875	0.272	0.732	0.199
10	−0.575	0.338	0.658	0.222

[a] Probability = 2.204(0.3)/3 = 0.2204.

This example illustrates the type of calculations that are necessary to to evaluate the choice probability of a three-alternative MNP model numerically. Namely, after obtaining the limit of integration and the argument of $\Phi(\cdot)$ within the integrand one has to calculate $\phi(\cdot)$ and $\Phi(\cdot)$ several times (ten in our example).[4]

[4] In addition, one must remember that $\bar{\mathbf{Z}}$ and $\mathbf{C}^{-1}$ must be calculated from $\mathbf{V}$ and $\mathbf{\Sigma}_\xi$ prior to the numerical evaluation of the integral; however, the computational effort involved in doing that is relatively small.

For problems with more than three alternatives, the approach seems less promising because one must approximate a multiple integral, which requires more evaluations of a more complex integrand.

Since the probability of choice must be evaluated several thousand times even for small problems it seems that the direct numerical approach can only be used effectively with rather small three-alternative problems.

Because of this, some researchers have investigated alternative approaches to evaluate $p_i(\mathbf{V}, \mathbf{\Sigma}_\xi)$ approximately. Two approaches that seem promising for different applications are reviewed next.

2.2.2 Monte Carlo Simulation Method

This method has been suggested by Lerman and Manski (1977); it consists in evaluating the MNP function $p_i(\mathbf{V}, \mathbf{\Sigma}_\xi)$ by performing experiments with random numbers. For each experiment, one generates a MVN $(\mathbf{V}, \mathbf{\Sigma}_\xi)$ random vector $\mathbf{U}$ using a string of pseudorandom numbers generated by a computer, looks at the components of $\mathbf{U}$, and records a success if the ith component is the largest. If the experiment is repeated many times, the fraction of successes will approach the choice probability $p_i(\mathbf{V}, \mathbf{\Sigma}_\xi)$. The method is, basically, equivalent to estimating the fraction of persons who choose alternative i in a segment of the population with constant $\mathbf{V}$ and $\mathbf{\Sigma}_\xi$ by observing the choices of many individuals in the subgroup.

In order to generate a MVN random variable with mean $\mathbf{V}$ and covariance $\mathbf{\Sigma}_\xi$, one can proceed as follows [see Fishman (1973), for example]; express $\mathbf{\Sigma}_\xi$ as

$$\mathbf{\Sigma}_\xi = \mathbf{C}_\xi \mathbf{C}_\xi^{\mathrm{T}},$$

where, if desired, $\mathbf{C}_\xi$ may be a lower triangular matrix with positive diagonal elements.

Generate I independent standard normal variates (subroutines that do so are standard in most computer installations) $v_1, v_2, \ldots, v_I$ and calculate $U_1, \ldots, U_I$ by

$$\mathbf{U} = \mathbf{v}\mathbf{C}_\xi^{\mathrm{T}} + \mathbf{V}.$$

We note that $\mathbf{U}$ is MVN, since it is a linear combination of independent normal variables, and that, as expected

$$E(\mathbf{U}) = \mathbf{V} + E(\mathbf{v})\mathbf{C}_\xi^{\mathrm{T}} = \mathbf{V}$$

and

$$\operatorname{cov}(\mathbf{U}) = \mathbf{C}_\xi \operatorname{cov}(\mathbf{v})\, \mathbf{C}_\xi^{\mathrm{T}} = \mathbf{C}_\xi \cdot \mathbf{I} \cdot \mathbf{C}_\xi^{\mathrm{T}} = \mathbf{C}_\xi \mathbf{C}_\xi^{\mathrm{T}} = \mathbf{\Sigma}_\xi,$$

where in the last expression, $\mathbf{I}$ is the identity matrix.

Example Let us perform three experiments for the same problem in Section 2.2.1 with

$$\mathbf{V} = (2, 2, 3) \qquad \text{and} \qquad \mathbf{\Sigma}_\xi = \begin{bmatrix} 2 & 0 & 1 \\ 0 & 2 & 1 \\ 1 & 1 & 3 \end{bmatrix}.$$

Since

$$\mathbf{\Sigma}_\xi = \frac{1}{\sqrt{2}} \begin{bmatrix} 2 & 0 & 0 \\ 0 & 2 & 0 \\ 1 & 1 & 2 \end{bmatrix} \begin{bmatrix} 2 & 0 & 1 \\ 0 & 2 & 1 \\ 0 & 0 & 2 \end{bmatrix} \frac{1}{\sqrt{2}},$$

we can use

$$\begin{aligned} U_1 &= 2 + \sqrt{2}\, v_1, \\ U_2 &= 2 + \sqrt{2}\, v_2, \\ U_3 &= 3 + v_1/\sqrt{2} + v_2/\sqrt{2} + \sqrt{2}\, v_3; \end{aligned}$$

and if from a normal random variate generator we have obtained the number string 0.11, 1.23, −0.50, 0.73, 0.65, 0.7, 1.51, −0.98, 0.32, . . . , we can perform experiments by using three of these numbers at a time. The first three experiments yield

observation 1 $\quad \mathbf{U} = (2.15, 3.74, 3.24)$, and the choice is $i = 2$;

observation 2 $\quad \mathbf{U} = (3.03, 2.92, 4.94)$, and $i = 3$;

observation 3 $\quad \mathbf{U} = (4.14, 1.01, 3.83)$, and $i = 1$.

After these three experiments, the estimated probabilities are $p_1 = \frac{1}{3}$, $p_2 = \frac{1}{3}$, and $p_3 = \frac{1}{3}$, but more experiments would result in values closer to the exact values: $p_1 = 0.22$, $p_2 = 0.22$, and $p_3 = 0.56$. ■

Since each experiment can be regarded as a Bernoulli trial with probability of success p_i, the total number of successes after N trials, N_i, is binomially distributed. The mean is $E(N_i) = Np_i$ and the variance $\operatorname{var}(N_i) = Np_i(1 - p_i)$. For large values of N, one can use the normal approximation to the binomial and be quite sure that

$$|N_i - Np_i| < 2[Np_i(1 - p_i)]^{1/2}.$$

Consequently, the relative error in estimating p_i is

$$\varepsilon_i(N) = 100\left|\frac{N_i}{N} - p_i\right| \Big/ p_i < 2\left(\frac{1 - p_i}{Np_i}\right)^{1/2} \approx 2\left(\frac{N - N_i}{NN_i}\right)^{1/2}.$$

This expression indicates that small probabilities ($p_i \to 0$) require larger values of N since the relative error is proportional to the square root of the reciprocal of the number of successes:

$$\varepsilon_i(N) \approx (200/\sqrt{N_i})\% \qquad \text{for small} \quad p_i\text{s}.$$

If in the example we admitted a 10% relative error in our calculation of p_1, we would have to repeat the experiment until we obtained $20^2 = 400$ successes, which, because $p_1 \approx 0.22$, would require approximately 1800 experiments. The simulation approach thus seems unsuitable for calibration purposes because it would be very costly.

In addition, since to calculate p_i one normally performs experiments until some prescribed number of successes is achieved [or a similar stopping rule is used, e.g., $\varepsilon_i(N) < 0.1$], the number of experiments is itself a random variable and this, as pointed out by Danganzo, *et al.* (1977b), introduces a small bias in the calculated values. This bias, however, is rather small [as suggested by the experiment in Daganzo *et al.* (1977b)] and becomes smaller with increased values of N_i and N.

The last drawback of calibration with simulation is that if in the initial stage of the search process the current value of $\boldsymbol{\theta}$ is very different from the true value $\boldsymbol{\theta}_o$, some of the observations in the data set may have such small probabilities that they may be impossible to calculate. Indeed, this happens since with a small synthetic data set with 50 observations, Daganzo *et al.* (1977b) found that, for three of the observations at an arbitrary starting point, N_i was equal to zero after 10,000 experiments. On the other hand, in the last stage of the process, near the optimum, one needs high accuracy to discriminate between values of $\boldsymbol{\theta}$ with similar $\log L(\boldsymbol{\theta})$ and this cannot be done with Monte Carlo simulation. Of course, it can be properly argued that if the likelihood function is very flat, the estimate of $\boldsymbol{\theta}$, $\hat{\boldsymbol{\theta}}$ is not very reliable (see Chapter 3), and one is not interested in determining it accurately anyway.

Although Monte Carlo simulation has some undesirable characteristics that prevent its use in calibrating MNP models, the technique is very useful for prediction purposes. It will be seen in Chapter 4 that when one has to evaluate the fraction of the population selecting an alternative, i.e., the expected choice probability $P_i(\boldsymbol{\theta})$ for a user sampled at random from the population, one can use the Monte Carlo method since in that case one can easily afford a large number of replications. Monte Carlo simulation is, in particular, a very convenient way to obtain confidence and prediction intervals for the forecasts (see Chapter 5).

2.2.3 *Approximation Method*

This particular approach is based on formulas [Clark (1961)] that approximate p_i very quickly for a reasonably large number of alternatives. The approach was suggested for an MNP route-choice prediction problem by Daganzo and Sheffi (1977) and subsequently an efficient estimation method was developed by Daganzo *et al.* (1977a). Further discussions of the method appear in Daganzo *et al.* (1977b) and Bouthelier (1978). Bouthelier's dissertation (1978) is particularly interesting since, in addition to pioneering several aspects of this approach, it summarizes the relevant information in previous publications.

Clark's Formulas

Assume that Ω_1, Ω_2, and Ω_3 are three MVN distributed random variables with known mean vector $\mathbf{m} = (m_1, m_2, m_3)$ and covariance matrix

$$\boldsymbol{\Sigma}_\Omega = \begin{bmatrix} \sigma_1^2 & \sigma_{12}^2 & \sigma_{13}^2 \\ \sigma_{21}^2 & \sigma_2^2 & \sigma_{13}^2 \\ \sigma_{31}^2 & \sigma_{32}^2 & \sigma_3^2 \end{bmatrix}.$$

Let $\tilde{\Omega}_2$ be the random variable taking the greatest value of Ω_1 and Ω_2, $\tilde{\Omega}_2 = \max\{\Omega_1; \Omega_2\}$. In connection with a stochastic network scheduling problem Clark (1961) calculated the first four moments of $\tilde{\Omega}_2$ and the covariance of $\tilde{\Omega}_2$ and Ω_3 as a function of $\mathbf{m}$ and $\boldsymbol{\Sigma}_\Omega$. The formulas for the first two moments of $\tilde{\Omega}_2$ (the third and fourth moments will not be used in MNP calculations) and the covariance of $\tilde{\Omega}_2$ and Ω_3 are

$$\tilde{m}_2 = m_2 + (m_1 - m_2)\Phi(\alpha) + a\phi(\alpha), \tag{2.24a}$$

$$\tilde{\tilde{m}}_2 = m_2^2 + \sigma_2^2 + (m_1^2 + \sigma_1^2 - m_2^2 - \sigma_2^2)\Phi(\alpha) + (m_1 + m_2)a\phi(\alpha), \tag{2.24b}$$

$$\tilde{\sigma}_2^2 = \tilde{\tilde{m}}_2 - \tilde{m}_2^2, \tag{2.24c}$$

and

$$\tilde{\sigma}_{23}^2 = \sigma_{23}^2 + (\sigma_{13}^2 - \sigma_{23}^2)\Phi(\alpha), \tag{2.24d}$$

where

$$a = [(\sigma_1^2 + \sigma_2^2 - 2\sigma_{12}^2)]^{1/2} \qquad \text{and} \qquad \alpha = (m_1 - m_2)/a.$$

In these formulas, $\tilde{m}_2$, $\tilde{\tilde{m}}_2$, $\tilde{\sigma}_2^2$, and $\tilde{\sigma}_{23}^2$ represent, respectively, the mean, second absolute moment and variance of $\tilde{\Omega}_2$, and the covariance of $\tilde{\Omega}_2$ and Ω_3.

If, as suggested by Clark, one approximates $\{\tilde{\Omega}_2, \Omega_3\}$ by a bivariate normal distribution with mean vector and covariance matrix given by Eqs. (2.24), one can apply Eqs. (2.24a–c) again to $\{\tilde{\Omega}_2, \Omega_3\}$ to obtain the mean and variance of $\tilde{\Omega}_3 = \max\{\tilde{\Omega}_2, \Omega_3\} = \max\{\Omega_1, \Omega_2, \Omega_3\}$.

As a matter of fact, the formulas can be applied recursively to a set of variables $\Omega_1, \ldots, \Omega_k$ to obtain the approximate mean and variance of the maximum $\tilde{\Omega}_k$.

At the $(i-1)$ step, one calculates

$$\tilde{m}_i = m_i + (\tilde{m}_{i-1} - m_i)\Phi(\alpha_i) + a_i\phi(\alpha_i),$$
$$\tilde{\tilde{m}}_i = m_i^2 + \sigma_i^2 + (\tilde{m}_{i-1} + \tilde{\tilde{\sigma}}_{i-1}^2 - m_i^2 - \sigma_i^2)\Phi(\alpha_i) + (\tilde{m}_{i-1} + m_i)a_i\phi(\alpha_i),$$
$$\tilde{\sigma}_i^2 = \tilde{\tilde{m}}_i - \tilde{m}_i^2,$$
$$\tilde{\sigma}_{ij}^2 = \sigma_{ij}^2 + (\tilde{\sigma}_{i-1,j}^2 - \sigma_{ij}^2)\Phi(\alpha_i) \qquad \text{for} \quad j = i+1, i+2, \ldots, k,$$

and

$$\tilde{\sigma}_{ji}^2 = \tilde{\sigma}_{ij}^2 \qquad \text{for} \quad j = i+1, i+2, \ldots, k$$

with

$$a_i = (\tilde{\sigma}_{i-1}^2 + \sigma_i^2 - 2\tilde{\sigma}_{i-1,i}^2)^{1/2} \qquad \text{and} \qquad \alpha_i = (\tilde{m}_{i-1} - m_i)/a_i.$$

We note that the ith step requires one evaluation of $\phi(\cdot)$ and $\Phi(\cdot)$, the calculation of $\tilde{m}_i$, $\tilde{\tilde{m}}_i$, and $(k-i)$ variance or covariance calculations.

Since it takes $k-1$ steps to calculate the mean and variance of $\tilde{\Omega}_k$, the total number of calculations consists of

(1) $k-1$ evaluations of $\phi(\cdot)$ and $\Phi(\cdot)$,
(2) $2(k-1)$ evaluations of $\tilde{m}$ and $\tilde{\tilde{m}}$, and
(3) $k(k-1)/2$ evaluations of variances and covariances.

It can be seen that for large values of k the number of calculations increases with the square of k. However, since a single calculation takes a very small amount of computer time, one can calculate $\tilde{m}_k$ and $\tilde{\sigma}_k^2$ efficiently for a substantial number of alternatives.

Application to the MNP Function

The choice probability $p_i(\mathbf{V}, \mathbf{\Sigma}_\xi)$ can be written as

$$p_i(\mathbf{V}, \mathbf{\Sigma}_\xi) = \Pr\left\{U_i > \max_{j \neq i}(U_j) \middle| \mathbf{V}, \mathbf{\Sigma}_\xi\right\}, \tag{2.25a}$$

or using the same transformation as in Section 2.2.1 as

$$p_i(\mathbf{V}, \mathbf{\Sigma}_\xi) = \Pr\left\{\max_{j=1,\ldots,I-1}(Z_j) \leq 0 \middle| \bar{\mathbf{Z}}, \mathbf{\Sigma}_Z\right\}. \tag{2.25b}$$

Using $\tilde{Z}_{I-1} = \max_{j=1,\ldots,I-1}(Z_j)$, and letting $\tilde{\mu}_{I-1}$ and $\tilde{\sigma}_{I-1}^2$ be the approximate mean and variance of $\tilde{Z}_{I-1}$ that one calculates with Clark's recursive formulas, one can approximate $\tilde{Z}_{I-1}$ by a normal random variable with the same mean and variance, and p_i by

$$p_i(\mathbf{V}, \mathbf{\Sigma}_\xi) \approx \Phi(-\tilde{\mu}_{I-1}/\tilde{\sigma}_{I-1}). \tag{2.26}$$

The effort involved in evaluating p_i is approximately the same as performing $I-2$ steps of Clark's recursive technique. For a problem with three alternatives we need

(1) one calculation of $\phi(\cdot)$,
(2) two calculations of $\Phi(\cdot)$,
(3) two evaluations of $\tilde{m}$ and $\tilde{\tilde{m}}$, and
(4) one evaluation of a variance or covariance.

These are trivial calculations with a computer and, as will be seen with the example below, much less cumbersome than those needed for the numerical-integration method.

It should be noted at this point that one can alternatively find the choice probability of, say, the last alternative, p_I, by operating with Clark's method directly on $\mathbf{V}$ and $\boldsymbol{\Sigma}_\xi$ to find

$$m^*_{I-1} = E\left[\max_{j<I}(U_j)\right],$$

$$\tilde{\sigma}^{2*}_{I-1} = \operatorname{var}\left[\max_{j<I}(U_j)\right],$$

$$\tilde{\sigma}^{2*}_{I-I,I} = \operatorname{cov}\left[\max_{j<I}(U_j), U_I\right],$$

and

$$p_I(\mathbf{V}, \boldsymbol{\Sigma}_\xi) = \Phi\left(\frac{V_I - m^*_{I-1}}{(\sigma_I^2 + \tilde{\sigma}^{2*}_{I-1} - 2\tilde{\sigma}^{2*}_{I-1,I})^{1/2}}\right). \tag{2.27}$$

The computational requirements of the first method are less than those of Eq. (2.27) since Eq. (2.26) requires fewer covariance calculations, and the calculation of $\bar{\mathbf{Z}}$ and $\boldsymbol{\Sigma}_Z$ can be done off line.

These two methods are now applied to the example of Section 2.2.1.

Example We evaluate p_1 for an MNP model with $\mathbf{V} = (2, 2, 3)$ and

$$\boldsymbol{\Sigma}_\xi = \begin{bmatrix} 2 & 0 & 1 \\ 0 & 2 & 1 \\ 1 & 1 & 3 \end{bmatrix}.$$

As was seen in Section 2.2.1, $\bar{\mathbf{Z}} = (0, 1)$ and $\boldsymbol{\Sigma}_Z = \begin{bmatrix} 4 & 2 \\ 2 & 3 \end{bmatrix}$. Clark's formulas, Eqs. (2.24a–c), yield

$$\mathrm{a} = 1.732, \qquad \alpha = -0.577,$$

$$\tilde{\mu}_2 = 1 - \Phi(-0.577) + 1.732\phi(-0.577) = 1.302,$$

$$\tilde{\tilde{\mu}}_2 = 4 + 1.732\phi(-0.577) = 4.585,$$

$$\tilde{\sigma}_2^2 = 2.890 \qquad \text{and} \qquad \tilde{\sigma}_2 = 1.700.$$

Equation (2.26) gives $p_1 \approx \Phi(-1.302/1.700) = 0.222$.

Note that this value of p_1 is very close to the one calculated with the integration method but that the computational effort is drastically reduced.

In order to apply Eq. (2.27), it is convenient to rearrange the elements of $\mathbf{V}$ and $\mathbf{\Sigma}_\xi$ so that the alternative under consideration is the last one. Such a permutation yields

$$\mathbf{V} = (3, 2, 2) \qquad \text{and} \qquad \mathbf{\Sigma}_\xi = \begin{bmatrix} 3 & 1 & 1 \\ 1 & 2 & 0 \\ 1 & 0 & 2 \end{bmatrix}.$$

Naturally, one will now calculate p_3 instead of p_1. The involved calculations are

$$\begin{aligned} a &= 1.73 \qquad \text{and} \qquad \alpha = 0.577, \\ E(\tilde{U}_2) &= 2 + \Phi(0.577) + 1.73 \cdot \phi(0.577) = 3.30, \\ E(\tilde{U}_2^2) &= 6 + 6\Phi(0.577) + 5 \cdot 1.73 \cdot \phi(0.577) = 13.23, \\ \text{var}(\tilde{U}_2) &= 2.34, \\ \text{cov}(\tilde{U}_2, U_3) &= \Phi(0.577) = 0.72, \end{aligned}$$

and

$$p_3 = \Phi[(2 - 3.3)/(2.34 + 2 - 1.44)^{1/2}] = \Phi(-1.3/1.7) = 0.222. \quad \blacksquare$$

Accuracy and Efficiency of the Method

The computer central processing unit (CPU) time of the approximation method is approximately given by

$$\text{time} \approx \alpha(I - 2)(I + 3),$$

where I is the number of alternatives and α is a parameter that depends on the computer installation. On an IBM 370 model 168 computer, the value of α was found to be 10^{-4} sec.

Thus, for a problem with five alternatives, time $\approx 24 \times 10^{-4}$ sec, and a calibration execution requiring 10^5 MNP function evaluations would take approximately four minutes of CPU time. The approximation method thus is computationally attractive even for problems with more than three alternatives.

Daganzo *et al.* (1977b), Bouthelier (1978), and Albright *et al.* (1977) have all explored the accuracy of the approximation method. Daganzo *et al.* and Bouthelier looked at the effect of approximating $\tilde{U}_2, \tilde{U}_3$, etc. by normal variates. They looked at the exact and approximated cumulative distribution functions of $\tilde{U}_j$ (for different values of j and independent Us) and concluded that the approximation is satisfactory except, perhaps, in cases where vari-

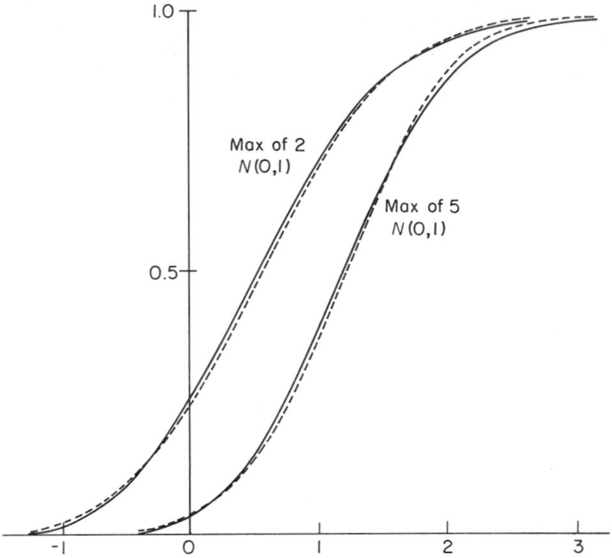

Fig. 2.3 Accuracy of Clark's approximation formulas. Case I: cumulative distribution function for the maximum of several independent standard normal random variables. Straight line: true; dashed line: approximation. [Source: Daganzo *et al.* (1977b).]

ables have very different variances and similar means. Figures 2.3 and 2.4 display some of the results in the abovementioned publications. It was also concluded by Daganzo *et al.* that the existance of positive correlations tends to enhance the results and that problems with few alternatives are more accurately approximated. In addition to this analytical evidence, Albright *et al.* (1977) have verified the accuracy of the approximation method with a series of Monte Carlo simulation experiments.

Although much emphasis has been placed on accuracy, it should be remembered that, whether or not the approximation method closely reproduces the MNP probabilities, it could be, to a certain extent, irrelevant; for if

$$0 \leq p_i(\mathbf{V}, \mathbf{\Sigma}_\xi) \leq 1 \qquad \text{and} \qquad \sum_{i=1}^{I} p_i(\mathbf{V}, \mathbf{\Sigma}_\xi) \approx 1,$$

the approximation method would satisfy Eqs. (1.5a) and (1.5b) and could be regarded as a discrete-choice model in its own right. Although more evidence is needed in this respect, Daganzo *et al.* (1977a) found that for a problem with ten alternatives $\sum_{i=1}^{10} p_i = 1.05$ and that the result was more or less independent of the order in which the alternatives were stacked for the recursive calculations.

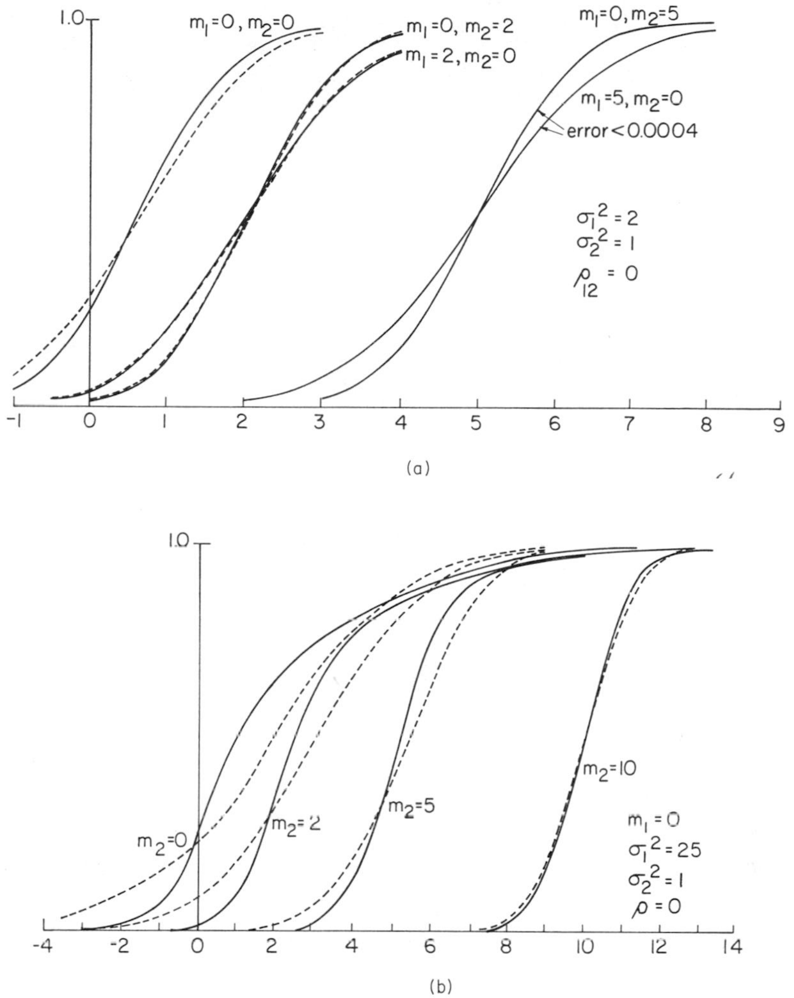

Fig. 2.4 Accuracy of Clark's approximation formulas. Case II: cumulative distribution function for the maximum of two independent normal variables with different means (m_1, m_2) and variances (σ_1^2, σ_2^2). Straight line: true; dashed line: approximation. [Source: Daganzo *et al.* (1977b).]

At present, the approximation approach seems to be the MNP function evaluation method that is best suited to calibrate models since for most applications it seems reasonably accurate and is the fastest of the three. An exception would be a three-alternative problem with negative correlations and/or very large variance differentials where the relatively large differences that would arise between the approximation and exact MNP probabilities could not be tolerated. Under these conditions, it would be better to use the more exact numerical-integration method. Note also that for two-alternative problems the integration and approximation methods coincide.

2.3 Likelihood Evaluation

Evaluation of the likelihood function generally involves calculation of a choice probability for each one of the observations in the data set, which must, of course, be done with one of the evaluation methods described in the previous section.

Evaluation of the likelihood function thus involves calculation of $\mathbf{V}$ and $\boldsymbol{\Sigma}_\xi$ for each one of the observations in the data set by entering into the specification of the model

$$\log p_1[E(\mathbf{Z}_{(n)}, \operatorname{cov}(\mathbf{Z}_{(n)})]$$

and calculating $\log p_{c_{(n)}}(\mathbf{V}_{(n)}(\boldsymbol{\theta}), \boldsymbol{\Sigma}_{\xi(n)}(\boldsymbol{\theta}))$.

The sum of these quantities gives the log-likelihood function for attribute-based samples [Eq. (2.5)].

Choice-based samples require, in addition, calculation of the fraction of the population that would select each alternative if the true parameter value was $\boldsymbol{\theta}$ [see Eq. (2.7a) and the related discussion regarding the calculation of such fractions—$P_i(\boldsymbol{\theta})$]. Alternatively, it is possible to use the pseudo-likelihood function given by Eq. (2.7b), which does not require calculation of $P_i(\boldsymbol{\theta})$. The selection of either one of these equations is dictated by the availability of information about the distribution of the attribute vector and the alternatives across the population.

In a random sample with ranked alternatives, one must calculate $E(\mathbf{Z}_{(n)})$ and $\operatorname{cov}(\mathbf{Z}_{(n)})$ instead of $\mathbf{V}$ and $\boldsymbol{\Sigma}_\xi$ for each observation. This is done by calculating $\boldsymbol{\Delta}_{(n)}$ and entering it in Eqs. (2.10). With this done, one calculates

$$\mathbf{V}_{(n)}(\boldsymbol{\theta}) = \mathbf{V}(\boldsymbol{\theta}, \mathbf{a}_{(n)}),$$
$$\boldsymbol{\Sigma}_{\xi(n)}(\boldsymbol{\theta}) = \boldsymbol{\Sigma}_\xi(\boldsymbol{\theta}, \mathbf{a}_{(n)}),$$

for each one of the observations.

The rest of this section applies only to attribute-based samples but the discussion is easy to generalize for other forms of the log-likelihood function.

2.3.1 *Model Specification*

In order to calculate the log-likelihood function for a given $\boldsymbol{\theta}$, it is necessary to know the attribute vector $\mathbf{a}_{(n)}$ and choice $c_{(n)}$ of every observation in the sample, and how $\mathbf{V}_{(n)}$ and $\boldsymbol{\Sigma}_{\xi(n)}$ depend on these (i.e., the data and the specification of the MNP model). A convenient way of handling this is the scheme depicted in Fig. 2.2, where the likelihood evaluation routine calls successively, for each data point, a specification routine that calculates $\mathbf{V}_{(n)}$ and $\boldsymbol{\Sigma}_{\xi(n)}$ from $\boldsymbol{\theta}$ and $\mathbf{a}_{(n)}$, and the MNP function evaluation routine.

Although most of the comments in this section would apply to any computer program, the specific input details correspond to a prototype FORTRAN program that has been developed by several researchers and the author [Daganzo *et al.* (1977a,b) and Daganzo and Schoenfeld (1978)]. In the aforementioned program, the specification routine must be provided by the user following some simple guidelines. Namely, given a choice $c_{(n)}$ (or a ranking $r_{(n)}$), an attribute vector $\mathbf{a}_{(n)}$, and a value of the parameter $\boldsymbol{\theta}$, the subroutine must return $\mathbf{V}_{(n)}$ and $\boldsymbol{\Sigma}_{\xi(n)}$. The program will automatically call this and the MNP function evaluation subroutines once for each observation and will aggregate the results to give $\log L(\boldsymbol{\theta})$.

In specifying $\mathbf{V}(\boldsymbol{\theta}, \mathbf{a})$ and $\boldsymbol{\Sigma}_{\xi}(\boldsymbol{\theta}, \mathbf{a})$ the user must make sure that the matrix $\boldsymbol{\Sigma}_{\xi}$ remains positive definite for all the feasible values of $\boldsymbol{\theta}$, since otherwise $\boldsymbol{\Sigma}_{\xi}$ would not represent a covariance matrix and the program would not return meaningful values.[5] This can be done in two ways:

(a) expressing $\boldsymbol{\Sigma}_{\xi}(\boldsymbol{\theta}, \mathbf{a})$ as the product of a matrix and its transpose,

$$\boldsymbol{\Sigma}_{\xi}(\boldsymbol{\theta}, \mathbf{a}) = \mathbf{C}_{\xi}(\boldsymbol{\theta}, \mathbf{a})\, \mathbf{C}_{\xi}^{\mathrm{T}}(\boldsymbol{\theta}, \mathbf{a});$$

(b) expressing $\boldsymbol{\Sigma}_{\xi}(\boldsymbol{\theta}, \mathbf{a})$ as a function of $\boldsymbol{\theta}$ and $\mathbf{a}$ directly, and placing bounds on each one of the parameters $\boldsymbol{\theta}$, $\boldsymbol{\theta}_{\min} < \boldsymbol{\theta} < \boldsymbol{\theta}_{\max}$, to ensure that $\boldsymbol{\Sigma}_{\xi}(\boldsymbol{\theta}, \mathbf{a})$ is positive definite.

Each method has its proper application place. Method (a) can always be applied but requires a matrix multiplication for each evaluation of $\boldsymbol{\Sigma}_{\xi}$, and since the matrix $\mathbf{C}_{\xi}(\boldsymbol{\theta}, \mathbf{a})$ is not a covariance matrix, it is difficult to interpret and specify reasonably. Method (b) is more intuitive to specify but for problems with several parameters it is hard to find the domain of $\boldsymbol{\theta}$ that makes $\boldsymbol{\Sigma}_{\xi}(\boldsymbol{\theta}, \mathbf{a})$ positive definite. Sheffi (1978a) and Sheffi and Daganzo (1978b) discuss ways of specifying MNP models by using networks as graphical aids.

The input to a MNP computer program will, thus, typically involve several things:

(1) a control card giving the number of observations, alternatives, parameters, attributes, and other information, such as the maximum allowable number of iterations, and a convergence criterion;

[5] Although positive-semidefinite matrices are covariance matrices too, the statistical regularity conditions imposed on the specification of a MNP model in Chapter 3 require that $\boldsymbol{\Sigma}_{\xi}$ be positive definite (see condition 3 in Section 3.2.2).

(2) a set of cards (one for each parameter) giving

$$\boldsymbol{\theta}_{\min}, \quad \text{an initial value of } \boldsymbol{\theta}, \quad \text{and} \quad \boldsymbol{\theta}_{\max};$$

(3) the data set (one card per observation) giving the attribute vector and an observed choice;

(4) either a FORTRAN subroutine giving the specification of $\mathbf{V}(\boldsymbol{\theta}, \mathbf{a})$ and $\boldsymbol{\Sigma}_\xi(\boldsymbol{\theta}, \mathbf{a})$, or a set of constants that would be used in an internally defined subroutine.

The computer program will then evaluate $\log L(\boldsymbol{\theta})$ at the initial point and, using a systematic search technique (discussed in the following section), move to different points $\boldsymbol{\theta}$ until a value $\hat{\boldsymbol{\theta}}$ that maximizes the likelihood is found.

2.3.2 Computer Input Preparation

As an example consider a three-alternative modal-split problem in which the attractivenss of mode i is proportional to the negative of the travel time:

$$V_1 = -\theta_1 A_1, \qquad V_2 = -\theta_1 A_2, \qquad V_3 = -\theta_1 A_3,$$

where A_i represents the travel time by mode i and θ_1 is a generic parameter representing the value of travel time in unattractiveness units.

Assuming that modes 1 and 2 are two public-transportation modes (say, bus and streetcar) and that mode 3 is the private automobile, it seems reasonable to expect modes 1 and 2 to share some neglected attributes that would not particularly affect mode 3, e.g., public-transportation discomfort and lack of privacy. It then makes sense to specify the covariance matrix $\boldsymbol{\Sigma}_\xi(\boldsymbol{\theta}, \mathbf{A})$ as

$$\boldsymbol{\Sigma}_\xi(\boldsymbol{\theta}, \mathbf{A}) = \begin{bmatrix} 1 & \theta_2 & 0 \\ \theta_2 & 1 & 0 \\ 0 & 0 & 1 \end{bmatrix},$$

where θ_2 represents the correlation of U_1 and U_2 (a large number would indicate that the common neglected attributes influence the perceived attractiveness heavily and a small number would indicate the opposite).

Since for this particular problem we are employing specification method (b), we need to make sure that $\boldsymbol{\Sigma}_\xi(\boldsymbol{\theta}, \mathbf{a})$ is positive definite. This can be done by calculating the main diagonal minors of $\boldsymbol{\Sigma}_\xi$ and finding the range of θ_2 for which they are positive. In our case, $\boldsymbol{\Sigma}_\xi$ is positive definite if $|\boldsymbol{\Sigma}_\xi| > 0$, which, of course, only happens if $|\theta_2| < 1$.

Since logically θ_1 need not be restricted, one could assign the following values to $\boldsymbol{\theta}_{\min}$ and $\boldsymbol{\theta}_{\max}$:

$$\boldsymbol{\theta}_{\min} = (-100, -1) \qquad \text{and} \qquad \boldsymbol{\theta}_{\max} = (100, 1).$$

Table 2.4

Trinomial Probit Calibration Data[a]

A_1	A_2	A_3	Choice	A_1	A_2	A_3	Choice
16.481	16.196	23.890	2	15.237	14.345	19.984	2
15.123	11.373	14.182	2	10.840	11.071	10.188	1
19.469	8.822	20.819	2	16.841	11.224	13.417	2
18.847	15.649	21.280	2	13.913	16.991	26.618	3
12.578	10.671	18.335	2	13.089	9.822	19.162	2
11.513	20.582	27.838	1	16.626	10.725	15.285	3
10.651	15.537	17.418	1	13.477	15.509	24.421	2
8.359	15.675	21.050	1	20.851	14.557	19.800	2
11.679	12.668	23.104	1	11.365	12.673	22.212	2
23.237	10.356	21.346	2	13.296	10.076	17.810	2
13.236	16.019	10.087	3	15.417	14.103	21.050	1
20.052	16.861	14.168	3	15.938	11.180	19.851	2
18.917	14.764	21.564	2	19.034	14.125	19.764	2
18.200	6.868	19.095	2	10.466	12.841	18.540	1
10.777	16.554	15.938	1	15.799	16.979	13.074	3
20.003	6.377	9.314	2	12.713	15.105	13.629	2
19.768	8.523	18.960	2	16.908	10.958	19.713	2
8.151	13.845	17.643	2	17.098	6.853	14.502	2
22.173	18.045	15.535	1	18.608	14.286	18.301	2
13.134	11.067	19.108	2	11.059	10.812	20.121	1
14.051	14.247	15.764	1	15.641	10.754	24.669	2
14.685	10.811	12.361	3	7.822	18.949	16.904	1
11.666	10.758	16.445	1	12.824	5.697	19.183	2
17.211	15.201	17.059	3	11.852	12.147	15.672	2
13.930	16.227	22.024	1	15.557	8.307	22.286	2

[a] Source: Daganzo *et al.* (1977).

Table 2.4 gives a hypothetical data set for this problem, and Table 2.5 gives the necessary computer input. The computer output is given at the end of the next section.

2.4 Maximization Methods and Computer Output Interpretation

2.4.1 Search Methods

Once a log-likelihood evaluation method has been adopted, it is possible to use standard optimization procedures to find the maximum of $\log L(\boldsymbol{\theta})$. The procedures discussed in this section are the *steepest-ascent*, *Newton–Raphson*, and *variable-metric* methods. In addition, one can use search

Table 2.5

Trinomial Probit Input Data with CHOMP

(a) Card sequence

8. Job Control cards

7. Initial value cards

6. Data set

5. Control card

4. Job control cards

3. Specification subroutine

2. Main program

1. Job control cards

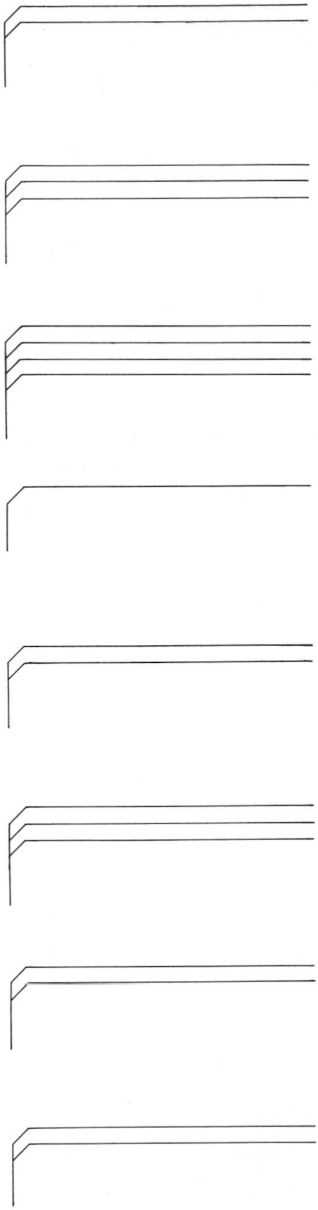

Table 2.5 (*continued*)

(b) Card contents

Description	Actual card contents for the example
FORTRAN Specification subroutine In this subtroutine $A(I, K)$ is the ith attribute of the kth observation, PAR(I) represents θ_i, $V(I)$ is the ith measured attractiveness function, and SIGMA (I, J) is an element of the covariance matrix.	SUBROUTINE SPEC (A, PAR, K, V, SIGMA) DIMENSION A(5,100), PAR(3), V(3), SIGMA (3, 3) V(1) = − PAR(1) * A(1, K) V(2) = − PAR(1) * A(2, K) V(3) = − PAR(1) * A(3, K) SIGMA (1, 1) = 1 SIGMA (1, 2) = PAR(2) RETURN END
Control card[a] $(NA, r, N, I, \varepsilon, \alpha, NIT, H)$	3 2 50 3 0.001 3.0 5 1
Data set (first and last cards only) (CHOICE, A_1, A_2, A_3)	2 16.481 16.196 23.89 2 15.557 8.307 22.286
Initial value cards[a] $(\theta, \theta_{\min}, \theta_{\max}, \partial\theta)$	0 − 100.00 100.00 0.0001 0 − 1.00 1.00 0.0100

[a] NA, r, N, and I are, respectively, the number of attributes, parameters, data points, and alternatives. ε is a small number used as a convergence criterion, α is a number that controls the line search (3 seems always to work well). NIT is the number of iterations, $H = 1$ requests that the covariance matrix of $\hat{\boldsymbol{\theta}}$ be calculated, and $\partial\theta$ are small numbers used to calculate the derivatives of $\log L(\boldsymbol{\theta})$ numerically.

methods that have been specifically developed for maximum-likelihood problems [such as the one used by Hausman and Wise (1978)], but these will not be covered in this book.

The steepest-ascent method calculates the direction in which the log-likelihood function increases the fastest and evaluates $\log L(\boldsymbol{\theta})$ several times along such direction until a maximum is found. In mathematical terms, we find the value of η for which $\log L(\boldsymbol{\theta}_\eta)$ is maximum, where

$$\boldsymbol{\theta}_\eta = \boldsymbol{\theta} + \eta\,\Delta\boldsymbol{\theta}, \tag{2.28}$$

η is a scalar and $\Delta\boldsymbol{\theta}$ is a vector that points in the direction in which $\log L(\boldsymbol{\theta}_\eta)$ increases the fastest when η is increased. From this new point $\boldsymbol{\theta}_\eta$, the process is repeated until a *stationary point* from which one cannot find an ascent direction is located.

From elementary calculus it is known that a function increases the fastest in the direction of the *gradient*, or vector of partial derivatives. That is, for the steepest-ascent method, $\Delta\boldsymbol{\theta}$ is given by

$$\Delta\boldsymbol{\theta} = \nabla_\theta \log L(\boldsymbol{\theta}), \tag{2.29}$$

where $\nabla_\theta \log L(\boldsymbol{\theta}) = [\partial \log L(\boldsymbol{\theta})/\partial\theta_1, \ldots, \partial \log L(\boldsymbol{\theta})/\partial\theta_r]$ is the gradient, which can be evaluated numerically.

Once $\Delta\boldsymbol{\theta}$ has been selected, one must find the value of η, η^*, that results in the largest increase of $\log L(\boldsymbol{\theta})$; i.e.,

$$\max_{\eta \geq 0} \log L(\boldsymbol{\theta} + \eta\, \Delta\boldsymbol{\theta}). \tag{2.30}$$

This is, however, a maximization of a function of one variable, which can be accomplished with a golden section search, for instance. An iteration of the steepest-ascent method involves calculating $\Delta\boldsymbol{\theta}$ with Eq. (2.29), η^* with Eq. (2.30), and the new value of $\boldsymbol{\theta}$, $\boldsymbol{\theta}_{\eta^*}$, with Eq. (2.28). The other two search

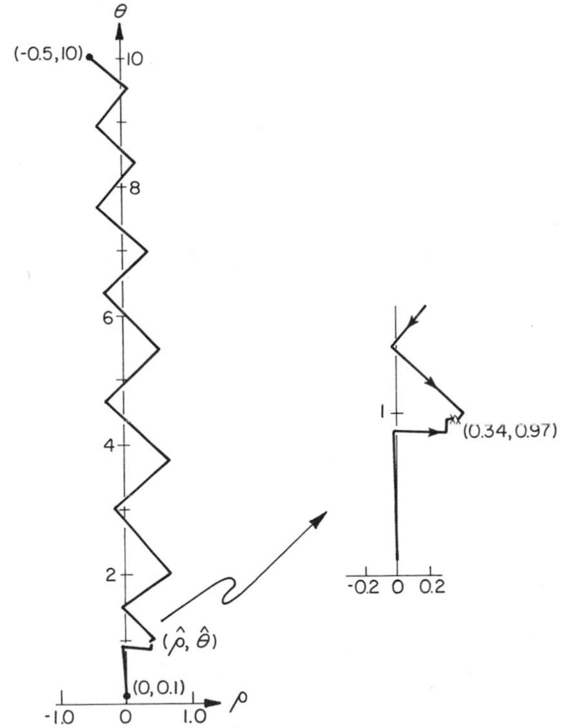

Fig. 2.5 Convergence pattern of the steepest-ascent method for a two-parameter (θ and ρ in the figure) trinomial probit model. [Source: Daganzo *et al.* (1977b).]

methods about to be reviewed follow the same pattern except that the formulas to calculate the search direction $\Delta\boldsymbol{\theta}$ and the *step size* η^* are different.

The steepest-ascent method is very reliable but needs many iterations to approach the optimum. This can be seen in Fig. 2.5, which displays the convergence steps of a problem similar to the one in the previous section for two different starting points [Daganzo *et al.*, (1977b)]. Since, as can be gathered from the discussion in the two previous sections, calculation of $\log L(\boldsymbol{\theta})$ is a very time-consuming operation, other methods, which converge in fewer steps and thus require fewer function evaluations, can be used advantageously for MNP analysis.

The *Newton–Raphson* method is used by some MNL computer packages because, when feasible, it is the fastest search method. With this method, $\boldsymbol{\theta}_{\eta^*}$ is obtained by approximating $\log L(\boldsymbol{\theta})$ by a quadratic function with gradient and *Hessian matrix* (i.e., matrix of partial second derivatives) equal to those of $\log L(\boldsymbol{\theta})$ at the current point and setting $\boldsymbol{\theta}_{\eta^*}$ equal to the maximum of the quadratic function. For the method to work, the Hessian matrix should be negative definite at each visited point, since otherwise the quadratic function does not have a unique, finite maximum. This is automatically achieved if the log-likelihood function is strictly concave (as in the case of MNL) or, otherwise, by starting with a parameter value $\boldsymbol{\theta}$ that is sufficiently close to the optimum.[6]

For the Newton–Raphson method η^* and $\Delta\boldsymbol{\theta}$ are

$$\eta^* = 1, \qquad \Delta\boldsymbol{\theta} = \nabla_\theta \log L(\boldsymbol{\theta})[\nabla_\theta^2 \log L(\boldsymbol{\theta})]^{-1}, \tag{2.31}$$

where $\nabla_\theta^2 \log L(\boldsymbol{\theta})$ represents the Hessian matrix.

The Newton–Raphson method is not suitable for most MNP analyses because the calculation of the Hessian matrix requires a phenomenal computational effort in most instances. The method is computationally attractive, however, for binary probit, and for trinomial probit with fixed and known covariance matrix because for these models the partial derivatives of $\log L(\boldsymbol{\theta})$ are available in closed form (see Section 2.4.3).

Variable-metric methods have some of the advantages of the two previously discussed methods since they do not require calculation of second derivatives but do exhibit some of the fast-converging characteristics of the Newton–Raphson method. In the Davidon–Fletcher–Powell (DFP) version [see Avriel (1976) for an accessible reference] the search direction at the $(i + 1)$st step is given by

$$\Delta\boldsymbol{\theta}_{i+1} = -\nabla_\theta \log L(\boldsymbol{\theta}_i)\mathbf{H}_i, \tag{2.32a}$$

[6] A search method stopping after the first iteration of the Newton–Raphson method is sometimes used by statisticians. It is called the *method of scoring* [see Rao (1965), Section 5g].

where $\mathbf{H}_i$ is an approximation for the inverse Hessian matrix, which is recursively updated according to the DFP updating formula

$$\mathbf{H}_i = \mathbf{H}_{i-1} + \frac{\mathbf{q}_i^{\mathrm{T}}\mathbf{q}_i}{\mathbf{q}_i\mathbf{q}_i'^{\mathrm{T}}} - \frac{\mathbf{H}_{i-1}\mathbf{q}_i'^{\mathrm{T}}\mathbf{q}_i'\mathbf{H}_{i-1}}{\mathbf{q}_i'\mathbf{H}_{i-1}\mathbf{q}_i'^{\mathrm{T}}}. \tag{2.32b}$$

In this formula $\mathbf{q}_i$ denotes $(\boldsymbol{\theta}_i - \boldsymbol{\theta}_{i-1})$ and $\mathbf{q}_i'$ denotes $[\boldsymbol{\nabla}_\theta \log L(\boldsymbol{\theta}_i) - \boldsymbol{\nabla}_\theta \log L(\boldsymbol{\theta}_{i-1})]$; at the first iteration one sets $\mathbf{H}_o$ equal to an arbitrary negative definite symmetric matrix (or positive definite for minimization problems). It should be noted that for MNP calibration programs, calculation of Eq. (2.32b) is a trivial task compared with calculation of $\boldsymbol{\nabla}_\theta \log L(\boldsymbol{\theta})$, and that consequently the computational effort involved in calculating $\Delta\boldsymbol{\theta}$ with a variable-metric algorithm is analogous to that of the steepest-ascent method. Since in a variable-metric algorithm the step size η^* is also calculated with (2.30) it can be concluded that the effort per iteration is the same with both methods. As is illustrated in Fig. 2.6, however, the number of steps required with a variable-metric algorithm is made smaller. The difference usually

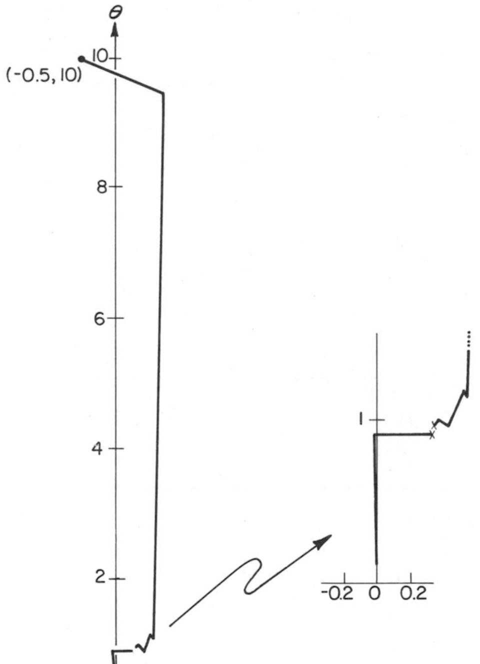

Fig. 2.6 Convergence pattern of a variable metric algorithm for a two-parameter (θ and ρ in the figure) trinomial probit model. [Source: Daganzo *et al.* (1977b).]

increases with the number of parameters to be estimated and with functions that are approximately quadratic.

As an exercise, we apply the three methods to

$$\max y = -29x_1^2 - 7x_2^2 + 18x_1x_2$$

starting at $x_1 = x_2 = 10$. The maximum of this function is at $x^* = (0, 0)$. The reader can verify the results in Table 2.6, which show the slowness of the steepest-ascent method, and that, indeed, $\mathbf{H}_i$ converges to $[\nabla^2 f(x)]^{-1}$.

2.4.2 Computer Output Interpretation and Cost Considerations

Since in addition to the maximum-likelihood estimator one normally wants an estimate of its variance, and since such an estimate is given in most cases by the negative of the inverse of the Hessian matrix of $\log L(\boldsymbol{\theta})$ at the optimum $\hat{\boldsymbol{\theta}}$ (see Chapter 3), a computer routine should produce $[-\nabla_\theta^2 \log L(\hat{\boldsymbol{\theta}})]^{-1}$ as an output. This can be done, either numerically once the optimum is reached or by using the matrix $\mathbf{H}$ if a variable-metric algorithm is used. For $\mathbf{H}$ to be a good approximation, however, the search procedure must have performed several steps near the optimum since otherwise the matrix $\mathbf{H}$ may not have been appropriately warmed up.

Instances in which $\mathbf{H}$ can be used reliably are not known yet since computational experience with MNP models is still very limited; such knowledge would be useful, however, since numerical evaluation of $\nabla_\theta^2 \log L(\hat{\boldsymbol{\theta}})$ is a rather time-consuming operation.

Since in an estimation program the computational cost per step increases linearly with the number of data points, it is cost effective to implement computer codes that only use part of the data (say one-tenth of it) to perform a preliminary search that should yield values of $\boldsymbol{\theta}$ and $\mathbf{H}$ close to $\hat{\boldsymbol{\theta}}$ and $[\nabla_\theta^2 \log L(\hat{\boldsymbol{\theta}})]^{-1}$. With these values as inputs, estimation with the entire data set will rarely require more than two or three iterations and the computational cost can be sharply reduced.

Table 2.7 gives the output corresponding to the problem in the previous section. At each iteration, the values of the parameters and the log-likelihood function are given. Note how the value of the likelihood function increases in absolute value immediately after phase I since more data points are considered from then on. At the end, the exact and approximate inverse Hessian matrices with a changed sign are given under the labels "exact and approximate estimated parameter covariance matrix."

The cost per step of a MNP calibration code, using the approximation method for MNP function evaluations and the DFP algorithm as a search method, can be estimated by means of the following formula, where I is the

Table 2.6

A Comparison of Three Search Techniques

Iteration number	Method employed	$\Delta\theta$	η^*	x	**H** DFP method
Initial values	Steepest-ascent (SA)			(10, 10)	$\begin{pmatrix} -1.0 & 0.0 \\ 0.0 & -1.0 \end{pmatrix}$
	Newton–Raphson (NR)			(10, 10)	
	Davidon Fletcher–Powell (DFP)			(10, 10)	
1	SA	(−400, 40)	0.0164	(3.457, 10.65)	$\begin{pmatrix} -0.113 & -0.294 \\ -0.294 & -0.903 \end{pmatrix}$
	NR	(−10, −10)	1	(0, 0)	
	DFP	(−400, 40)	0.0164	(3.457, 10.65)	
2	SA	(−8.8, −88)	0.091	(2.66, −2.66)	$\begin{pmatrix} -0.034 & -0.031 \\ -0.031 & -0.117 \end{pmatrix}$
	NR	Optimum reached			
	DFP	(−26.9, −82.1)	0.130	(−0.048, 0.006)	
3	SA	(−28.3, 2.83)	0.061	(0.92, 2.83)	$\begin{pmatrix} -0.029 & -0.037 \\ -0.037 & -0.117 \end{pmatrix}$
	NR	Optimum reached			
	DFP	(0.070, −0.009)	0.686	(0, 0)	
Exact solution				(0, 0)	$\begin{pmatrix} -0.029 & -0.037 \\ -0.037 & -0.117 \end{pmatrix}$

number of alternatives, N is the number of sample points, and r is the number of parameters:

$$\text{time} = \alpha(r + 10)N(I - 2)(I + 3).$$

The formula follows from the one in Section 2.2.3, taking into account that each log-likelihood evaluation requires N applications of Clark's formulas, and that each step requires r log-likelihood evaluations to calculate the gradient and approximately ten to perform the one dimensional search. Since, as mentioned in Section 2.2.3, for a reasonably fast computer $\alpha \approx 10^{-4}$ sec, one can apply the method to problems with more than three alternatives, ten or more parameters, and several hundred data points.

The direct numerical Hessian evaluation at the end of the program requires a minimum of $r(r - 1)/2$ log-likelihood function evaluations in the neighborhood of $\hat{\boldsymbol{\theta}}$, which for problems with many parameters is as time-consuming as performing two or three steps.

Thus, even though it is now possible to calibrate a MNP model with existing techniques, further refinements could reduce computational costs considerably. The next subsection discusses a refinement for MNP problems with known covariance matrix $\boldsymbol{\Sigma}_\xi$.

2.4.3 *Shortcut Gradient and Hessian Calculating Methods*[7]

Let us assume that the covariance matrix of the error terms is positive definite and known for each observation in the data set and that the specification of the measured-attractiveness vector is linear in the parameters.[8] That is, the perceived-attractiveness vector $\mathbf{U}$ can be expressed as

$$\mathbf{U} = \boldsymbol{\theta}[\mathbf{A}] + \boldsymbol{\xi},$$

where $\mathbf{U}$ and $\boldsymbol{\xi}$ are row vectors of dimension I, $\boldsymbol{\theta}$ is a row vector of dimension r, $[\mathbf{A}]$ is a $(r \times I)$-dimensional matrix of constants and attributes, and $\boldsymbol{\xi}$ is MVN distributed with zero mean and covariance matrix $\boldsymbol{\Sigma}_\xi$ independent of $\boldsymbol{\theta}$.

First note that the log-likelihood function of an attribute-based sample [Eq. (2.5)] can be written as[9]

$$\log L(\boldsymbol{\theta}) = \sum_{n=1}^{N} \log p_{c_{(n)}}[\mathbf{V}(\boldsymbol{\theta}, \mathbf{a}_{(n)}), \boldsymbol{\Sigma}_{\xi_{(n)}}]$$

[7] This subsection contains substantial mathematical derivations, but it can be skipped without loss of continuity.

[8] Although the derivations in this section could be generalized to models with nonlinear specifications, this was not done because the notation becomes much more involved and the logic is the same.

[9] The discussion that follows could be generalized to include the other sampling methods discussed previously. Instead, they are briefly discussed at the end of the subsection.

Table 2.7

Sample Computer Output

```
NO. OF ATTRIBUTES=      3
NO. OF PARAMETERS=      2
NO. OF SAMPLE POINTS=     50
NO. OF ALTERNATIVES=     3
EPSILON=     .00100
ALPHA=    3.00000
NO. OF ITERATIONS=      5
PROGRAM SELECTION=     -0

PARAMETER NO.  1
INITIAL VALUE=    0.
MIN. ALLOWABLE VALUE=-100.00000
MAX. ALLOWABLE VALUE= 100.00000
PARAMETER INCREMENT=      .00010

PARAMETER NO.  2
INITIAL VALUE=    0.
MIN. ALLOWABLE VALUE=   -1.00000
MAX. ALLOWABLE VALUE=    1.00000
PARAMETER INCREMENT=     .01000

SAMPLE DATA=CHOICE,ATTRIBUTE 1,ATTRIBUTE 2...
     2   16.48100   16.19600   23.89000
     2   15.12300   11.37300   14.18200
     2   19.46900    8.82200   20.81900
     2   18.84700   15.64900   21.28000
     2   12.57800   10.67100   18.35500
     1   11.51300   20.58200   27.83800
     1   10.65100   15.53700   17.41800
     1    8.35900   15.67500   21.05000
     1   11.67900   12.66800   23.10400
     2   23.23700   10.35600   21.34600
     3   13.23600   16.01900   10.08700
     3   20.05200   16.86100   14.16800
     2   18.91700   14.76400   21.56400
     2   18.20000    6.86800   19.09500
     1   10.77700   16.55400   15.93800
     2   20.00300    6.37700    9.31400
     2   19.76800    8.25300   18.96000
     2    8.15100   13.84500   17.64300
     1   22.17300   18.04500   15.53500
     2   13.13400   11.06700   19.10800
     1   14.05100   14.24700   15.76400
     3   14.68500   10.81100   12.36100
     1   11.66600   10.75800   16.44500
     3   17.21100   15.20100   17.05900
     1   13.93000   16.22700   22.02400
     2   15.23700   14.34500   19.98400
     1   10.84000   11.04100   10.18800
     2   16.84100   11.22400   13.41700
     3   13.91300   16.99100   26.61800
     2   13.08900    9.82200   19.16200
     3   16.62600   10.72500   15.28500
     2   13.47700   15.50900   24.42100
     2   20.85100   14.55700   19.80000
     2   11.36500   12.67300   22.21200
     2   13.26900   10.07600   17.81000
     1   15.41700   14.10300   21.05000
     2   15.93800   11.18000   19.85100
     2   19.03400   14.12500   19.76400
     1   10.46600   12.84100   18.54000
     3   15.79900   16.97900   13.07400
     2   12.71300   15.10500   13.62900
     2   16.90800   10.95800   19.71300
     2   17.09800    6.85300   14.50200
     2   18.60800   14.28600   18.30100
     1   11.05900   10.81200   20.12100
     2   15.64100   10.75400   24.66900
     1    7.82200   18.94900   16.90400
     2   12.82400    5.69700   19.18300
     2   11.85200   12.14700   15.67200
     2   15.55700    8.30700   22.28600
```

```
BEGIN OUTPUT

LOG LIKELIHOOD AT STARTING POINT=                -22.06697


ITERATION  1

LOG LIKELIHOOD=          -15.90499

PAR. NO.                 PAR. VALUE
     1                      .17755
     2                     -.00264


ITERATION  2

LOG LIKELIHOOD=          -15.30301

PAR. NO.                 PAR. VALUE
     1                      .19712
     2                      .54513


ITERATION  3

LOG LIKELIHOOD=          -15.21489

PAR. NO.                 PAR. VALUE
     1                      .17655
     2                      .62885


ITERATION  4

LOG LIKELIHOOD=          -15.21308

PAR. NO.                 PAR. VALUE
     1                      .17552
     2                      .61153

END PHASE I


ITERATION  5

LOG LIKELIHOOD=          -34.00635

PAR. NO.                 PAR. VALUE
     1                      .23209
     2                      .61064


ITERATION  6

LOG LIKELIHOOD=          -33.89499

PAR. NO.                 PAR. VALUE
     1                      .23680
     2                      .48043


ITERATION  7

LOG LIKELIHOOD=          -33.89442

PAR. NO.                 PAR. VALUE
     1                      .23835
     2                      .47568

OPTIMUM REACHED******END EXECUTION


ESTIMATED PARAMETER COVARIANCE MATRIX
PAR. NOS.                COVARIANCE(APPROX.)              COVARIANCE(EXACT)
  1, 1                          .00202                    .20620E-02
  2, 1                         -.00458                   -.38776E-02
  2, 2                          .06985                    .99593E-01
```

and that the gradient of $\log L(\boldsymbol{\theta})$ is

$$\nabla_\theta \log L(\boldsymbol{\theta}) = \sum_{n=1}^{N} \nabla_\theta \log p_{c(n)}[\mathbf{V}(\boldsymbol{\theta}, \mathbf{a}_{(n)}), \boldsymbol{\Sigma}_{\xi(n)}]$$

or taking derivatives with respect to $\mathbf{V}$ and then with respect to $\boldsymbol{\theta}$ (using the chain differentiation rule), we have

$$\nabla_\theta \log L(\boldsymbol{\theta}) = \sum_{n=1}^{N} \nabla_V \log p_{c(n)}(\mathbf{V}_{(n)}, \boldsymbol{\Sigma}_{\xi(n)})[\mathbf{a}_{(n)}]^{\mathrm{T}}, \tag{2.33}$$

where ∇_V denotes the vector of partial derivatives with respect to $\mathbf{V}$, and we have used the fact that $\mathbf{V}_{(n)} = \boldsymbol{\theta}[\mathbf{a}_{(n)}]$.

Analogously, we can write the Hessian matrix as

$$\nabla_\theta^2 \log L(\boldsymbol{\theta}) = \sum_{n=1}^{N} [\mathbf{a}_{(n)}]\nabla_V^2 \log p_{c(n)}(\mathbf{V}_{(n)}, \boldsymbol{\Sigma}_{\xi(n)})[\mathbf{a}_{(n)}]^{\mathrm{T}}. \tag{2.34}$$

It is possible to calculate the gradient and Hessian of $\log L(\boldsymbol{\theta})$ simultaneously with $\log L(\boldsymbol{\theta})$ by finding $\nabla_V \log p_{c(n)}(\mathbf{V}_{(n)}, \boldsymbol{\Sigma}_{\xi(n)})$ and $\nabla_V^2 \log p_{c(n)}(\mathbf{V}_{(n)}, \boldsymbol{\Sigma}_{\xi(n)})$ for each observation during the likelihood-evaluation process. Such strategy will be particularly useful when the number of alternatives is smaller than the number of parameters since in such a case ∇_V and ∇_V^2 are easier to apply than ∇_θ and ∇_θ^2. Further economy of computation can be achieved if efficient ways of calculating ∇_V and ∇_V^2 are found.

A shortcut evaluation method of $\nabla_V \log p_i(\mathbf{V}, \boldsymbol{\Sigma}_\xi)$ and $\nabla_V^2 \log p_I(\mathbf{V}, \boldsymbol{\Sigma}_\xi)$, which was suggested by McFadden (1977), is introduced next.

Consider the MNP function $p_i(\mathbf{V}, \boldsymbol{\Sigma}_\xi)$, given by Eqs. (2.14 and 2.15), and write its partial derivative with respect to V_j as

$$\frac{\partial p_i(\mathbf{V}, \boldsymbol{\Sigma}_\xi)}{\partial V_j} = \int_{u_1<u_i} \cdots \int_{u_i=-\infty}^{\infty} \cdots \int_{u_I<u_i} \frac{\partial \phi(\mathbf{u} \mid \mathbf{V}, \boldsymbol{\Sigma}_\xi)}{\partial V_j}\, d\mathbf{u}, \qquad j \neq i.$$

Since $\mathbf{u}$ and $\mathbf{V}$ enter in the same way but with opposite signs in $\phi(\mathbf{u} \mid \mathbf{V}, \boldsymbol{\Sigma}_\xi)$, one has

$$\frac{\partial p_i(\mathbf{V}, \boldsymbol{\Sigma}_\xi)}{\partial V_j} = \int_{u_1<u_i} \cdots \int_{u_j<u_i} \cdots \int_{u_i=-\infty}^{\infty} \cdots \int_{u_I<u_i} -\frac{\partial \phi(\mathbf{u} \mid \mathbf{V}, \boldsymbol{\Sigma}_\xi)}{\partial u_j}\, d\mathbf{u}, \qquad j \neq i,$$

which after changing the order of integration and integrating with respect to u_j reduces to

$$-\int_{u_1<u_i} \cdots \int_{u_{j-1}<u_i} \int_{u_{j+1}<u_i} \cdots \int_{u_i=-\infty}^{\infty} \cdots \int_{u_I<u_i} \phi(\mathbf{u} \mid \mathbf{V}, \boldsymbol{\Sigma}_\xi)\Big|_{u_j=-\infty}^{u_j=u_i} du_1 \cdots du_{j-1}\, du_{j+1} \cdots du_I, \qquad j \neq i. \tag{2.35}$$

The integrand of Eq. (2.35) can be written

$$\phi(\mathbf{u}\,|\,\mathbf{V},\boldsymbol{\Sigma}_\xi)\Big|_{u_j=-\infty}^{u_j=u_i} = [(2\pi)^I|\boldsymbol{\Sigma}_\xi|]^{-1/2}$$

$$\cdot \exp\{-\tfrac{1}{2}(u_1 - V_1, \ldots, u_i - V_j, \ldots, u_i - V_i, \ldots, u_I - V_I)$$

$$\cdot \boldsymbol{\Sigma}_\xi^{-1} \begin{bmatrix} u_1 - V_1 \\ \vdots \\ u_i - V_j \\ \vdots \\ u_i - V_i \\ \vdots \\ u_I - V_I \end{bmatrix} \}, \qquad j \neq i, \tag{2.36a}$$

and we note that the exponent in this expression is an $(I-1)$-dimensional quadratic equation in $u_1, u_2, \ldots, u_{j-1}, u_{j+1}, \ldots,$ and u_I, which can be written

$$\mathbf{u}(j)\mathbf{Q}\mathbf{u}(j)^{\mathrm{T}} - 2\mathbf{u}(j)\mathbf{R}^{\mathrm{T}} + \mathbf{V}\boldsymbol{\Sigma}_\xi^{-1}\mathbf{V}^{\mathrm{T}}, \tag{2.36b}$$

where $\mathbf{u}(j)$ represents the vector $(u_1, u_2, \ldots, u_{j-1}, u_{j+1}, \ldots, u_I)$, $\mathbf{Q}$ is an $(I-1) \times (I-1)$-dimensional, positive definite matrix related to $\boldsymbol{\Sigma}_\xi^{-1}$, and $\mathbf{R}^{\mathrm{T}}$ is a column vector that depends on $\boldsymbol{\Sigma}_\xi^{-1}$ and $\mathbf{V}$.[10] It is easy to show that the matrix $\mathbf{Q}$ can be obtained by adding row j of $\boldsymbol{\Sigma}_\xi^{-1}$ to row i and then column j to column i. The vector $\mathbf{R}$ can be obtained by deleting the jth element of $\mathbf{V}\boldsymbol{\Sigma}_\xi^{-1}$ and adding it to the ith element.

Equation (2.36b) can be alternatively written

$$[\mathbf{u}(j) \quad \mathbf{R}\mathbf{Q}^{-1}]\mathbf{Q}[\mathbf{u}(j)^{\mathrm{T}} - \mathbf{Q}^{-1}\mathbf{R}^{\mathrm{T}}] - \mathbf{R}\mathbf{Q}^{-1}\mathbf{R}^{\mathrm{T}} + \mathbf{V}\boldsymbol{\Sigma}_\xi^{-1}\mathbf{V}^{\mathrm{T}},$$

or, letting $\boldsymbol{\Sigma}_\xi^{-1}(ij) = \mathbf{Q}$, $\mathbf{V}(ij) = \mathbf{R}\mathbf{Q}^{-1}$, and $K(ij) = \mathbf{R}\mathbf{Q}^{-1}\mathbf{R}^{\mathrm{T}} - \mathbf{V}\boldsymbol{\Sigma}_\xi^{-1}\mathbf{V}^{\mathrm{T}}$, as

$$[\mathbf{u}(j) - \mathbf{V}(ij)]\boldsymbol{\Sigma}_\xi^{-1}(ij)[\mathbf{u}(j) - \mathbf{V}(ij)]^{\mathrm{T}} - K(ij).$$

The indexes i and j denote the alternative of the MNP function and the partial derivative being considered. Entering with this expression into Eqs. (2.35) and (2.36) yields

$$\frac{\partial p_i(\mathbf{V},\boldsymbol{\Sigma}_\xi)}{\partial V_j} = -\left(\frac{|\boldsymbol{\Sigma}_\xi(ij)|}{2\pi|\boldsymbol{\Sigma}_\xi|}\right)^{1/2} \exp\left(\frac{K(ij)}{2}\right)$$

$$\cdot \int_{u_1<u_i} \cdots \int_{u_{j-1}<u_i} \int_{u_{j+1}<u_i} \cdots \int_{u_i=-\infty}^{\infty}$$

$$\cdots \int_{u_I<u_i} \phi[\mathbf{u}(j)\,|\,\mathbf{V}(ij), \boldsymbol{\Sigma}_\xi(ij)]\, d\mathbf{u}(j), \qquad j \neq i.$$

[10] The matrix $\mathbf{Q}$ is positive definite because, for any $(I-1)$-dimensional vector $\mathbf{u}(j) \neq 0$, we can define an I-dimensional vector $\mathbf{u} \neq 0$ [with $u_j = u_i$ and same elements as $\mathbf{u}(j)$] which due to the relationship between Eqs. (2.36a) and (2.36b) satisfies $\mathbf{u}(j)\mathbf{Q}\mathbf{u}(j)^{\mathrm{T}} = \mathbf{u}\boldsymbol{\Sigma}_\xi^{-1}\mathbf{u}^{\mathrm{T}} > 0$ [which is positive by the definiteness of $\boldsymbol{\Sigma}_\xi^{-1}$].

The integral in this expression, however, is the MNP function corresponding to the $(i-1)$th alternative (or ith if $j > i$) of a MNP model with $I - 1$ alternatives, mean $\mathbf{V}(ij)$, and covariance matrix $\mathbf{\Sigma}_\xi(ij)$. Thus, we write

$$\frac{\partial p_i(\mathbf{V}, \mathbf{\Sigma}_\xi)}{\partial V_j} = -\left(\frac{|\mathbf{\Sigma}_\xi(ij)|}{2\pi|\mathbf{\Sigma}_\xi|}\right)^{1/2} \exp\left(\frac{K(ij)}{2}\right) p_{i'}[\mathbf{V}(ij), \mathbf{\Sigma}_\xi(ij)], \qquad j \neq i, \tag{2.37}$$

where $i' = i - 1$ if $j < i$ and $i' = i$ if $j > i$. This equation is easier to calculate than a numerical derivative since it involves the probability of choice for a model with $I - 1$ alternatives (instead of I). The computational savings are most noticeable for models with few alternatives, with the most dramatic simplification occurring for $I = 3$; in that case, the derivative requires calculation of a trivial binary probit function.

Before illustrating Eq. (2.37) with an example, we note that if $\mathbf{\Sigma}_\xi$ is the same for all the observations in the data set, the values of $\mathbf{\Sigma}_\xi(ij)$, $\mathbf{\Sigma}_\xi^{-1}(ij)$, and the square root in Eq. (2.37) can be calculated off line for all possible combinations of i and j, with consequent further computational simplification. The derivative with respect to V_i can be obtained by noting that

$$p_i = 1 - \sum_{k \neq i} p_k$$

and that

$$\frac{\partial p_i(\mathbf{V}, \mathbf{\Sigma}_\xi)}{\partial V_i} = - \sum_{k \neq i} \frac{\partial p_k(\mathbf{V}, \mathbf{\Sigma}_\xi)}{\partial V_i}. \tag{2.38}$$

Of course, the derivatives of $\log p_i(\mathbf{V}, \mathbf{\Sigma}_\xi)$ are simply obtained by dividing Eqs. (2.37) and (2.38) by $p_i(\mathbf{V}, \mathbf{\Sigma}_\xi)$.

Since $\mathbf{\Sigma}_\xi(ij)$ is positive definite (see footnote 10), the left-hand side of Eq. (2.37) is always strictly negative and the left-hand side of Eq. (2.38) is always strictly positive. This means that for MNP models in which $\mathbf{\Sigma}_\xi$ is nonsingular, the choice probability of an alternative is a strictly increasing function of the measured attractiveness of the corresponding alternative, and a strictly decreasing function of the measured attractiveness of the other alternatives. This is an important property of the MNP model, which will be used in Chapter 3 as supporting evidence for Conjecture 3.1.

As an illustration we now calculate $\partial p_i / \partial V_2$ for the example presented in Section 2.2.

Example Calculate $\partial p_1 / \partial V_2$ at $\mathbf{V} = (2, 2, 3)$ if

$$\mathbf{\Sigma}_\xi = \begin{pmatrix} 2 & 0 & 1 \\ 0 & 2 & 1 \\ 1 & 1 & 3 \end{pmatrix}.$$

We invert $\mathbf{\Sigma}_\xi$ and calculate $\mathbf{\Sigma}_\xi^{-1}(1,2)$ and $\mathbf{\Sigma}_\xi(1,2)$:

$$\mathbf{\Sigma}_\xi^{-1} = \frac{1}{8}\begin{pmatrix} 5 & 1 & -2 \\ 1 & 5 & -2 \\ -2 & -2 & 4 \end{pmatrix},$$

$$\mathbf{\Sigma}_\xi^{-1}(1,2) = \frac{1}{8}\begin{pmatrix} 12 & -4 \\ -4 & 4 \end{pmatrix} = \frac{1}{2}\begin{pmatrix} 3 & -1 \\ -1 & 1 \end{pmatrix}, \qquad \text{and} \qquad \mathbf{\Sigma}_\xi(1,2) = \begin{pmatrix} 1 & 1 \\ 1 & 3 \end{pmatrix}.$$

We then calculate $\mathbf{R}$, $\mathbf{V}(1,2)$, and $K(1,2)$:

$$\begin{aligned} \mathbf{V}\mathbf{\Sigma}_\xi^{-1} &= \tfrac{1}{8}(6,6,4), \\ \mathbf{R} &= \tfrac{1}{2}(3,1), \\ \mathbf{V}(1,2) &= \mathbf{R}\mathbf{\Sigma}_\xi(1,2) = \frac{1}{2}(3,1)\begin{pmatrix} 1 & 1 \\ 1 & 3 \end{pmatrix} = (2,3), \end{aligned}$$

and

$$K(1,2) = \frac{1}{4}(3,1)\begin{pmatrix} 1 & 1 \\ 1 & 3 \end{pmatrix}\begin{pmatrix} 3 \\ 1 \end{pmatrix} - \frac{1}{8}(2,2,3)\begin{pmatrix} 5 & 1 & -2 \\ 1 & 5 & -2 \\ -2 & -2 & 4 \end{pmatrix}\begin{pmatrix} 2 \\ 2 \\ 3 \end{pmatrix} = 0.^{11}$$

Since $|\mathbf{\Sigma}_\xi| = 8$, $|\mathbf{\Sigma}_\xi(1,2)| = 2$, and $i' = 1$, Eq. (2.37) reduces to

$$\frac{\partial p_1}{\partial V_2} = -0.200 p_1\left[(2,3), \begin{pmatrix} 1 & 1 \\ 1 & 3 \end{pmatrix}\right] = -0.200\Phi\left(\frac{-1}{\sqrt{2}}\right) = -0.048.$$

The reader can easily check this result by calculating the derivative numerically, using either Clark's formulas or the integration method. For $V = (2, 2.1, 3)$, the approximation yields $p_1 \approx 0.217$ and the integration method $p_1 \approx 0.2156$; in both cases $\Delta p_1/\Delta V_2 \approx -0.05$. ■

In instances where the approximation formulas do not closely approximate the MNP probabilities, but the approximation method is used anyway, there is no guarantee that the shortcut technique will approximate satisfactorily the derivatives of the approximation model. Experimentation will dictate whether this is a significant problem or not. On the other hand, the shortcut technique should present no problem when used in conjunction with the numerical-integration approach.

The shortcut derivative-evaluation method can be applied to likelihood functions of choice-based samples and random samples with ranked alternatives. For choice-based samples, one can calculate the gradient of the first

[11] This value need not equal zero. The reader can verify that for this same example $K(2,3) = \frac{17}{4}$.

term of Eq. (2.7a) with the shortcut method and then add to it the gradient of the second term, which can be easily calculated numerically from Eq. (2.7c). Alternatively, if one uses the estimator proposed by Manski and Lerman (1977), the task is trivial, since the estimator only involves maximization of a weighted sum of logarithms of choice functions [Eq. (2.7b)].

For ranked alternative data, the component of the log-likelihood function corresponding to one observation is the logarithm of a MNP function [see Eqs. (2.10), which give the measured attractiveness vector and covariance matrix]. It can be seen that if $\mathbf{\Sigma}_\xi$ is independent of $\boldsymbol{\theta}$, so will $\text{cov}(\mathbf{Z}_{(n)})$ and therefore the shortcut method can be applied without problems. However, $\text{cov}(\mathbf{Z}_{(n)})$ will change from observation to observation and one cannot derive $\mathbf{\Sigma}_\xi(ij)$ off line with this type of data. The chain-differentiation rule also yields a slightly different version of Eq. (2.33):

$$\nabla_\theta \log L(\boldsymbol{\theta}) = \sum_{n=1}^{N} \nabla_{E(\mathbf{Z}_{(n)})} \log p_1[E(\mathbf{Z}_{(n)}), \text{cov}(\mathbf{Z}_{(n)})]\, \mathbf{\Delta}_{(n)}^{\mathrm{T}}[\mathbf{a}_{(n)}]^{\mathrm{T}}. \tag{2.39}$$

For problems in which the calculation of $\mathbf{\Sigma}_\xi(i,j)$ can be performed off line, calculation of the gradient with the shortcut method takes approximately as much time as calculation of I choice functions for a problem with $I-1$ alternatives. For the approximation method this is

$$\text{time for gradient} \approx \alpha I(I-3)(I+2)N \quad \text{sec},$$

and the time for one iteration of a variable metric algorithm (allowing for ten log-likelihood evaluations for the line search) is

$$\text{time} \approx \alpha N[I(I-3)(I+2) + 10(I-2)(I+3)],$$

which can be compared with the numerical-derivative formula approach on a ratio basis. Since both search procedures visit the same sequence of points, they converge in the same number of steps and the ratio also indicates the relative calibration cost with the numerical and shortcut approaches. Table 2.8 summarizes the results for different values of the number of parameters r and alternatives I. It can be seen that the maximum economy is achieved for problems with few alternatives and several parameters. Although gradient computations are much more efficient with the shortcut method, some of the dramatic computation impact is lost by the one-dimensional search required by the variable-metric search. A much more noticeable difference would result if the line search could be obviated with the Newton–Raphson method. The Newton–Raphson method, however, requires the Hessian at each visited point and thus can only be used if the Hessian is easy to calculate.

Hessian calculations are also important because the negative definiteness at $\hat{\boldsymbol{\theta}}$ ensures that we are at a local maximum of the log-likelihood func-

Table 2.8

Computational Economy with Shortcut Gradient Calculations Using the Approximation Method and a Variable-Metric Algorithm

(Calibration time without shortcut)/(Calibration time with shortcut)

Number of alternatives	Number of parameters				
	2	4	6	8	10
3	1.2	1.4	1.6	1.8	2.0
4	1.02	1.2	1.38	1.54	1.71
5	0.93	1.08	1.24	1.39	1.55
6	0.86	1.00	1.14	1.28	1.43

tion and the negative of its inverse gives an estimate of the covariance matrix of the estimator.

We now discuss how the Hessian matrix can be calculated and how one can apply the technique to develop a very efficient trinomial probit algorithm that may use the numerical integration method.

Taking derivatives in Eq. (2.37) one has

$$\frac{\partial^2 p_i(\mathbf{V}, \boldsymbol{\Sigma}_\xi)}{\partial V_j \partial V_k} = -\left(\frac{|\boldsymbol{\Sigma}_\xi(ij)|}{2\pi|\boldsymbol{\Sigma}_\xi|}\right)^{1/2} \exp\left[\frac{K(ij)}{2}\right]$$
$$\cdot \boldsymbol{\nabla}_{V(ij)} p_{i'}[\mathbf{V}(ij), \boldsymbol{\Sigma}_\xi(ij)] \frac{\partial \mathbf{V}^{\mathrm{T}}(ij)}{\partial V_k} \qquad \forall i \neq j. \tag{2.40}$$

A similar formula would be obtained from Eq. (2.38) if $i = j$. Since $\mathbf{V}(ij)$ is a linear combination of $\mathbf{V}$, the last factor in Eq. (2.40) is a constant vector that can be calculated off line. Calculation of Eq. (2.40) is thus computationally equivalent to calculating the gradient of a MNP function with respect to $\mathbf{V}$ for a problem with $I - 1$ alternatives. This is an involved proposition for problems with several alternatives, since one must calculate $(I + 1)I/2$ partial derivatives. The Newton–Raphson search is thus not likely to result in computational savings except for problems with two, three, and perhaps four alternatives, since in these cases Eq. (2.40) would assume a closed form.

The trinomial probit model is particularly interesting because $p_1[\mathbf{V}(ij), \boldsymbol{\Sigma}_\xi(ij)]$ is a binary probit function that can be expressed as the cumulative normal function $\Phi(\cdot)$ of a simple function of $\mathbf{V}(ij)$ and $\boldsymbol{\Sigma}_\xi(ij)$ (see Section 1.3.3). Consequently, the second derivative requires only a single evaluation of $\phi(\cdot)$ and some multiplications and additions. Furthermore, since for the binary model the two entires of $\boldsymbol{\nabla}_{V(ij)} p_i$ are of equal absolute value and opposite sign, only one of them need be calculated.

The Hessian of $\log p_i$ is obtained from the Hessian and gradient of p_i with the chain differentiation rule which for this case is

$$\nabla_V^2 \log p_i = (1/p_i^2)[(\nabla_V p_i)^{\mathrm{T}}(\nabla_V p_i) - p_i \nabla_V^2 p_i].$$

In addition to the results of Eq. (2.40) this equation needs the values of p_i and $\nabla_V p_i$; this is not a problem, however, since this information is already available. The Hessian of $\log L(\boldsymbol{\theta})$ is of course obtained with Eq. (2.34), as was done with the numerical-evaluation method.

Since the gradient and Hessian calculations for a trinomial probit model with fixed covariance matrix are very simple, it seems reasonable to use the Newton–Raphson method. The method is particularly useful with the numerical-integration approach because the marginal effort required to obtain the gradient and Hessian is small and $\log L(\boldsymbol{\theta})$ has to be evaluated only once per iteration.

For example, a problem that converges in five steps (not unusual for the Newton–Raphson method) with 500 data points would require just 2500 trinomial probit function evaluations, or approximately 25,000 evaluations of $\Phi(x)$. This is to be compared with the 10 to 20 times higher cost *per step* of the variable-metric algorithm with numerical derivatives.

The Newton–Raphson method converges quickly on well-behaved "smooth" and concave functions and has proven its usefulness in MNL calibration codes. However, since the properties of $\log L(\boldsymbol{\theta})$ for the trinomial probit model have not been studied successfully yet, it is difficult to assess how effectively the Newton–Raphson method can be applied to a MNP model. The next section discusses the scant knowledge that exists regarding the unimodality of log

2.5 Properties of the Log-Likelihood Function

Although the steepest-ascent and variable-metric algorithms discussed in the previous section converge to a stationary point of the log-likelihood function, in general, there is no guarantee that such a point will be either a local or a global maximum [see Theorem 10.1 of Avriel (1976, p. 293)]. However, if the log-likelihood function is concave, there is no need to perform any further analysis because every stationary point of a concave function is also a global maximum. Concave log-likelihood functions arise with the MNL model and, as is shown later in this section, with the binary probit model.

For general likelihood functions, a stationary point can either be a local minimum, a local maximum or a "*saddle point*," i.e., a point that is neither a minimum nor a maximum. The type of stationary point is given by the definiteness of the Hessian matrix (thereby the importance of Hessian calculation methods). If the Hessian of the log-likelihood function does not have full rank, one cannot tell whether a local maximum or minimum has been reached. However, if it has full rank, a positive-definite Hessian indicates a local minimum, a negative definite, a local maximum, and an indefinite saddle point. This is easily seen because the Taylor-series expansion of $\log L(\boldsymbol{\theta})$ in the neighborhood of the stationary point $\boldsymbol{\theta}^*$ can be written

$$\log L(\boldsymbol{\theta}^* + \Delta\boldsymbol{\theta}) \approx \log L(\boldsymbol{\theta}^*) + \tfrac{1}{2}\Delta\boldsymbol{\theta}\, \mathbf{V}_\theta^2 \log L(\boldsymbol{\theta}^*)\, \Delta\boldsymbol{\theta}^{\mathrm{T}} \qquad \Delta\boldsymbol{\theta} \to 0,$$

and $\log L(\boldsymbol{\theta}^* + \Delta\boldsymbol{\theta}) >$ (or $<$) $\log L(\boldsymbol{\theta}^*)$ for all small $\Delta\boldsymbol{\theta}$ if and only if

$$\tfrac{1}{2}\Delta\boldsymbol{\theta}\, \mathbf{V}_\theta^2 \log L(\boldsymbol{\theta}^*)\, \Delta\boldsymbol{\theta}^{\mathrm{T}} > (\text{or} <)\ 0$$

for all $\Delta\boldsymbol{\theta}$. This is of course true if and only if $\mathbf{V}_\theta^2 \log L(\boldsymbol{\theta}^*)$ is positive (negative) definite.

The negative definiteness of $\mathbf{V}_\theta^2 \log L(\boldsymbol{\theta}^*)$ can be determined by inspection of either its principal diagonal minors or its eigenvalues (see Appendix D). If the Hessian matrix is not negative definite, we may not be at a maximum and the search procedure must continue. The search direction, however, cannot be determined from the gradient of $\log L(\boldsymbol{\theta})$ at the stationary point since it is zero there; it can, instead, be determined by maximizing the difference $\log L(\boldsymbol{\theta}^* + \Delta\boldsymbol{\theta}) - \log L(\boldsymbol{\theta}^*)$ while holding the length of $\Delta\boldsymbol{\theta}$ constant and small. Such a direction is given by the eigenvector of $\mathbf{V}_\theta^2 \log L(\boldsymbol{\theta}^*)$ that corresponds to the largest eigenvalue.[12]

The search procedure then continues normally until a negative-definite Hessian matrix corresponding to a local maximum is found.

Unless it is known a priori that the log-likelihood function is unimodal (every local maximum is global), the only way to check whether the maximum is unique is by starting the search from several different points until one is reasonably sure that there is no other point that is also a maximum. This process can be rather time consuming but the cost can be cut by using only part of the data while carrying it out. In the future, analysis and experience will probably identify conditions under which MNP models have unimodal log-likelihood functions and the search for their maxima will be simplified.

[12] Since for small $\Delta\boldsymbol{\theta}$, $\log L(\boldsymbol{\theta}^* + \Delta\boldsymbol{\theta}) - \log L(\boldsymbol{\theta}^*)$ is given by $\tfrac{1}{2}\Delta\boldsymbol{\theta}\, \mathbf{V}_\theta^2 \log L(\boldsymbol{\theta}^*)\Delta\boldsymbol{\theta}^{\mathrm{T}}$, $\Delta\boldsymbol{\theta}$ is directly proportional to the vector of unit length, $\|\mathbf{x}\| = 1$, that maximizes $\mathbf{x}\, \mathbf{V}_\theta^2 \log L(\boldsymbol{\theta}^*)\mathbf{x}^{\mathrm{T}}$. Since the Hessian is symmetric and real, it can be expressed as $\mathbf{V}_\theta^2 \log L(\boldsymbol{\theta}^*) = \mathbf{BDB}^{\mathrm{T}}$, where $\mathbf{D}$ is a diagonal matrix of eigenvalues, and $\mathbf{B}$ is a square matrix, such that $\mathbf{BB}^{\mathrm{T}} = \mathbf{I}$, whose rows are the eigenvectors. Since the quantity to be maximized can be expressed as $\mathbf{yDy}^{\mathrm{T}}(\mathbf{y} = \mathbf{xB})$, one can find $\mathbf{y}$ first, and then $\mathbf{x} = \mathbf{yB}^{\mathrm{T}}$. Since $\mathbf{D}$ is diagonal, $\mathbf{y}$ is a vector of zeros with a one in the location corresponding to the largest element of $\mathbf{D}$. The vector $\mathbf{x}$ is obviously given by the corresponding column of $\mathbf{B}^{\mathrm{T}}$ (row of $\mathbf{B}$) which is by definition the eigenvector corresponding to the largest eigenvalue.

A preliminary result, involving the binary probit model, is given below. We first prove the following lemma.

Lemma 2.1 The functions $\log \Phi(z)$ and $\log[1 - \Phi(z)]$ are strictly concave functions of z.

Proof Since such functions are continuous, a necessary condition for strict concavity is that the second derivative be negative. Since $1 - \Phi(z) = \Phi(-z)$, the second derivative of $\log[1 - \Phi(z)]$ coincides with that of $\log \Phi(-z)$, and it suffices to show that $d^2 \log \Phi(z)/dz^2 < 0$. The second derivative is

$$\frac{d^2 \log \Phi(z)}{dz^2} = \frac{d}{dz}\left[\frac{\phi(z)}{\Phi(z)}\right] = \frac{\phi'(z)\Phi(z) - \phi^2(z)}{\Phi(z)^2},$$

where $\phi'(z)$ represents the derivative of $\phi(z)$. This expression is negative if

$$\phi^2(z) > \phi'(z)\Phi(z). \tag{2.41}$$

Since for any finite z,

$$\phi(z) > 0, \qquad 0 < \Phi(z) < 1, \qquad \text{and} \qquad \phi'(z) = -z\phi(z),$$

Eq. (2.41) trivially holds for $z \geq 0$.

For $z < 0$, Eq. (2.41) can be replaced by

$$\Phi(z) < \phi(z)/|z|, \qquad z < 0, \tag{2.42}$$

but this identity is a well-known property of $\Phi(z)$ [see Feller (1968, Vol. 1, p. 175), for example), which is proved here for completeness:

$$\begin{aligned}
\Phi(z) &= \frac{1}{\sqrt{2\pi}} \int_{-\infty}^{z} \exp\left(-\frac{1}{2}t^2\right) dt \\
&= \frac{1}{\sqrt{2\pi}} \int_{-\infty}^{z} \frac{-t}{|t|} \exp\left(-\frac{1}{2}t^2\right) dt \qquad \text{if} \quad z < 0 \\
&< \frac{1}{\sqrt{2\pi}} \int_{-\infty}^{z} \frac{-t}{|z|} \exp\left(-\frac{1}{2}t^2\right) dt \qquad \text{if} \quad z < 0 \\
&= \phi(z)/|z| \qquad \text{if} \quad z < 0,
\end{aligned}$$

which concludes the proof. ■

We can now study the concavity of binary probit models. Since, as was explained in Chapter 1, every random utility binary probit model can be reduced to a form

$$\begin{aligned}
p_1 &= \Phi[V(\boldsymbol{\theta}, \mathbf{A})], \\
p_2 &= 1 - \Phi[V(\boldsymbol{\theta}, \mathbf{A})],
\end{aligned}$$

where $V(\cdot,\cdot)$ is a function that depends on $\mathbf{V}(\cdot,\cdot)$ and $\boldsymbol{\Sigma}_\xi(\cdot,\cdot)$, we state the following theorem:

Theorem 2.1 The log-likelihood function of a binary probit model corresponding to an attribute-based sample is a concave function of $\boldsymbol{\theta}$ if the function $V(\boldsymbol{\theta}, \mathbf{A})$ is a linear in $\boldsymbol{\theta}$.

Proof We first note that for any observation n with choice $c_{(n)}$ and attribute vector $\mathbf{a}_{(n)}$

$$\log P_{C_{(n)}}(\boldsymbol{\theta}, \mathbf{a}_n) = \begin{cases} \log \Phi[V(\boldsymbol{\theta}, \mathbf{a}_{(n)})] & \text{if } \; c_{(n)} = 1 \\ \log\{1 - \Phi[V(\boldsymbol{\theta}, \mathbf{a}_{(n)})]\} & \text{if } \; c_{(n)} = 2 \end{cases}$$

is a concave function of V (see Lemma 2.1). Since a concave function of a linear function is concave (see Appendix D), $\log P_{c_{(n)}}(\boldsymbol{\theta}, \mathbf{a}_{(n)})$ is concave in $\boldsymbol{\theta}$.

Since $\log L(\boldsymbol{\theta})$ is a sum of concave functions, $\log L(\boldsymbol{\theta}) = \sum_{n=1}^{N} \log P_{c_{(n)}}(\boldsymbol{\theta}, \mathbf{a}_{(n)})$ is itself concave, and the proof is complete. ■

For choice-based samples, it is not known whether $\log L(\boldsymbol{\theta})$ is concave in a general case. However, we can state the following corollary, which concerns the pseudolikelihood function $\log L_p(\boldsymbol{\theta})$.

Corollary 2.1 With the same restrictions as above, Eq. (2.7b) is concave.

Proof Equation (2.7b) is a linear combination (with nonnegative constants) of concave functions, which is itself concave. ■

The following also follows immediately from the theorem.

Corollary 2.2 A binary probit model with linear-in-the-parameters measured attractiveness and fixed covariance matrix has a concave log-likelihood function.

Proof In this case $V(\boldsymbol{\theta}, \mathbf{A})$ is obviously linear in $\boldsymbol{\theta}$. ■

2.6 Summary

This chapter has presented the state of the art in calibration of multinomial probit models. Although the techniques and problems are meticulously described, the information in the chapter should not be regarded as final since current ongoing research may result in substantial improvements to the methods and techniques presented. As a matter of fact, a main purpose of this chapter is to describe the state of the art of MNP calibration calculations, so that further thinking on the subject will be stimulated. Estimation of multinomial probit models is now possible thanks to the speed of modern-day computers and to some efficient software that has recently been developed. It seems that, at least for the time being, there are two MNP function evaluation methods that can be used. The numerical-integration method, in conjunction with analytical evaluation of gradients and Hessian, can be used for trinomial probit models with linear-in-the-parameters specifications and known covariance matrix. The recommended search procedure is the Newton–Raphson method, since it requires a minimum number of log-likelihood evaluations. The approximation method can be economically applied to general problems with more than three alternatives and several hundred data points. A variable-metric or similar algorithm that does not require Hessian calculations seems most appropriate since, so far, experience with it has been satisfactory. A third MNP function-evaluation method (Monte Carlo simulation) has been also proposed, but its applicability seems to be restricted to prediction problems.

At the time of this writing, there already are a few computer programs for estimation of MNP models. CHOMP is a research-oriented computer program developed by the author and his associates that uses the approximation method and a variable metric algorithm. The output of CHOMP includes the maximum-likelihood estimate $\hat{\boldsymbol{\theta}}$ and an estimate of its covariance matrix. Some economy with large data sets is achieved by using only some of the data in the initial stages of the search.

The unimodality of $\log L(\boldsymbol{\theta})$ has been established only for the binary probit model with a linear-in-the-parameters specification of $V(\boldsymbol{\theta}, \mathbf{a})$. Since experience with problems with more than three alternatives is still limited, one must proceed with caution because multiple maxima and/or saddle points may be encountered.

Advances in MNP model calibration can be expected in the near future with emphasis, perhaps, on enhancing the accuracy and efficiency of choice-probability calculations and improving the understanding of the unimodality of $\log L(\boldsymbol{\theta})$.

Some bibliographical notes on the computational aspects of MNP calibration follow.

The papers by Hausman and Wise (1978) and Andrews and Langdon (1976) contain, respectively, what appears to be the first calibration of a MNP model with more than two alternatives and a clear description of the numerical-integration method for three alternatives. Section 2.2.1 is based on the research of these authors. The simulation approach of Section 2.2.2 was proposed by Lerman and Manski (1977). The papers by Daganzo *et al.* (1977a, 1977b) and Bouthelier's dissertation (1978, Chapter 2) provide much of the background for the discussion in Section 2.2.3. For the theoretically oriented reader, Clark's original paper (1961) is highly recommended, in particular, the appendix containing the derivation of the approximation formulas. Clark's formulas were first applied to a choice model by Daganzo and Sheffi (1977).

The shortcut gradient calculation technique of Section 2.4.2 was proposed by McFadden (1977), who also gives a concise review of other discrete choice model calibration issues. The user's manual and listing of CHOMP (the previously mentioned calibration code) are given by Daganzo and Schoenfeld (1978). CHOMP is based roughly on the original experimental code developed by Daganzo *et al.* (1977a).

Chapter 3 Statistical Aspects of Multinomial Probit Model Calibration

It was mentioned in Chapter 1 that application of a MNP model required three steps: specification, calibration, and prediction. Since specification is is a step that has to be done based on one's intuitive or technical knowledge of a problem, and the type of application greatly influences the model form, an in-depth discussion of useful MNP specifications for different applications areas will not be given in this book. Chapter 2 addressed this issue indirectly by showing how a gap-acceptance study could be cast as a MNP problem, thereby illustrating how technical knowledge can help in model specification. In many applications, however, it is not possible to derive such a clear-cut specification and an investigation of the effect of possible specification errors in the accuracy of the model is warranted. This chapter deals with such issues as well as with several other statistical aspects of MNP model calibration. Of no concern will be how one obtains the estimates, since the mechanical aspects of calibration have already been covered in Chapter 2.

3.1 Model Specification Considerations

We assume for the rest of this section that the true model[1] has a measured-attractiveness vector that is linear in the parameters and that consequently can be expressed as

$$\mathbf{V} = \mathbf{a}[\theta], \tag{3.1}$$

[1] As was mentioned in Chapter 1, and is usual in econometrics, we assume there is such a thing as a true model and a true parameter value.

where $[\boldsymbol{\theta}]$ represents an $s \times I$ matrix whose entries are either known constants or elements of $\boldsymbol{\theta}$, and as usual $\mathbf{V}$ is an I-dimensional row vector of measured-attractiveness values and $\mathbf{a}$ an s-dimensional vector of attributes, which, in order to allow for the representation of constants in the specification of $\mathbf{V}$, starts with numeral 1. The covariance matrix of the true model $\boldsymbol{\Sigma}_\xi$ will be allowed to depend on $\boldsymbol{\theta}$ but not on $\mathbf{a}$. Although these qualifications restrict the scope of the models that are the subject of our discussion, they still apply to many situations. For example, the modal-split numerical example of Sections 2.3.2 and 2.4.2 satisfies all the requirements. In a non-MNP context, the assumptions of this section are standard in most disaggregate demand modeling efforts to date since, with the MNL model, computer programs are prepared for linear-in-the-parameters specifications of the measured-attractiveness vector only, and as was seen in Chapter 1 the covariance matrix of an MNL model is fixed and known. Furthermore, the requirement that the covariance matrix of the true model is not a function of $\mathbf{a}$ is not as restrictive as it may seem, because one of the objectives of this section is, precisely, to find instances where, due to the characteristics of the data and/or the nature of the problem, it may be wise to use a specification that does depend on $\mathbf{a}$.

In the discussion that follows, several MNP specification issues will be covered, in particular, errors in the data, errors in the specification of the model, population taste variations, and parameter estimability.

3.1.1 Errors in the Data

The model considered in this section is

$$\mathbf{U} = \mathbf{a}[\boldsymbol{\theta}] + \boldsymbol{\xi}, \tag{3.2}$$

where as usual $\mathbf{U}$ is the perceived attractiveness and $\boldsymbol{\xi}$ an unobservable error-term vector that is MVN distributed with mean zero and covariance matrix $\boldsymbol{\Sigma}_\xi(\boldsymbol{\theta})$. The question being addressed is What is the appropriate course of action we should take if we suspect certain major inaccuracies in the measurement, or reporting, of $\mathbf{a}$ in our data? In other words, if our data set consists of a reported attribute vector $\mathbf{a}^*_{(n)}$ for the nth observation ($n = 1, 2, \ldots, N$), which differs from the true, unknown attribute vector value $\mathbf{a}_{(n)}$ by an amount $\boldsymbol{\eta}_{(n)}$:

$$\mathbf{a}^*_{(n)} = \mathbf{a}_{(n)} + \boldsymbol{\eta}_{(n)}, \tag{3.3}$$

is there a way of modifying the model to avoid biases in the estimation of $\boldsymbol{\theta}$? The answer is, under certain conditions, yes.

If $\boldsymbol{\eta}_{(n)}$ varies across the population according to a MVN distribution with mean $\bar{\boldsymbol{\eta}}$ and covariance matrix $\boldsymbol{\Sigma}_\eta$, Eq. (3.2) becomes

$$\mathbf{U}_{(n)} = \mathbf{a}^*_{(n)}[\boldsymbol{\theta}] + \xi^*_{(n)} \qquad \xi^*_{(n)} = \xi_{(n)} - \boldsymbol{\eta}_{(n)}[\boldsymbol{\theta}], \tag{3.4}$$

where ξ^* is unobserved with mean and covariance matrix given by

$$E(\xi^*) = -\bar{\boldsymbol{\eta}}[\boldsymbol{\theta}], \tag{3.5a}$$

$$\operatorname{cov}(\xi^*) = \boldsymbol{\Sigma}_\xi(\boldsymbol{\theta}) + [\boldsymbol{\theta}]^{\mathrm{T}}\boldsymbol{\Sigma}_\eta[\boldsymbol{\theta}]. \tag{3.5b}$$

If the values of $\bar{\boldsymbol{\eta}}$ and $\boldsymbol{\Sigma}_\eta$ can be guessed (e.g., $\bar{\boldsymbol{\eta}}$ may be known to be zero and $\boldsymbol{\Sigma}_\eta$ diagonal with known entries), one can estimate $[\boldsymbol{\theta}]$ correctly with the available data using the following MNP model form:

$$\mathbf{V}^*(\boldsymbol{\theta}, \mathbf{a}^*) = (\mathbf{a}^*_{(n)} - \bar{\boldsymbol{\eta}})[\boldsymbol{\theta}], \tag{3.6a}$$

$$\boldsymbol{\Sigma}^*_\xi(\boldsymbol{\theta}) = \boldsymbol{\Sigma}_\xi(\boldsymbol{\theta}) + [\boldsymbol{\theta}]^{\mathrm{T}}\boldsymbol{\Sigma}_\eta[\boldsymbol{\theta}]. \tag{3.6b}$$

Once $\boldsymbol{\theta}$ has been estimated it is possible to replace it into the original specification of the model, Eq. (3.2), to obtain a calibrated choice function dependent on **a**.

If the values of $\bar{\boldsymbol{\eta}}$ and $\boldsymbol{\Sigma}_\eta$ are not known, it is still possible to calibrate a MNP model with

$$\mathbf{V}^*(\boldsymbol{\theta}, \mathbf{a}^*) = \mathbf{a}^*_{(n)}[\boldsymbol{\theta}] + \boldsymbol{\theta}_v, \tag{3.7a}$$

$$\boldsymbol{\Sigma}^*_\xi(\boldsymbol{\theta}) = \boldsymbol{\Sigma}_\xi(\boldsymbol{\theta}) + \boldsymbol{\theta}_\Sigma, \tag{3.7b}$$

where $\boldsymbol{\theta}_v$ is an I-dimensional vector of additional parameters corresponding to the constant vector $\bar{\boldsymbol{\eta}}[\boldsymbol{\theta}]$, and $\boldsymbol{\theta}_\Sigma$ is a positive-semidefinite matrix that replaces $[\boldsymbol{\theta}]^{\mathrm{T}}\boldsymbol{\Sigma}_\eta[\boldsymbol{\theta}]$.

Unfortunately, inclusion of $\boldsymbol{\theta}_v$ and $\boldsymbol{\theta}_\Sigma$ in the specification makes the parameters that appeared only in $\boldsymbol{\Sigma}_\xi(\boldsymbol{\theta}_\Sigma)$, or only as independent constants in **V**, unestimable [Section 3.1.4. discusses estimatibility problems in general and Eqs. (3.7) as an example]. Since this precludes obtaining a choice function based on Eq. (3.2), the calibrated choice function must be derived from Eqs. (3.7). It will therefore be a function of **a*** (not **a**), which is a variable whose distribution across the population must be forecasted for prediction purposes. This is not desirable because in many instances the distribution of **a*** is so difficult to forecast that, in order to carry out a prediction, one has to guess the distribution of **a*** with a procedure involving as many subjective decisions as the one needed to guess the values of $\bar{\boldsymbol{\eta}}$ and $\boldsymbol{\Sigma}_\eta$ in the data. Thus, unless the distribution of **a*** can be forecasted easily, it is much more desirable to guess $\bar{\boldsymbol{\eta}}$ and $\boldsymbol{\Sigma}_\xi$ and use Eqs. (3.6) to estimate $\boldsymbol{\theta}$ since the resulting model involves fewer parameters.

Example The modal-split model of Section 2.3.2 can be defined in terms of $\boldsymbol{\theta}$ and $\mathbf{a}$ as

$$\mathbf{a} = (1, a_1, a_2, a_3), \qquad \boldsymbol{\theta} = (\theta_1, \theta_2),$$

$$[\boldsymbol{\theta}] = \begin{bmatrix} 0 & 0 & 0 \\ -\theta_1 & 0 & 0 \\ 0 & -\theta_1 & 0 \\ 0 & 0 & -\theta_1 \end{bmatrix}, \qquad \boldsymbol{\Sigma}_\xi(\boldsymbol{\theta}) = \begin{bmatrix} 1 & \theta_2 & 0 \\ \theta_2 & 1 & 0 \\ 0 & 0 & 1 \end{bmatrix}.$$

If the data in Table 2.4 contained measurement errors in the columns giving a_1, a_2, and a_3, these values would have to be regarded as being $\mathbf{a}^*$, and the specification of the model modified accordingly.

Assuming that the differences between the table values and the true values are independent identically distributed normal variables with zero mean and variance proportional to $\mathbf{a}^*$:

$$\boldsymbol{\eta} \sim \mathrm{MVN}\left(\mathbf{0}, \theta_3 \begin{bmatrix} 0 & 0 & 0 & 0 \\ 0 & a_1^* & 0 & 0 \\ 0 & 0 & a_2^* & 0 \\ 0 & 0 & 0 & a_3^* \end{bmatrix}\right),$$

one can obtain $\mathbf{V}^*(\boldsymbol{\theta}, \mathbf{a})$ and $\boldsymbol{\Sigma}_\xi^*(\boldsymbol{\theta})$ from Eqs. (3.6):

$$\mathbf{V}^*(\boldsymbol{\theta}, \mathbf{a}) = \mathbf{a}^*[\boldsymbol{\theta}] = (-\theta_1 a_1^*, -\theta_1 a_2^*, -\theta_1 a_3^*)$$

and

$$\boldsymbol{\Sigma}_\xi^*(\boldsymbol{\theta}) = \begin{bmatrix} 1 & \theta_2 & 0 \\ \theta_2 & 1 & 0 \\ 0 & 0 & 1 \end{bmatrix} + \begin{bmatrix} 0 & -\theta_1 & 0 & 0 \\ 0 & 0 & -\theta_1 & 0 \\ 0 & 0 & 0 & -\theta_1 \end{bmatrix}$$

$$\times \begin{bmatrix} 0 & 0 & 0 & 0 \\ 0 & \theta_3 a_1^* & 0 & 0 \\ 0 & 0 & \theta a_2^* & 0 \\ 0 & 0 & 0 & \theta_3 a_3^* \end{bmatrix} \begin{bmatrix} 0 & 0 & 0 \\ -\theta_1 & 0 & 0 \\ 0 & -\theta_1 & 0 \\ 0 & 0 & -\theta_1 \end{bmatrix}$$

$$= \begin{bmatrix} 1 + a_1^*\theta_1^2\theta_3 & \theta_2 & 0 \\ \theta_2 & 1 + a_2^*\theta_1^2\theta_3 & 0 \\ 0 & 0 & 1 + a_3^*\theta_1^2\theta_3 \end{bmatrix}.$$

Calibration of these functions with the data in Table 2.4 would yield values of $\hat{\theta}_1$, $\hat{\theta}_2$, and $\hat{\theta}_3$ that could be substituted in both the original and modified models for prediction purposes.

When the appropriate allowances for errors in the data are not made, the resulting parameter estimates will generally be biased. Unfortunately, closed form formulas to predict the bias are not yet available because $\hat{\theta}$ does not assume a closed form as it does in the case of multiple regression. Nevertheless, it helps knowing that one can avoid the possible biases by modifying the MNP model in a simple way.

The Missing Data Problem

A not-infrequent occurrence in many estimation problems is the absence of some attributes in some observations of the data set. For instance, in studies requiring socioeconomic data it is not uncommon for many people not to know, or not to be willing to disclose the value of attributes such as income. In such cases, if there are only a few observations with missing data, it is possible to omit these observations from the data set and proceed in the normal way. If many observations contain missing data, however, the accuracy of the results will suffer, and it may be worthwhile to use one of two techniques, similar to those used when there were errors in the data, that can use all the data points in the sample. They are *guessing*, and *using the data.*

If a good guess can be made for the missing attribute, we can include the guess as part of the sample and correct the covariance matrix to take into account the possible error. The technique is identical to the one leading to Eqs. (3.6). Let, in this section only, $\mathbf{a}'_{(n)}$ denote the components of $\mathbf{a}_{(n)}$ that are not guessed, $\mathbf{a}''_{(n)}$ the guesses, $[\boldsymbol{\theta}''_{(n)}]$ the rows of $[\boldsymbol{\theta}]$ that correspond to guessed attributes for the nth observation, and $[\boldsymbol{\theta}'_{(n)}]$ the remaining rows. Using this notation, the perceived-attractiveness vector can be expressed as

$$\mathbf{U}_{(n)} = \mathbf{a}'_{(n)}[\boldsymbol{\theta}'_{(n)}] + \mathbf{a}''_{(n)}[\boldsymbol{\theta}''_{(n)}] + \boldsymbol{\eta}''_{(n)}[\boldsymbol{\theta}''_{(n)}] + \boldsymbol{\xi}_{(n)}, \tag{3.8}$$

where $\boldsymbol{\eta}''_{(n)}$ represents the error in the estimation of $\mathbf{a}''_{(n)}$. If the accuracy of the guessing process can be assessed, it may be possible to obtain the distribution of $\mathbf{U}_{(n)}$, which under the usual conditions of normality and zero mean for $\boldsymbol{\eta}''_{(n)}$ corresponds to a MNP model with

$$\mathbf{V}^*_{(n)} = \mathbf{a}'_{(n)}[\boldsymbol{\theta}'_{(n)}] + \mathbf{a}''_{(n)}[\boldsymbol{\theta}''_{(n)}], \tag{3.9a}$$

$$\boldsymbol{\xi}^*_{(n)} = \boldsymbol{\xi}_{(n)} + \boldsymbol{\eta}''_{(n)}[\boldsymbol{\theta}''_{(n)}], \tag{3.9b}$$

and

$$\boldsymbol{\Sigma}^*_{\xi(n)} = \boldsymbol{\Sigma}_{\xi} + [\boldsymbol{\theta}''_{(n)}]^{\mathrm{T}}\boldsymbol{\Sigma}_{\eta''_{(n)}}[\boldsymbol{\theta}''_{(n)}]. \tag{3.9c}$$

If a good guess cannot be made, it may be possible to estimate the mean and variance of the missing attributes conditional on the observed attributes from inspection of the complete observations in the data set. We can then set $\mathbf{a}''_{(n)}$ equal to the mean, $\Sigma_{\eta''_{(n)}}$ equal to the covariance matrix, and use Eqs. (3.9) for estimation. This technique is similar to the *zero-order regression estimation* method of the general linear model when some observations are missing. Carrying it out is, of course, more easily said than done, because the sample may not contain enough complete observations similar to the one with missing attributes. For observations where only one attribute is missing, however, the task may not be quite so difficult, since then one has to estimate only a mean and a variance. It is important to note that in deriving the values of $\mathbf{a}''_{(n)}$ and $\Sigma_{\eta''_{(n)}}$ for both the guessing and data-use methods (or any hybrid thereof) *the adopted values should not be influenced by the choice of the observation*, for otherwise the likelihood equation representing the probability of the choice given the attributes will no longer be meaningful.

3.1.2 Specification Errors

It is not easy to state a priori the effect of omitting an attribute from the true specification of a MNP model on the parameters associated with other attributes. However, as happened with errors in the data, under certain fairly general conditions, it is possible to correct the specification of a model to avoid errors. The problem is analogous to that of using a data set with some attributes missing in all the observations.

We express the perceived attractiveness of the correctly specified model as

$$\mathbf{U} = \mathbf{a}'[\boldsymbol{\theta}'] + \mathbf{a}''[\boldsymbol{\theta}''] + \xi, \tag{3.10}$$

where the attributes of $\mathbf{a}''$ are, mistakenly, being omitted from the specification. If the distribution of $\mathbf{A}''$, conditional on $\mathbf{a}'$, can be considered to be MVN with mean vector and covariance matrix dependent on $\mathbf{a}'$ one can conceptually reduce Eq. (3.10) to a MNP model in the same way as was done with Eq. (3.8). This is difficult to do in practice, however, because one rarely has an exhaustive list of the neglected attributes (as they were called in Chapter 1); and even if many of them were known, it would be difficult to determine the form of their dependence on $\mathbf{a}'$.

These problems are alleviated if, as is often the case, one can reasonably assume that the neglected attributes are independent of the rest. In such a case the term $\mathbf{a}''[\boldsymbol{\theta}'']$ can be treated as a constant vector plus a zero-mean error term, both to be determined from the estimation process

$$\mathbf{a}''[\boldsymbol{\theta}''] = \boldsymbol{\theta}'' + \xi'', \qquad \xi'' \sim \mathrm{MVN}(0, \Sigma_{\xi''}). \tag{3.11}$$

For estimation, $\boldsymbol{\theta}''$ is added to the first row of $[\boldsymbol{\theta}']$, which premultiplied by $\mathbf{a}'$ yields the corrected measured-attractiveness vector $\mathbf{V}^*$. The corrected covariance matrix Σ_ξ^* is given by $\Sigma_\xi + \Sigma_{\xi''}$. The resulting model is still

MNP and therefore it should be possible to obtain satisfactory estimates for $[\boldsymbol{\theta}']$. Multinomial probit is the only discrete choice model in existence today that, by admitting a full parametrization of the covariance matrix of the error terms, can capture properly the consequences of neglected attributes. We now show that the example that was calibrated in Section 2.3.2 could correspond to a MNP model with some neglected attributes.

Example The true specification of a three-alternative modal-choice problem could be as follows:

alternative 1 (bus)	$U_1 = -\theta_1 T_1 + C_T + \xi_1;$
alternative 2 (streetcar)	$U_2 = -\theta_1 T_2 + C_T + \xi_2;$
alternative 3 (automobile)	$U_3 = -\theta_1 T_3 + C_A + \xi_3.$

In these equations T_i represents the travel time by the ith mode in appropriate units, C_{T} represents the comfort associated by a person with transit travel (in attractiveness units), and C_{A} the comfort of auto travel. Since it is difficult to provide an objective measure for comfort that is quantifiable, the variables C_{A} and C_{T} will be omitted from the model specification (i.e., they will become neglected attributes) and will be inserted into the error terms.

Assuming the ξ_i's are independent, identically distributed normal variables with zero mean and the same variance $\sigma_\xi^2 = \theta_2$, and that C_{T} and C_{A} are also mutually independent normal variables (independent of T_1, T_2, and T_3, too) with unknown means and variances,

$$E(C_T) = \theta_3, \qquad E(C_A) = \theta_4, \qquad \operatorname{var}(C_T) = \operatorname{var}(C_A) = \theta_5,$$

we can proceed to write the corresponding MNP model.

The partitioning of $\mathbf{a}$ and $[\boldsymbol{\theta}]$ yields

$$\mathbf{a}' = (1, T_1, T_2, T_3), \qquad \mathbf{a}'' = (C_T, C_A),$$

$$[\boldsymbol{\theta}'] = \begin{bmatrix} 0 & 0 & 0 \\ -\theta_1 & 0 & 0 \\ 0 & -\theta_1 & 0 \\ 0 & 0 & -\theta_1 \end{bmatrix}, \qquad [\boldsymbol{\theta}''] = \begin{bmatrix} 1 & 1 & 0 \\ 0 & 0 & 1 \end{bmatrix}.$$

The mean of $\mathbf{a}''[\boldsymbol{\theta}'']$ is

$$\boldsymbol{\theta}'' = E(\mathbf{a}'')[\boldsymbol{\theta}''] = (\theta_3, \theta_3, \theta_4)$$

and the covariance matrix is

$$\boldsymbol{\Sigma}_{\xi''} = [\boldsymbol{\theta}'']^{\mathrm{T}} \boldsymbol{\Sigma}_{a''} [\boldsymbol{\theta}''] = \begin{bmatrix} \theta_5 & \theta_5 & 0 \\ \theta_5 & \theta_5 & 0 \\ 0 & 0 & \theta_5 \end{bmatrix}.$$

Consequently, we have

$$\mathbf{V}^* = (1, T_1, T_2, T_3)\begin{bmatrix} \theta_3 & \theta_3 & \theta_4 \\ -\theta_1 & 0 & 0 \\ 0 & -\theta_1 & 0 \\ 0 & 0 & -\theta_1 \end{bmatrix}$$

and

$$\mathbf{\Sigma}_\xi^* = \begin{bmatrix} \theta_2 + \theta_5 & \theta_5 & 0 \\ \theta_5 & \theta_2 + \theta_5 & 0 \\ 0 & 0 & \theta_2 + \theta_5 \end{bmatrix}.$$

This is a more general form of the example in Section 2.3.2 because there we assumed that $\theta_3 = \theta_4 = 0$. Aside from that, the models are identical for all we have to do is measure travel time in a system of units for which $\theta_2 + \theta_5 = 1$. ■

Other specification errors, for example, those involving misspecification of the covariance matrix, are more difficult to study. Of particular interest is the specification error that occurs when the measured-attractiveness vector is not a linear function of $\boldsymbol{\theta}$, but a linear form is adopted nevertheless.

We first show that it is always possible to use, at least conceptually, a linear specification involving some extra parameters instead of the nonlinear specification in $\boldsymbol{\theta}$. We will also assume without loss of generality that the linear specification used is the approximation of the nonlinear function in the neighborhood of the origin $\boldsymbol{\theta} = \mathbf{0}$.

Let the true specification of V_i be $V_i = V_i(\boldsymbol{\theta}, \mathbf{a})$, which can be written, by means of a series expansion, as

$$V_i = V_i(\mathbf{0}, \mathbf{a}) + \boldsymbol{\nabla}_{\boldsymbol{\theta}} V_i(\mathbf{0}, \mathbf{a})\boldsymbol{\theta}^{\mathrm{T}} + \boldsymbol{\theta}\boldsymbol{\nabla}_{\boldsymbol{\theta}}^2 V_i(\mathbf{0}, \mathbf{a})\boldsymbol{\theta}^{\mathrm{T}} + \cdots.$$

Note that both the gradient and Hessian of V_i evaluated at $\boldsymbol{\theta} = \mathbf{0}$ are functions of $\mathbf{a}$ only.

If for simplicity we ignore the higher-order terms (third order, etc.), it is possible to model V_i with a linear specification, provided one introduces some additional parameters θ'_{jk} to replace the $\theta_j \cdot \theta_k$ terms in the third term of V_i. One can specify V_i as

$$V_i \approx V_i\Big|_{\boldsymbol{\theta}=\mathbf{0}} + \sum_{j=1}^{I}\left(\frac{\partial V_i}{\partial \theta_j}\Big|_{\boldsymbol{\theta}=\mathbf{0}} \theta_j\right) + \sum_{j=1}^{I}\sum_{k=1}^{I}\left(\theta'_{jk}\frac{\partial^2 V_i}{\partial \theta_j \partial \theta_k}\Big|_{\boldsymbol{\theta}=\mathbf{0}}\right), \tag{3.12}$$

which is a linear specification with parameters θ_j and θ'_{jk}, and explanatory variables

$$V_i\big|_{\boldsymbol{\theta}=\mathbf{0}}, \qquad \frac{\partial V_i}{\partial \theta_j}\Big|_{\boldsymbol{\theta}=\mathbf{0}}, \qquad \text{and} \qquad \frac{\partial^2 V_i}{\partial \theta_j \partial \theta_k}\Big|_{\boldsymbol{\theta}=\mathbf{0}}.$$

Since very often the linear specification used involves only the first two terms of Eq. (3.12), the resulting error would be equivalent to neglecting the attributes $(\partial^2 V_i/\partial\theta_j\,\partial\theta_k)_{\boldsymbol{\theta}=\mathbf{0}}$ from the specification of the model, which is a problem that has already been explored. The previous discussion, however, does not entirely apply here since one cannot reasonably assume independence of the neglected attributes and the ones that are included. There is little more that can be said about nonlinearities except, perhaps, that one must exercise care whenever the curvature of $\mathbf{V}(\boldsymbol{\theta}, \mathbf{a})$ is felt to be important over the relevant range of $\mathbf{a}$.

3.1.3 Taste Variations

A type of nonlinearity that is often used in demand modeling, consists in letting the values of the coefficients of the attributes change with the value of $\mathbf{a}$. If, for instance, in a mode-choice model, a_i represents travel time by automobile and its coefficient θ_i represents the contribution towards attractiveness of one unit of travel time (i.e., the "value" of travel time) it seems reasonable to speculate that such a coefficient should depend on the socioeconomic status of the individual. In our case we could define the coefficient as an increasing function of income, and thus we could use $\theta_i a_j$ (a_j represents income) instead of θ_i for a more realistic specification of the model.

These variations in the coefficients are sometimes called *systematic taste variations*, because they are included to represent the differences among people in the way they appraise the various components of the attractiveness of an alternative. Systematic taste variations can and have been used in MNL models since, as long as the coefficients of every attribute are linear functions of $\boldsymbol{\theta}$, the resulting specification will also be linear in $\boldsymbol{\theta}$. In another type of taste variation that is often considered in demand modeling the coefficients of the attribute vector are allowed to change from person to person *in an unpredictable way*. Because of this feature, this second type of taste variation is called *random taste variation* or, simply, *taste variation*.

To analyze random taste variations, it is convenient to represent the specification of the model by [note the difference—in form only—between Eqs. (3.1) and (3.13)]

$$U_{(n)} = (\boldsymbol{\theta} + \Delta\boldsymbol{\theta}_{(n)})[\mathbf{a}]_{(n)} + \xi_{(n)}, \tag{3.13}$$

where $\boldsymbol{\theta}$ is the parameter vector, $[\mathbf{a}]_{(n)}$ is an $r \times I$ matrix whose entries are either known constants or attributes (the jth column contains the attributes appearing in the jth measured-attractiveness function), and $\Delta\boldsymbol{\theta}_{(n)}$ is the fluctuation of the vector of coefficients around the population mean value $\boldsymbol{\theta}$, corresponding to the nth individual in the sample. Since the vector $\Delta\boldsymbol{\theta}_{(n)}$

is not observable and changes from individual to individual it can be included as part of the error term. Thus Eq. (3.13) defines a random utility model with

$$\mathbf{V}^* = \boldsymbol{\theta}[\mathbf{a}] \tag{3.14a}$$

and

$$\xi^* = \Delta\boldsymbol{\theta}[\mathbf{a}] + \xi. \tag{3.14b}$$

If the elements of $\Delta\boldsymbol{\theta}$ are MVN distributed with mean zero (by construction) and covariance matrix $\boldsymbol{\Sigma}_{\Delta\theta}$, Eqs. (3.14) define a MNP model with covariance matrix

$$\boldsymbol{\Sigma}_\xi^* = [\mathbf{a}]^{\mathrm{T}}\boldsymbol{\Sigma}_{\Delta\theta}[\mathbf{a}] + \Sigma_\xi. \tag{3.14c}$$

In some cases the matrix $\boldsymbol{\Sigma}_{\Delta\theta}$ may be known, but most often it is left to be estimated, at least in part.

3.1.4 *Parameter Estimability*

In the last three subsections we discussed ways of avoiding errors in the specification of models and enhancing their realism. Even for models whose specification approximates reality well, however, there are instances where the values of some of the parameters cannot be derived from data because the model fits the data equally well for different values of $\boldsymbol{\theta}$.

For instance, in the binary probit model whose specification is given by

$$\begin{aligned} U_1 &= (\theta_1 + \theta_2) + \theta_3 a_1 + \xi_1, \\ U_2 &= \theta_4 + \xi_2, \qquad \xi \sim \mathrm{MVN}(\mathbf{0}, \theta_5 \mathbf{I}), \end{aligned} \tag{3.15}$$

it is not possible to estimate the values of θ_1, θ_2, and θ_4, because exactly the same choice functions are obtained as long as $\theta_1 + \theta_2 - \theta_4$ remains constant.

The choice functions for this model can be expressed as

$$p_1 = \Phi\left(\frac{V_1 - V_2}{\sqrt{2\theta_5}}\right) = \Phi\left(\frac{\theta_1 + \theta_2 - \theta_4 + \theta_3 a_1}{\sqrt{2\theta_5}}\right),$$

$$p_2 = 1 - p_i,$$

which reduce to the same functions of a_1 whether $\hat{\boldsymbol{\theta}} = (\hat{\boldsymbol{\theta}}_1, \hat{\boldsymbol{\theta}}_2, \hat{\boldsymbol{\theta}}_3, \hat{\boldsymbol{\theta}}_4, \hat{\boldsymbol{\theta}}_5)$ or $\hat{\boldsymbol{\theta}}(x, y) = (x, y, \hat{\theta}_3, x + y + \hat{\theta}_4 - \hat{\theta}_1 - \hat{\theta}_2, \hat{\theta}_5)$. Since parameter estimates $\hat{\boldsymbol{\theta}}$ and $\hat{\boldsymbol{\theta}}(x, y)$ give an equally good fit to the data, it is impossible to determine the correct values of x and y, and of θ_1, θ_2, and θ_4. As a matter of fact, with the specification in Eq. (3.15) none of the parameters in it can be determined, because any combination of parameters yielding the same value for $\theta_i/\sqrt{\theta_5}\,(i = 1, 2, 3, 4)$ also yields the same choice function.

In general, it can be said that whenever the choice functions can be expressed as a function of a smaller set of parameters, $\boldsymbol{\theta}'$, related to the old parameters by $\boldsymbol{\theta}' = \boldsymbol{\theta}'(\boldsymbol{\theta})$,

$$P_i(\boldsymbol{\theta}, \mathbf{a}) \equiv P_i'[\boldsymbol{\theta}'(\boldsymbol{\theta}), \mathbf{a}], \qquad i = 1, \ldots, I,$$

the old set of parameters is not estimable because the specification in terms of $\boldsymbol{\theta}'$ is entirely equivalent to that of $\boldsymbol{\theta}$; and even if $\boldsymbol{\theta}'$ could be estimated, $\boldsymbol{\theta}$ could not be derived from it.

Verifying the estimability of the parameters of a MNP model could be difficult, since to do that it is necessary to analyze the choice function; and with three or more alternatives, the choice function of a MNP model does not assume a closed form. Fortunately, as was discussed in Chapter 2, the MNP choice function can be expressed as

$$P_i(\boldsymbol{\theta}, \mathbf{a}) = \Pr\{U_i > U_j, \forall j \neq i \,|\, E(\mathbf{U}) = \mathbf{V}(\boldsymbol{\theta}, \mathbf{a}), \operatorname{cov}(\mathbf{U}) = \boldsymbol{\Sigma}_\xi(\boldsymbol{\theta}, \mathbf{a})\}, \tag{3.16}$$

where $P_i(\boldsymbol{\theta}, \mathbf{a})$ depends on $\boldsymbol{\theta}$ and $\mathbf{a}$ through $\mathbf{V}(\boldsymbol{\theta}, \mathbf{a})$ and $\boldsymbol{\Sigma}_\xi(\boldsymbol{\theta}, \mathbf{a})$ only. Thus, an obvious check is to make sure that there is no change of variable that can reduce the number of parameters in the expressions for $\mathbf{V}$ and $\boldsymbol{\Sigma}_\xi$.

Equations (3.7a) and (3.7b) of a previously discussed example can be examined in this way. It is not possible to estimate $\boldsymbol{\Sigma}_\xi$ and $\boldsymbol{\Sigma}_\eta$ simultaneously (assuming all of the elements of both of them are to be estimated separately) because Eq. (3.7b) can be expressed as a function of a smaller number of parameters. The same can be said of Eq. (3.7a), where the vector $\boldsymbol{\theta}_v$ was added to the specification of the measured attractiveness. Any independent constants that appeared in the model are made inestimable by the addition of $\boldsymbol{\theta}_v$. In the example given by Eqs. (3.15) either θ_1 or θ_2 could be omitted with this test. A more appropriate specification would then be

$$U_1 = \theta_1 + \theta_3 a_1 + \xi_1, \tag{3.17a}$$

$$U_2 = \theta_4 + \xi_2, \tag{3.17b}$$

$$\boldsymbol{\xi} \sim \mathrm{MVN}(\mathbf{0}, \theta_5 \mathbf{I}). \tag{3.17c}$$

Further scrutiny of the properties of Eq. (3.16) enables us to devise other tests. For instance, if the same random variable is subtracted from the attractiveness of all the alternatives, the probability of choice does not change, since the subtraction affects both sides of the inequality $\mathrm{U}_i > U_j$, $\forall j \neq i$. It was seen in Chapter 2 that if U_i was subtracted from all the alternatives the MNP function could be expressed as

$$p_i(\mathbf{V}, \boldsymbol{\Sigma}_\xi) = \Phi(\mathbf{0} \,|\, \bar{\mathbf{Z}}, \boldsymbol{\Sigma}_Z), \tag{3.18}$$

where the right-hand side of Eq. (3.18) represents the cumulative distribution function of a MVN($\bar{\mathbf{Z}}, \boldsymbol{\Sigma}_Z$) variate evaluated at the origin and $\bar{\mathbf{Z}}$ and $\boldsymbol{\Sigma}_Z$ are given by Eqs. (2.16), which are reproduced below:

$$\bar{Z}_j = V_{j'} - V_i, \qquad j = 1, \ldots, I-1, \tag{2.16a}$$

$$\operatorname{cov}(Z_j, Z_k) = \sigma^2_{j'k'} - \sigma^2_{ik'} - \sigma^2_{ij'} + \sigma^2_{ii}, \qquad j, k = 1, \ldots, I-1. \tag{2.16b}$$

A prime in these equations denoted the jth (or kth) element of a row or column, when the ith one has been deleted. Since the choice probability depends on $\boldsymbol{\theta}$ and $\mathbf{a}$ through $\mathbf{V}$ and $\boldsymbol{\Sigma}_\xi$, and these affect it through $\bar{\mathbf{Z}}$ and $\boldsymbol{\Sigma}_Z$ only, the same checks that were applied to $\mathbf{V}$ and $\boldsymbol{\Sigma}_\xi$ can be applied to $\bar{\mathbf{Z}}$ and $\boldsymbol{\Sigma}_Z$.[2]

Subtracting U_1 from the revised specification of the example defined by Eqs. (3.17) yields

$$\bar{Z}_1 = \theta_4 - \theta_1 - \theta_3 a_1, \tag{3.19a}$$

$$\operatorname{var}(Z_1) = 2\theta_5, \tag{3.19b}$$

and we see that θ_1 can be omitted from the specification since (3.19) can be expressed as a function of three parameters only, $\theta_4 - \theta_1$, θ_3, and θ_5.

The model can thus be specified as

$$U_1 = \theta_3 a_1 + \xi_1, \tag{3.20a}$$

$$U_2 = \theta_4 + \xi_2, \tag{3.20b}$$

$$\xi \sim \mathrm{MVN}(\boldsymbol{\theta}, \theta_5 \mathrm{I}), \tag{3.20c}$$

with a further reduction in the number of parameters.

Another transformation that is useful to check is multiplying the perceived-attractiveness vector by a positive constant (i.e., changing the units of measurement) since that will not affect the choice probability. Thus two MNP functions with $(\mathbf{V}, \boldsymbol{\Sigma}_\xi)$ and $(k\mathbf{V}, k^2\boldsymbol{\Sigma}_\xi)$ as arguments will yield the same results, provided $k > 0$. An appropriate choice of k may reveal some further estimability problems. For the example in Eqs. (3.20) and $k = 1/\sqrt{\theta_5}$ the model reduces to

$$U_1 = (\theta_3/\sqrt{\theta_5})a_1 + \xi_1,$$
$$U_2 = (\theta_4/\sqrt{\theta_5}) + \xi_2,$$
$$\xi \sim \mathrm{MVN}(\mathbf{0}, \mathbf{I})$$

[2] As a consequence of this check, and taking into account that $\boldsymbol{\Sigma}_\xi$ is symmetric, the reader can prove that if $\boldsymbol{\Sigma}_\xi$ is not a function of $\mathbf{a}$ it can have at most $I(I-1)/2$ estimable parameters that do not appear in $\mathbf{V}$. This means a maximum of one free parameter in $\boldsymbol{\Sigma}_\xi$ for binary probit, and a maximum of three for trinomial probit.

indicating that one can use a model with two constants only:

$$U_1 = \theta_3 a_1 + \xi_1, \tag{3.21a}$$

$$U_2 = \theta_4 + \xi_2, \tag{3.21b}$$

$$\xi \sim \text{MVN}(\mathbf{0}, \mathbf{I}). \tag{3.21c}$$

No further simplifications can be made to this specification, which on an a priori basis should be estimable. Note that to perform these estimability checks we never had to write the choice function, and consequently they can be performed rather easily even for multinomial models. Close scrutiny of $\mathbf{V}$ and $\mathbf{\Sigma}_\xi$, however, may not necessarily result in an estimable model because a model that is *a priori estimable* may not be so with the available data. In such cases we say we have multicollinearity in the data. If the data set corresponding to Eq. (3.21) contains N observations in which all of them have the same value for a_1 $[a_{(n)1} = a,\ n = 1, 2, \ldots, I]$ the log-likelihood function $\log L(\theta_3, \theta_4)$ can be expressed as

$$\log L(\theta_3, \theta_4) = \sum_{n=1}^{N} P_{c_{(n)}}(\theta_3, \theta_4, a_{(n)})$$

$$= \sum_{n=1}^{N} \{\Phi[(\theta_3 a_{(n)1} - \theta_4)/\sqrt{2}]\}^{2-c(n)}\{1 - \Phi[(\theta_3 a_{(n)1} - \theta_4)/\sqrt{2}]\}^{c(n)-1},$$

which, since $a_{(n)1}$ is constant, is a function of $(\theta_3 a - \theta_4)$ only. Thus, any combination of θ_3 and θ_4 such that $\theta_3 a - \theta_4$ is constant will yield the same values of $\log L(\boldsymbol{\theta})$ and cannot be distinguished with maximum-likelihood estimation.

In real problems one will usually not have the time or the ability (in cases with more than two alternatives) to test for multicollinearity by hand and, as is done for regression, it is desirable to have an automatic check during the calibration process. A reasonable way of testing the estimability of a model consists of verifying that the log-likelihood function is strictly concave in the neighborhood of $\hat{\boldsymbol{\theta}}$, as in such case all points around $\hat{\boldsymbol{\theta}}$ yield lower log likelihoods and there cannot be any combination of parameters yielding the same value. This check is automatically done in calibration codes, since they provide the inverse of the Hessian of $\log L(\hat{\boldsymbol{\theta}})$, which will contain some unusually large entries if either the model is not a priori estimable or there is multicollinearity. The next section contains a computer example of an inestimable parameter vector.

It should be remarked, however, that, rigorously speaking, the strict concavity of $\log L(\boldsymbol{\theta})$ at $\hat{\boldsymbol{\theta}}$ is *neither a necessary nor sufficient condition for estimability*. As is discussed in the next section for the true parameter vector $\boldsymbol{\theta}_o$ to be estimable, $\log L(\boldsymbol{\theta})$ must be strictly concave at $\boldsymbol{\theta}_o$; only then can we be sure that a strict local maximum of $\log L(\boldsymbol{\theta})$ will exist very close to $\boldsymbol{\theta}_o$.[3] Of course this is difficult to verify because the true value of $\boldsymbol{\theta}_o$ is unknown.

3.2 Statistical Properties of MNP Estimators

We now investigate the accuracy of the maximum-likelihood estimates. This will be done for random samples in detail and for other sampling mechanisms in an abbreviated form.

Since the results of the sampling process and ensuing calibration procedure (i.e., $\mathbf{a}_{(1)}, \ldots, \mathbf{a}_{(N)}, c_{(1)}, \ldots, c_{(n)}$, and $\hat{\boldsymbol{\theta}}$) can be regarded as outcomes of an experiment (i.e., the sampling-calibration process); and since such outcomes would change from experiment to experiment in an unpredictable way, one can regard the attribute vectors, choices, and maximum likelihood estimator as random variables[4] ($\mathbf{A}_{(1)}, \ldots, \mathbf{A}_{(n)}, C_{(1)}, \ldots, C_{(N)}$, and $\hat{\boldsymbol{\Theta}}$) whose values become known only after sampling and calibrating thc MNP model.

Throughout this section we will explore the statistical properties of $\hat{\boldsymbol{\Theta}}$, which will give us a clue as to the closeness of $\hat{\boldsymbol{\theta}}$ and the true value of $\boldsymbol{\theta}$, $\boldsymbol{\theta}_o$. Specifically, it will be shown that under certain conditions $\hat{\boldsymbol{\Theta}}$ is a *consistent* estimator of $\boldsymbol{\theta}_o$; i.e.,

$$\lim_{N \to \infty} \Pr\{|\hat{\boldsymbol{\Theta}} - \boldsymbol{\theta}_o| < \varepsilon\} = 1 \qquad \forall \varepsilon > 0. \tag{3.22}$$

Equation (3.22) simply states that the probability that $\hat{\boldsymbol{\Theta}}$ differs significantly from $\hat{\boldsymbol{\theta}}_o$ can be made arbitrarily small by increasing the sample size. It is a desirable property of estimators because it ensures that whatever accuracy is desired can be obtained. The consistency property, however, is not very informative because Eq. (3.22) does not indicate the magnitude of error that one can expect for a certain sample size; it only says that if $N \to \infty$, then $\varepsilon \to 0$. In this section, thus, we will also explore the approximate distribution of $\hat{\boldsymbol{\Theta}}$ for large values of N. This will enable us to build approximate confidence regions for $\boldsymbol{\theta}_o$ and test hypotheses, as is extensively discussed in Section 3.4.

[3] The reader can verify that if in Eqs. (3.21) U_2 was defined as $U_2 = \theta_4 + \theta_6 + a_2 \max(0, \theta_6) + \xi_2$, the strict (or nonstrict) concavity of $\log L(\boldsymbol{\theta})$ at the maximum $\hat{\boldsymbol{\theta}}$ would be misleading if the true value of θ_6 were negative (positive) but θ_6 were positive (negative). For MNP models it is not known when relationships similar to that between θ_4 and θ_6 occur between the parameters in the covariance matrix and those in the attractiveness vector.

[4] We normally use capital letters for random variables and lower case for the values they take.

3.2.1 *Asymptotic Properties of the Maximum Likelihood Estimator*[5]

Let $(X_{(1)}, \ldots, X_{(N)})$ be a random sample from a distribution function $F(x|\boldsymbol{\theta}_o)$, where $\boldsymbol{\theta}_o$ is unknown. Let us assume that $\boldsymbol{\theta}_o$ is vector valued and that so is the random variable X, which can have both discrete and continuous components. Define the joint mass-density function of X, $f(x|\boldsymbol{\theta}_o)$, as

$$f(x|\boldsymbol{\theta}_o) = \Pr\{X' = x' \text{ and } X'' \in [x'', x'' + dx'')\}/dx_1'' \cdots dx_l'',$$

where primes denote the discrete components of X, double primes the continuous components of X, and l the number of continuous components. Then the likelihood of a sample $(x_{(1)}, \ldots, x_{(N)})$ is

$$L(x_{(1)} \cdots x_{(N)}|\boldsymbol{\theta}) = \prod_{n=1}^{N} f(x_{(n)}|\boldsymbol{\theta}),$$

which for convenience we abbreviate by $L(\mathbf{x}|\boldsymbol{\theta})$.[6]

We now state in the form of a theorem some basic results of maximum likelihood theory which will be utilized in the sequel. The interested reader will find proofs of the theorem in standard probability and statistics books such as Wilks (1962) and Rao (1965). Particularly noteworthy for its clarity of presentation and conciseness is Theil's exposition (Theil, 1971, pp. 384–397), which develops the theory for a one-parameter case.

Theorem 3.1 If regularity conditions (a)–(d) hold, the maximum-likelihood estimator $\hat{\boldsymbol{\Theta}}$ of $\boldsymbol{\theta}_o$ from a random sample $\mathbf{X} = (X_{(1)}, \ldots, X_{(N)})$ of $f(x|\boldsymbol{\theta}_o)$ has the following properties:

Properties (1) It is consistent.

(2) For large values of N it is approximately MVN distributed with mean $\boldsymbol{\theta}_o$.

(3) It is asymptotically efficient. That is, no other *unbiased* (with mean $\boldsymbol{\theta}_o$) estimator $\tilde{\boldsymbol{\Theta}}$ can have a smaller covariance matrix for very large samples. More precisely, as $N \to \infty$, $[\text{cov}(\tilde{\boldsymbol{\Theta}}) - \text{cov}(\hat{\boldsymbol{\Theta}})]$ is a positive-semidefinite matrix.

(4) Minus the inverse Hessian of $\log L(\mathbf{x}|\boldsymbol{\theta})$ at $\boldsymbol{\theta} = \hat{\boldsymbol{\theta}}$ is a consistent estimate of $\text{cov}(\boldsymbol{\Theta})$.

(5) For large values of N, $-2[\log L(\mathbf{X}|\boldsymbol{\theta}_o)/\log L(\mathbf{X}|\hat{\boldsymbol{\Theta}})]$ has approximately a χ^2 distribution with as many degrees of freedom as parameters.

[5] The reader interested exclusively in applications of the MNP model may skip the body of this subsection and read the summary provided in Section 3.2.2.

[6] For the rest of this subsection we depart from our convention in notation in two ways: First, although the random variable X is vector valued, a boldface $\mathbf{X}$ will only be used to represent all the sample; and second, the notation $L(x|\boldsymbol{\theta})$ is preferred to $L(\boldsymbol{\theta})$ to emphasize that the likelihood value corresponds to a given data set.

Regularity Conditions (a) The third derivatives of $f(x|\boldsymbol{\theta})$ with respect to the elements of $\boldsymbol{\theta}$ must exist in an open neighborhood of $\boldsymbol{\theta}_o$.

(b) The third derivatives of $\log f(x|\boldsymbol{\theta})$ must be bounded:

$$\left|\frac{\partial^3 \log f(x|\boldsymbol{\theta})}{\partial\theta_i\,\partial\theta_j\,\partial\theta_k}\right| < u_{ijk}(x)$$

with $E_X[u_{ijk}(X)] < \mu_{ijk}$, for all combinations of i, j, and k in an open neighborhood of $\boldsymbol{\theta}_o$.

(c) The range of X must not depend on $\boldsymbol{\theta}$ so that integration and differentiation can be interchanged as shown below in an open neighborhood of $\boldsymbol{\theta}_o$:

$$\nabla_\theta \int_{-\infty}^{\infty} \cdots \int_{-\infty}^{\infty} L(\mathbf{x}|\boldsymbol{\theta})\,dx = \int_{-\infty}^{\infty} \cdots \int_{-\infty}^{\infty} \nabla_\theta L(\mathbf{x}|\boldsymbol{\theta})\,dx.$$

Of course, in this expression, the integral operator should be visualized as representing the summation operator for the discrete components of x.
(d) $E_X[-\nabla_\theta^2 \log f(X|\boldsymbol{\theta}_o)]$ must be a positive-definite matrix.[7] ■

In the remainder of this subsection we show that Theorem 3.1 applies to MNP models with random sampling and discuss how Conditions (a)–(d) can be checked in a simple way (Bouthelier, 1978, has investigated the properties of MNP estimates, as well). The main results are summarized in Section 3.2.2.

For a random sample of size N, the maximum-likelihood estimate $\hat{\boldsymbol{\theta}}$ is obtained by solving[8]

$$\max_{\boldsymbol{\theta}} \sum_{n=1}^{N} \log P_{c(n)}(\boldsymbol{\theta}, \mathbf{a}_{(n)}), \tag{3.23a}$$

which is equivalent to solving

$$\max_{\boldsymbol{\theta}} \prod_{n=1}^{N} \Pr\{C_{(n)} = c_{(n)} | \mathbf{A}_{(n)} = \mathbf{a}_{(n)}; \hat{\boldsymbol{\Theta}} = \boldsymbol{\theta}\}$$

or, letting $X_{(n)}$ represent the joint attribute and choice vector $(C_{(n)}\mathbf{A}_{(n)})$,

$$\max_{\boldsymbol{\theta}} \prod_{n=1}^{N} [f_{X_{(n)}}(x_{(n)}|\boldsymbol{\theta})/F_{A_n}(\mathbf{a}_{(n)}|\boldsymbol{\theta})],$$

where $f_{X_{(n)}}(x_{(n)}|\boldsymbol{\theta})$ represents the joint mass-density function of $X_{(n)}$ and $F_{A_n}(\mathbf{a}_{(n)}|\boldsymbol{\theta})$ is the mass-density function of $\mathbf{A}_{(n)}$, both of them conditional on $\boldsymbol{\theta}$.

[7] Actually, we only have to require that $E_X[-\nabla_\theta^2 \log f(X|\boldsymbol{\theta}_o)]$ be nonsingular because if conditions (a)–(c) hold, it can be shown that $E_X[-\nabla_\theta^2 \log f(X|\boldsymbol{\theta}_o)] = \operatorname{cov}[\nabla_\theta \log f(X|\boldsymbol{\theta}_o)]$, which must necessarily be positive semidefinite.

[8] If the log likelihood has multiple maxima there is at least one solution that satisfies Theorem 3.1. That solution is the maximum-likelihood estimator.

Since **A** is independent of $\boldsymbol{\theta}$, the factor $\prod_{n=1}^{N}[F_{A_n}(\mathbf{a}_{(n)}|\boldsymbol{\theta})]^{-1}$ enters the equation as a positive constant independent of $\boldsymbol{\theta}$ that can be ignored, and Eq. (3.23a) can be replaced by

$$\max_{\boldsymbol{\theta}} \prod_{n=1}^{N} f_{X_{(n)}}(x_{(n)}|\boldsymbol{\theta}).$$

Since, by definition of a random sampling process, the variables $X_{(n)}$ are independent and identically distributed, Theorem 3.1 applies.[9] We now check to see whether Conditions (a)–(d) are satisfied for MNP models.

We first note that

$$f_X(x|\boldsymbol{\theta}) = P_c(\boldsymbol{\theta}, \mathbf{a})F(\mathbf{a})$$

and that consequently the derivatives of $\log f_X(x|\boldsymbol{\theta})$ and $\log P_c(\boldsymbol{\theta}, \mathbf{a})$ with respect to $\boldsymbol{\theta}$ coincide.

Regularity Conditions (a) Since the choice function can be expressed in terms of a MNP function

$$P_c(\boldsymbol{\theta}, \mathbf{a}) = p_c[\mathbf{V}(\boldsymbol{\theta}, \mathbf{a}), \boldsymbol{\Sigma}_\xi(\boldsymbol{\theta}, \mathbf{a})],$$

which has finite derivatives if $\boldsymbol{\Sigma}_\xi$ is positive definite [as inspection of Eq. (2.15) shows], $P_c(\boldsymbol{\theta}, \mathbf{a})$ will satisfy Condition (a) if the third derivatives of **V** and $\boldsymbol{\Sigma}_\xi$ with respect to $\boldsymbol{\theta}$ exist. Thus, Condition (a) will be met if $\boldsymbol{\Sigma}_\xi$ is positive definite and the third derivatives of **V** and $\boldsymbol{\Sigma}_\xi$ with respect to $\boldsymbol{\theta}$ exist for all values of **a** and $\boldsymbol{\theta}$. In cases where $\boldsymbol{\Sigma}_\xi$ is not positive definite for all the values of $\boldsymbol{\theta}$ but there is an open domain defined by $\boldsymbol{\theta}_{\min}$ and $\boldsymbol{\theta}_{\max}$ (cf. Chapter 2) in which $\boldsymbol{\Sigma}_\xi$ is positive definite, Condition (a) will be met if $\boldsymbol{\theta}_o$ belongs to this domain and **V** and $\boldsymbol{\Sigma}_\xi$ are three times differentiable within the domain.

(b) Since $\log(\cdot)$ is analytical if its argument is positive, the derivatives of $\log P_c(\boldsymbol{\theta}, \mathbf{a})$ will exist if those of $P_c(\boldsymbol{\theta}, \mathbf{a})$ exist, as long as $P_c(\boldsymbol{\theta}, \mathbf{a}) > 0$ [Condition (c) below ensures that $P_c(\boldsymbol{\theta}, \mathbf{a})$ is always positive]. Thus, an argument similar to the one used with Condition (a) ensures that if the fourth derivatives of **V** and $\boldsymbol{\Sigma}_\xi$ with respect to $\boldsymbol{\theta}$ and **a** exist, and $\boldsymbol{\Sigma}_\xi$ is positive definite, as specified in Condition (a),

$$\frac{\partial^3 \log f_X(x|\boldsymbol{\theta})}{\partial\theta_i\,\partial\theta_j\,d\theta_k} = \frac{\partial^3 \log P_c(\boldsymbol{\theta}, \mathbf{a})}{\partial\theta_i\,\partial\theta_j\,\partial\theta_k}$$

exists and is a continuous function of $\boldsymbol{\theta}$ and **a**.

[9] Although in a random sampling process $F_{A_n}(\mathbf{a})$ coincides with the population probability mass density function of **A**, $F(\mathbf{a})$, the theorem requires only that the distribution of $\mathbf{A}_{(n)}$ be the same for all the sample points. This fact will be used in Section 3.2.2 when we analyze nonrandom sampling strategies.

If the feasible values of $\mathbf{A}$ are contained in a compact (closed and bounded) set $\mathscr{A}$, the third derivative will be bounded in the compact set defined by

$$\mathscr{B} = \{(\boldsymbol{\theta}, \mathbf{a}) : |\boldsymbol{\theta} - \boldsymbol{\theta}_o| \leq \delta, \mathbf{a} \in \mathscr{A}\} \qquad \text{for some } \delta > 0$$

for any given value of the choice c.

Thus we can write

$$\left| \frac{\partial^3 \log P_c(\boldsymbol{\theta}, \mathbf{a})}{\partial \theta_i \, \partial \theta_j \, \partial \theta_k} \right| < u_{ijk}(c) < \infty$$

and since the set of $u_{ijk}(c)$s only has a finite number of members it has a finite upper bound, $\mu_{ijk} > u_{ijk}(c)$.

Obviously, then $E_X[u_{ijk}(X)] < \mu_{ijk}$ and Condition (b) is met.

Thus, a sufficient condition for Condition (b) is that $\boldsymbol{\Sigma}_\xi$ be positive definite, the fourth derivatives of $\mathbf{V}$ and $\boldsymbol{\Sigma}_\xi$ with respect to $\boldsymbol{\theta}$ and $\mathbf{a}$ exist, and that the feasible values of $\mathbf{a}$ are contained in a compact set. However, if as with Condition (a) there is an open domain defined by $\boldsymbol{\theta}_{\min}$ and $\boldsymbol{\theta}_{\max}$ in which $\boldsymbol{\Sigma}_\xi$ is positive definite, it suffices to verify the differentiability conditions within the domain as long as $\boldsymbol{\theta}_o$ belongs to it.

(c) Since

$$f_X(x \,|\, \boldsymbol{\theta}) = P_c(\boldsymbol{\theta}, \mathbf{a}) F(\mathbf{a}),$$

the range of $X = (C, \mathbf{A})$ will be independent of $\boldsymbol{\theta}$ for all the feasible values of $\boldsymbol{\theta}(\boldsymbol{\theta}_{\min} < \boldsymbol{\theta} < \boldsymbol{\theta}_{\max})$, as long as $P_c(\boldsymbol{\theta}, \mathbf{a})$ is strictly positive for all values of c and all feasible values of $\mathbf{a}$ and $\boldsymbol{\theta}$. This will happen if $\mathbf{V}$ and $\boldsymbol{\Sigma}_\xi$ are finite ($\boldsymbol{\Sigma}_\xi$ positive definite, too) because then the choice probability is positive for all the alternatives. This can be seen from Eq. (2.15) because if $\mathbf{V}$ and $\boldsymbol{\Sigma}_\xi$ are finite and $\boldsymbol{\Sigma}_\xi$ is nonsingular the integrand is positive. Under these conditions the interchangeability of integration and differentiation follows inasmuch as $\nabla_\theta L(x \,|\, \boldsymbol{\theta})$ is continuous [provided $f_X(x \,|\, \boldsymbol{\theta})$ satisfies Condition (a)].

For Condition (c) to be met it is thus sufficient that the specification of $\mathbf{V}$ and $\boldsymbol{\Sigma}_\xi$ gives finite values whenever $\mathbf{a}$ and $\boldsymbol{\theta}$ are finite (a condition implied by the differentiability assumptions) and that $\boldsymbol{\theta}_o$ and all feasible values of $\mathbf{a}$ be finite.

(d) It is not easy to derive a sufficient condition to ensure that

$$-E_{C,A}[\nabla^2_\theta \log P_c(\boldsymbol{\theta}_o, \mathbf{A})] \tag{3.24}$$

is a positive-definite matrix for an arbitrary MNP model. However, it is always possible to define a necessary condition and, for binary probit, even a sufficient condition. One can also be reasonably sure of Condition (d) by checking the calibration results. This is explained below.

Necessary Condition For expression (3.24) to denote a positive-definite matrix it is necessary that $\boldsymbol{\theta}_o$ be a priori estimable since otherwise the second directional derivative of $\log P_c(\boldsymbol{\theta}, \mathbf{a})$ will vanish in at least one direction, $\Delta\boldsymbol{\theta}$, for all values of $\mathbf{a}$ and c:

$$\Delta\boldsymbol{\theta}\,[\nabla_{\theta}^2 \log P_c(\boldsymbol{\theta}, \mathbf{a})]\,\Delta\boldsymbol{\theta}^{\mathrm{T}} = 0 \qquad \forall(c, \mathbf{a});$$

and if that happens:

$$\Delta\boldsymbol{\theta}\,\{-E_{C,A}[\nabla_{\theta}^2 \log P_C(\boldsymbol{\theta}, \mathbf{A})]\}\,\Delta\boldsymbol{\theta}^{\mathrm{T}} = 0,$$

which indicates Eq. (3.24) is not positive definite.

Sufficient Condition For Eq. (3.24) to be positive definite it is sufficient that $\log P_c(\boldsymbol{\theta}, \mathbf{a})$ be a strictly concave function of $\boldsymbol{\theta}$, since then its Hessian is negative definite for all values of c and $\mathbf{a}$, and (3.24) is positive definite. In Section 2.5 we demonstrated the concavity of $\log P_c(\boldsymbol{\theta}, \mathbf{a})$ for binary probit models with specifications linear in the parameters.

It is now shown that if, in addition, the binary probit model is estimable and there is no multicollinearity, i.e., the distribution of $\mathbf{A}$ is not degenerate, expression (3.24) is positive definite.

If the a priori estimable choice functions are expressed as $p_1 = \Phi(\boldsymbol{\theta}\mathbf{a}^{\mathrm{T}})$ and $p_2 = \Phi(-\boldsymbol{\theta}\mathbf{a}^{\mathrm{T}})$ ($\boldsymbol{\theta}$ and $\mathbf{a}$ are of the same dimension, r, and do not have any repeated elements) we have

$$\nabla_{\theta}^2 \log P_i(\boldsymbol{\theta}, \mathbf{a}) = \mathbf{a}^{\mathrm{T}}[\nabla_x^2 \log \Phi(x)|_{x=\pm\boldsymbol{\theta}\mathbf{a}^{\mathrm{T}}}]\mathbf{a}, \qquad i = 1, 2,$$

and, since $\nabla_x^2 \log \Phi(x) < 0$, $\Delta\boldsymbol{\theta}\,[\nabla_{\theta}^2 \log P_i(\boldsymbol{\theta}, \mathbf{a})]\,\Delta\boldsymbol{\theta}^{\mathrm{T}}$ will vanish only if $\Delta\boldsymbol{\theta}\,\mathbf{a}^{\mathrm{T}} = 0$. Thus, for expression (3.24) not to be a definite matrix it would be necessary that $\Pr\{\Delta\boldsymbol{\theta}\,\mathbf{A}^{\mathrm{T}} = 0\} = 1$ for some $\Delta\boldsymbol{\theta} \neq 0$, since otherwise there is a finite probability that $-\nabla_{\theta}^2 \log P_i(\boldsymbol{\theta}, \mathbf{A})$ is positive definite and its expectation would be positive definite. But for $\Pr\{\Delta\boldsymbol{\theta}\,\mathbf{A}^{\mathrm{T}} = 0\}$ to equal 1 for some $\Delta\boldsymbol{\theta} \neq 0$, the probability density of $\mathbf{A}^{\mathrm{T}}$ would have to be concentrated in a hyperplane of $\mathscr{R}^r$ defined by $\Delta\boldsymbol{\theta}\,\mathbf{A}^{\mathrm{T}} = 0$, in which case there would be multicollinearity. We can rest assured that this does not occur if the data attribute matrix, $(\mathbf{a}_{(1)}, \ldots, \mathbf{a}_{(N)})$, is of rank r.[10]

Unfortunately, for the general MNP problem it is not possible to derive a similar sufficient condition because the concavity of the log-MNP function has not been established. However, the Hessian of the log-likelihood

[10] It is easy to show following the same arguments that if the specification of a MNL model is expressed as $\mathbf{V} = \boldsymbol{\theta}[\mathbf{a}]$, where $[\mathbf{a}]$ is an $r \times I$ matrix with zeros on the first column, whose entries are either known constants or elements of $\mathbf{a}$, a sufficient condition for estimability of a MNL model (condition d) is $\Pr\{\Delta\boldsymbol{\theta}[\mathbf{A}] = \mathbf{0}\} \neq 1$, $\forall\Delta\boldsymbol{\theta} \neq \mathbf{0}$.

function,

$$\nabla_\theta^2 \log L(\mathbf{x} \mid \boldsymbol{\theta}) = \nabla_\theta^2 \log L(\boldsymbol{\theta}),$$

is a good approximation for $NE_X[\nabla_\theta^2 \log f_X(X \mid \boldsymbol{\theta})]$ since the former is the sum of N independent identically distributed observations of $\nabla_\theta^2 \log f_X(X \mid \boldsymbol{\theta})$; consequently, a nonsingular Hessian over the domain of reasonable values of $\boldsymbol{\theta}$ is a strong indication that Condition (d) is satisfied, (remember that if the Hessian is nonsingular it is negative definite at $\boldsymbol{\theta}_o$ [c.f. footnote 7]).

In instances where $\hat{\boldsymbol{\theta}}$ takes a reasonable value (i.e., we know it is close to $\boldsymbol{\theta}_o$) it may be appropriate to check the strict concavity of the log-likelihood function at $\hat{\boldsymbol{\theta}}$ only; this is an easy thing to do since the output of a MNP code includes $-[\nabla_\theta^2 \log L(\hat{\boldsymbol{\theta}})]^{-1}$, which should be positive definite.

3.2.2 Summary and Example

Under the regularity conditions defined below, the maximum-likelihood estimator $\hat{\boldsymbol{\Theta}}$ of a MNP model calibrated with a random sample[11] has the following properties:

(1) It is consistent.

(2) It is asymptotically MVN distributed with mean $\boldsymbol{\theta}_o$.

(3) It is asymptotically efficient (no other estimator has a smaller covariance matrix).

(4) $-[\nabla_\theta^2 \log L(\mathbf{x} \mid \hat{\boldsymbol{\theta}})]^{-1}$ is a consistent estimate of $\mathrm{cov}(\hat{\boldsymbol{\Theta}})$.

(5) $-2[\log L(\mathbf{X} \mid \boldsymbol{\theta}_o)/\log L(\mathbf{X} \mid \hat{\boldsymbol{\Theta}})]$ is asymptotically $\chi^2_{(r)}$ distributed, where r is the dimensionality of $\boldsymbol{\theta}$.

Sufficient Regularity Conditions

The discussion regarding Conditions (a)–(d) of Theorem 3.1 in the previous subsection can be collapsed into the following set of sufficient regularity conditions.

(1) The values of the attribute vector **a** that can actually occur are bounded.[12]

(2) $\boldsymbol{\theta}_o$ must belong to the feasibility domain defined by $\boldsymbol{\theta}_{\min}$ and $\boldsymbol{\theta}_{\max}$; $\boldsymbol{\theta}_{\min} < \boldsymbol{\theta}_o < \boldsymbol{\theta}_{\max}$ (cf. Section 2.3.1).

[11] For models with ranked alternatives, the same analysis shows that Theorem 3.1 applies under a similar set of regularity conditions, as long as a random sampling procedure is still followed.

[12] Note that Condition (1) precludes the inclusion in a model of dummy attributes taking on infinite values.

(3) $\mathbf{V}(\boldsymbol{\theta}, \mathbf{a})$ and $\boldsymbol{\Sigma}_\xi(\boldsymbol{\theta}, \mathbf{a})$ must be four times differentiable functions of $\boldsymbol{\theta}$ and $\mathbf{a}$, and $\boldsymbol{\Sigma}_\xi(\boldsymbol{\theta}, \mathbf{a})$ must be positive definite for all the feasible values of $\boldsymbol{\theta}$, $\boldsymbol{\theta}_{\min} < \boldsymbol{\theta} < \boldsymbol{\theta}_{\max}$, and $\mathbf{a}$.

(4) For large samples, $-\boldsymbol{\nabla}_\theta^2 \log L(\mathbf{x} \mid \boldsymbol{\theta}_o)$ must be positive definite. This can be verified by establishing the nonsingularity of $\boldsymbol{\nabla}_\theta^2 \log L(\mathbf{x} \mid \boldsymbol{\theta})$, empirically, over a range of $\boldsymbol{\theta}$ that would include $\boldsymbol{\theta}_o$. Of course, if one is reasonably sure that $\hat{\boldsymbol{\theta}}$ is close to $\boldsymbol{\theta}_o$, checking that $\boldsymbol{\nabla}_\theta^2 \log L(\mathbf{x} \mid \hat{\boldsymbol{\theta}})$ is negative definite may be enough. For binary probit a more rigorous test can be carried out (see the discussion in the previous section).

A short trinomial probit example that illustrates the ideas in Sections 3.1 and 3.2.1 is presented next.

Example We reconsider at this stage the example that was provided in Chapter 2 (Sections 2.3.2 and 2.4.2) and the data set contained in Table 2.4.

If the specification of the model was inadvertently set

$$V_1 = -(\theta_1 + \theta_2)a_1,$$
$$V_2 = -(\theta_1 + \theta_2)a_2,$$
$$V_3 = -(\theta_1 + \theta_2)a_3,$$

with

$$\boldsymbol{\Sigma}_\xi = \begin{bmatrix} 1 & \theta_3 & 0 \\ \theta_3 & 1 & 0 \\ 0 & 0 & 1 \end{bmatrix},$$

the parameter vector $\boldsymbol{\theta} = (\theta_1, \theta_2, \theta_3)$ would not be estimable because it is possible to express $\mathbf{V}$ and $\boldsymbol{\Sigma}_\xi$ as a function of $\theta_1' = \theta_1 + \theta_2$ and $\theta_2' = \theta_3$ only. Since regularity conditions (1)–(3) are met [it is reasonable to assume that for the population under study $0 \le a_I \le a_{\text{big}}$, $i = 1, 2, 3$, and that therefore Condition (1) applies] the model is estimated with the hope of checking regularity condition (4) a posteriori.

After a few iterations the following values are obtained:

$$\hat{\boldsymbol{\theta}} = (0.12, 0.12, 0.48),$$
$$\log L(\hat{\boldsymbol{\theta}}) = -33.895,$$

and

$$\boldsymbol{\nabla}_\theta^2 \log L(\hat{\boldsymbol{\theta}}) = \begin{bmatrix} -133.2 & -133.2 & -10.19 \\ -133.2 & -133.2 & -10.19 \\ -10.19 & -10.19 & -10.83 \end{bmatrix}.$$

The Hessian is obviously singular indicating that regularity condition (4) is not met and that there might be an identification problem. In existing computer packages the output includes an estimated covariance matrix of

$\hat{\boldsymbol{\Theta}}$ which is simply minus the inverse Hessian [see Theorem 3.1, Property (4)]. In cases like these an attempt to calculate $[\nabla_\theta^2 \log L(\hat{\boldsymbol{\theta}})]^{-1}$ would yield an error message, but due to computer round-off error in the calculation of $\nabla_\theta^2 \log L(\hat{\boldsymbol{\theta}})$ calculations sometimes proceed yielding another, approximately singular, matrix containing some unusually large entries. In the CDC 6400 computer where these calculations were carried out we obtained

$$-[\nabla_\theta^2 \log L(\hat{\boldsymbol{\theta}})]^{-1} \approx \begin{bmatrix} 17592 & -17592 & -0.002 \\ -17592 & 17592 & -0.002 \\ -0.002 & -0.002 & 0.098 \end{bmatrix} \approx \operatorname{cov}(\hat{\boldsymbol{\Theta}}),$$

where in addition to the singularity of the matrix and its large entries one can notice the perfect negative correlation between the first two elements of $\hat{\boldsymbol{\Theta}}$. This, of course, suggests a functional relationship between these elements, which in our case is

$$\hat{\Theta}_1 + \hat{\Theta}_2 = \text{const},$$

corresponding to an estimability problem.

With this evidence one can usually correct the specification of the model. In our case setting

$$V_1 = -\theta_1 T_1, \qquad V_2 = -\theta_1 T_2, \qquad V_3 = -\theta_1 T_3$$

and

$$\Sigma_\xi = \begin{bmatrix} 1 & \theta_2 & 0 \\ \theta_2 & 1 & 0 \\ 0 & 0 & 1 \end{bmatrix}$$

results in an estimable problem (same as in Sections 2.3.2 and 2.4.2) that yields

$$\hat{\boldsymbol{\theta}} = (0.24, 0.48),$$
$$\log L(\hat{\boldsymbol{\theta}}) = -33.895$$

and

$$\operatorname{cov}(\hat{\boldsymbol{\Theta}}) \approx \begin{bmatrix} 0.002 & -0.004 \\ -0.004 & 0.1 \end{bmatrix}.$$

Since regularity condition (4) seems to be met (the log-likelihood function of this problem seemed well behaved and strictly concave throughout) the previous result can be adopted.

When instead of the 50 data points one uses many more with the same specification, according to the consistency property, we expect the entries of the covariance matrix of $\hat{\mathbf{\Theta}}$ to decrease. This, indeed, happens since for a 500-point data set the results were

$$\hat{\theta} = (0.27, 0.51),$$
$$\log L(\hat{\theta}) = -338.85,$$

and

$$\operatorname{cov}(\hat{\mathbf{\Theta}}) \approx \begin{bmatrix} 0.0002 & -0.0004 \\ -0.0004 & 0.009 \end{bmatrix}.$$

Since the regularity condition are met, assuming that no specification errors have been committed, the estimator $\hat{\mathbf{\Theta}}$ with 500 data points (and perhaps the one with 50 too) is approximately BVN distributed with mean $\boldsymbol{\theta}_o$ and covariance matrix as given above. Property (3) ensures that $\operatorname{cov}(\hat{\mathbf{\Theta}})$ is on the average the smallest matrix we can get with 500 data points. ■

3.2.3 Properties of Nonrandom Sample Estimators

When the sampling process is not random, Theorem 3.1 must be reconsidered. Assume that we are sampling at random from a subgroup of the whole population of individuals. Under such circumstances the sampling distribution of $\mathbf{A}$ will not coincide with the population distribution of $\mathbf{A}$ and the sample and population distributions of $X = (C, \mathbf{A})$ will also differ. This, however, makes little difference in our case since $X_{(1)}, \ldots, X_{(N)}$ are still independent and identically distributed, and, as long as the regularity conditions are met, Theorem 3.1 still applies. When the subgroup is homogeneous ($\mathbf{A} \approx \bar{\mathbf{a}}$), regularity condition (4) may cause problems, however, since even for an estimable problem one may have multicollinearity, and, as happens in regression analysis, there may be large variances associated with $\hat{\mathbf{\Theta}}$.

Stratified sampling is another instance where the sample distribution of $\mathbf{A}$ does not coincide with the population, but where unlike in the previous case Theorem 3.1 does not seem to apply because $\mathbf{A}_{(1)}, \ldots, \mathbf{A}_{(N)}$ (and consequently $X_{(1)}, \ldots, X_{(N)}$) are not identically distributed.

Imagine, however, that instead of predetermining the number of observations in each stratum we only decide the desired fraction of the sample that must be assigned to each stratum ($f_{(k)}$ will denote the desired fraction of observations in stratum k) and that the actual number of observations is obtained by sampling from a multinomial distribution with probabilities $f_{(k)}$. For large samples the actual fraction of observations in each stratum would then be relatively close to the desired fraction, and, furthermore, if we visualize the assignment of observations to strata as part of the sampling mechanism leading to $\mathbf{A}_{(1)}, \ldots, \mathbf{A}_{(N)}$ the random variables $(\mathbf{A}_{(1)}, \ldots, \mathbf{A}_{(N)})$

would be independent and identically distributed; therefore, Theorem 3.1 would apply. Of course, $\hat{\mathbf{\Theta}}$ should be interpreted as a random variable, which to be observed requires determining the number of observations in each stratum from the desired fractions $f_{(k)}$, in addition to gathering the data and carrying out the estimation procedure. The procedure just described will be called a *random stratified sampling* process.

Multicollinearity problems will not arise with random stratified samples if the strata and corresponding sampling mechanism are adequately designed. As a matter of fact, a proper sample design will usually result in better estimates than a random sample since more observations can be placed where needed.

In cases for which the number of observations within each stratum is fixed for the sample it can be shown that for sufficiently large samples Theorem 3.1 also applies. All one has to do is redefine X in such a way that the stratified sampling process reduces to a random sampling of Xs. This can be done by letting X represent the attributes and choices of several observations from different strata. For example, if we have two classes with 30 and 60 observations each, we can define each observation of X as one observation from class 1 and two from class 2, so that

$$\begin{aligned} X_1 &= (\mathbf{a}_{(1)}, c_{(1)}), (\mathbf{a}_{(31)}, c_{(31)}), (\mathbf{a}_{(32)}, c_{(32)}), \\ X_2 &= (\mathbf{a}_{(2)}, c_{(2)}), (\mathbf{a}_{(33)}, c_{(33)}), (\mathbf{a}_{(34)}, c_{(34)}), \\ &\vdots \\ X_{30} &= (\mathbf{a}_{(30)}, c_{(30)}), (\mathbf{a}_{(59)}, c_{(59)}), (\mathbf{a}_{(60)}, c_{(60)}), \end{aligned}$$

where we have assumed that observations 1–30 belong to class 1 and observation 31–90 to class 2. The stratified sampling mechanism can then be visualized as a random sampling of 30Xs and Theorem 3.1 applies. Redefining X in such way, however, changes the meaning of a large sample because we now require a large number of observations *within each subgroup*. Such redefinition makes large samples harder to come by, especially when one has many subgroups. In order to be able to relax these requirements formally, it would be necessary to analyze the problem in depth to place restrictions on the sequence $\mathbf{a}_{(1)}, \ldots, \mathbf{a}_{(N)}$ that will make Theorem 3.1 apply. This might be difficult to do, but if it is reasonable to expect only minor differences between this estimator and the random stratified sampling estimator with desired sample fraction $f_{(k)}$, equal to the actual sample fractions, one may apply Theorem 3.1 nevertheless.

Choice-Based Sampling

For choice-based samples that are estimated with maximum likelihood [Eq. (2.7a) in Chapter 2] it is easy to show that Theorem 3.1 will apply under the regularity conditions at the beginning of Section 3.2.2 if $\log P_c(\boldsymbol{\theta})$ is a four-times-differentiable function of $\boldsymbol{\theta}$.

This is always true when $P_c(\boldsymbol{\theta}, \mathbf{a})$ is four-times differentiable [as happens if Condition (a) is met] because (see Section 1.2)

$$P_c(\boldsymbol{\theta}) = \int_{\mathbf{a}} P_c(\boldsymbol{\theta}, \mathbf{a}) F(\mathbf{a})\, d\mathbf{a},$$

where $F(\mathbf{a})$ is the *population* distribution of $\mathbf{A}$. Thus, the regularity conditions at the beginning of Section 3.2.2 also apply to choice-based samples calibrated by maximum likelihood.

Manski and Lerman (1977) showed that when the proxy function $\log L_p(\boldsymbol{\theta})$ is used [see Eq. (2.7b)], and under similar regularity conditions, the estimator of $\boldsymbol{\theta}_o$, $\hat{\boldsymbol{\Theta}}_p$

(1) is consistent,
(2) is asymptotically MVN distributed with mean $\boldsymbol{\theta}_o$, and
(3) the negative of the inverse Hessian of the proxy function is a consistent estimate of $\operatorname{cov}(\hat{\boldsymbol{\Theta}}_p)$.

The same remarks that were made about stratified and random stratified sampling apply here. This is particularly important in this case because in choice-based samples the number of observations per alternative is usually determined a priori.

On the other hand, the number of strata (i.e., choices) is so small that having many observations in each stratum is not a very restrictive condition.

3.3 Model Updating

If a model has been calibrated with a data set containing N observations and subsequently N' more observations are made available one could improve the accuracy of the estimates by recalibrating the model with the combined data set of $N + N'$ observations. This is not always possible, however, because in many instances the old observations will not be available and because even if they were, calibration of disaggregate demand models (MNP models in particular) is still such a computer time- (and memory-) consuming operation that shortcut calibration procedures using only the new data, and the results of old calibrations, would be attractive. If, after calibration of the model with new data, we can find a way to combine the results of the old and new model to yield a combined, better model we would have succeeded in developing a shortcut recalibration process.

The information corresponding to a calibrated (old) model consists of an estimate $\hat{\boldsymbol{\theta}}_{\text{old}}$, and the approximate distribution of the estimator: $\hat{\boldsymbol{\theta}}_{\text{old}} \sim$

MVN$[\boldsymbol{\theta}_o, \text{cov}(\hat{\boldsymbol{\Theta}}_{\text{old}})]$, $\boldsymbol{\theta}_o$ unknown. Of course, different results will, in general, be obtained from a new data set. These will include another estimate, $\hat{\boldsymbol{\theta}}_{\text{new}}$, and the distribution of the estimator:

$$\hat{\boldsymbol{\Theta}}_{\text{new}} \sim \text{MVN}[\boldsymbol{\theta}_o, \text{cov}(\hat{\boldsymbol{\Theta}}_{\text{new}})], \qquad \boldsymbol{\theta}_o \quad \text{unknown.}$$

These two estimators can be combined in many different ways in order to get another unbiased estimator, but some of these combinations might be less efficient (i.e., have a larger variance) that one of the original estimators. Therefore, one must proceed carefully.

Atherton and Ben-Akiva (1976) proposed an expression for the case of one parameter based on Bayesian statistical postulates and Lerman *et al.* (1976) extended it to the case of several parameters. The expression we are about to derive is the same as the one proposed by these researchers but here it is shown, by classical statistics only, that the derived updated estimate and covariance matrix can be interpreted as an approximation of the MLE and its variance if the whole data set had been used.

Our goal, thus, is to choose $\hat{\boldsymbol{\theta}}$ so that it approximates the maximum-likelihood estimate that would have been obtained if the samples had been combined prior to calibration. This is done as follows:

Since by the way MLE works the estimates of cov$(\hat{\boldsymbol{\Theta}})$ given in the output represent $-[\nabla^2_\theta \log L(\hat{\boldsymbol{\theta}})]^{-1}$, for values of $\boldsymbol{\theta}$ near $\boldsymbol{\theta}_{\text{old}}$, a Taylor-series expansion yields

$$\log L_{\text{o}}(\boldsymbol{\theta}) \approx \log L_{\text{o}}(\hat{\boldsymbol{\theta}}_{\text{old}}) - \tfrac{1}{2}(\boldsymbol{\theta} - \hat{\boldsymbol{\theta}}_{\text{old}})[\text{cov}(\hat{\boldsymbol{\Theta}}_{\text{old}})]^{-1}(\boldsymbol{\theta} - \hat{\boldsymbol{\theta}}_{\text{old}})^{\text{T}}, \tag{3.25a}$$

where we have taken into account that $\nabla_\theta \log L_o(\hat{\boldsymbol{\theta}}_{\text{old}}) = 0$; the subscript "o" denotes the likelihood function corresponding to the old data set and the subscript "n" will be used below for the new data set.

The log-likelihood function of the new data set can be similarly approximated for values of $\boldsymbol{\theta}$ near $\hat{\boldsymbol{\theta}}_{\text{new}}$:

$$\log L_{\text{n}}(\boldsymbol{\theta}) \approx \log L_{\text{n}}(\hat{\boldsymbol{\theta}}_{\text{new}}) - \tfrac{1}{2}(\boldsymbol{\theta} - \hat{\boldsymbol{\theta}}_{\text{new}})[\text{cov}(\hat{\boldsymbol{\Theta}}_{\text{new}})]^{-1}(\boldsymbol{\theta} - \hat{\boldsymbol{\theta}}_{\text{new}})^{\text{T}}. \tag{3.25b}$$

Since the log-likelihood function is a sum of terms corresponding to each observation, the log-likelihood function corresponding to the combined data set can be approximated for values of $\boldsymbol{\theta}$ close to both $\boldsymbol{\theta}_{\text{new}}$ and $\boldsymbol{\theta}_{\text{old}}$ by

$$\begin{aligned}\log L(\boldsymbol{\theta}) \approx{}& \log L_{\text{o}}(\hat{\boldsymbol{\theta}}_{\text{old}}) - \tfrac{1}{2}(\boldsymbol{\theta} - \hat{\boldsymbol{\theta}}_{\text{old}})[\text{cov}(\hat{\boldsymbol{\Theta}}_{\text{old}})]^{-1}(\boldsymbol{\theta} - \hat{\boldsymbol{\theta}}_{\text{old}})^{\text{T}} \\ &+ \log L_{\text{n}}(\hat{\boldsymbol{\theta}}_{\text{new}}) - \tfrac{1}{2}(\boldsymbol{\theta} - \hat{\boldsymbol{\theta}}_{\text{new}})[\text{cov}(\hat{\boldsymbol{\Theta}}_{\text{new}})]^{-1}(\boldsymbol{\theta} - \boldsymbol{\theta}_{\text{new}})^{\text{T}}.\end{aligned} \tag{3.26}$$

Equation (3.26) will be valid only for some values of $\boldsymbol{\theta}$ (close to both $\hat{\boldsymbol{\theta}}_{\text{new}}$ and $\hat{\boldsymbol{\theta}}_{\text{old}}$) if the values of $\hat{\boldsymbol{\theta}}_{\text{new}}$ and $\hat{\boldsymbol{\theta}}_{\text{old}}$ are reasonably close; the consistency property of MLE ensures that this will happen if N and N' are large.

We now find the value of $\boldsymbol{\theta}$ that maximizes the right-hand side of Eq. (3.26) and use it as an approximation to $\hat{\boldsymbol{\theta}}$. Set the gradient equal to zero:

$$\mathbf{0} = \nabla_\theta \log L(\hat{\boldsymbol{\theta}}) \approx -(\hat{\boldsymbol{\theta}} - \hat{\boldsymbol{\theta}}_{\text{old}})[\text{cov}(\hat{\boldsymbol{\theta}}_{\text{old}})]^{-1} - (\boldsymbol{\theta} - \hat{\boldsymbol{\theta}}_{\text{new}})[\text{cov}(\hat{\boldsymbol{\Theta}}_{\text{new}})]^{-1}.$$

Rearranging some terms one has

$$(\hat{\boldsymbol{\theta}} - \hat{\boldsymbol{\theta}}_{\text{old}})\{[\text{cov}(\hat{\boldsymbol{\Theta}}_{\text{old}})]^{-1} + [\text{cov}(\hat{\boldsymbol{\Theta}}_{\text{new}})]^{-1}\} \approx (\hat{\boldsymbol{\theta}}_{\text{new}} - \hat{\boldsymbol{\theta}}_{\text{old}})[\text{cov}(\hat{\boldsymbol{\Theta}}_{\text{new}})]^{-1}$$

or

$$\hat{\boldsymbol{\theta}} \approx \hat{\boldsymbol{\theta}}_{\text{old}} + (\hat{\boldsymbol{\theta}}_{\text{new}} - \hat{\boldsymbol{\theta}}_{\text{old}})[\text{cov}(\hat{\boldsymbol{\Theta}}_{\text{new}})]^{-1}\{[\text{cov}(\hat{\boldsymbol{\Theta}}_{\text{old}})]^{-1} + [\text{cov}(\hat{\boldsymbol{\Theta}}_{\text{new}})]^{-1}\}^{-1}, \tag{3.27a}$$

which is an approximation for the combined sample MLE.

The variance of $\hat{\boldsymbol{\Theta}}$ is approximately given by the negative of the inverse Hessian of Eq. (3.26), which, since it is the sum of two quadratic forms with constant Hessians, is

$$\text{cov}(\hat{\boldsymbol{\Theta}}) \approx \{[\text{cov}(\hat{\boldsymbol{\Theta}}_{\text{old}})]^{-1} + [\text{cov}(\hat{\boldsymbol{\Theta}}_{\text{new}})]^{-1}\}^{-1}. \tag{3.27b}$$

Equations (3.27) could be applied recursively to more than two data sets in a straightforward manner, but this is not necessary because simple direct formulas exist. Letting k denote the data set and K the number of these, $\hat{\boldsymbol{\theta}}$ is the solution of

$$\mathbf{0} = \nabla_\theta \log L(\hat{\boldsymbol{\theta}}) \approx -\sum_{k=1}^{K} (\hat{\boldsymbol{\theta}} - \hat{\boldsymbol{\theta}}_k)[\text{cov}(\hat{\boldsymbol{\Theta}}_k)]^{-1},$$

and the estimate of $\text{cov}(\hat{\boldsymbol{\Theta}})$ is given by a second application of ∇_θ to the right-hand side of this expression:

$$\text{cov}(\hat{\boldsymbol{\Theta}}) \approx \left\{\sum_{k=1}^{K} [\text{cov}(\hat{\boldsymbol{\Theta}}_k)]^{-1}\right\}^{-1}. \tag{3.28a}$$

Solution of the likelihood equation yields

$$\hat{\boldsymbol{\theta}} \approx \left\{\sum_{k=1}^{k} \hat{\boldsymbol{\theta}}_k[\text{cov}(\hat{\boldsymbol{\Theta}}_k)]^{-1}\right\}\text{cov}(\hat{\boldsymbol{\Theta}}), \tag{3.28b}$$

which coincides with Atherton's expression.

Example For a binary probit gap-acceptance study such as the one worked out at the beginning of Chapter 2, data from two different intersections were gathered and both the critical gap T and its variance σ_ξ^2 (see the beginning of Section 2.1) were estimated for five movements [left turns, right turns, etc.; see Daganzo (1978b)]. Then, the whole data set was used to

Table 3.1

Summary of Results of a Binary Probit Gap-Acceptance Study[a]

Parameter Vector Definition $\boldsymbol{\theta} = (\theta_1; \theta_2)$
$\boldsymbol{\theta}$ = [mean critical gap, T (sec); variance of critical gap, σ_ξ^2 (sec^2)]

Traffic stream	Number of observations	$\hat{\boldsymbol{\theta}}$	cov($\hat{\boldsymbol{\Theta}}$)
Left onto LeConte	40	(8.40, 35.68)	$\begin{bmatrix} 2.22 & 12.56 \\ 12.56 & 522.0 \end{bmatrix}$
Left onto Virginia	73	(6.29, 6.66)	$\begin{bmatrix} 0.47 & 1.10 \\ 1.10 & 8.17 \end{bmatrix}$
Straight across Virginia (Eastbound)	48	(6.22, 4.24)	$\begin{bmatrix} 0.69 & 0.60 \\ 0.60 & 5.19 \end{bmatrix}$
Right onto LeConte	157	(6.03, 7.17)	$\begin{bmatrix} 0.23 & 0.07 \\ 0.07 & 5.56 \end{bmatrix}$
Straight across Virginia (Westbound)	63	(5.96, 4.79)	$\begin{bmatrix} 0.42 & 0.35 \\ 0.35 & 4.44 \end{bmatrix}$
Total of several intersections	451	(6.4, 7.8)	$\begin{bmatrix} 0.08 & 0.13 \\ 0.13 & 1.78 \end{bmatrix}$

[a] Source: Daganzo, 1978b.

determine T and σ_ξ^2 assuming that these values did not change from intersection to intersection. The results of the calibration are summarized in Table 3.1. We now update our parameter vector $\hat{\boldsymbol{\theta}} = (\hat{T}, \hat{\sigma}_\xi)$ based on the five models and compare the results with the exact one. Although the whole data set includes 48 observations more than the individual data sets (these 48 observations corresponded to several traffic streams that could not be analyzed separately because none of them had a sufficiently large number of observations) the results should be reasonably close.

Formulas (3.28) are applied and the intermediate calculations are carried out in Table 3.2. From those results one obtains

$$\text{cov}(\hat{\boldsymbol{\Theta}}) \approx \begin{bmatrix} 0.09 & 0.10 \\ 0.10 & 1.33 \end{bmatrix}$$

and $\hat{\boldsymbol{\theta}} \approx (6.2, 5.16)$.

The slight disagreement of these results with the ones in Table 3.1 may be due to either the few observations in some of the data sets (in particular the

Table 3.2

Model Updating Calculations[a]

Traffic stream	$[\mathrm{cov}(\hat{\boldsymbol{\Theta}})]^{-1}$	$\hat{\theta}[\mathrm{cov}(\hat{\boldsymbol{\Theta}})]^{-1}$
Left onto LeConte	$\begin{bmatrix} 0.52 & -0.013 \\ -0.013 & 0.0022 \end{bmatrix}$	(3.93; −0.03)
Left onto Virginia	$\begin{bmatrix} 3.06 & -0.41 \\ -0.41 & 0.18 \end{bmatrix}$	(16.53; −1.4)
Straight across Virginia (Eastbound)	$\begin{bmatrix} 1.63 & -0.19 \\ -0.19 & 0.21 \end{bmatrix}$	(9.32; −0.26)
Right onto LeConte	$\begin{bmatrix} 4.34 & -0.055 \\ -0.055 & 0.18 \end{bmatrix}$	(26.04; 0.96)
Straight across Virginia (Westbound)	$\begin{bmatrix} 2.58 & -0.20 \\ -0.20 & 0.24 \end{bmatrix}$	(14.42; −0.06)
Sum	$\begin{bmatrix} 12.13 & -0.87 \\ -0.87 & 0.81 \end{bmatrix}$	(70.24; −0.79)

[a] Data from Table 3.1.

left-turning stream onto LeConte) or to a significant variation in critical gap from intersection to intersection; in any case the differences are perfectly acceptable for a practical application. ■

3.4 Goodness-of-Fit Measures and Tests

3.4.1 Confidence Intervals and Hypothesis Tests

Since for a model satisfying the regularity conditions $\hat{\boldsymbol{\Theta}}$ is approximately MVN distributed with mean $\boldsymbol{\theta}_o$ and covariance matrix $\boldsymbol{\Sigma}_\theta$ (we use $\boldsymbol{\Sigma}_\theta$ as an abbreviation for the estimated covariance matrix of $\hat{\boldsymbol{\Theta}}$) any linear combination of $\hat{\boldsymbol{\Theta}}$ will also be approximately MVN distributed. Letting $\boldsymbol{\Delta}$ be an arbitrary matrix of constants with as many rows as parameters, the linear combination $\hat{\boldsymbol{\Theta}}\boldsymbol{\Delta}$ is approximately distributed as follows:

$$\hat{\boldsymbol{\Theta}}\boldsymbol{\Delta} \sim \mathrm{MVN}(\boldsymbol{\theta}_o\boldsymbol{\Delta}, \boldsymbol{\Delta}^{\mathrm{T}}\boldsymbol{\Sigma}_\theta\boldsymbol{\Delta}).$$

Consequently, if $\boldsymbol{\Delta}^{\mathrm{T}}\boldsymbol{\Sigma}_\theta\boldsymbol{\Delta}$ has full rank the quadratic function of $\hat{\boldsymbol{\Theta}}\boldsymbol{\Delta}$ defined below has approximately a χ^2 distribution with degrees of freedom equal to the dimension of $\hat{\boldsymbol{\Theta}}\boldsymbol{\Delta}$, d (see Appendix C):

$$(\hat{\boldsymbol{\Theta}}\boldsymbol{\Delta} - \boldsymbol{\theta}_o\boldsymbol{\Delta})(\boldsymbol{\Delta}^{\mathrm{T}}\boldsymbol{\Sigma}_{\theta}\boldsymbol{\Delta})^{-1}(\hat{\boldsymbol{\Theta}}\boldsymbol{\Delta} - \boldsymbol{\theta}_o\boldsymbol{\Delta})^{\mathrm{T}} \sim \chi^2_{(d)},$$

and it is possible to derive *confidence regions*[13] for the linear combination of $\boldsymbol{\theta}$, $\boldsymbol{\theta}_o\boldsymbol{\Delta}$. Since we can write

$$\Pr\{(\hat{\boldsymbol{\Theta}}\boldsymbol{\Delta} - \boldsymbol{\theta}_o\boldsymbol{\Delta})(\boldsymbol{\Delta}^{\mathrm{T}}\boldsymbol{\Sigma}_{\theta}\boldsymbol{\Delta})^{-1}(\hat{\boldsymbol{\Theta}}\boldsymbol{\Delta} - \boldsymbol{\theta}_o\boldsymbol{\Delta})^{\mathrm{T}} \leq \chi^2_{1-\alpha,\, d}\} = 1 - \alpha, \quad (3.29\text{a})$$

where $\chi^2_{1-\alpha,\, d}$ represents the $(1 - \alpha)100$ percentile of $\chi^2_{(d)}$, the quadratic equation in $\hat{\boldsymbol{\theta}}\boldsymbol{\Delta}$, below, defines a $(1 - \alpha)$ confidence region for $\boldsymbol{\theta}_o\boldsymbol{\Delta}$:

$$(\hat{\boldsymbol{\theta}}\boldsymbol{\Delta} - \boldsymbol{\theta}\boldsymbol{\Delta})(\boldsymbol{\Delta}^{\mathrm{T}}\boldsymbol{\Sigma}_{\theta}\boldsymbol{\Delta})^{-1}(\hat{\boldsymbol{\theta}}\boldsymbol{\Delta} - \boldsymbol{\theta}\boldsymbol{\Delta})^{\mathrm{T}} \leq \chi^2_{1-\alpha,\, d}. \quad (3.29\text{b})$$

Furthermore, since $\boldsymbol{\Sigma}_{\theta}$ is positive definite, $(\boldsymbol{\Delta}^{\mathrm{T}}\boldsymbol{\Sigma}_{\theta}\boldsymbol{\Delta})^{-1}$ is positive definite (see Appendix A), and Eq. (3.29) defines an ellipsoid in d dimensions.

By selecting the right matrix $\boldsymbol{\Delta}$, one can derive confidence intervals for a combination of parameters. For instance, if $\boldsymbol{\Delta} = \mathbf{I}$, Eq. (3.29b) yields a confidence interval for $\boldsymbol{\theta}_o$, whereas if $\boldsymbol{\Delta} = (1, 0, 0, 0, \ldots, 0)^{\mathrm{T}}$, Eq. (3.29b) gives a confidence interval for the first component of $\boldsymbol{\theta}$.

In general, the ith column of $\boldsymbol{\Delta}$ should correspond to the ith parameter *of interest* (say, θ_j) with all the elements zero except the jth one. There should be as many columns as parameters in the confidence region.

Equation (3.29b) can, of course, be used to test hypotheses since a null hypothesis $\mathrm{H}_o: \boldsymbol{\theta}\boldsymbol{\Delta} = \boldsymbol{\theta}_o\boldsymbol{\Delta}$ ($\boldsymbol{\theta}_o\boldsymbol{\Delta}$ is a known vector of dimension d) can be rejected at the α significance level if[14]

$$(\hat{\boldsymbol{\theta}}\boldsymbol{\Delta} - \boldsymbol{\theta}_o\boldsymbol{\Delta})[\boldsymbol{\Delta}^{\mathrm{T}}\boldsymbol{\Sigma}_{\theta}\boldsymbol{\Delta}]^{-1}(\hat{\boldsymbol{\theta}}\boldsymbol{\Delta} - \boldsymbol{\theta}_o\boldsymbol{\Delta})^{\mathrm{T}} \geq \chi^2_{1-\alpha,\, d}. \quad (3.30)$$

Since, under H_o, the left-hand side of Eq. (3.30) is an observation from a $\chi^2_{(d)}$ variable [see Eq. (3.29a)] the null hypothesis will be rejected when it is true $100\alpha\%$ of the time.

It is also possible to test certain hypotheses by using Property (5) of Theorem 3.1, which states that if H_o is true ($\mathrm{H}_o: \boldsymbol{\theta} = \boldsymbol{\theta}_o$),

$$2 \log[L(\hat{\boldsymbol{\Theta}})/L(\boldsymbol{\theta}_o)] \sim \chi^2_{(r)},$$

where r is the number of parameters. Therefore, the null hypothesis can be rejected at the α level if

$$2 \log[L(\hat{\boldsymbol{\theta}})/L(\boldsymbol{\theta}_o)] \geq \chi^2_{1-\alpha,\, r}. \quad (3.31)$$

[13] A $(1 - \alpha)100\%$ confidence region for a parameter $\boldsymbol{\theta}_o\boldsymbol{\Delta}$ is a region in the $\boldsymbol{\theta}\boldsymbol{\Delta}$ space (defined as a set function of $\hat{\boldsymbol{\theta}}$) that will cover $\boldsymbol{\theta}_o\boldsymbol{\Delta}$ $(1 - \alpha)100\%$ of the time if the experiment of obtaining $\hat{\boldsymbol{\theta}}$ and calculating the set function is repeated many times. Thus, if $1 - \alpha$ is close to unity, we can be reasonably sure that $\boldsymbol{\theta}_o\boldsymbol{\Delta}$ is contained in the region.

[14] The level of significance gives the probability that H_o is rejected given that it is true.

Although the left-hand side of Eq. (3.30) with $\mathbf{\Delta} = \mathbf{I}$ and the left-hand side of (3.31) do not necessarily coincide, they are very close for large samples and either test can be used. This can be seen with a Taylor-series expansion about $\hat{\boldsymbol{\theta}}$ of Eq. (3.31). If we neglect third- and higher-order terms (which is reasonable for large samples because then $\hat{\boldsymbol{\theta}} \approx \boldsymbol{\theta}_o$), Eq. (3.31) becomes

$$2[\log L(\hat{\boldsymbol{\theta}}) - \log L(\boldsymbol{\theta}_o)] \approx 2\log L(\hat{\boldsymbol{\theta}}) - 2\log L(\hat{\boldsymbol{\theta}}) - 2\mathbf{V}_\theta \log L(\hat{\boldsymbol{\theta}})(\boldsymbol{\theta}_o - \hat{\boldsymbol{\theta}}) \\ - (\boldsymbol{\theta}_o - \hat{\boldsymbol{\theta}})[\mathbf{V}_\theta^2 \log L(\hat{\boldsymbol{\theta}})](\boldsymbol{\theta}_o - \hat{\boldsymbol{\theta}})^{\mathrm{T}} \geq \chi^2_{1-\alpha,\, r}$$

which, since $\mathbf{V}_\theta \log L(\hat{\boldsymbol{\theta}}) = \mathbf{0}$ and $\mathbf{V}_\theta^2 \log L(\hat{\boldsymbol{\theta}}) = -\mathbf{\Sigma}_\theta^{-1}$, establishes the approximate equivalence of Eqs. (3.30) and (3.31) for large samples.

It is also possible to derive an equivalent of Eq. (3.31) and Property (5) in Theorem 3.1 when fewer than r parameters have to be tested. This equivalent is

$$-2\log[L(\hat{\boldsymbol{\theta}})/L(\hat{\boldsymbol{\theta}}_d)] \geq \chi^2_{1-\alpha,\, d}, \tag{3.32}$$

where $\hat{\boldsymbol{\theta}}_d$ is the value of $\boldsymbol{\theta}$ that maximizes the log-likelihood function subject to the restriction that the components of $\hat{\boldsymbol{\theta}}$ that correspond to the parameters that are being tested be set equal to the tested values; as before, d is the number of parameters tested.

Application of Eqs. (3.32) and (3.30) is, however, still equivalent and since calculation of $\hat{\boldsymbol{\theta}}_d$ is rather expensive in a MNP model (it requires a second calibration) we recommend using Eq. (3.30) for testing hypotheses.

Example We shall obtain a 90% confidence region for θ_1 and θ_2 for the example in Section 3.2.2. In addition, we shall test the hypothesis $\mathrm{H}_o{:}\theta_{o1} = \theta_{o2}$.

The results of the calibration process were

$$\hat{\boldsymbol{\theta}} = (0.27, 0.51) \qquad \mathbf{\Sigma}_\theta = \begin{bmatrix} 0.0002 & -0.0004 \\ -0.0004 & 0.009 \end{bmatrix}.$$

To obtain the confidence region we set $\mathbf{\Delta} = \left[\begin{smallmatrix} 1 & 0 \\ 0 & 1 \end{smallmatrix}\right]$ in Eq. (3.29b) and obtain

$$(0.27 - \theta_1, 0.51 - \theta_2)\begin{bmatrix} 5488 & 244 \\ 244 & 122 \end{bmatrix}\begin{pmatrix} 0.27 - \theta_1 \\ 0.51 - \theta_2 \end{pmatrix} \leq \chi^2_{0.9,2} = 4.61,$$

which is the equation of the interior of an ellipse centered at (0.27, 0.51). The confidence region is plotted in Fig. 3.1.

Testing H_o is equivalent to testing $H_o{:}\theta_1 - \theta_2 = 0$ and we use

$$\mathbf{\Delta}^{\mathrm{T}} = (1, -1)$$

since then $\boldsymbol{\theta\Delta} = \theta_1 - \theta_2$, as desired. The rest of the process is straightforward; we may use Eq. (3.29b) for a confidence interval and/or Eq. (3.30)

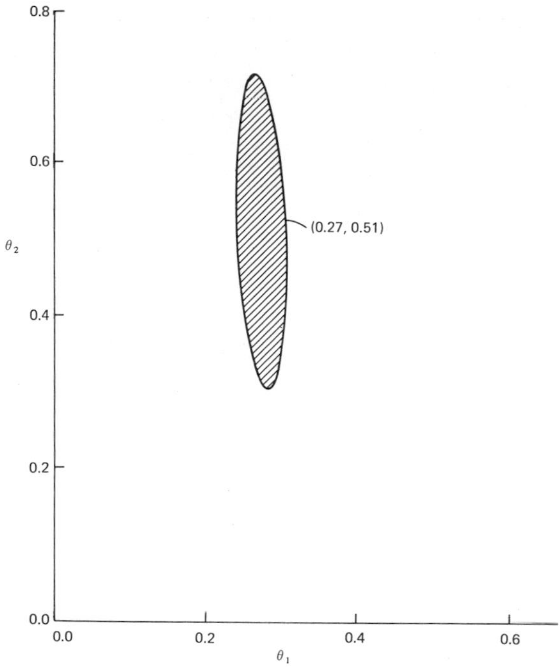

Fig. 3.1 90% confidence region for a two-parameter binary probit model.

for a hypothesis test. Doing the latter with $\hat{\boldsymbol{\theta}}\boldsymbol{\Delta} = -0.24$, $\boldsymbol{\theta}_o\boldsymbol{\Delta} = 0$, and $d = 1$, we obtain the test statistic

$$(-0.24)\left[(1, -1)\begin{pmatrix} 0.0002 & -0.0004 \\ -0.0004 & 0.009 \end{pmatrix}^{-1}\begin{pmatrix} 1 \\ -1 \end{pmatrix}\right](-0.24)$$

$$= (0.24)^2 \times 100 = 5.76 \geq \chi^2_{0.9,1} = 2.71,$$

and the null hypothesis can be rejected. ■

As in regression analyses, tests of whether the coefficient of a certain attribute is significantly different from zero can be used to help decide whether the attribute should be included in a model on the basis of statistical fit. In Section 1.6 we discussed that and other criteria for attribute inclusion in models.

3.4.2 Goodness-of-Fit Measures

We now review measures that can be used to ascertain the overall goodness of fit of MNP models. These measures are similar to the correlation coefficient of regression analysis in that they take larger values the larger the explanatory power of the attributes in the model and have a minimum value taken when the attributes do not explain anything.

A perfect-fit model from a forecaster's point of view would consist of a choice function $P_i(\hat{\boldsymbol{\theta}}, \mathbf{a})$, that could predict perfectly the choice of each observation in the data set, i.e.,

$$\mathrm{P}_{c(n)}(\hat{\boldsymbol{\theta}}, \mathbf{a}_{(n)}) \approx 1, \qquad n = 1, \ldots, N.$$

This would be analogous to a multiple-regression model in which all the observations fall on the regression plane and the dependent variable can, thus, be perfectly predicted.

Note, however, that for this to happen in a regression model the variance of the unobserved disturbances has to be very small and the model must be correctly specified. In MNP analysis the same thing occurs; for a perfect fit we would need a perfect specification and $\boldsymbol{\Sigma}_\xi \to 0$. Since even for a perfectly specified model $\boldsymbol{\Sigma}_\xi$ may be substantially different from zero we should not be discouraged by imperfect fit since the pseudocorrelation coefficients we shall introduce are not indicators of model correctness, only of fit to the data.

A logical candidate for an indicator of goodness of fit (i.e., high data probabilities) is the log-likelihood function itself, $\log L(\hat{\boldsymbol{\theta}})$. This indicator is always negative and approaches zero with a perfect fit. However, a model that has been calibrated with much data will usually exhibit larger log-likelihood values, which makes it difficult to compare models calibrated with different data sets. Some normalization of it would seem desirable.

The following approach seems reasonable (see Tardiff, 1976, for a discussion of the binary case). We calculate the highest log-likelihood that could be obtained from a model excluding all explanatory variables (although with as many parameters as necessary), and compare that with the log-likelihood of our model. The difference will be the improvement in log-likelihood due to the explanatory attributes.

Before proceeding, though, we must pause to prove a lemma and suggest a conjecture which will enable us to calculate the maximum attainable likelihood of a model without attributes, by hand.

Lemma 3.1 For any random utility model, the implicit function theorem of calculus holds between the set of finite *reduced attractiveness vectors*, $\mathbf{V}' = (V_2 - V_1, V_3 - V_1, \ldots, V_I - V_1)$, and the corresponding image set of *reduced choice probability vectors*, $\mathbf{p}' = (p_2, p_3, \ldots, p_I)$, provided that for every alternative i

$$0 < \frac{\partial p_i}{\partial V_i} < \infty \qquad \text{and} \qquad -\infty < \frac{\partial p_i}{\partial V_j} < 0, \qquad \forall j \neq i.$$

Proof The fundamental theorem on implicit functions holds if the Jacobian of the transformation $\mathbf{p}'(\mathbf{V}')$, $|\partial(\mathbf{p}')/\partial(\mathbf{V}')|$, is finite and different from zero.

Consider the Jacobian matrix of $\mathbf{p}(\mathbf{V})$. By the hypothesis of the lemma we know that its diagonal entries are strictly positive, the off-diagonal entries are strictly negative, and all of them are finite. Furthermore, the row sums add up to zero since $\sum_{i=1} p_i(\mathbf{V}) = 1$.

Since $\mathbf{p} = \mathbf{p}(\mathbf{V})$ can be written

$$(p_1, \mathbf{p}') = \mathbf{p}(0, \mathbf{V}')$$

the Jacobian matrix of $\mathbf{p}'(\mathbf{V}')$ is obtained by deleting the first row and column of $\partial(\mathbf{p})/\partial(\mathbf{V})$. The elements of this matrix, $\partial(\mathbf{p}')/\partial(\mathbf{V}')$, have the same properties as those of $\partial(\mathbf{p})/\partial(\mathbf{V})$, except the row sums are strictly positive.

For a matrix with this structure the points in the *Gerschgorin disks* have positive real parts, and consequently, all the eigenvalues must be different from zero, ruling out a singular Jacobian matrix. Since the Jacobian is also finite (all its elements are finite) the theorem on implicit functions applies and the proof is complete. ■

This lemma is a necessary condition for a well-behaved one-to-one mapping between the set of all possible reduced-choice probability vectors and reduced-attractiveness vectors to exist for a given random-utility model.

Since the lemma holds for any MNP model with a positive definite covariance matrix [Eqs. (2.37 and 2.38) and the ensuing discussion show that the condition on $\partial p_i/\partial V_j$ specified in the lemma is satisfied] it seems reasonable to put forth the following conjecture.

Conjecture 3.1 For a MNP model with a positive-definite covariance matrix, there is a one-to-one relationship between the set of all finite reduced-attractiveness vectors and the set of all reduced-choice probability vectors for which all the probabilities (including p_1) are different from zero.

The following fact, in conjunction with Lemma 3.1, also supports the plausibility of this conjecture.

Fact 3.1 Conjecture 3.1 holds for the binary and trinomial probit models, as well as for the MNL model.

Proof The fact holds if there is an (inverse) relationship between $\mathbf{p}'$ and $\mathbf{V}'$.

[15] According to the *Gerschgorin theorem* [see Stein (1967) for example] the jth eigenvalue of a square matrix $\mathbf{A}$ must lie in a circle on the complex plane that is centered at $(a_{jj}, 0)$ and has radius given by the sum of the absolute values of the off-diagonal elements on the jth row.

For the MNL model this inverse relationship is

$$V_i - V_1 = \log(p_i/p_1), \qquad i = 2, \ldots, I.$$

For the binary probit model it is

$$V_2 - V_1 = \sigma\Phi^{-1}(p_2),$$

where $\sigma = (\mathrm{var}(\xi_1 - \xi_2))^{1/2}$.

For the trinomial probit model, it is possible to give a similar proof without actually deriving the inverse relationship. This can be done by expressing $p_i(\mathbf{V}')$ in the form of Eq. (2.17) and inspecting the properties of the equation (Daganzo, 1979b). ■

Let $P_i(\hat{\boldsymbol{\theta}}, \mathbf{0})$ be the choice function of a model without attributes, which is specified so that the choice probability vector can take every possible set of values. According to Conjecture 3.1 and Fact 3.1 this can be done by, for example, setting

$$V_i = \boldsymbol{\theta}_i$$

with $\boldsymbol{\theta}_1 \equiv 0$ and selecting $\boldsymbol{\Sigma}_\xi$ as a positive-definite matrix.

The highest log-likelihood is given by

$$\max_{\boldsymbol{\theta}} \sum_{n=1}^{N} \log P_{c(n)}(\hat{\boldsymbol{\theta}}, \mathbf{0})$$

or, since any desired set of probabilities can be attained by selecting the right value of $\hat{\boldsymbol{\theta}}$, we can use $p_i, i = 1, \ldots, I$, as the independent variables and, if desired, obtain $\hat{\boldsymbol{\theta}}$ afterwards. Thus, we can solve instead:

$$\max_{p_i} \sum_{n=1}^{N} \log p_{c(n)},$$

$$\text{subject to} \quad \sum_{i=1}^{I} p_i = 1 \text{ and } 0 < p_i < 1, i = 1, \ldots, I,$$

which, letting N_i be the observations in the sample choosing alternative i, is equivalent to

$$\max_{p_i} \sum_{i=1}^{I} N_i \log p_i$$

$$\text{subject to} \quad \sum_{i=1}^{I} p_i = 1 \text{ and } 0 < p_i < 1, i = 1, \ldots, I.$$

This yields $p_i = N_i/N$, and the maximum possible value of the log-likelihood function if no explanatory variables are included (*the background log-likelihood*):

$$\log L = \sum_{i=1}^{I} N_i \log \frac{N_i}{N} = N\left\{\sum_{i=1}^{I} \frac{N_i}{N} \log \frac{N_i}{N}\right\}. \tag{3.33a}$$

Conjecture 3.1 and Fact 3.1 indicate that the background log-likelihood can actually be obtained since there are values of $\boldsymbol{\theta}$ that yield: $p_1 = N_1/N, \ldots$ $p_I = N_I/N$.

The normalization

$$\rho_l^2 = \frac{-\log L(\hat{\boldsymbol{\theta}}) + \log L}{\log L} = -\frac{\log L(\hat{\boldsymbol{\theta}})}{\log L} + 1, \tag{3.33b}$$

which represents the fraction of background log likelihood that is explained by the model, is independent of sample size. It ranges from zero (or perhaps even negative for a model that does not contain constants in the specification of the measured attractiveness) to one, and is easy to interpret.

For models with specifications that are linear in the parameters and contain independent constants in the measured attractiveness functions, ρ_l^2 is sure to exceed zero since $\log L$ is the maximum value of the log likelihood that is obtained when all the parameters except the constants are set equal to zero.

Since the distribution of $\log L(\hat{\boldsymbol{\Theta}})$ is known for any given value of $\boldsymbol{\theta}_o$ (see Theorem 3.1), so is the distribution of ρ_l^2 which can be used as a test statistic. The resulting tests are, however, equivalent to the ones based on Eq. (3.30) and less convenient to apply because they necessitate more calculations.

Some authors have proposed to use different measures of goodness of fit. Stopher (1975) proposed the use of a *correlation ratio* and Burns *et al.* (1976) the use of a *correlation coefficient*. These measures, however, require that the data are grouped before computation, and therefore may be difficult to apply in cases where there are several attributes and more than two alternatives.

The normalization of $\log L(\hat{\boldsymbol{\theta}})$ given by Eq. (3.33) is not either the only one that is currently being used. Also popular is calculating $\log L(\mathbf{0})$ and using that in Eq. (3.33b) instead of $\log L$. In logit models with linear specifications this is equivalent to setting $p_i = 1/I$, $i = 1, \ldots, I$ and $\log L = -N\log(I)$ instead of Eq. (3.33a).

In MNP models the form of p_i depends on the form of $\boldsymbol{\Sigma}_\xi$ when $\boldsymbol{\theta} = \mathbf{0}$ and thus a general form for $\log L(\mathbf{0})$ cannot be given. This normalization is a little bit more difficult to interpret than Eq. (3.33b) because the value of ρ^2 corresponding to a totally unexplanatory model is neither zero nor any other constant.

The reader can check that for the example introduced in Section 3.2.2

$$\log L(\hat{\boldsymbol{\theta}}) = 33.895,$$
$$N = 50, \qquad N_1 = 14, \qquad N_2 = 29, \qquad \text{and} \qquad N_3 = 7.$$

Consequently then,

$$\log L = -47.381 \qquad \text{and} \qquad \rho_l^2 = 0.285.$$

Finally, we propose another measure of goodness of fit, which like Eq. (3.33b) ranges from zero to one but has a more intuitive physical interpretation.

The expression

$$\overline{p}(\mathbf{a}) = \exp\left\{\frac{1}{N}\log L(\hat{\boldsymbol{\theta}})\right\} = \left[\prod_{n=1}^{N} P_{c(n)}(\hat{\boldsymbol{\theta}}, \mathbf{a}_{(n)})\right]^{1/N}$$

can be interpreted as the (geometric) average choice probability in the sample and thus ranges from zero to one. Analogously,

$$\overline{p} = \exp\{N^{-1}\log L\}$$

can be interpreted as the average choice probability of the chosen alternative in the last model without any explanatory variables. Of course, $1 - \overline{p}$, is the average background probability of the rejected alternatives, representing the overall amount of uncertainty in the data, and

$$\rho_p^2 = (\overline{p}(\mathbf{a}) - \overline{p})/(1 - \overline{p})$$

can be interpreted as the reduction in such uncertainty resulting from the new model.

For the example in Section 3.2.2

$$\overline{p}(\mathbf{a}) = \exp\{-33.895/50\} = 0.51,$$
$$\overline{p} = \exp\{-47.381/50\} = 0.39,$$

showing that the average probability of a chosen alternative can be increased to 0.51 by inclusion of explanatory variables, from the background value of 0.39. Although this information by itself is easy to understand in physical terms, one may compute ρ_p^2 if desired; in our case $\rho_p^2 = 0.196$, showing that the attributes of the model reduce the overall uncertainty in the data by about 20%. With disaggregate demand models the values of ρ_l^2 and ρ_p^2 are typically smaller than the coefficient of determination in regression analyses since in studies of human behavior $\boldsymbol{\Sigma}_\xi$ is usually large.

The values of ρ^2 are not, however, indicators of model correctness. To test the correctness of the model one would have to retrieve the actual disturbance vector $\xi_{(n)}$ for each observation in the sample, to check whether they are MVN distributed according to the hypotheses of the model. In regression analyses one does that by analyzing the residuals of the data with respect to the estimated regression equation. A similar check is, unfortunately, impractical for MNP models because the values of U_i for the individuals in the sample, $U_{(n)i}$, are not observed in the data and it is not possible to determine the residuals of an observation from $\{U_{(n)i} - V_i(\hat{\boldsymbol{\theta}}, \mathbf{a}_{(n)})\}$. The information we do have, that $\{U_{c_{(n)}} \geq U_i \; \forall i \neq c_{(n)}\}$ for every data point, could conceivably be used to construct a model appropriateness test. The information in the data is so small, however, that the test would not likely be very powerful, making such an effort hardly worthwhile.

This is why in specifying MNP models one has to rely much more on good judgment than on statistical fit, as was pointed out in Chapter 1.

3.4.3 Behavioral Models—Myth or Reality?

Disaggregate demand models have some desirable properties, such as data efficiency and ease of application.[16] Unfortunately, by sheer repetition, more than by anything else, it is now unquestioningly accepted by many that disaggregate demand models are also "behavioral," i.e., a choice function depicts causes and effects of human behavior in that it represents how the response of an individual changes when some of the attributes (stimuli) in it are changed. This section is included to challenge that widely accepted tenet and, hopefully, to make researchers and practitioners a little more skeptical of the results of a model.

If we want to study the behavior of a group of individuals, we must observe how they respond to different stimuli, but for the study to be meaningful the *same* group of individuals would have to be observed repeatedly. Under these ideal laboratorylike conditions, one could make statistical inferences about behavior and claim that a resulting model is behavioral.

Unfortunately, however, disaggregate demand models are usually calibrated with cross-sectional data including observations of *different* individuals in different situations. Therefore, it will not be uncommon for the choice function of a model to represent differences from individual to individual rather than behavior. Such choice functions, although providing a good fit to the data, may not be behavioral.

In the above-mentioned binary probit modal-split study of the city of Mérida, Venezuela, it was found that the choice probability of public

[16] Although by no means a typical example, it is illustrative to know that the fraction of all trips in the rush hour made by private automobile and public transportation was predicted for the 210 origin–destination pairs in the city of Mérida, Venezuela, by a staff of 30 graduate students and the author in *eight working days*. In addition to the design and execution of a home interview survey (no suitable data were available for a modal-split study), this period had to be used to familiarize the students with disaggregate demand models since none of them had used such techniques before.

transportation increased with the transit access time and that such a phenomenon persisted with several alternate specifications that were tried (as a matter of fact, transit access time was the best explanatory variable in all the specifications). This seemingly surprising fact was later associated with the layout of the city, which has transit routes flowing through the more affluent parts of town. The access time behaved, thus, as a proxy variable for socioeconomic status and, consequently, we could not claim that the choice function represented behavior as far as the transit access time stimulus was concerned.[17] Of course, one can argue that such a phenomenon could probably be removed if one had included in the model the right socioeconomic variable; but, since such variable would be highly correlated with transit access time, its inclusion would undoubtedly create multicollinearity problems, which would still make the estimation of behavior impossible. In the Mérida model, inclusion of several socioeconomic variables failed to decrease the significance of transit access time, which could probably be attributed to our failure to identify the right explanatory variable. Nevertheless, the fact remains that with the available cross-sectional data, behavioral inferences with respect to transit access time could not be made.

Even in instances where the choice function seems to depict behavior in a qualitative way, there is no assurance that the magnitude of the coefficients of any policy variable are the right ones because that variable may be a proxy for another neglected attribute, without the dramatic effects described above.

As a matter of fact, only if the explanatory variables under consideration are totally uncorrelated with neglected attributes and there are no specification errors and multicollinearity problems can we say that the model depicts behavior. Our intuitive belief in these facts is the only assurance we can have of the behavioral content of a model. In other words, a discrete choice model may or may not depict behavior, but the fact that it has been calibrated from disaggregate data does not provide such an assurance.

3.5 Summary

The most relevant issues connected with the specification and calibration of MNP models are covered in this chapter. In Section 3.1 we discuss the specification aspects and argue that MNP models are quite robust because

[17] It should be noted that although any policy analysis of mode choice involving such a model and changes to transit access time would be meaningless, the results of the model were still useful to establish the existing modal split. This is true in general of disaggregate demand models. Although they can always be used to establish patterns of choice in the population they are calibrated from (not behavior), in order to be relevant for policy analysis and to have the transferability property (see Section 1.2.1) they must be "behavioral," i.e., they must also reproduce patterns of choice in different situations.

they can be applied under several circumstances, including errors in the data and neglected attributes. Some necessary and some sufficient conditions are also put forward in this section for the estimability of the parameter vector. Although Section 3.1 is not based on any particular reference the reader will find related discussions in Manski (1973) and Hausman and Wise (1978).

In Section 3.2 we are concerned with the statistical properties of the maximum-likelihood estimator of a MNP model. Chapter 3 of Bouthelier's dissertation (Bouthelier, 1978) covers much of Section 3.2.1 and includes in it the proof of Theorem 3.1. McFadden (1973) discusses the statistical properties of the MNL model. The reader interested in choice-based sampling will find a thorough explanation of these models in Manski and Lerman (1977). The model-updating problem discussed in Section 3.3 was first investigated for a one-parameter case by Atherton and Ben-Akiva (1976) using Bayesian decision theory. Lerman *et al.* (1976) subsequently gave a parameter-updating formula for the multiparameter case. Although the formula given in this book coincides with the formulas provided by these authors, we chose to interpret them as an approximation to the maximum likelihood estimator rather than as a Bayes' estimator.

In Section 3.4 we are concerned with procedures to evaluate the validity of a calibrated model. In it, we show how to develop confidence regions and perform hypothesis tests using the results from the previous sections. Two measures of overall goodness of fit that can play a role similar to the correlation coefficient in regression analyses were also presented. In addition to the papers mentioned in the text the reader may find valuable the review of goodness-of-fit measures given by Hauser (1978) from an information-theoretic approach. The section concludes with some remarks about the behavioral content of MNP models calibrated with cross-sectional data.

Chapter 4 Prediction: Mechanical Aspects

In many MNP applications, knowledge of the choice function is the ultimate piece of information and many a study would terminate after calibration. For instance, in traffic-flow theory, knowledge of the critical gap and its variance is all one needs for studying unsignalized intersections and passing zones on two-lane bidirectional roads; in toxicology, knowledge of the critical dosage of a drug that will cause death in 50% of the population of rats may be the only thing that is needed of a binary probit model. In both of these instances, the use of a MNP model terminates with the calibration process and its interpretation. In demand forecasting, there are also instances where the final answer results directly from the calibration process; for instance, to estimate the monetary value of travel time some researchers have calibrated binary probit (and logit) models of route choice between two highways, one of which has a toll. In these models, the choice function is

$$p_1 = \Phi[\theta_1 \,\mathrm{TOLL} + \theta_2(T_2 - T_1)], \qquad \theta_1 > 0, \qquad \theta_2 > 0,$$

where we assume that the toll is on highway 2 and T_i is the travel time by route i. Assuming that the model is behavioral, i.e., it represents causes and effects (cf. Section 3.4.3), one could say that the quantity in brackets in the above equation represents the relative attractiveness of highway 1 with respect to highway 2. Since such a quantity does not change if one changes the toll one unit as long as the travel time differential is changed by θ_1/θ_2 units, for the population under study the value θ_2/θ_1 would represent an average monetary value of travel time. A study of the value of travel time would therefore terminate there.

In many instances, however, one is not only interested in the value of $\boldsymbol{\theta}$ per se, but also in the numbers of people from the population (or any subgroup thereof) that select each one of the alternatives. In addition, one will also be interested in other measures that characterize the situation, such as the elasticity of demand (or usage), the total (and average) satisfaction derived by the population from the set of alternatives available to them, and its elasticity. Chapter 1 explored some of these figures of merit.

We shall now explore how to use a choice function to obtain the above-mentioned information when some of the attributes in the choice function vary across the population. In our analysis we shall assume that the choice function of the MNP model is known with certainty; that is, there are no specification errors and the values of the estimated parameters are very close to the true parameter values. Furthermore, we shall consider only very large groups of people; this results in deterministic predictions, since the laws of large numbers ensure identical forecasts for groups of people with the same distribution of the attribute vector and same number of individuals. In the following chapter, we shall explore the consequences of uncertainty in the value of $\boldsymbol{\theta}$ and in the distribution of the attribute vector, and the variability of the figures of merit for small groups of individuals.

A figure of merit for a heterogeneous group of individuals, such as the total usage or the average satisfaction, can always be equated to an expectation of a similar figure of merit defined for homogeneous groups of individuals. For instance, as was shown in Section 1.2, the expected[1] usage of alternative i, y_i, is related to the expected value of the choice probability function according to [see Eqs. (1.4a) and (1.4b) in Chapter 1]

$$y_i = M \int_a P_i(\boldsymbol{\theta}, \mathbf{a}) F(\mathbf{a})\, d\mathbf{a}, \tag{4.1a}$$

$$y_i = E_A[P_i(\boldsymbol{\theta}, \mathbf{A})]M = E_A[MP_i(\boldsymbol{\theta}, \mathbf{A})], \tag{4.1b}$$

where M is the number of individuals in the group and $F(\mathbf{a})$ is the density function of the attribute vector across the individuals of the group. This confirms the previous statement, since y_i is given by the average of $MP_i(\boldsymbol{\theta}, \mathbf{a})$ across the group, and $MP_i(\boldsymbol{\theta}, \mathbf{a})$ is the usage for a homogeneous group with $\mathbf{A} - \mathbf{a}$.

In general, a generic figure of merit defined for a homogeneous population group with $\mathbf{A} = \mathbf{a}$ will be a function of $\boldsymbol{\theta}$ and $\mathbf{a}$, which as in Chapter 1 we denote by $T(\boldsymbol{\theta}, \mathbf{a})$. For a heterogeneous group, and as was also shown in Section 1.5, the corresponding figure of merit can be expressed as

$$T(\boldsymbol{\theta}) = E_A[T(\boldsymbol{\theta}, \mathbf{A})], \tag{4.2}$$

where the expectation is taken with respect to the distribution of $\mathbf{A}$ in the group under study.

[1] The word "expected" is used here because the actual usage is a random variable that would normally differ for a different group of individuals with same distribution of the attribute vector. However, since in this chapter we exclusively study large groups, the word will be dropped from now on.

4.1 Two Common Figures of Merit

The most commonly used figures of merit are the usage and the overall level of satisfaction. These two variables and their elasticities are analyzed below for homogeneous groups of individuals and expressions for $T(\boldsymbol{\theta}, \mathbf{a})$ are obtained. Sections 4.2 and 4.3 discuss calculation of Eq. (4.2).

4.1.1 The Demand Function

The demand function of alternative i, $D_i(\boldsymbol{\theta}, \mathbf{a})$, for a homogeneous group of individuals with $\mathbf{A} = \mathbf{a}$ is $D_i(\boldsymbol{\theta}, \mathbf{a}) = MP_i(\boldsymbol{\theta}, \mathbf{a})$ since we can do away with the expectations in Eq. (4.1b). Similarly, if we are interested in the joint usage of several alternatives and we let $\mathscr{I}'$ be the set of such alternatives, we can define the pooled demand function as

$$D(\boldsymbol{\theta}, \mathbf{a}) = M \sum_{i \in \mathscr{I}'} P_i(\boldsymbol{\theta}, \mathbf{a}). \tag{4.3}$$

The elasticity of demand with respect to attribute a_k is

$$\varepsilon_{a_k}^{D(\boldsymbol{\theta}, \mathbf{a})} = \frac{\partial D(\boldsymbol{\theta}, \mathbf{a})}{\partial a_k} \frac{a_k}{D(\boldsymbol{\theta}, \mathbf{a})}, \qquad k = 1, \ldots, s,$$

where $D(\boldsymbol{\theta}, \mathbf{a})$ is given by (4.3); or, using vector notation,

$$\boldsymbol{\varepsilon}^{D(\boldsymbol{\theta}, \mathbf{a})} = \boldsymbol{\nabla}_a \log D(\boldsymbol{\theta}, \mathbf{a}) \begin{bmatrix} a_1 & 0 & \cdots & 0 \\ 0 & a_2 & \cdots & 0 \\ \vdots & & \ddots & \vdots \\ 0 & 0 & \cdots & a_s \end{bmatrix}. \tag{4.4}$$

Equation (4.4) can be evaluated numerically for MNP models with the techniques that were used to calculate the gradient of the choice functions in calibration programs.

Closed-form elasticities can be obtained for the binary probit model; if as explained in Section 1.3.3 the specification is expressed as $p_1 = \Phi[V(\boldsymbol{\theta}, \mathbf{a})]$ and $p_2 = \Phi[-V(\boldsymbol{\theta}, \mathbf{a})]$, the elasticity of demand is

$$\boldsymbol{\varepsilon}^{D_1} = \frac{\phi(V(\boldsymbol{\theta}, \mathbf{a})]}{\Phi[V(\boldsymbol{\theta}, \mathbf{a})]} \boldsymbol{\nabla}_a V(\boldsymbol{\theta}, \mathbf{a}) \begin{bmatrix} a_1 & & 0 \\ & \ddots & \\ 0 & & a_s \end{bmatrix} \tag{4.5a}$$

and

$$\boldsymbol{\varepsilon}^{D_2} = -\frac{\phi[V(\boldsymbol{\theta}, \mathbf{a})]}{\Phi[-V(\boldsymbol{\theta}, \mathbf{a})]} \boldsymbol{\nabla}_a V(\boldsymbol{\theta}, \mathbf{a}) \begin{bmatrix} a_1 & & 0 \\ & \ddots & \\ 0 & & a_s \end{bmatrix}. \tag{4.5b}$$

If the measured attractiveness functions are linear functions of **a**, they can be expressed as

$$\mathbf{V} = \mathbf{a}[\boldsymbol{\theta}],$$

where $[\boldsymbol{\theta}]$ is an $s \times 2$ matrix whose entries are known constants (remember that the elements of $\boldsymbol{\theta}$ are known). If the covariance matrix $\boldsymbol{\Sigma}_\xi$ is independent of **a**, we can define a constant σ^2 equal to the variance of $\xi_1 - \xi_2$, which is given by

$$\sigma^2 = (1, -1)\boldsymbol{\Sigma}_\xi\binom{1}{-1} = \sigma_1^2 + \sigma_2^2 - 2\sigma_{12}^2,$$

and express $V(\boldsymbol{\theta}, \mathbf{a})$ as $\mathbf{a}[\boldsymbol{\theta}]\binom{1}{-1}\sigma^{-1}$. This is, of course, equivalent to the expression for $V(\boldsymbol{\theta}, \mathbf{a})$ given in Section 1.3.3. The gradient appearing in Eqs. (4.5) is then

$$\nabla_a V(\boldsymbol{\theta}, \mathbf{a}) = \sigma^{-1}(1, -1)[\boldsymbol{\theta}]^{\mathrm{T}}. \tag{4.5c}$$

For the trinomial probit model with covariance matrix independent of **a**, it is also possible to derive a closed-form elasticity formula with the shortcut gradient evaluation method of Section 2.4.2. Since

$$P_i(\boldsymbol{\theta}, \mathbf{a}) = p_i[\mathbf{V}(\boldsymbol{\theta}, \mathbf{a}), \boldsymbol{\Sigma}_\xi],$$

the chain-differentiation rule yields

$$\nabla_a P_i(\boldsymbol{\theta}, \mathbf{a}) = \nabla_V p_i(\mathbf{V}, \boldsymbol{\Sigma})\left[\frac{\partial(V_1 \cdots V_I)}{\partial(a_1 \cdots a_s)}\right]^{\mathrm{T}},$$

where $[\partial(V_1 \cdots V_I)/\partial(a_1 \cdots a_s)]$ is the Jacobian matrix of $\mathbf{V}(\boldsymbol{\theta}, \mathbf{a})$, and $\nabla_V p_i(\mathbf{V}, \boldsymbol{\Sigma})$ is available in closed form by Eqs. (2.37) and (2.38). Dividing this expression by $P_i(\boldsymbol{\theta}, \mathbf{a})$ yields $\nabla_a \log P_i(\boldsymbol{\theta}, \mathbf{a})$, which can be entered in Eq. (4.4) for a closed-form elasticity formula. The multinomial logit model also has closed form elasticities.[2]

A general property of the gradient is that the derivative of the MNP function, $p_i(\mathbf{V}, \boldsymbol{\Sigma})$, with respect to V_j is negative if $j \neq i$ and positive if $j = i$ (see Section 2.4.3). Thus, if an attribute appears only in the attractiveness of one alternative with a positive (negative) coefficient the elasticity of the usage of the corresponding alternative with respect to the attribute will be positive (negative). The elasticities of the usage of all other alternatives will be of the opposite sign.

[2] The reader can check that if $\mathbf{V} = \mathbf{a}[\boldsymbol{\theta}]$ the elasticity vector is

$$\boldsymbol{\varepsilon}^{D_i} = (-p_1, -p_2, \ldots, 1 - p_i, \ldots, -p_I)[\boldsymbol{\theta}]^{\mathrm{T}} \begin{bmatrix} a_1 & & 0 \\ & \ddots & \\ 0 & & a_s \end{bmatrix}.$$

4.1.2 The Satisfaction

It has been suggested (see Williams, 1977 for example) that the actual benefit derived from a choice situation by a given individual is the perceived attractiveness of the chosen alternative since in most applications it can be safely postulated that choice makers derive satisfaction only from the alternative they choose. The satisfaction for a random choice maker from the homogeneous group is U_i if $_i$ is the chosen alternative. But since by definition of random utility model the perceived attractiveness of the chosen alternative is the largest, the satisfaction is given by $\max(U_i)$, $i = 1, \ldots, I$. Defining the overall satisfaction of the group as the sum of the individual satisfactions, the laws of large numbers ensure that the overall satisfaction is M times the expected satisfaction of a randomly selected individual. The expected satisfaction, which we call *the satisfaction*, is

$$S(\boldsymbol{\theta}, \mathbf{a}) = E\left[\max_i(U_i)\right], \tag{4.6}$$

where, for the MNP model, $\mathbf{U} \sim \text{MVN}[\mathbf{V}(\boldsymbol{\theta}, \mathbf{a}), \boldsymbol{\Sigma}_\xi(\boldsymbol{\theta}, \mathbf{a})]$. For binary probit models, it is possible to express $S(\boldsymbol{\theta}, \mathbf{a})$ in closed form by use of Clark's formulas [Eqs. (2.24)] as follows:

$$S(\boldsymbol{\theta}, \mathbf{a}) = V_2(\boldsymbol{\theta}, \mathbf{a}) + [V_1(\boldsymbol{\theta}, \mathbf{a}) - V_2(\boldsymbol{\theta}, \mathbf{a})]\Phi[V(\boldsymbol{\theta}, \mathbf{a})] + \sigma\phi[V(\boldsymbol{\theta}, \mathbf{a}], \tag{4.7}$$

where $\sigma = (\sigma_1^2 + \sigma_2^2 - 2\sigma_{12}^2)^{1/2}$ and $V(\boldsymbol{\theta}, \mathbf{a}) = [V_1(\boldsymbol{\theta}, \mathbf{a}) - V_2(\boldsymbol{\theta}, \mathbf{a})]/\sigma$.

For general MNP models, it is necessary to calculate $S(\boldsymbol{\theta}, \mathbf{a})$ either numerically, by simulation, or by approximation with Eqs. (2.24). The process is similar to that of calculating the choice probabilities because it also has two stages. First, one calculates $\mathbf{V} = \mathbf{V}(\boldsymbol{\theta}, \mathbf{a})$ and $\boldsymbol{\Sigma}_\xi = \boldsymbol{\Sigma}_\xi(\boldsymbol{\theta}, \mathbf{a})$ with the specification of the model, and then the expected value of the maximum component of a $\text{MVN}(\mathbf{V}, \boldsymbol{\Sigma}_\xi)$ random vector. The function relating the satisfaction to $\mathbf{V}$ and $\boldsymbol{\Sigma}_\xi$ will be called henceforth the *MNP satisfaction function*

$$E[\max(U_i)|\mathbf{V}, \boldsymbol{\Sigma}_\xi| = s(\mathbf{V}, \boldsymbol{\Sigma}_\xi)].$$

One must be very careful with the definition of satisfaction because two choice models yielding the same choice function can have different satisfactions depending on how the measured attractiveness functions and the covariance matrix are defined. This happens because, unfortunately, a set of choice probabilities does not uniquely define $\mathbf{V}$ and $\boldsymbol{\Sigma}_\xi$ (or $\mathbf{V}$ for a MNL model) and, consequently, it is not possible to express $S(\boldsymbol{\theta}, \mathbf{a})$ as a function of the choice probability vector. This can be seen by means of an example if one notes that when a constant is added to all the measured attractiveness values of a random utility model the basic form of the choice function is not affected, but in the formula for satisfaction such a constant alters the final result. That is, if a constant k is added to the elements of the measured attractiveness vector, the resulting, different, random utility model has a perceived attractiveness vector $\mathbf{U}^*$ given by

$$U_i^* = U_i + k, \qquad i = 1, \ldots, I.$$

Although this does not alter the choice probabilities (the constant k cancels out in the choice probability expression—see Eq. (1.6), for example), it modifies the satisfaction by exactly k attractiveness units:

$$S^*(\boldsymbol{\theta}, \mathbf{a}) = E\left[\max_i (U_i + k)\right] = E[\max(U_i) + k] = S(\boldsymbol{\theta}, \mathbf{a}) + k.$$

Of course one could conceivably avoid part of this problem by comparing $S(\boldsymbol{\theta}, \mathbf{a})$ to the satisfaction of a benchmark subgroup (say with $\mathbf{a} = \mathbf{0}$) in which case the constant k would cancel out. Unfortunately, the problem persists because k can be an arbitrary function of $\mathbf{a}$ and as seen with the following example different choices of k change the value of $S(\boldsymbol{\theta}, \mathbf{a}) - S(\boldsymbol{\theta}, \mathbf{0})$.

Example Assume that the correct measured attractiveness of a binary model of choice between public transit (alternative 1) and private automobile (alternative 2) is as follows:

Model a $V_1 = \theta_1 - \theta_2 a_1,$
$V_2 = -\theta_2 a_2 + \theta_3 a_3,$

where a_1 and a_2 are the door-to-door travel times by public transit and automobile, and a_3 represents the income of the choice maker. Alternatively, one could subtract $\theta_3 a_3$ from V_1 and V_2 to obtain a choice model with the same choice probability functions:

Model b $V_1 = \theta_1 - \theta_2 a_1 - \theta_3 a_3,$
$V_2 = -\theta_2 a_2.$

If we use momentarily the subscripts a and b to denote the satisfaction under models a and b, and remember that $S_a(\boldsymbol{\theta}, \mathbf{a}) - S_b(\boldsymbol{\theta}, \mathbf{a}) = \theta_3 a_3$, we have

$$\begin{aligned}[S_a(\boldsymbol{\theta}, \mathbf{a}) - S_a(\boldsymbol{\theta}, \mathbf{0})] - [S_b(\boldsymbol{\theta}, \mathbf{a}) - S_b(\boldsymbol{\theta}, \mathbf{0})] &= [S_a(\boldsymbol{\theta}, \mathbf{a}) - S_b(\boldsymbol{\theta}, \mathbf{a})] \\ &\quad - [S_a(\boldsymbol{\theta}, \mathbf{0}) - S_b(\boldsymbol{\theta}, \mathbf{0})] \\ &= \theta_3 a_3,\end{aligned}$$

and we see that $S(\boldsymbol{\theta}, \mathbf{a}) - S(\boldsymbol{\theta}, \mathbf{0})$ is not the same for Models a and b. ■

Therefore, for the satisfaction measure to be meaningful, in addition to having a correctly specified set of choice functions, the perceived-attractiveness vector must truly depict attraction. Despite these qualifications, $S(\boldsymbol{\theta}, \mathbf{a})$ is a very useful value because as shown in Section 4.5, even in cases where it lacks meaning, it can be used for certain supply–demand equilibration procedures. Furthermore, if the covariance matrix of the perceived-attractiveness vector is fixed and known, as happens with MNL models, the measure $S'(\boldsymbol{\theta}, \mathbf{a}) = S(\boldsymbol{\theta}, \mathbf{a}) - V_1(\boldsymbol{\theta}, \mathbf{a})$, which we call the *relative satisfaction*,[3] is independent of the way in which one specifies $\mathbf{V}(\boldsymbol{\theta}, \mathbf{a})$ and can therefore be used without difficulty. $S'(\boldsymbol{\theta}, \mathbf{a})$ can be interpreted as the increase in satisfaction resulting from addition of alternatives $2, 3, \ldots, I$ to the choice set.

We now prove the uniqueness of $S'(\boldsymbol{\theta}, \mathbf{a})$ by showing that if $\mathbf{V}(\boldsymbol{\theta}, \mathbf{a})$ and $\mathbf{V}^*(\boldsymbol{\theta}, \mathbf{a})$ are two specifications yielding the same choice probability functions, $S'(\boldsymbol{\theta}, \mathbf{a}) = S^{*\prime}(\boldsymbol{\theta}, \mathbf{a})$.

If $\mathbf{V}^*$ and $\mathbf{V}$ yield the same choice probabilities,

$$p_i[\mathbf{V}^*(\boldsymbol{\theta}, \mathbf{a}), \boldsymbol{\Sigma}_\xi] = p_i[\mathbf{V}(\boldsymbol{\theta}, \mathbf{a}), \boldsymbol{\Sigma}_\xi] = P_i(\boldsymbol{\theta}, \mathbf{a}), \qquad i = 1, \ldots, I.$$

According to Conjecture 3.1 and Fact 3.1 the reduced measured-attractiveness vector is the same for both specifications and consequently

$$V_i^*(\boldsymbol{\theta}, \mathbf{a}) - V_1^*(\boldsymbol{\theta}, \mathbf{a}) = V_i(\boldsymbol{\theta}, \mathbf{a}) - V_1(\boldsymbol{\theta}, \mathbf{a}), \qquad i = 1, \ldots, I.$$

The satisfaction corresponding to this new attractiveness vector is denoted $S_o(\boldsymbol{\theta}, \mathbf{a})$. It is related to $S(\boldsymbol{\theta}, \mathbf{a})$ by

$$S_o(\boldsymbol{\theta}, \mathbf{a}) = S(\boldsymbol{\theta}, \mathbf{a}) - V_1(\boldsymbol{\theta}, \mathbf{a})$$

because the two specifications only differ by a constant $V_1(\boldsymbol{\theta}, \mathbf{a})$, which was subtracted from the measured attractiveness vector. Similarly,

$$S_o(\boldsymbol{\theta}, \mathbf{a}) = S^*(\boldsymbol{\theta}, \mathbf{a}) - V_i^*(\boldsymbol{\theta}, \mathbf{a})$$

and therefore

$$S_o(\boldsymbol{\theta}, \mathbf{a}) = S'(\boldsymbol{\theta}, \mathbf{a}) = S^{*\prime}(\boldsymbol{\theta}, \mathbf{a}). \quad \blacksquare$$

This establishes the uniqueness of $S'(\boldsymbol{\theta}, \mathbf{a})$ for MNP models with fixed and known covariance matrices; the result also holds for MNL models. For the previous example, the reader can verify that, indeed, $S'_a(\boldsymbol{\theta}, \mathbf{a}) \equiv S'_b(\boldsymbol{\theta}, \mathbf{a})$.

Because the significance of an "attractiveness unit" is hard to grasp, it is desirable to obtain an indication of its value compared with more usual measures of benefits, such as monetary value or time. Such an indication is provided by the coefficients of attributes representing money or time, if such attributes enter in the specification of the model; assuming of course,

[3] We can also define the satisfaction relative to alternative i by subtracting $V_i(\boldsymbol{\theta}, \mathbf{a})$ from $S(\boldsymbol{\theta}, \mathbf{a})$. However, the term relative satisfaction is used in this book in connection with alternative 1, without loss of generality.

that there are no problems with cross-sectional data and that the model is truly behavioral.

We now turn our attention to the derivatives of $S(\boldsymbol{\theta}, \mathbf{a})$ and $S'(\theta, \mathbf{a})$. The following theorem gives insight into the behavior of satisfaction and will help calculate its derivatives. The proof is adapted from Sheffi and Daganzo (1978a).

Theorem 4.1 For a random utility model with additive disturbances ξ (the only kind considered in this book), the partial derivative of the satisfaction with respect to the measured attractiveness of an alternative equals its probability of choice:

$$\frac{\partial E[\max_{i=1,\ldots,I}(U_i)]}{\partial V_j} = p_j, \qquad j = 1, \ldots, I.$$

Proof The partial derivative of the satisfaction with respect to the measured attractiveness of the jth alternative can be expressed as

$$\frac{\partial E[\max_{i=1,\ldots,I}(V_i + \xi_i)]}{\partial V_j} = \frac{\partial}{\partial V_j} \int_{\mathbf{x}} \max_{i-1,\ldots,I} (V_i + x_i) F_\xi(\mathbf{x})\, d\mathbf{x},$$

where $F_\xi(\mathbf{x})$ denotes the density function of the error terms.

Letting $\Gamma_j(\mathbf{x}, \mathbf{V})$ be the indicator function,

$$\Gamma_j(\mathbf{x}, \mathbf{V}) = \begin{cases} 1 & \text{if} \quad V_j + x_j > V_i + x_i \quad \forall i \neq j \\ 0 & \text{otherwise,} \end{cases}$$

it is possible to interchange the derivative and integral operators in the above expression and to simplify it as follows:

$$\begin{aligned} &\int_{\mathbf{x}} \frac{\partial}{\partial V_j} \left[\max_{i=1,\ldots,I} (V_i + x_i) \right] F_\xi(\mathbf{x})\, d\mathbf{x} \\ &= \int_{\mathbf{x}} \Gamma_j(\mathbf{x}, \mathbf{V}) F_\xi(\mathbf{x})\, d\mathbf{x} \\ &= \Pr\{V_j + \xi_j > V_i + \xi_i\ \forall i \neq j\} \\ &= p_i. \quad \blacksquare \end{aligned}$$

This result is intuitively appealing because it indicates that the level of satisfaction always increases when an alternative is improved and that the increase is proportional to the popularity of the alternative. In our case it will be even more significant because it will mean that we can calculate the derivatives of satisfaction fairly easily even for heterogeneous groups.

Theorem 4.1 can also be used to derive the expression for satisfaction of random utility models with fixed distribution of the error terms by solving a system of partial differential equations. Letting $s(\mathbf{V})$ denote the satisfaction associated with the measured attractiveness vector $\mathbf{V}$, we can write for the MNL model

$$\frac{\partial s(\mathbf{V})}{\partial V_i} = \frac{\exp(V_i)}{\sum_{j=1}^{I} \exp(V_j)}, \qquad i = 1, \ldots, I,$$

with boundary condition $s(\mathbf{V}) = 0$ if $\mathbf{V} = (0, -\infty, -\infty, \ldots, -\infty)$. This yields $s(\mathbf{V}) = \log \sum_{i=1}^{I} \exp(V_i)$ in agreement with Eq. (1.10). The reader can verify that for the trinomial GEV model of Section 1.3.2, one has

$$s(\mathbf{V}) = \log(\exp(V_1) + \{\exp[V_2/(1-\rho)] + \exp[V_3/(1-\rho)]\}^{1-\rho})$$

and that the expression given for the binary probit model meets

$$\frac{\partial s(\mathbf{V})}{\partial V_1} = \Phi(V) = p_1.$$

If the specification of $\mathbf{V}$ is linear in $\mathbf{a}$, i.e., it can be expressed as $\mathbf{V} = \mathbf{a}[\boldsymbol{\theta}]$ and $\boldsymbol{\Sigma}_\xi$ does not depend on $\mathbf{a}$, the gradient of $S(\boldsymbol{\theta}, \mathbf{a})$ with respect to $\mathbf{a}$ is given by the chain-differentiation rule and the convenient form

$$\nabla_a S(\boldsymbol{\theta}, \mathbf{a}) = [P_1(\boldsymbol{\theta}, \mathbf{a}), \ldots, P_I(\boldsymbol{\theta}, \mathbf{a})][\boldsymbol{\theta}]^{\mathrm{T}}, \tag{4.8}$$

which simply involves calculation of choice functions. In more-complicated cases the gradient can be calculated numerically.

Although Theorem 4.1 states that the increase in satisfaction obtained from an increase in attractiveness is independent of how the model is specified, the value of the derivative with respect to an attribute depends on the way the model is specified. It is easy to see that for model *a*

$$\frac{\partial S(\boldsymbol{\theta}, \mathbf{a})}{\partial a_3} = p_2 \theta_3$$

and for model *b*

$$\frac{\partial S(\boldsymbol{\theta}, \mathbf{a})}{\partial a_3} = -\theta_3 p_1.$$

Thus care must also be taken in the analysis of the derivatives of $S(\boldsymbol{\theta}, \mathbf{a})$.

Since $S'(\boldsymbol{\theta}, \mathbf{a})$ is independent of the specification used, however, its derivative is independent of model form; for models *a* and *b* the reader can check that $\partial S'(\boldsymbol{\theta}, \mathbf{a})/\partial a_3 = \theta_3 p_2$. This means that the added satisfaction provided by alternative 2 increases with higher-income groups. In other words, higher-income groups benefit more from the existence of automobiles than low-income groups. However, unless one can tell from knowledge of the problem whether model a or model b is the true one, one cannot tell how much more satisfaction is derived by wealthy individuals than by poor individuals from the general situation.

Although for many applications there are other figures of merit, in addition to the satisfaction and demand, that may be of interest (Section 1.5 discussed the average number of automobiles owned by a family), it is not possible to discuss them. It should be remembered, however, that the mechanics of prediction, discussed in Sections 4.2 and 4.3, would be identical for any figure of merit $T(\boldsymbol{\theta}, \mathbf{a})$ that depends on $\boldsymbol{\theta}$ and $\mathbf{a}$ through $\mathbf{V}$ and $\boldsymbol{\Sigma}_\xi$ only.

4.1.3 Heterogeneous Population Groups

Equation (4.2) can be applied to predict the usage and the satisfaction of heterogeneous groups of people. However, before explaining how to do that in Sections 4.2 and 4.3, we show how Eq. (4.2) can also be used to predict the derivatives of usage and satisfaction of heterogeneous population groups.

Assume that we wish to calculate the elasticity of usage with respect to a certain policy attribute A_p whose value a_p is the same for all the population. In such a case the integration in Eq. (4.1a) can be restricted to all attributes except A_p provided $F(\mathbf{a})$ is interpreted as the density of $\mathbf{A}$ exclusive of A_p, and a_p is fixed in $P_i(\boldsymbol{\theta}, \mathbf{a})$. The equation is

$$y_i(a_p) = M \int_a P_i(\theta, \mathbf{a}) F(\mathbf{a})\, d\mathbf{a},$$

and taking derivatives on both sides with respect to a_p, we obtain

$$y_i'(a_p) = M \int_a \frac{\partial P_i(\boldsymbol{\theta}, \mathbf{a})}{\partial a_p} F(\mathbf{a})\, d\mathbf{a}, \tag{4.9}$$

showing that if we set $T(\boldsymbol{\theta}, \mathbf{a}) = \partial P_i(\boldsymbol{\theta}, \mathbf{a})/\partial a_p$ and $T(\boldsymbol{\theta}) = y_i'(a_p)/M$, Eq. (4.2) applies. This formula is particularly useful for trinomial probit models in which a_p does not appear in $\boldsymbol{\Sigma}_\xi$, since in such case $\partial P_i(\boldsymbol{\theta}, \mathbf{a})/\partial a_p$ assumes a closed form and hand evaluation of $y_i'(a_p)$ with Eq. (4.9) is much less time consuming than another evaluation of y_i in the neighborhood of a_p. Qualitatively, the formula shows that if a_p appears with a negative coefficient in V_j $(j \neq i)$ and/or with a positive coefficient in V_i, the derivative inside the integral will always be positive and, consequently, so will be the elasticity of usage.

The same analysis can be performed with respect to the satisfaction of a MNP model for which the policy variable a_p does not appear in the covariance matrix. In such a case, the average satisfaction of one individual is

$$S(\boldsymbol{\theta}) = \int_{\mathbf{a}} S(\boldsymbol{\theta}, \mathbf{a}) F(\mathbf{a})\, d\mathbf{a},$$

and if **V** is linear in a_p and *the coefficients of* a_p *are not functions of other attributes*, using Eq. (4.8), after interchanging differentiation and integration, yields

$$\frac{\partial S(\boldsymbol{\theta})}{\partial a_p} = \int_{\mathbf{a}} [\boldsymbol{\theta}]_p \begin{bmatrix} P_1(\boldsymbol{\theta}, \mathbf{a}) \\ \vdots \\ P_I(\boldsymbol{\theta}, \mathbf{a}) \end{bmatrix} F(\mathbf{a})\, d\mathbf{a},$$

where $[\boldsymbol{\theta}]_p$ represents the pth row of $[\boldsymbol{\theta}]$, i.e., the constant coefficients of a_p in each of the measured-attractiveness functions. Bringing $[\boldsymbol{\theta}]_p$ out of the integral and using Eq. (4.1a), we finally obtain

$$\frac{\partial S(\boldsymbol{\theta})}{\partial a_p} = [\boldsymbol{\theta}]_p \begin{bmatrix} y_1 \\ \vdots \\ y_I \end{bmatrix} / M. \tag{4.10}$$

Equation (4.10) is useful because it is a function of variables that are immediately available and obviates a special prediction procedure for $\partial S(\boldsymbol{\theta})/\partial a_p$. In addition, Eq. (4.10) indicates that $S(\boldsymbol{\theta})$ is related to *consumers' surplus*.

Let a_p denote the price of using one of the alternatives, say i, and thus be a variable appearing only in V_i. As previously required we assume that the coefficient of a_p is constant. If a_p is expressed in units of attractiveness it will enter V_i with a -1 coefficient and Eq. (4.10) would yield

$$\frac{\partial[MS(\boldsymbol{\theta})]}{\partial a_p} = -y_i(a_p). \tag{4.11}$$

Assuming everything else is fixed, $y_i(a_p)$ is a one-dimensional demand function relating usage to price, and the "area under the curve"

$$\int_{x=0}^{a_p^*} y_i(x)\, dx = M[S(\boldsymbol{\theta})|_{a_p=0} - S(\boldsymbol{\theta})|_{a_p=a_p}] \tag{4.12}$$

is the change in consumers' surplus to the users of alternative i when the price is dropped from a_p to zero, as it represents their willingness to pay. Since Eq. (4.12) can also be interpreted as the increase in satisfaction for the whole population when the price is dropped from a_p to zero, the equivalence of the satisfaction measure and consumers' surplus should be apparent. It should be noted, however, that for more realistic models in which the coefficient of a_p is allowed to depend on socioeconomic attributes the satisfaction is not equivalent to consumers' surplus because Eq. (4.12) does not hold.

The measure $S(\boldsymbol{\theta})$ is more useful for policy analysis than other measures of consumer benefits because if the choice-set is exhaustive (i.e., it includes not choosing anything), the population of choice makers includes everybody in the population, and because with the proper selection of $F(\mathbf{a})$, $S(\boldsymbol{\theta})$ can be calculated for different subgroups of the population. Thus, using $S(\boldsymbol{\theta})$, it is possible to study the repercussions of different policies not only on the whole population but also on minority groups.

A similar comment can be made regarding $S'(\boldsymbol{\theta}) = E_A[S'(\boldsymbol{\theta}, \mathbf{A})]$. The value of $S'(\boldsymbol{\theta})$ represents the average increase in satisfaction resulting from inclusion of alternatives 2 to I in the choice set and is related to $S(\boldsymbol{\theta})$ by

$$S'(\boldsymbol{\theta}) = S(\boldsymbol{\theta}) - E_A[V_1(\boldsymbol{\theta}, \mathbf{A})] \tag{4.13}$$

since by definition $S'(\boldsymbol{\theta}, \mathbf{a}) = S(\boldsymbol{\theta}, \mathbf{a}) - V_1(\boldsymbol{\theta}, \mathbf{a})$. Equation (4.13) is particularly easy to evaluate for linear specifications for then $E_A[V_1(\boldsymbol{\theta}, \mathbf{A})] = V_1[\boldsymbol{\theta}, E(\mathbf{A})]$.

For linear specifications, the derivative of $S'(\boldsymbol{\theta})$ with respect to a_p is

$$\frac{\partial S'(\boldsymbol{\theta})}{\partial a_p} = \frac{\partial S(\boldsymbol{\theta})}{\partial a_p} - [\boldsymbol{\theta}]_{p1}$$

where $[\boldsymbol{\theta}]_{p1}$ is the coefficient of a_p in $V_1(\boldsymbol{\theta}, \mathbf{a}_p)$. Naturally, the derivatives coincide if $V_1(\boldsymbol{\theta}, \mathbf{A})$ is independent of A_p.

The next section includes a numerical example illustrating many of the ideas that have been introduced.

4.2 General Prediction Techniques

4.2.1 *Classification by Attributes*

This method was briefly described in Chapter 1 because it is very simple and helps to illustrate the difference between aggregate and disaggregate demand models. The method is applicable to any discrete choice model. Its description will be illustrated with an example.

Given a figure of merit $T(\boldsymbol{\theta}, \mathbf{a})$ associated with the individuals of a homogeneous group, we can express its expected value for a heterogeneous group as

$$T(\boldsymbol{\theta}) = \int_{\mathbf{a}} T(\boldsymbol{\theta}, \mathbf{a}) F(\mathbf{a})\, d\mathbf{a},$$

where $F(\mathbf{a})$ is the mass–density function of the attribute vector across the members of the group.

Let us approximate $F(\mathbf{a})$ by a discrete mass function defined as follows:

$$F(\mathbf{a}) \approx \begin{cases} m^{(k)}/M & \text{if} \quad \mathbf{a} = \mathbf{a}^{(k)}, \quad k = 1, 2, \ldots, K, \\ 0 & \text{otherwise,} \end{cases}$$

where the $\mathbf{a}^{(k)}$s are values of the attribute vector representative of certain members of the group, $m^{(k)}$ is the number of members of the group with attribute vector approximately equal to $\mathbf{a}^{(k)}$, and M is the size of the group.

The values $m^{(k)}$ must satisfy

$$\sum_{k=1}^{K} m^{(k)} = M,$$

so that the approximation to $F(\mathbf{a})$ is a proper probability mass function. If the values $m^{(k)}$ and $\mathbf{a}^{(k)}$ are available, the prediction equation becomes

$$T(\boldsymbol{\theta}) \approx \sum_{k=1}^{K} T(\boldsymbol{\theta}, \mathbf{a}^{(k)}) \frac{m^{(k)}}{M}, \tag{4.14}$$

which is the formula for the *classification by attributes method.*

The name of the approach is based on the physical interpretation of Eq. (4.14), which predicts $T(\boldsymbol{\theta})$ after classifying the individuals of the heterogeneous group into K quasi-homogeneous classes with attribute vector $\mathbf{a}^{(k)}$, and $m^{(k)}$ individuals each.

Example We now illustrate the technique with a trinomial mode-choice problem. This example will be used throughout this chapter. Each individual living in the square zone depicted in Fig. 4.1 has three basic choices when a major sporting event is featured in the downtown area:

(1) not to travel;
(2) to walk to the transit station located at the northeast corner of the area and board the train;
(3) to drive a car (conditional on the decision maker auto-ownership status) to the freeway access located at the southwest corner of the area and go to downtown.

The square zone under consideration has a rectangular-grid street system parallel to the sides. The population in this area is $M = 10{,}000$ decision makers, who are uniformly distributed throughout the area; 70% of the population own cars and 30% do not; these percentages are also uniformly distributed in the area.

Let us suppose that the following MNP model has been specified, calibrated, and after some consideration judged to represent choice-making behavior reasonably well:[4]

$$\begin{aligned} U_1 &= 0 + \xi_1 && \text{(not to travel)},\\ U_2 &= 3 - 6A_{\mathrm{T}} - 6R_{\mathrm{T}} + \xi_2 && \text{(transit)},\\ U_3 &= 3.5 - 6A_{\mathrm{A}} - 6R_{\mathrm{A}} + A0 + \xi_3 && \text{(car)}, \end{aligned}$$

[4] The MNP model specification given below is not likely to be realistic because the choice probabilities are much too sensitive to the level of service attributes. This will result in rather low satisfaction values but is useful for pedagogical purposes to ensure that the mode choice probabilities vary substantially within the zone.

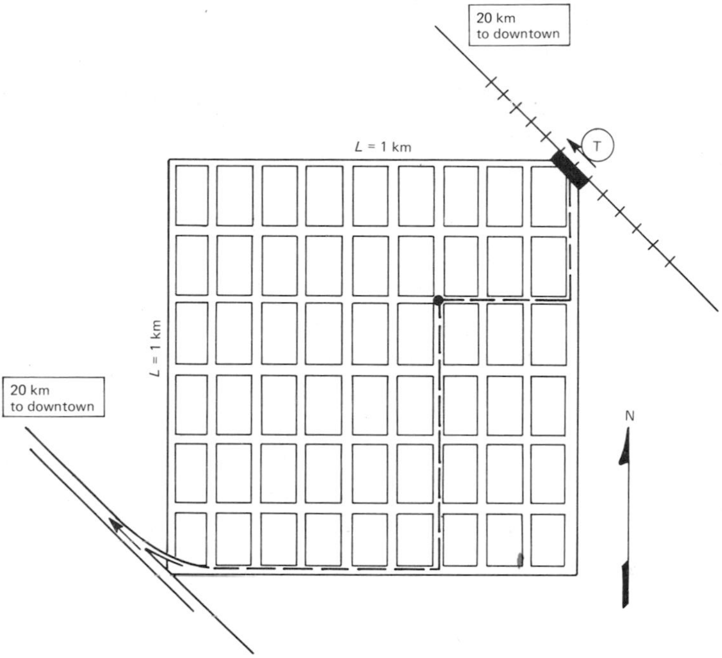

Fig. 4.1 Hypothetical suburb connected to the city center by freeway and train.

with

$$\boldsymbol{\Sigma}_\xi = \begin{bmatrix} 0.1 & 0 & 0 \\ 0 & 0.1 & 0 \\ 0 & 0 & 0.1 \end{bmatrix}.$$

The units of the access time (time spent within the zone) to transit A_T, the access time by auto A_A, the travel time outside the zone by transit R_T, and auto R_A, are all in hours. AO is a dummy socioeconomic variable that is zero for car owners and -1000 (a very large but finite value) for non–car owners. AO ensures that non–car owners do not drive to the sporting event.

The following numerical values have been considered for this example:

length of the square side	$L = 1$ km
walking speed	$S_T = 4$ km/hr
driving speed inside the zone	$S_A = 40$ km/hr
waiting time plus in-vehicle travel time for transit	$R_T = 20$ min
freeway driving time	$R_A = 30$ min

Letting the attribute vector be $\mathbf{A} = (1, A_T, A_A, R_T, R_A, AO)$ the specification can be written $\mathbf{U} = \mathbf{A}[\boldsymbol{\theta}] + \boldsymbol{\xi}$ with

$$[\boldsymbol{\theta}]^T = \begin{bmatrix} 0 & 0 & 0 & 0 & 0 & 0 \\ 3 & -6 & 0 & -6 & 0 & 0 \\ 3.5 & 0 & -6 & 0 & -6 & 1 \end{bmatrix}.$$

We now divide the population into subgroups with similar attribute vector. This can usually be done in different ways but in this particular case careful inspection of the problem results in just a few classes.

We first notice that since attributes A_T, A_A, and AO are the only ones that vary across the population, they are the only ones we need to be concerned about. The simplicity of the example enables us to segment the population quite easily into groups with approximately equal driving and walking access times. Figure 4.2 represents three possible equal area partitions of the zone with 1, 3, and 10 subzones each. Since the fraction of car owners is homogeneously distributed we can assume that it is 70% in each one of the subzones. The values of $m^{(k)}$ and $\mathbf{a}^{(k)}$ are obtained by inspection of the figure.

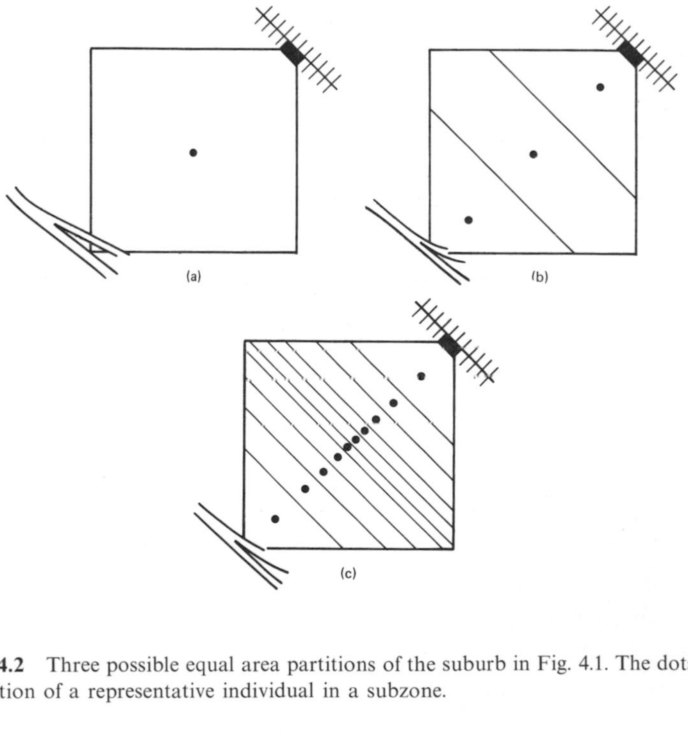

Fig. 4.2 Three possible equal area partitions of the suburb in Fig. 4.1. The dots represent the location of a representative individual in a subzone.

$a_T^{(k)}$ and $a_A^{(k)}$ are obtained by measuring the grid distance from the center of gravity of the subzone to the southwest and northeast corners of the square and dividing the result by the appropriate speed.

$m^{(k)}$ is proportional to the area of the subzone times 0.7 (if we consider a group of car owners) or 0.3 (if it is a group of non–car owners).

The values are summarized in Table 4.1 for the three partition case. In the table the values have been entered in $\mathbf{V} = \mathbf{a}[\boldsymbol{\theta}]$, and $\mathbf{V}^{(k)}$ is also given for all the classes. Had the matrix $\boldsymbol{\Sigma}_\xi$ depended on $\mathbf{a}$, $\boldsymbol{\Sigma}_\xi^{(k)}$ should also have been computed for each class. In our case, however, $\boldsymbol{\Sigma}_\xi$ is constant and that does not have to be done.

Let us now calculate $P_i(\boldsymbol{\theta})$, $S(\boldsymbol{\theta})$, $S'(\boldsymbol{\theta})$, and their derivatives. For $P_i(\boldsymbol{\theta})$ we enter in Eq. (4.14) with $T(\boldsymbol{\theta}, \mathbf{a}^{(k)}) = P_i(\boldsymbol{\theta}, \mathbf{a}^{(k)})$ $(i = 1, 2, 3)$ and for $S(\boldsymbol{\theta})$ we use $T(\boldsymbol{\theta}, \mathbf{a}^{(k)}) = S(\boldsymbol{\theta}, \mathbf{a}^{(k)})$. Note that $S'(\boldsymbol{\theta})$ coincides with $S(\boldsymbol{\theta})$ since for this problem $V_1(\boldsymbol{\theta}, \mathbf{a}) \equiv 0$. Table 4.2 gives the values of $P_i(\boldsymbol{\theta}, \mathbf{a}^{(k)})$ and $S(\boldsymbol{\theta}, \mathbf{a}^{(k)})$, which were derived with the approximate formulas described in Section 2.2.3.

It is interesting to see how the satisfaction from travel increases with proximity to the transit station for those segments of the population that do not own a car but reaches a minimum in the middle of the zone for car owners.

This result is reasonable since satisfaction reaches a minimum where the travel time to downtown by the best mode is maximum. That location is the middle subzone for car owners and the southwest zone for non–car owners. The satisfaction units can be converted to hours of saved travel time by dividing them by six (we are assuming that the model is behavioral) as indicated by the generic coefficient of the time attributes in the specification of the model. The values in minutes are given in parenthesis in Table 4.2.

Table 4.1

Intermediate Calculations of the Classification by Attributes Prediction Method

	Northeast zone		Central zone		Southwest zone	
class (k)	1	2[a]	3	4[a]	5	6[a]
class size ($m^{(k)}$)	2333	1000	2333	1000	2333	1000
$a_T^{(k)}$ (hr)	0.136	0.136	0.250	0.250	0.364	0.364
$a_A^{(k)}$ (hr)	0.0364	0.0364	0.025	0.025	0.0136	0.0136
$ao^{(k)}$	0	−1000	0	−1000	0	−1000
$V_1^{(k)}$	0	0	0	0	0	0
$V_2^{(k)}$	0.184	0.184	−0.500	−0.500	−1.184	−1.184
$V_3^{(k)}$	0.182	−999.72	0.350	−999.65	0.418	−999.52

[a] Non–car-owner class.

Table 4.2

Final Calculations of the Classification by Attributes Prediction Method.

Subzone	Class (k)	$P_1(\boldsymbol{\theta}, \mathbf{a}^{(k)})$	$P_2(\boldsymbol{\theta}, \mathbf{a}^{(k)})$	$P_3(\boldsymbol{\theta}, \mathbf{a}^{(k)})$	$S(\boldsymbol{\theta}, \mathbf{a}^{(k)})$[a]
Northeast	1	0.16	0.34	0.50	0.45 (4.5)
	2[b]	0.34	0.66	0	0.29 (2.9)
Central	3	0.20	0.03	0.77	0.41 (4.1)
	4[b]	0.87	0.13	0	0.03 (0.3)
Southwest	5	0.17	0	0.83	0.46 (4.6)
	6[b]	1.00	0	0	0.00 (0.00)

[a] The numbers in parentheses are minutes.
[b] Non–car-owner group.

The choice probabilities also follow an interesting pattern. As we move away from the transit station car owners shift from transit to the automobile but non–car owners simply choose not to travel since they are transit "captives."

The elasticity of the demand for each of the three alternatives can be obtained with Eq. (4.4). As an example, consider the elasticity of the demand for travel by transit for the individuals in group 4 (non–car owners in the center of the square zone) with respect to the in-vehicle travel time by transit R_{T}.

Because within this subgroup alternative 3 can be ignored for most practical purposes, we can use the binary probit elasticity formula [Eqs. (4.5a)–(4.5c)]:

$$[\boldsymbol{\theta}]\begin{bmatrix} 1 \\ -1 \end{bmatrix} = \begin{bmatrix} 0 & 3 \\ 0 & -6 \\ 0 & -6 \end{bmatrix}\begin{bmatrix} 1 \\ -1 \end{bmatrix} = \begin{bmatrix} -3 \\ 6 \\ 6 \end{bmatrix},$$

$$V(\boldsymbol{\theta}, \mathbf{a}) = \sigma^{-1}\mathbf{a}[\boldsymbol{\theta}]\begin{bmatrix} 1 \\ -1 \end{bmatrix} = (1, 0.25, 0.333)\begin{bmatrix} -3 \\ 6 \\ 6 \end{bmatrix}\frac{1}{0.477} = 1.12,$$

$$\boldsymbol{\varepsilon}^{D_2} = -\frac{\phi(1.12)}{\Phi(-1.12)}(-3, 6, 6)\begin{bmatrix} 1 & 0 & 0 \\ 0 & 0.25 & 0 \\ 0 & 0 & 0.333 \end{bmatrix}\frac{1}{0.477}$$

$$= -3.4(-3, 1.5, 2) = (10.2, -5.1, -6.8).$$

Thus a 1% increase in riding time would be expected to cause a 6.8% decrease in the transit ridership of group 4.

The derivative of the satisfaction is much easier to obtain, as it is given by Eq. (4.8), which requires only a matrix multiplication. For group 4 we obtain

$$\nabla_a S(\boldsymbol{\theta}, \mathbf{a}^{(4)}) = (0.87, 0.13, 0.0) \begin{bmatrix} 0 & 0 & 0 & 0 & 0 & 0 \\ 3 & -6 & 0 & -6 & 0 & 0 \\ 3.5 & 0 & -6 & 0 & -6 & 1 \end{bmatrix}$$

$$= (0.4, -0.8, 0, -0.8, 0, 0),$$

expressed in attractiveness units per unit change in the value of the attribute. Expressing attractiveness in hours,

$$\nabla_a S(\boldsymbol{\theta}, \mathbf{a}^{(4)}) = (0.067, -0.13, 0, -0.13, 0, 0),$$

and we see that an increase in R_{T} of 1 hr decreases the average satisfaction of the individuals in class 4 by 0.13 hr. This was expected since the fraction of individuals in the zone that choose transit is also 0.13.

Let us now aggregate all these measures for the whole population. The formulas for $P_i(\boldsymbol{\theta})$ and $S(\boldsymbol{\theta})$ are

$$P_i(\boldsymbol{\theta}) = \sum_{k=1}^{6} \frac{P_i(\boldsymbol{\theta}, \mathbf{a}^{(k)})}{10{,}000} m^{(k)}$$

and

$$S(\boldsymbol{\theta}) = S'(\boldsymbol{\theta}) = \sum_{k=1}^{6} \frac{S(\boldsymbol{\theta}, \mathbf{a}^{(k)})}{10{,}000} m^{(k)},$$

which with the values of $m^{(k)}$ given in Table 4.1 and the values of $P_i(\boldsymbol{\theta}, \mathbf{a}^{(k)})$ and $S(\boldsymbol{\theta}, \mathbf{a}^{(k)})$ given in Table 4.2 yield

$$P_1(\boldsymbol{\theta}) = 0.34 \qquad P_2(\boldsymbol{\theta}) = 0.17 \qquad P_3(\boldsymbol{\theta}) = 0.49$$

and

$$S(\boldsymbol{\theta}) = 0.34 \text{ (attractiveness units)} = 3.4 \text{ (min/individual)}.$$

The usages and total satisfaction are obtained by multiplying these results by 10,000. The derivative of demand with respect to transit riding time (a policy variable that is the same for all the population) can be obtained with Eq. (4.14), setting $T(\boldsymbol{\theta}, \mathbf{a}^{(k)}) = \partial P_i(\boldsymbol{\theta}, \mathbf{a}^{(k)})/\partial R_{\mathrm{T}}$. Alternatively, one can change R_{T} by a small amount, recalculate the usage, and approximate in this way the derivative. The derivative of demand for transit of non–car owners is found below by the first method. For subgroup 4, the value was obtained with the elasticity calculations; it was

$$\frac{\partial P_2(\boldsymbol{\theta}, \mathbf{a}^{(4)})}{\partial R_{\mathrm{T}}} = -\phi(1.12) \times 6 = -1.3.$$

In the same way we find

$$\frac{\partial P_2(\boldsymbol{\theta}, \mathbf{a}^{(2)})}{\partial R_\mathrm{T}} = -2.2 \qquad \text{and} \qquad \frac{\partial P_2(\boldsymbol{\theta}, \mathbf{a}^{(6)})}{\partial R_\mathrm{T}} = -0.11,$$

and since there is the same number of individuals in the three classes, Eq. (4.14) yields $\partial P_2(\boldsymbol{\theta})/\partial R_\mathrm{T} = -(2.2 + 1.3 + 0.1)/3 = -1.2$. The derivative of usage is $-1.2 \times 3000 = -3600$ passengers/hr $= -60$ passengers/min.

The derivative of the satisfaction is easier to obtain. It equals $-6 \times P_2(\boldsymbol{\theta}) = -1.2$ attractiveness units/hr; or 0.2 min/min.

Note that since the derivative of satisfaction with respect to a policy variable a_p is so easily obtained, it is very easy to assess how minor policy changes would affect different population subgroups. For this particular example, it would be relatively easy to study the effects of increasing the frequency of trains, metering the ramp on the entrance of the freeway, and in general any policy resulting in minor alterations to R_T and/or R_A.

If desired, one can also obtain the derivatives of $P(\boldsymbol{\theta})$ and $S(\boldsymbol{\theta})$ with respect to variables that change across the population (such as the auto-ownership percentage, or changes in driving time through the zone). In such instances, however, the distribution of the attribute vector changes when the attribute is changed and one must either calculate the derivatives numerically or modify Eqs. (4.9) and (4.10) accordingly. ■

The problem with the classification by attributes approach is that for models with several variables the number of classes needed for a reasonable accuracy can become very large.

To illustrate the effect that the number of classes has on the results of the forecast, the usage of the three modes was calculated for the partitions with one and ten subzones. The results are summarized in Fig. 4.3. Assuming that the partition with ten subzones provides an accurate estimate of usage, it can be seen that the transit ridership prediction error for the one class partition was 64% on the low side and for the three class partition 3% on the high side. The relative error of the two other alternatives is smaller. This is in general typical of discrete-choice models where forecasting errors tend to manifest themselves on the usage of low probability alternatives.

4.2.2 *Other General Prediction Methods*

In order to avoid the encumbrance of a large number of classes, other approaches have been devised. Two of these methods are *stochastic simulation* and *classification by* $\mathbf{V}$ and $\boldsymbol{\Sigma}_\xi$.

In the stochastic simulation method, one replicates an imaginary experiment in which one would select persons at random from the population to

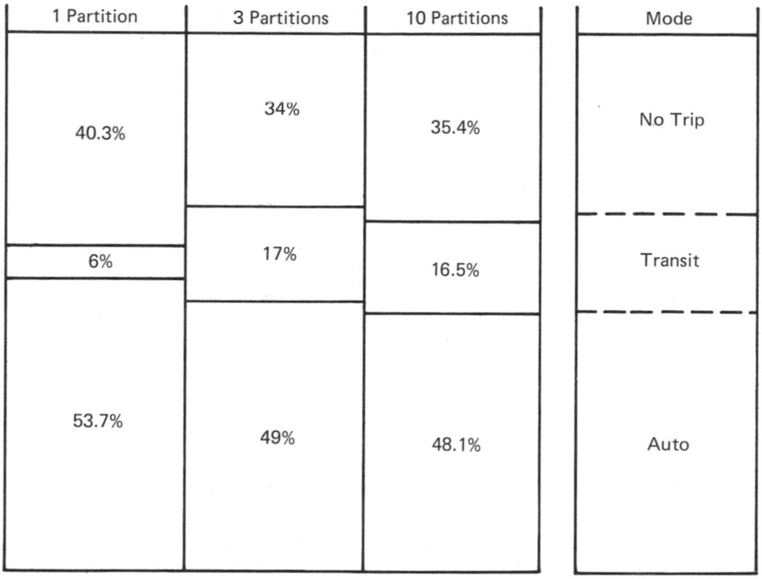

Fig. 4.3 Prediction results with different numbers of classes.

observe their choices and (if it were possible) their satisfactions. After many repetitions of such a process, one could easily provide approximate values of $P_i(\boldsymbol{\theta})$ and $S(\boldsymbol{\theta})$.

To carry out the experiment in a computer one has to devise a way of generating $F(\mathbf{a})$ distributed random attribute vectors from a table of random numbers or a psuedorandom-number generator. There are standard procedures to do this, which are extensively discussed in the simulation literature (see Fishman (1973) for example). Obtaining a value of $\mathbf{A}$, $\mathbf{a}^{(n)}$ in such a way parallels the real-life action of selecting an individual from the population. Since such an individual can be thought of as characterizing a homogeneous subgroup of the population with alternative shares, $P_i(\boldsymbol{\theta}, \mathbf{a}^{(n)})$, and average satisfaction $S(\boldsymbol{\theta}, \mathbf{a}^{(n)})$, in accordance with Eq. (4.2) one can approximate $P_i(\boldsymbol{\theta})$ and $S(\boldsymbol{\theta})$ by averaging these values. Letting $\mathbf{a}^{(n)}$ be the attribute vector of the nth observation and N the total number of observations, one can estimate $P(\boldsymbol{\theta})$ and $S(\boldsymbol{\theta}, \mathbf{a})$ by

$$P_i(\boldsymbol{\theta}) \approx \sum_{n=1}^{N} P_i(\boldsymbol{\theta}, \mathbf{a}^{(n)})/N, \qquad S(\boldsymbol{\theta}) \approx \sum_{n=1}^{N} S(\boldsymbol{\theta}, \mathbf{a}^{(n)})/N, \tag{4.15}$$

where $P_i(\boldsymbol{\theta}, \mathbf{a}^{(n)})$ and $S(\boldsymbol{\theta}, \mathbf{a}^{(n)})$ can be obtained with the approximate formulas. Since the right-hand sides of Eqs. (4.15) represent the sample means of two sets of independent identically distributed random variables, t-tests and confidence intervals can be built on $P_i(\boldsymbol{\theta})$ and $S(\boldsymbol{\theta})$ for large values of N.

Equations (4.15) can be used conveniently for MNL and binary probit models because $P_i(\boldsymbol{\theta}, \mathbf{a})$ and $S(\boldsymbol{\theta}, \mathbf{a})$ assume an exact closed form. For MNP models an alternative way of estimating $P(\boldsymbol{\theta})$ and $S(\boldsymbol{\theta})$ that does not require calculation of choice functions consists in finding the actual choice and satisfaction of the individual every time an attribute vector is sampled and working with the resulting strings of values. To do that one enters in the specification of the model with $\mathbf{a}^{(n)}$ to obtain $\mathbf{V}^{(n)}$ and $\boldsymbol{\Sigma}_\xi^{(n)}$ and then uses the simulation method described in Section 2.2.2 to obtain the vector of perceived utilities $\mathbf{U}^{(n)} = (U_1^{(n)}, \ldots, U_I^{(n)})$, the satisfaction $S^{(n)} = \max_{i=1,\ldots,I}(U_i^{(n)})$, and an index $c_i^{(n)}$, which equals 1 if alternative i is chosen and 0 otherwise.

The estimates of $P_i(\boldsymbol{\theta})$ and $S(\boldsymbol{\theta})$ are

$$P_i(\boldsymbol{\theta}) \approx \sum_{n=1}^{N} c_i^{(n)}/N, \qquad S(\boldsymbol{\theta}) \approx \sum_{n=1}^{N} S^{(n)}/N. \tag{4.16}$$

As in the previous case, one can perform t-tests and find confidence intervals; but since the $c_i^{(k)}$s are *Bernoulli* random variables with success probability equal to $P(\boldsymbol{\theta})$, we can give a simple expression of error size.

With very high probability, the relative error is smaller than two standard deviations, $2\{[1 - P_i(\boldsymbol{\theta})]/[P_i(\boldsymbol{\theta})N]\}^{1/2}$, which as in the example of Section 4.2.1, indicates that there is an inherent difficulty in predicting the usage of alternatives with low probability. To predict transit usage in the previous example with less than 10% error we would need $N \approx 2000$ observations. Although this is computationally feasible, the simulation approach may not be attractive for smaller choice probabilities and/or in cases where extensive sensitivity analyses have to be performed. Furthermore, although it does not require calculation of $m^{(k)}$ for a large number of groups as the classification by attributes approach, it necessitates the preparation of a computer program to generate the string of $\mathbf{a}^{(k)}$s.

The classification by $\mathbf{V}$ and $\boldsymbol{\Sigma}_\xi$ approach has been proposed for the MNL model by Reid (see Reid (1978) for a discussion) and can also be applied to the MNP model. Since the MNP choice function can be expressed as a MNP function of $\mathbf{V}(\boldsymbol{\theta}, \mathbf{a})$ and $\boldsymbol{\Sigma}_\xi(\boldsymbol{\theta}, \mathbf{a})$, $p_i(\mathbf{V}, \boldsymbol{\Sigma}_\xi)$, it could be advantageous to classify the population into groups of people, $k = 1, \ldots, K$, with similar values of $\mathbf{V}$ and $\boldsymbol{\Sigma}_\xi$ and predict $P_i(\boldsymbol{\theta})$ by

$$P_i(\boldsymbol{\theta}) \approx \sum_{k=1}^{K} \frac{m^{(k)}}{M} p_i(\mathbf{V}^{(k)}, \boldsymbol{\Sigma}_\xi^{(k)}), \tag{4.17a}$$

where as before $m^{(k)}$ is the number of individuals in class k.

For the satisfaction, or any other figure of merit depending on $\mathbf{a}$ through $\mathbf{V}$ and $\boldsymbol{\Sigma}_\xi$ only, one has

$$S(\boldsymbol{\theta}) \approx \sum_{k=1}^{K} \frac{m^{(k)}}{M} s(\mathbf{V}^{(k)}, \boldsymbol{\Sigma}_\xi^{(k)}), \tag{4.17b}$$

where $s(\mathbf{V}, \boldsymbol{\Sigma}_\xi)$ is the MNP satisfaction function, relating $\mathbf{V}$ and $\boldsymbol{\Sigma}_\xi$ to the satisfaction. These two equations indeed give the desired results because they can be visualized as approximations for $E_{V,\Sigma_\xi}[p_i(\mathbf{V}, \boldsymbol{\Sigma}_\xi)]$ and $E_{V,\Sigma_\xi}[s(\mathbf{V}, \boldsymbol{\Sigma}_\xi)]$, which are equivalent to $E_A[P_i(\boldsymbol{\theta}, \mathbf{A})]$ and $E_A[S(\boldsymbol{\theta}, \mathbf{A})]$, respectively.[5]

The classification by $\mathbf{V}$ and $\boldsymbol{\Sigma}_\xi$ approach is attractive for models in which $\boldsymbol{\Sigma}_\xi$ is independent of $\mathbf{a}$ since then one only needs to cross classify the population according to $(V_1, \ldots, V_I)$.[6] The method is advantageous in cases where I is small and we have a large number of attributes because then the number of classes might be drastically reduced.

A problem with the above method, however, is that the distribution of $\mathbf{V}$ is not usually known (otherwise there would be no need to estimate $\boldsymbol{\theta}$), and consequently one has to obtain the values of $m^{(k)}$ from the distribution of the attribute vector $F(\mathbf{a})$ and the parameters of the model. This is a time-consuming operation that requires cross classification of the population across attributes, calculation of $\mathbf{V}$ for each one of the classes, assignment of the individuals of each one of the attribute based classes to an attractiveness class, and compilation of the number of individuals in each of the attractiveness classes. Since this process is equally time consuming as compilation of the $m^{(k)}$s for the attribute-based classes the method is not particularly advantageous when a computer is used to evaluate Eqs. (4.14) because the time and effort needed to calculate $m^{(k)}$ in the classification-by-attributes approach is usually the controlling factor.

In hand calculations, however, the method is attractive for MNP models with three or four alternatives and many attributes that vary across the population. In this case calculation of the choice probabilities and the satisfaction is so cumbersome that a reduction in the number of times the MNP function has to be evaluated does result in a reduction of effort.

4.2.3 Discussion

In the preceding part of this chapter, it was implicitly assumed that the distribution of the attribute vector $F(\mathbf{a})$ was exogenously available. Although such may be the case in certain applications, in many others, especially those involving long-term forecasts of socioeconomic data, it is naive to expect to be able to obtain $F(\mathbf{a})$ accurately since, even for the present, the distribution of socioeconomic attributes (such as income and family size) in a zone is

[5] The expectations with respect to $\mathbf{A}$ and $(\mathbf{V}, \boldsymbol{\Sigma}_\xi)$ are the same because p_i and S depend on $\mathbf{A}$ through $\mathbf{V}$ and $\boldsymbol{\Sigma}_\xi$ only.

[6] Actually one only needs to cross classify across the reduced measured attractiveness vector $\mathbf{V}' = (V_2 - V_1, \ldots, V_I - V_1)$ since groups of people having the same values for $\mathbf{V}'$ will also exhibit the same choice probabilities.

rarely available. For socioeconomic attributes, one may have information on their mean and, perhaps, their variance but very rarely anything else. Level-of-service attributes and policy variables tend to be easier to forecast. The distribution of the former can often be determined, as was done in the previous example, from the geography of the zone and the characteristics of the alternatives. Policy variables, of course, are by definition exogenous variables.

In order to avoid problems caused by lack of information on the distribution of a certain attribute, the availability of such information must be considered a prerequisite for the inclusion of attributes in the specification of a model.

Because of these problems and because of the involved calculations required by the general prediction techniques, researchers have developed approximate shortcut prediction techniques that only use the mean $\bar{\mathbf{A}}$ and covariance matrix of the attribute vector $\boldsymbol{\Sigma}_A$. These characteristics are less difficult to forecast than $F(\mathbf{a})$ although estimating some of the off-diagonal terms of $\boldsymbol{\Sigma}_A$ may sometimes be difficult. Techniques and data sources to forecast the moments of the attribute vector across the population vary from discipline to discipline and will not be reviewed in this book.

In addition to forecasting $\bar{\mathbf{A}}$ and $\boldsymbol{\Sigma}_A$, a good forecaster will usually attach a degree of accuracy to these values by figuring out maximum and minimum reasonable values and, perhaps, even giving a subjective distribution of the estimates. Since the values of $\bar{\mathbf{A}}$ and $\boldsymbol{\Sigma}_A$ influence the forecast their subjective distribution can be used to obtain a subjective distribution of the forecasts. This uncertainty regarding the values of $\bar{\mathbf{A}}$ and $\boldsymbol{\Sigma}_A$will be ignored in the rest of this chapter but will be considered in Chapter 5.

4.3 Shortcut Prediction Techniques

We shall assume throughout this section that the specification of the model is linear and that the covariance matrix $\boldsymbol{\Sigma}_\xi$ is independent of the attribute vector. Thus

$$\mathbf{U} = \mathbf{a}[\boldsymbol{\theta}] + \xi, \tag{4.18}$$

where $\mathrm{cov}(\xi) = \boldsymbol{\Sigma}_\xi$ and as before $[\boldsymbol{\theta}]$ is an $s \times I$ matrix of constants. It will be further assumed that the distribution of $\mathbf{A}$ across the group of people under study can be approximated by a MVN distribution with known mean $\bar{\mathbf{A}}$ and covariance matrix $\boldsymbol{\Sigma}_A$. We first explore the case of binary logit and probit models, and then the MNP case. The discussion of the MNP model is expanded to include components of $\mathbf{A}$ that cannot reasonably be approximated by normal distributions, and specifications of $\boldsymbol{\Sigma}_\xi$ that depend on $\mathbf{A}$.

4.3.1 Binary Logit and Probit Models

Following Westin (1974), let us write the equations of the binary logit model as

$$p_1 = (1 + e^{-V})^{-1}, \qquad p_2 = 1 - p_1, \tag{4.19a}$$

and

$$S' = \log(e^{V_1} + e^{V_2}) - V_1 = \log(1 + e^{-V}) \tag{4.19b}$$

where S' is the mean relative satisfaction, and $V = V_1 - V_2$.

Since the attribute vector influences only p_1, p_2, and S' through V, it is possible to express $P_1(\boldsymbol{\theta})$, $P_2(\boldsymbol{\theta})$ and $S'(\boldsymbol{\theta})$ as

$$P_1(\boldsymbol{\theta}) = E_V[(1 + e^{-V})^{-1}], \qquad P_2(\boldsymbol{\theta}) = 1 - P_1(\boldsymbol{\theta}) \tag{4.20a}$$

and

$$S'(\boldsymbol{\theta}) = E_V[\log(1 + e^{-V})]. \tag{4.20b}$$

Furthermore, since $\mathbf{A}$ is MVN distributed with mean $\bar{\mathbf{A}}$ and covariance matrix $\boldsymbol{\Sigma}_A$, $\mathbf{V}$ is MVN distributed with mean $\bar{\mathbf{V}} = \bar{\mathbf{A}}[\boldsymbol{\theta}]$ and covariance matrix $\boldsymbol{\Sigma}_V = [\boldsymbol{\theta}]^{\mathrm{T}}\boldsymbol{\Sigma}_A[\boldsymbol{\theta}]$, and $V = V_1 - V_2$ is also normally distributed with mean and variance given by

$$\bar{V} = \bar{\mathbf{V}}\begin{pmatrix} 1 \\ -1 \end{pmatrix} \qquad \text{and} \qquad \sigma_V^2 = (1, -1)\boldsymbol{\Sigma}_V\begin{pmatrix} 1 \\ -1 \end{pmatrix}.$$

Equations (4.20a) and (4.20b) can be evaluated by a statistical change of variable. This is done by plotting the cumulative distribution functions of

$$p_1(V) = (1 + e^{-V})^{-1} \qquad \text{and} \qquad s'(V) = \log(1 + e^{-V})$$

from that of V, and by calculating their means numerically.

Example Assume that in the example of Section 4.2.1 we want to calculate the fraction of transit users among the non–car owners and their relative satisfaction. Let us further assume that the binary probit model defined by U_1 and U_2 in the example is replaced by a binary logit model with similar choice function. Since for logit models $\boldsymbol{\Sigma}_\xi = \frac{1}{3}\pi^2\mathbf{I}$, and the logistic and normal equations are reasonably close when they have the same mean and variance, the binary logit model approximates well the binary probit model as long as the latter has $\boldsymbol{\Sigma}_\xi = \frac{1}{3}\pi^2\mathbf{I}$. In our case, if we redefine the attractiveness units to be smaller by a factor of $\pi/\sqrt{0.3}$, the probit model can be rewritten as

$$V_1 = 0, \qquad V_2 = 17.2 - 34.4A_{\mathrm{T}} - 34.4R_{\mathrm{T}}, \qquad \boldsymbol{\Sigma}_\xi = \tfrac{1}{3}\pi^2\mathbf{I},$$

as if both U_1 and U_2 had been multiplied by $\pi/\sqrt{0.3}$. This model is approximately equivalent to a binary logit model with the above V_1 and V_2. We will use such a model for the example. For this binary problem, the attribute vector is:

$$\mathbf{A} = (1, A_{\mathrm{T}}, R_{\mathrm{T}}),$$

where R_{T} is fixed at $R_{\mathrm{T}} = 0.33$ and A_{T} is the sum of two independent identically distributed rectangular random variables with range from zero to $L/S_{\mathrm{T}} = 0.25$ hr (see Fig. 4.1). Consequently,

$$E(A_{\mathrm{T}}) = 0.25,$$

$$\mathrm{var}(A_{\mathrm{T}}) = 2\frac{0.25^2}{12} = 0.01,$$

$$\bar{V} = -17.2 + 34.4(0.25) + 34.4(0.33) = 2.75,$$

and

$$\sigma_V^2 = 34.4^2 \times 0.01 = 11.83.$$

If we approximate the distribution of A_{T} by a normal distribution, the cumulative distribution function of V is

$$F_V(x) \approx \Phi\left(\frac{x - 2.75}{3.44}\right).$$

From Eqs. (4.19) we have

$$\Pr\{P_1 \le x\} = \Pr\{(1 + e^{-V})^{-1} \le x\} = \Pr\left\{V \le -\log\left(\frac{1}{x} - 1\right)\right\}$$

$$= \Phi\left(\frac{-2.75 - \log(1/x - 1)}{3.44}\right), \qquad 0 \le x \le 1, \qquad (4.21a)$$

and

$$\Pr\{S' \le x\} = \Pr\{\log(1 + e^{-V}) \le x\} = \Pr\{V \ge -\log(e^x - 1)\}$$

$$= \Phi\left\{\frac{2.75 + \log(e^x - 1)}{3.44}\right\}, \qquad x \le 0. \qquad (4.21b)$$

These equations are plotted in Fig. 4.4, and since both P_1 and S' are nonnegative random variables, their mean is given by the shaded area in the figure:

$$P_1(\boldsymbol{\theta}) = 0.76, \qquad P_2(\boldsymbol{\theta}) = 1 - P_1(\boldsymbol{\theta}) = 0.24$$

$$S'(\boldsymbol{\theta}) = 0.54 \text{ (attractiveness units)} = 0.54 \times 60/34.4 = 0.94 \quad \text{min.}$$ ■

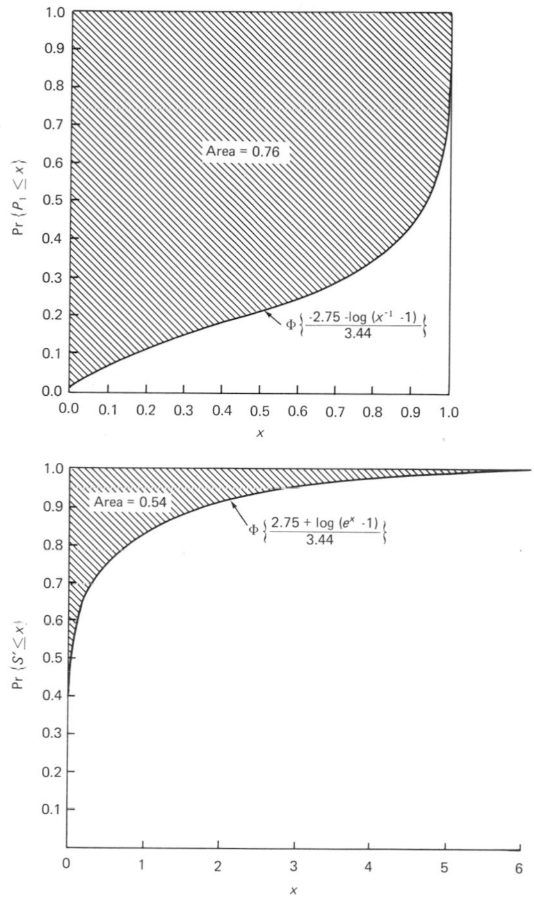

Fig. 4.4 Graphical execution of Westin's binary logit shortcut prediction method.

Equations (4.21) have the general form

$$\Pr\{P_1 \le x\} = \Phi\left[\frac{-\bar{V} - \log(x^{-1} - 1)}{\sigma_V}\right], \qquad 0 \le x \le 1, \qquad (4.22a)$$

$$\Pr\{S' \le x\} = \Phi\left[\frac{\bar{V} + \log(e^x - 1)}{\sigma_V}\right], \qquad x \ge 0. \qquad (4.22b)$$

In any problem all one has to do is calculate $\bar{V}$ and σ_V, plot Eqs. (4.22), and calculate the area above the curves.

The technique is even simpler for the binary probit model (McFadden and Reid, 1975). Let us define

$$V = (V_1 - V_2)/\sigma,$$

where $\sigma^2 = \mathrm{var}(U_1 - U_2) = (1, -1)\mathbf{\Sigma}_\xi\binom{1}{-1}$ (note the difference between the definition of V for logit and probit models). Consider now the choice function and the relative satisfaction of the binary probit model, which, as reference to Eqs. (1.18) and (4.7) shows, is

$$p_1 = \Phi(V), \qquad p_2 = 1 - p_1,$$
$$S' = \sigma[-V\Phi(-V) + \phi(V)].$$

Alternatively, and letting ξ be a standard normal variable, we write p_1 and S' in a form more convenient to be manipulated:

$$p_1(V) = \Pr\{\xi \leq V \mid V\} = \Pr\{\xi - V \leq 0 \mid V\}$$

and

$$s'(V) = \sigma E_\xi[\max(0, \xi - V) \mid V].$$

This last expression can be verified from Eq. (2.24a). The expressions for $P_1(\boldsymbol{\theta})$ and $S'(\boldsymbol{\theta})$ are

$$P_1(\boldsymbol{\theta}) = E_V[\Pr\{\xi - V \leq 0 \mid V\}]$$

and

$$S'(\boldsymbol{\theta}) = \sigma E_V\{E_\xi[\max(0, \xi - V) \mid V]\}.$$

The expression for $P_1(\boldsymbol{\theta})$ reduces to the unconditional probability

$$P_1(\boldsymbol{\theta}) = \int_{x=-\infty}^{\infty} \Pr\{\xi - V \leq 0 \mid V = x\} f_V(x)\, dx = \Pr\{\xi - V \leq 0\},$$

which, since ξ and V are normally distributed, is

$$P_1(\boldsymbol{\theta}) = \Phi[\bar{V}/(1 + \sigma_V^2)^{1/2}], \tag{4.23a}$$

where $\bar{V} = (\bar{V}_1 - \bar{V}_2)/\sigma$ and $\sigma_V^2 = \mathrm{var}(V_1 - V_2)/\sigma^2$. These values are obtained as in the binary logit case.

Since $\xi - V$ is a normal random variable with mean $-\bar{V}$ and variance $1 + \sigma_V^2$, the expression for the relative satisfaction,

$$S'(\boldsymbol{\theta}) = \sigma E[\max(0, \xi - V)],$$

can be simplified by means of Eq. (2.24a) to

$$S'(\boldsymbol{\theta}) = \sigma\left[-\bar{V}\Phi\left(\frac{-\bar{V}}{(1 + \sigma_V^2)^{1/2}}\right) + (1 + \sigma_V^2)^{1/2}\phi\left(\frac{\bar{V}}{(1 + \sigma_V^2)^{1/2}}\right)\right]. \tag{4.23b}$$

If the satisfaction is to be expressed in units of any given attribute, Eq. (4.23b) should be divided by the coefficient of such an attribute in the specification of $\mathbf{V}$.

Example We repeat the calculations of the previous example, only this time the original probit formulation is not altered:

$$V_1 = 0, \qquad V_2 = 3 - 6A_T - 6R_T,$$
$$\mathbf{\Sigma}_\xi = 0.1\mathbf{I}.$$

We find $\sigma^2 = 0.2$ and in the same way as was done for logit:

$$\bar{V} = [-3 + 6(0.25) + 6(0.33)]/\sqrt{0.2} = 1.12$$

and

$$\sigma_{\bar{V}}^2 = 6^2(0.01/0.2) = 1.8.$$

Equations (4.23) yield

$$P_1(\boldsymbol{\theta}) \approx \Phi(0.66) = 0.74, \qquad P_2(\boldsymbol{\theta}) = 1 - P_1(\boldsymbol{\theta}) = 0.26,$$

and

$$S'(\boldsymbol{\theta}) = S(\boldsymbol{\theta}) = 0.12 \text{ (attractiveness units)} = 12 \times \tfrac{60}{6} = 1.2 \quad \text{min.}$$

These values are close to the binary logit values because the two choice functions are similar; they also agree reasonably well with the three-partition results of the previous section (see Table 4.2):

$$P_1(\boldsymbol{\theta}) = (0.34 + 0.87 + 1.00)/3 = 0.74, \qquad P_2(\boldsymbol{\theta}) = 0.26,$$

and

$$S(\boldsymbol{\theta}) = (0.29 + 0.03 + 0.00)/3 = 0.10 \text{ (attractiveness units)} = 1.0 \quad \text{min.}$$

The difference in satisfaction is due to the few classes used in the classification method rather than to the inaccuracies of the shortcut method. The reader can verify that using the ten-subzone partition $S(\boldsymbol{\theta}) = 1.2$. ■

4.3.2 MNP Shortcut Method

We now present a prediction method (Bouthelier and Daganzo, 1979) that can be applied to MNP models in which some of the attributes are not normally distributed and/or do not enter the specification of **V** in a linear form.

Let us partition the attribute vector into two classes $\mathbf{A}'$ and $\mathbf{A}''$, of which $\mathbf{A}''$ is the set of attributes that cannot be reasonably approximated by normal distributions and $\mathbf{A}'$ is the set of attributes that for any given value of $\mathbf{A}''$ can be jointly approximated by a MVN distribution. Without loss of generality we assume that the elements of $\mathbf{A}'$ are the first s' attributes of $\mathbf{A}$ and the elements of $\mathbf{A}''$ the remaining s'' attributes ($s = s' + s''$); thus $\mathbf{A} = (\mathbf{A}', \mathbf{A}'')$.

In the remainder of this discussion it is also assumed that the covariance matrix $\boldsymbol{\Sigma}_\xi$ must be independent of $\mathbf{a}'$ and that the specification of $\mathbf{V}$ is linear in $\mathbf{a}'$ for all values of $\mathbf{a}''$, that is,

$$\mathbf{V} = \mathbf{a}'[\boldsymbol{\theta}(\mathbf{a}'')],$$

where $[\boldsymbol{\theta}(\mathbf{a}'')]$ is a, $s' \times I$ matrix of known functions of $\mathbf{a}''$.

When in a particular problem we partition $\mathbf{A}$, there may be some attributes that are normally distributed but must be included in $\mathbf{A}''$ to ensure that $\boldsymbol{\Sigma}_\xi$ is independent of $\mathbf{a}'$ and/or $\mathbf{V}$ is a linear function of $\mathbf{a}'$. When doing this in practice one must try to include as few attributes as possible in the $\mathbf{A}''$ vector for, as we are about to see, this will simplify matters a great deal.

We write $\bar{\mathbf{A}}'(\mathbf{a}'')$ for the conditional mean of $\mathbf{A}'$ given that $\mathbf{A}'' = \mathbf{a}''$ and $\boldsymbol{\Sigma}_{A'}(\mathbf{a}'')$ for the conditional covariance matrix. Thus, for a fixed value of $\mathbf{A}''$ ($\mathbf{A}'' = \mathbf{a}''$) the attribute vector $\mathbf{A}'$ is MVN distributed:

$$(\mathbf{A}' \mid \mathbf{A}'' = \mathbf{a}'') \sim \text{MVN}[\bar{\mathbf{A}}'(\mathbf{a}''), \boldsymbol{\Sigma}_{A'}(\mathbf{a}'')],$$

and for a person sampled at random from the subgroup of the population having $\mathbf{A}'' = \mathbf{a}''$ the perceived attractiveness vector is also MVN distributed:

$$(\mathbf{U} \mid \mathbf{A}'' = \mathbf{a}'') \sim \text{MVN}(\bar{\mathbf{A}}'(\mathbf{a}'')[\boldsymbol{\theta}(\mathbf{a}'')], [\boldsymbol{\theta}(\mathbf{a}'')]^{\mathrm{T}}\boldsymbol{\Sigma}_{A'}(\mathbf{a}'')[\boldsymbol{\theta}(\mathbf{a}'')] + \boldsymbol{\Sigma}_\xi(\boldsymbol{\theta}, \mathbf{a}'')\}.$$

This last property enables us to calculate $P_i(\boldsymbol{\theta} \mid \mathbf{A}'' = \mathbf{a}'')$ and $S(\boldsymbol{\theta} \mid \mathbf{A}'' = \mathbf{a}'')$ by evaluating the MNP function or satisfaction function with the approximation formulas, or any other method. The expressions are:

$$P_i(\boldsymbol{\theta} \mid \mathbf{A}'' = \mathbf{a}'') = p_i[\bar{\mathbf{U}}(\mathbf{a}''), \boldsymbol{\Sigma}_U(\mathbf{a}'')], \qquad i = 1, 2, \ldots, I, \tag{4.24a}$$

and

$$S(\boldsymbol{\theta} \mid \mathbf{A}'' = \mathbf{a}'') = s[\bar{\mathbf{U}}(\mathbf{a}''), \boldsymbol{\Sigma}_U(\mathbf{a}'')], \tag{4.24b}$$

where we have abbreviated the mean and covariance of $(\mathbf{U} \mid \mathbf{A}'' = \mathbf{a}'')$ by $\bar{\mathbf{U}}(\mathbf{a}'')$ and $\boldsymbol{\Sigma}_U(\mathbf{a}'')$.

If s'' is small it is not difficult to classify the population into a few classes with similar $\mathbf{A}''$ to yield $P_i(\boldsymbol{\theta})$ and $S(\boldsymbol{\theta})$:

$$P_i(\boldsymbol{\theta}) \approx \sum_{k=1}^{K} P_i(\boldsymbol{\theta} \mid \mathbf{A}'' = \mathbf{a}''^{(k)}) \frac{m^{(k)}}{M}, \tag{4.24c}$$

$$S(\boldsymbol{\theta}) \approx \sum_{k=1}^{K} S(\boldsymbol{\theta} \mid \mathbf{A}'' = \mathbf{a}''^{(k)}) \frac{m^{(k)}}{M}. \tag{4.24d}$$

The technique, thus, can be summarized as follows:

(1) Partition $\mathbf{A}$, make sure that $\boldsymbol{\Sigma}_\xi$ does not depend on $\mathbf{a}'$, and write $\mathbf{V}$ as $\mathbf{a}[\boldsymbol{\theta}(\mathbf{a}'')]$.

(2) Partition the population into K classes according to $\mathbf{a}''$ and calculate

$$\bar{\mathbf{U}}(\mathbf{a}'') = \bar{\mathbf{A}}'(\mathbf{a}'')[\boldsymbol{\theta}(\mathbf{a}'')]$$

and

$$\boldsymbol{\Sigma}_U(\mathbf{a}'') = [\boldsymbol{\theta}(\mathbf{a}'')]^{\mathrm{T}}\boldsymbol{\Sigma}_{A'}(\mathbf{a}'')[\boldsymbol{\theta}(\mathbf{a}'')] + \boldsymbol{\Sigma}_{\xi}(\boldsymbol{\theta}, \mathbf{a}'')$$

for the different classes with $\mathbf{a}'' = \mathbf{a}''^{(k)}$.

(3) Calculate $P_i(\boldsymbol{\theta} | \mathbf{A}'' = \mathbf{a}'')$ and $S(\boldsymbol{\theta} | \mathbf{A}'' = \mathbf{a}'')$ for each class with Eqs. (4.24a) and (4.24b), and enter in Eqs. (4.24c) and (4.24d) to obtain $P_i(\boldsymbol{\theta})$ and $S(\boldsymbol{\theta})$.

Example We now calculate $P_1(\boldsymbol{\theta})$, $P_2(\boldsymbol{\theta})$, and $P_3(\boldsymbol{\theta})$ for the example in Section 4.2.1.

Step 1 Since AO is an obviously nonnormal random variable it is included in $\mathbf{A}''$; all other variables are included in $\mathbf{A}'$ and the partition is

$$\mathbf{A}' = (1, A_{\mathrm{T}}, A_{\mathrm{A}}, R_{\mathrm{T}}, R_{\mathrm{A}}),$$
$$\mathbf{A}'' = (AO).$$

With this definition,

$$[\boldsymbol{\theta}(\mathbf{a}'')] = \begin{bmatrix} 0 & 3 & 3.5 + ao \\ 0 & -6 & 0 \\ 0 & 0 & -6 \\ 0 & -6 & 0 \\ 0 & 0 & -6 \end{bmatrix}.$$

Step 2 We need only two classes, one for $AO = 0$ and another for $AO = -1000$.

We now calculate $\bar{\mathbf{A}}'(\mathbf{a}'')$ and $\boldsymbol{\Sigma}_{A'}(\mathbf{a}'')$. Since in this example the populations of non–car owners and car owners are both uniformly distributed, the mean vector and variance–covariance matrix of the normally distributed attributes are independent of AO.

Obviously, A_{T} and A_{A} are not independent since the sum of the distances from each and every household in the zone to the freeway access ramp and the transit station is $2L$ (see Fig. 4.1):

$$S_{\mathrm{T}}A_{\mathrm{T}} + S_{\mathrm{A}}A_{\mathrm{A}} = 2L.$$

The distance d between a random household and a corner of the zone is the sum of two uniformly distributed random variables, resulting in a triangular distribution with mean L and variance $L^2/6$.[7] Then, for the

[7] In cases where the geometry of a zone is not so regular simple manual simulations yield answers readily. Alternatively, one can use graphical methods as suggested by Daganzo (1977a).

numerical values chosen for this example we have

$$A_{\mathrm{T}} = \tfrac{1}{4}d, \qquad E(A_{\mathrm{T}}) = \tfrac{1}{4}, \qquad \mathrm{var}(A_{\mathrm{T}}) = \tfrac{1}{96},$$
$$A_{\mathrm{A}} = \tfrac{1}{40}d, \qquad E(A_{\mathrm{A}}) = \tfrac{1}{40}, \qquad \mathrm{var}(A_{\mathrm{A}}) = \tfrac{1}{9600},$$

and since A_{T} and A_{A} are linearly related,

$$\mathrm{cov}(A_{\mathrm{T}}, A_{\mathrm{A}}) = -\sqrt{\mathrm{var}(A_{\mathrm{T}})\,\mathrm{var}(A_{\mathrm{A}})} = -\tfrac{1}{960}.$$

We can now write

$$\bar{\mathbf{A}}'(\mathbf{a}'') = (1, 0.25, 0.025, 0.33, 0.5)$$

and

$$\boldsymbol{\Sigma}_{A'}(\mathbf{a}'') = \begin{bmatrix} 0 & 0 & 0 & 0 & 0 \\ 0 & \frac{1}{96} & -\frac{1}{960} & 0 & 0 \\ 0 & -\frac{1}{960} & \frac{1}{9600} & 0 & 0 \\ 0 & 0 & 0 & 0 & 0 \\ 0 & 0 & 0 & 0 & 0 \end{bmatrix},$$

which with the known values of $[\boldsymbol{\theta}(\mathbf{a}'')]$ and $\boldsymbol{\Sigma}_{\xi}(\boldsymbol{\theta}, \mathbf{a}'')$ yields

$$\bar{\mathbf{U}}(\mathbf{a}'') = (0, -0.5, 0.35 + ao)$$

and

$$\boldsymbol{\Sigma}_{U}(a'') = \begin{bmatrix} 0.1 & 0 & 0 \\ 0 & 0.48 & -0.04 \\ 0 & -0.04 & 0.104 \end{bmatrix}.$$

Step. 3 As indicated by Eqs. (4.24a) and (4.24b), we now use the approximation method to calculate the market shares and the satisfaction when $AO = 0$ and $AO = -1000$.

If $AO = 0$, then $m/M = 0.7$, and

$$P_1(\boldsymbol{\theta} \,|\, AO = 0) = 0.18, \qquad P_2(\boldsymbol{\theta} \,|\, AO = 0) = 0.13, \qquad P_3(\boldsymbol{\theta} \,|\, AO = 0) = 0.69,$$

and

$$S(\boldsymbol{\theta} \,|\, AO = 0) = 0.44.$$

If $AO = -1000$, then $m/M = 0.3$, and the results coincide with the binary probit example in the previous subsection, namely,

$$P_1(\boldsymbol{\theta} \,|\, AO = -1000) = 0.74, \qquad P_2(\boldsymbol{\theta} \,|\, AO = -1000) = 0.26,$$
$$P_3(\boldsymbol{\theta} \,|\, AO = -1000) = 0.00,$$

and

$$S(\boldsymbol{\theta} \,|\, AO = -1000) = 0.12.$$

Equations (4.24c) and (4.24d) yield

$$P_1(\boldsymbol{\theta}) = 0.35,\ P_2(\boldsymbol{\theta}) = 0.17,\ P_3(\boldsymbol{\theta}) = 0.48$$

and

$$S(\boldsymbol{\theta}) = 0.34 \text{ (attractiveness units)} = 3.4 \quad \text{min.}$$

Note how well the probabilities coincide with those resulting from the 10-partition (20-class) method in Fig. 4.3. This seems to indicate that approximating some nonnormal random variables by normal variables is a reasonable thing to do as long as the variables that are being approximated are reasonably well-behaved (unimodal and smooth). ■

The technique can also be applied to calculate the elasticity of demand, since by Eq. (4.9)

$$\varepsilon_{a_p}^{D_i} = \frac{a_p}{y_i}\frac{\partial y_i(a_p)}{\partial a_p} = ME_A\left[\frac{\partial P_i(\boldsymbol{\theta}, \mathbf{A})}{\partial A_p}\right]\frac{y_i}{a^p}$$

$$= ME_A\left\{\nabla_V p_i(\mathbf{V}, \boldsymbol{\Sigma}_\xi)\left[\frac{\partial(\mathbf{V})}{\partial A_p}\right]^{\mathrm{T}}\right\}\frac{y_i}{a_p},$$

which for linear specifications can be written

$$\varepsilon_{a_p}^{D_i} = M\frac{y_i}{a_p}\ E_V[\nabla_V p_i(\mathbf{V}, \boldsymbol{\Sigma}_\xi)][\boldsymbol{\theta}]_p^{\mathrm{T}},$$

where $[\boldsymbol{\theta}]_p^{\mathrm{T}}$ is a column vector containing the coefficients of A_p in $V(\boldsymbol{\theta}, \mathbf{A})$. $E_V[\nabla_V p_i(\mathbf{V}, \boldsymbol{\Sigma}_\xi)]$ can be calculated with the shortcut method in the same way as $P(\boldsymbol{\theta})$ or $S(\boldsymbol{\theta})$; the only difference is Step 3. Alternatively, one can calculate $P_i(\boldsymbol{\theta})$ again for a different value of a_p ($a_p = a_p + \Delta a_p$) and set

$$\varepsilon_{a_p}^{D_i} \approx \frac{y(a_p + \Delta a_p) - y(a_p)}{\Delta a_p}\frac{a_p}{y_p}.$$

Both methods of calculation require a similar amount of effort.

The derivatives of $S(\boldsymbol{\theta})$ are directly obtained from the usage of each of the alternatives

4.4 Prediction of Equilibrium

It is common in many applications of demand analysis to find that some of the attributes that influence the usage of an alternative depend on the number of individuals that select the alternative. In the transportation field, for instance, as the number of people that use an alternative increases, congestion appears and the attractiveness of the alternative decreases with the level-of-service attributes that are affected by congestion. The example considered in the previous section could exhibit this phenomenon if the travel time on the freeway, say, depended heavily on its use. In that case R_A would increase with y_3 according to a function $R_A(y_3)$, its value would not be known a priori, and the prediction methods explained in the previous section could not be carried out. In other applications involving consumer purchasing behavior the price of an item (alternative) will normally enter with a minus sign in its attractiveness; but if we are studying the demand of such a large group of people that the amount of purchases affect the market price of the items, the prices will not be known a priori and prediction cannot take place. Because of this economic interpretation we will call the variable attributes "prices" and will denote them by π_i. In this section we show how to find a set of prices that are consistent with demand. We will assume that each alternative has at most one price π_i associated with it, that the price enters the specification of the measured attractiveness with a negative coefficient, but that it does not enter $\boldsymbol{\Sigma}_\xi$. The set of alternatives that have prices will be denoted by $\mathscr{I}_\pi$. By selecting the right units of measurement for each price π_i, we can also ensure without loss of generality that its coefficient is -1. Thus, the specification we consider is

$$
\begin{aligned}
U_i &= V_i(\boldsymbol{\theta}, \mathbf{a}) - \pi_i + \xi_i \qquad && \text{if alternative } i \text{ has a price } (i \in \mathscr{I}_\pi), \\
U_i &= V_i(\boldsymbol{\theta}, \mathbf{a}) + \xi_i && \text{if alternative } i \text{ does not have a price } (i \notin \mathscr{I}_\pi), \\
& && \quad \text{i.e., } \pi_i \equiv 0.
\end{aligned}
\tag{4.25}
$$

where $\boldsymbol{\Sigma}_\xi$ is positive definite and independent of $\boldsymbol{\pi}$; note that the measured-attractiveness functions have been redefined, for the purposes of this section only, to exclude the price vector. They are assumed to take finite values for the range of $\mathbf{a}$. Note that since π_i is independent of $\mathbf{a}$ the prices must be the same for the whole population.

Before a prediction can take place, we must find the *equilibrium price vector* $\boldsymbol{\pi}^*$:

$$\pi_i^* = \pi_i(y_i) \qquad \text{if} \quad i \in \mathscr{I}_\pi, \tag{4.26a}$$

$$y_i = y_i(\boldsymbol{\pi}^*) = MP_i(\boldsymbol{\theta}, \boldsymbol{\pi}^*), \tag{4.26b}$$

where $y_i(\boldsymbol{\pi}^*)$ is the demand function, i.e., the function relating usage to the price vector, and $P_i(\boldsymbol{\theta}, \boldsymbol{\pi}^*)$ represents the probability that a user selected at random from the population chooses alternative i when the prices are $\boldsymbol{\pi}^*$. The equilibrium prices generate a demand which results in the original prices and thus "clears the market." Equations (4.26) will henceforth be called the equilibrium equations.

Before stating in the form of a theorem a result that will help us solve Eqs. (4.26), we prove the following preliminary results:

Lemma 4.1 The function relating the satisfaction to the measured attractiveness vector, $s(\mathbf{V})$, of any random utility model is a convex function of $\mathbf{V}$.

Proof Since $s(\mathbf{V}) = E_\xi[\max_i(V_i + \xi_i)]$, we can write

$$s(\mathbf{V}) = \int_{\mathbf{x}} \max_i \{V_i + x_i\} F_\xi(\mathbf{x})\, d\mathbf{x},$$

where $F_\xi(\mathbf{x})$ represents the mass–density function of $\boldsymbol{\xi}$. Since the expression $\max_i\{V_i + x_i\}$ is convex in V_i for any value of x_i, and $F_\xi(\mathbf{x})$ is always nonnegative, $s(\mathbf{V})$ is a convex combination (a linear combination with nonnegative coefficients) of convex functions which is also convex. (See also paragraph 4.2 in Appendix D.) ■

Corollary 4.1 For a heterogeneous group of individuals and under the the conditions stipulated at the onset of this section, the average satisfaction $S(\boldsymbol{\theta}, \boldsymbol{\pi})$ is a convex function of $\boldsymbol{\pi}$.

Proof

$$S(\boldsymbol{\theta}, \boldsymbol{\pi}) = E_{A,\xi}\{\max_i [V_i(\boldsymbol{\theta}, \mathbf{A}) - \pi_i + \xi_i]\}$$

and since $\max[V_i(\boldsymbol{\theta}, \mathbf{A}) - \pi_i + \xi_i]$ is convex in π_i the same argument of the lemma shows that $S(\boldsymbol{\theta}, \boldsymbol{\pi})$ is convex. ■

We now assume that the price functions are monotonically increasing continuous functions of y_i such that $\pi_i(0)$ is finite and equal to $\pi_{i,\min}$ and $\pi_i(\infty) = \infty$. Furthermore, if we denote by $\pi_i^{-1}(\cdot)$ the (also continuous and increasing) inverse price functions (see Fig. 4.5), and we let $\boldsymbol{\pi}_{\min}$ be the vector of minimum values $\pi_{i,\min}$, we can prove the following lemma:

Lemma 4.2 The gradient of the function

$$H(\boldsymbol{\pi}) = MS(\boldsymbol{\theta}, \boldsymbol{\pi}) + \sum_{i \in \mathscr{I}_\pi} \int_{\pi_{i,\min}}^{\pi_i} \pi_i^{-1}(w)\, dw, \qquad \boldsymbol{\pi} > \boldsymbol{\pi}_{\min} \tag{4.27}$$

vanishes at a point $\boldsymbol{\pi} > \boldsymbol{\pi}_{\min}$ where $H(\boldsymbol{\pi})$ reaches a global minimum.

Proof The logic of the proof is as follows. We first establish the existence of values of π_i, $\pi_{i,\max}$ $\forall i \in \mathscr{I}_\pi$, that yield $H(\boldsymbol{\pi}) > H(\boldsymbol{\pi}_{\min})$ for all $\boldsymbol{\pi} \geq \boldsymbol{\pi}_{\min}$ and whenever $\pi_i > \pi_{i,\max}$ for some $i \in \mathscr{I}_\pi$. This enables us to restrict the search for the global optimum to the set $\boldsymbol{\Pi} = \{\boldsymbol{\pi} : \boldsymbol{\pi}_{\min} \leq \boldsymbol{\pi} \leq \boldsymbol{\pi}_{\max}\}$. Next, we show that the minimum of $H(\boldsymbol{\pi})$ in $\boldsymbol{\Pi}$ is reached in the interior of $\boldsymbol{\Pi}$ and that consequently the gradient of $H(\boldsymbol{\pi})$ vanishes there. With this, the proof will be completed. The details follow.

Since $S(\boldsymbol{\theta}, \boldsymbol{\pi})$ is given by $E_A\{\max_i[V_i(\boldsymbol{\theta}, \mathbf{A}) - \pi_i]\}$ and the maximum function is convex, Jensen's inequality [see Feller (1971, Vol. II), for example]

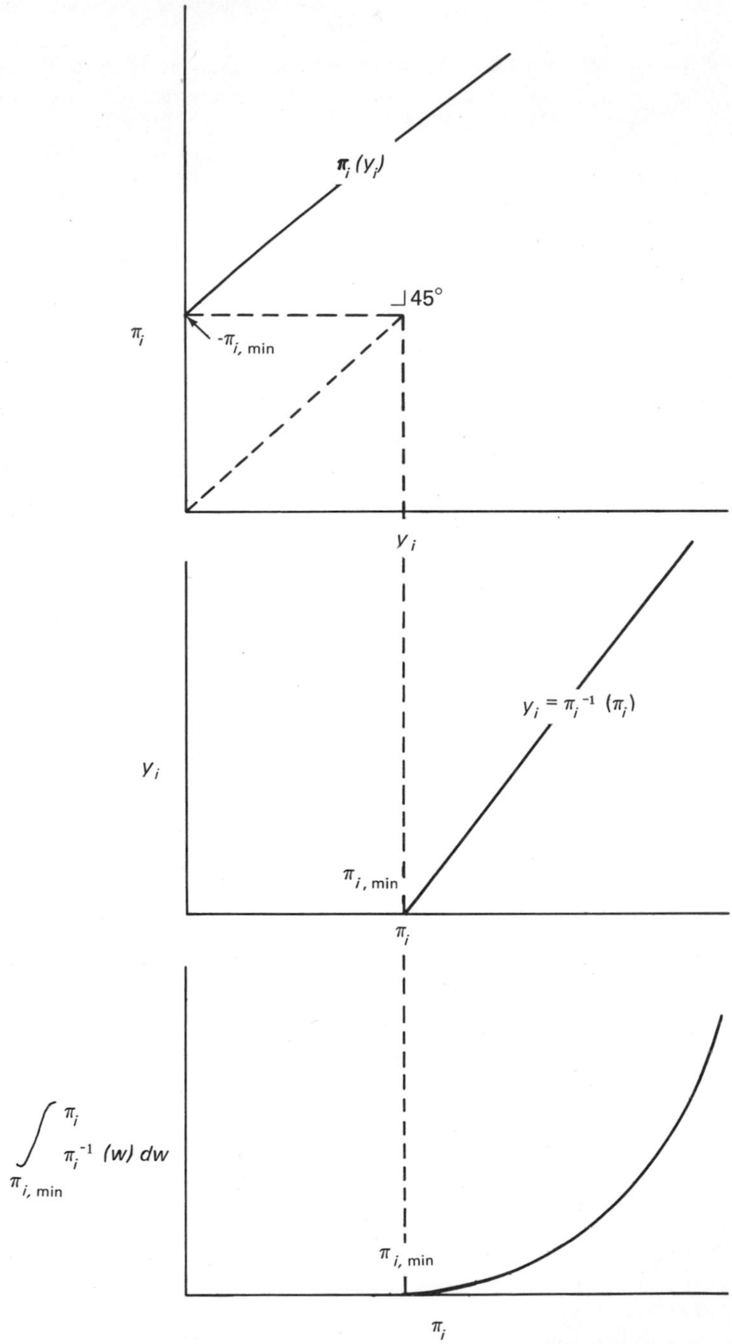

Fig. 4.5 An increasing price function, its inverse, and the integral of the latter.

ensures that

$$S(\boldsymbol{\theta}, \boldsymbol{\pi}) \geq \max_i \{E_A[V_i(\boldsymbol{\theta}, \mathbf{A})] - \pi_i\} = \max_i \{V_i(\boldsymbol{\theta}) - \pi_i\}.$$

Furthermore, since

$$\max_i [V_i(\boldsymbol{\theta}) - \pi_i] \geq \max_i [V_i(\boldsymbol{\theta})] - \max_i (\pi_i),$$

we can write

$$H(\boldsymbol{\pi}) \geq M\left\{\max_i [V_i(\boldsymbol{\theta})] - \max_i (\pi_i)\right\} + M \sum_i \pi_i$$
$$+ \sum_{i \in \mathscr{I}_\pi} \left[\int_{\pi_{i,\min}}^{\pi_i} \pi_i^{-1}(w)\, dw - \pi_i M\right], \qquad \boldsymbol{\pi} \geq \boldsymbol{\pi}_{\min},$$

and since $(\sum_i \pi_i) - \max_i(\pi_i)$, which is the sum of the $I - 1$ smallest π_is, is larger than the sum of the $I - 1$ smallest $\pi_{i,\min}$s, we can write

$$H(\boldsymbol{\pi}) \geq M\left\{\max_i [V_i(\boldsymbol{\theta})] + \left(\sum_i \pi_{i,\min}\right) - \max_i (\pi_{i,\min})\right\}$$
$$+ \sum_{i \in \mathscr{I}_\pi} \left[\int_{\pi_{i,\min}}^{\pi_i} \pi_i^{-1}(w)\, dw - M\pi_i\right], \qquad \boldsymbol{\pi} \geq \boldsymbol{\pi}_{\min}$$

or

$$H(\boldsymbol{\pi}) \geq k + \sum_{i \in \mathscr{I}_\pi} H_i(\pi_i), \qquad \boldsymbol{\pi} \geq \boldsymbol{\pi}_{\min},$$

where k is fixed (not a function of $\boldsymbol{\pi}$) and

$$H_i(\pi_i) = \int_{\pi_{i,\min}}^{\pi_i} \pi_i^{-1}(w)\, dw - \pi_i M, \qquad \pi_i \geq \pi_{i,\min},$$

since the function $H_i(\pi_i)$ has a continuous derivative increasing from $-M$ to ∞, it has a finite absolute minimum $\tilde{H}_i$ at a finite value of π_i. Thus, we can write

$$H(\boldsymbol{\pi}) \geq k + \sum_{i \in \mathscr{I}_\pi} \tilde{H}_i + \sum_{i \in \mathscr{I}_\pi} [H_i(\pi_i) - \tilde{H}_i], \qquad \boldsymbol{\pi} \geq \boldsymbol{\pi}_{\min},$$

or since the quantities in brackets are nonnegative,

$$H(\boldsymbol{\pi}) \geq k + \sum_{i \in \mathscr{I}_\pi} \tilde{H}_i + [H_i(\pi_i) - \tilde{H}_i],$$
$$\text{for any } i \in \mathscr{I}_\pi, \qquad \text{and} \qquad \boldsymbol{\pi} \geq \boldsymbol{\pi}_{\min},$$

where the right-hand side is a lower bound on $H(\boldsymbol{\pi})$ for $\boldsymbol{\pi} \geq \boldsymbol{\pi}_{\min}$, that depends only on π_i.

Since $\lim_{\pi_i \to \infty} H_i(\pi_i) = \infty$, the lower bound can be made as large as desired by increasing π_i, and it is possible to find a value of π_i, $\pi_{i,\max}$, for which the lower bound will exceed $H(\boldsymbol{\pi}_{\min})$.

Therefore, if $\boldsymbol{\pi} \geq \boldsymbol{\pi}_{\min}$ and $\pi_i \geq \pi_{i,\max}$, $H(\boldsymbol{\pi}) > H(\boldsymbol{\pi}_{\min})$.

We can thus restrict our search for the global minimum of $H(\boldsymbol{\pi})$ to the compact set $\boldsymbol{\Pi} = \{\boldsymbol{\pi}:\boldsymbol{\pi}_{\min} \leq \boldsymbol{\pi} \leq \boldsymbol{\pi}_{\max}\}$. Since $H(\boldsymbol{\pi})$ is continuous in $\boldsymbol{\Pi}$ the minimum exists. This completes the first part of the proof.

We now show that the minimum belongs to the interior of $\boldsymbol{\Pi}$ and that consequently $\boldsymbol{\nabla}_{\pi} H(\boldsymbol{\pi}) = \mathbf{0}$ at the minimum.

Taking derivatives in Eq. (4.27) and using Eq. (4.10) we have

$$\frac{\partial H(\boldsymbol{\pi})}{\partial \pi_i} = -y_i(\boldsymbol{\pi}) + \pi_i^{-1}(\pi_i), \qquad i \in \mathscr{I}_{\pi}.$$

Since for MNP and MNL models the choice probability cannot be equal to zero for a finite $\mathbf{V}$ [see the discussion on Condition (c) in Section 3.2.1], $y_i(\boldsymbol{\pi})$ is always positive. Furthermore, since $\pi_i^{-1}(\pi_{i,\min}) = 0$,

$$\frac{\partial H(\boldsymbol{\pi})}{\partial \pi_i} < 0 \qquad \text{if} \quad \pi_i = \pi_{i,\min},$$

and $H(\boldsymbol{\pi})$ can always be decreased if one of the components of $\boldsymbol{\pi}$ equals its minimum value by increasing that component a small amount. Consequently, the minimum of $H(\boldsymbol{\pi})$ is reached at a point strictly larger than $\boldsymbol{\pi}_{\min}$. As a matter of fact, such a point must belong to the interior of $\boldsymbol{\Pi}$ because if one of its components i equaled $\pi_{i,\max}$, $H(\boldsymbol{\pi}) > H(\boldsymbol{\pi}_{\min})$ and the point could not be the minimum. The proof is now complete. ■

We can now prove the following:

Theorem 4.2 Under the conditions of Lemma 4.2, the unique minimum of $H(\boldsymbol{\pi})$ is also the unique equilibrium price vector $\boldsymbol{\pi}^*$.

Proof We first show that $H(\boldsymbol{\pi})$ is strictly convex for $\boldsymbol{\pi} \geq \boldsymbol{\pi}_{\min}$. Since $\pi_i^{-1}(w)$ is increasing,

$$\int_{\pi_{i,\min}}^{\pi_i} \pi_i^{-1}(w)\, dw$$

is a strictly convex function of π_i for $\pi_i \geq \pi_{i,\min}$, and

$$\sum_{i \in \mathscr{I}_{\pi}} \int_{\pi_{i,\min}}^{\pi_i} \pi_i^{-1}(w)\, dw$$

is a strictly convex function of $\boldsymbol{\pi}$ for $\boldsymbol{\pi} \geq \boldsymbol{\pi}_{\min}$. This ensures that $H(\boldsymbol{\pi})$ is strictly convex in the convex set $\tilde{\boldsymbol{\Pi}}$ defined by $\boldsymbol{\pi} \geq \boldsymbol{\pi}_{\min}$ because, as shown in Corollary 4.1, $S(\boldsymbol{\theta}, \boldsymbol{\pi})$ is convex.

The problem

$$\min_{\pi \in \Pi} [H(\pi)]$$

is thus a convex programming problem with a strictly convex objective function which can only have one local–global minimum [see Avriel (1976) for example]. By Lemma 4.2 such a minimum exists and is reached in the interior of $\tilde{\Pi}$. Since such a minimum is unique, it is also the only point of $\tilde{\Pi}$ where the gradient of $H(\pi)$ vanishes.

The proof can, now, be completed because the equilibrium equations

$$y_i(\pi^*) = \pi_i^{-1}(\pi_i^*), \qquad i \in \mathscr{I}_\pi,$$

can be rewritten as $\nabla_\pi H(\pi^*) = \mathbf{0}$ [note that $\partial H(\pi)/\partial \pi_i = -y_i(\pi) + \pi_i^{-1}(\pi_i)$], and since $\nabla_\pi H(\pi)$ vanishes exactly once in $\tilde{\Pi}$, π^* is unique and coincides with the unique minimum of $H(\pi)$. ■

The minimum of Eq. (4.27) can be easily found by mathematical programming techniques. The variable metric algorithm described in Section 2.4.1 is particularly useful because $\nabla_\pi H(\pi)$ is readily available,

$$\frac{\partial H(\pi)}{\partial \pi_i} = \pi_i^{-1}(\pi) - y_i(\pi)$$

(it requires calculation of the usage for the given π), and $H(\pi)$ only needs calculation of $S(\theta, \pi)$. The Newton–Raphson method can also be used if the derivatives of $y_i(\pi)$ are easily calculated. For most problems these methods converge after four or five iterations.

Assuming that $S(\theta, \pi)$ has to be calculated five or six times at each iteration and letting one effort unit equal the work needed to do a prediction of the choice probability vector, $\mathbf{P}(\theta, \pi)$, the total work involves about 25 calculations of S and five calculations of $\mathbf{P}$, or $5 + 25/I$ effort units. Thus, calculating the equilibrium prices is approximately 10 times more time consuming than predicting when the prices are known. Although this may seem difficult when done by hand, it is a trivial calculation when done by computer with the shortcut prediction method.

The following is a simplified version of the example in the previous section.

Example Assume that all the people of the zone in Fig. 4.1 own automobiles, $AO \equiv 0$, and that the travel time on the freeway increases with the number of users from the zone that travels to downtown, y_3, according to

$$R_A = 0.5 + y_3/6000 \quad \text{hr}.$$

Similarly, the transit travel time follows a similar relationship with the transit usage y_2:

$$R_T = 0.333 + y_2/12000 \quad \text{hr.}$$

We first rewrite the specification of the model as in Eq. (4.25):

$$\begin{aligned} U_1 &= \xi_1, \\ U_2 &= 3 - 6A_T - \pi_2 + \xi_2, \\ U_3 &= 3.5 - 6A_A - \pi_3 + \xi_3, \end{aligned}$$

with $\mathbf{\Sigma}_\xi = 0.1\mathbf{I}$. Of course $\pi_2 = 6R_T$ and $\pi_3 = 6R_A$, which yield the price functions

$$\pi_2 = 2 + y_2/2000$$

and

$$\pi_3 = 3 + y_3/1000.$$

These correspond to the integrals

$$\int_{\pi_{2,\min}}^{\pi_2} \pi_2^{-1}(w)\,dw = \int_2^{\pi_2} (w - 2)2000\,dw = 1000(\pi_2 - 2)^2,$$
$$\int_{\pi_{3,\min}}^{\pi_3} \pi_3^{-1}(w)\,dw = \int_3^{\pi_3} (w - 3)1000\,dw = 500(\pi_3 - 3)^2.$$

The shortcut aggregation procedure yields for a random choice maker (see step 2 of the example in Section 4.3.2)

$$\bar{\mathbf{U}} = (0, 1.5 - \pi_2, 3.35 - \pi_3)$$

and

$$\mathbf{\Sigma}_U = \begin{bmatrix} 0.1 & 0 & 0 \\ 0 & 0.48 & -0.04 \\ 0 & -0.04 & 0.104 \end{bmatrix}.$$

$S(\boldsymbol{\theta}, \boldsymbol{\pi})$ is obtained by finding the mean of the maximum of the three components of a vector-valued random variable $\mathbf{U}$ having the above mean vector and covariance matrix. With this, the preliminary calculations have been completed, and we may start the search process. The variable metric algorithm described in Section 2.4.1 will be used.

We start the search process at $\boldsymbol{\pi} = (2, 3) = \boldsymbol{\pi}_{\min}$ by calculating the derivatives and value of $H(\boldsymbol{\pi})$ at $\boldsymbol{\pi} = (2, 3)$.

Since $\bar{\mathbf{U}} = (0, -0.5, 0.35)$ coincides with the value for the car owners of the example in Section 4.3.2, no new calculations have to be performed.

The results are

$$MS(\boldsymbol{\theta}, \boldsymbol{\pi}_{\min}) = 10{,}000 \times 0.44 = 4400,$$

$$y_1 = 10{,}000 \times 0.18 = 1800, \qquad y_2 = 10{,}000 \times 0.13 = 1300,$$

and

$$y_3 = 10{,}000 \times 0.69 = 6900.$$

This yields

$$H(\boldsymbol{\pi}_{\min}) = 4400 + 0 + 0 = 4400,$$

$$\left.\frac{\partial H(\boldsymbol{\pi})}{\partial \pi_2}\right|_{\pi_2 = 2} = -y_2 + \pi_2^{-1}(2) = -1300,$$

$$\left.\frac{\partial H(\boldsymbol{\pi})}{\partial \pi_3}\right|_{\pi_3 = 3} = -y_3 + \pi_3^{-1}(3) = -6900.$$

Since the function is to be minimized, the direction of search is given by $-\nabla H(\boldsymbol{\pi}) = (1300, 6900)$. As required by the variable metric algorithm, the approximate inverse Hessian of $H(\boldsymbol{\pi})$ is initially set equal to an arbitrary positive definite matrix $\mathbf{H}_o$, which we chose to be the identity matrix $\mathbf{I}$. We then find the point along the search direction that maximizes $H(\boldsymbol{\pi})$, i.e., find the scalar η^* that maximizes $H[\boldsymbol{\pi}(\eta)]$, where $\boldsymbol{\pi}(\eta) = (2, 3) + \eta(1300, 6900)$.

Since for $\eta = 0$, $H = 4400$; for $\eta = 10^{-4}$, $H = 1518$; and for $\eta = 3 \times 10^{-4}$, $H = 2688$, we know that

$$0 \le \eta^* \le 3 \times 10^{-4}.$$

After some iterations of the golden section method, which can easily be carried out on a programmable pocket calculator if $H(\boldsymbol{\pi})$ is programmed into it, we find that

$$\eta^* = 1.42 \times 10^{-4} \qquad \text{and} \qquad H[\boldsymbol{\pi}(\eta^*)] = 1323.2.$$

Thus the result at the end of the first iteration is $\pi_1 = (2.18, 3.98)$. The gradient at this point can be calculated numerically; it is

$$\left.\nabla_\pi H(\boldsymbol{\pi})\right|_{\boldsymbol{\pi} = (2,3,42)} = (-1340, 267).$$

The revised inverse Hessian is given by the DFP updating formula [Eq. (2.32b)] which yields

$$\mathbf{H}_1 = \begin{bmatrix} 1 & 0.0056 \\ 0.0056 & 0.000168 \end{bmatrix},$$

and the new search direction is

$$-\nabla H(\boldsymbol{\pi})\begin{bmatrix} 1 & 0.0056 \\ 0.0056 & 0.000168 \end{bmatrix} = (1340, 8).$$

The process is repeated a few more times by finding new values of η^*, $\boldsymbol{\pi}$, and a search direction before convergence is achieved. The convergence pattern is displayed in Fig. 4.6. The optimum is $H^* = 1144$ and the equilibrium prices are $\pi_2^* \simeq 2.45$ and $\pi_3^* \simeq 3.93$.

The approximate value of $\nabla^2 H(\boldsymbol{\pi}^*)$ is

$$\begin{bmatrix} 4000 & -90 \\ -90 & 3600 \end{bmatrix}.$$

The usage of the three alternatives at equilibrium is

$$y^* = (8170, 900, 930)$$

and the satisfaction at equilibrium is $S^*(\boldsymbol{\theta}) = 0.0509$ attractiveness units (or 0.5 min/individual). The great reduction in travel and satisfaction is due to the choice makers' aversion to congestion in this particular model (as was

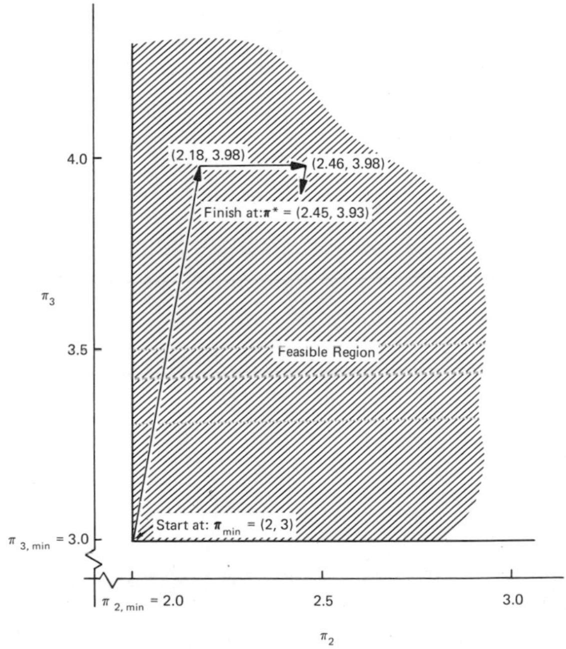

Fig. 4.6 Convergence pattern of the search for an equilibrium price vector.

mentioned earlier, the example is not realistic but was chosen because it illustrates the mechanics of prediction rather well).

The elasticity of y_2 and y_3 with respect to the equilibrium prices can be obtained from $\nabla^2 H(\boldsymbol{\pi}^*)$ since

$$\frac{\partial^2 H(\boldsymbol{\pi}^*)}{\partial \pi_i \, \partial \pi_j} = -\frac{\partial y_i}{\partial \pi_j^*} + \delta_{ij}\pi_i^{-1}(\pi_i^*), \qquad i, j \in \mathscr{I}_\pi,$$

where δ_{ij} is Kronecker's delta ($\delta_{ij} = 1$ if $i = j$, and 0 otherwise). Thus

$$\varepsilon_{\pi_j^*}^{D_i} = \left[-\frac{\partial^2 H(\pi^*)}{\partial \pi_i \, \partial \pi_j} + \delta_{ij} y_i^* \right] \frac{\pi_j^*}{y_i^*}.$$

For our example we might be interested in encouraging transit usage y_2; the corresponding elasticities are -8.4 with respect to the travel time by transit and 0.4 with respect to freeway travel time. ■

4.5 Calibration Revisited

The shortcut prediction method can also be used advantageously for two important calibration problems, which are discussed below.

4.5.1 Calibration with Grouped Data

If, as often is the case, instead of disaggregate data, one has data on groups of individuals, including

(1) the number of people in a group, n_j,
(2) the number of people selecting each alternative, n_{ij}, and
(3) the distribution of the attribute vector across the group, $F_j(\mathbf{a})$,

the maximum likelihood process described in Chapter 2 cannot be applied because we do not know which individuals of the group selected what alternatives. Thus, the maximum-likelihood equation must be modified to use the available information. The discussion that follows is based on Bouthelier and Daganzo (1979).

We can visualize n_{ij} as an outcome of a random variable N_{ij}, which is determined by randomly selecting a group of n_j people from a population of individuals with distribution of the attribute vector $F_j(\mathbf{a})$, and observing the number that choose alternative i. The likelihood equation is then

$$L(\boldsymbol{\theta}) = \Pr[N_{ij} = n_{ij}, \forall i, j \,|\, \boldsymbol{\theta}].$$

Assuming that individuals act independently, and that n_j is small compared with the population size, we see that for a given group j, N_{ij} is a multinomial random variable and

$$L(\boldsymbol{\theta}) = \prod_{j=1}^{J} \left\{ \frac{n_j!}{\prod_{i=1}^{I} n_{ij}!} \prod_{i=1}^{I} [P_{ij}(\boldsymbol{\theta})]^{n_{ij}} \right\}, \tag{4.28}$$

where $P_{ij}(\boldsymbol{\theta})$ represents the probability that an individual sampled at random from a group with attribute vector distribution $F_j(\mathbf{a})$ chooses alternative i, and J is the number of groups.

The log-likelihood function (except for an additive constant) is

$$\log L(\boldsymbol{\theta}) = \sum_{j=1}^{J} \sum_{i=1}^{I} n_{ij} \log P_{ij}(\boldsymbol{\theta}). \tag{4.29}$$

The shortcut method can be used to evaluate $P_{ij}(\boldsymbol{\theta})$:

$$P_{ij}(\boldsymbol{\theta}) = \sum_{k=1}^{K} P_{ij}(\boldsymbol{\theta} \,|\, \mathbf{A}'' = \mathbf{a}''^{(k)}) \frac{m_j^{(k)}}{n_j},$$

where $m_j^{(k)}$ is the number of individuals in class k of group j and for notational simplicity we have assumed that the same nonnormal attribute vector and the same classes are used for all the groups. In this last expression $P_{ij}(\boldsymbol{\theta} \,|\, \mathbf{A}'' = \mathbf{a}''^{(k)})$ is a MNP function that can be calculated as explained in Chapter 2. The log-likelihood equation is

$$\log L(\boldsymbol{\theta}) = \sum_{i=1}^{I} \sum_{j=1}^{J} n_{ij} \log\left[\sum_{k=1}^{K} P_{ij}(\boldsymbol{\theta} \,|\, \mathbf{A}'' = \mathbf{a}''^{(k)}) m_j^{(k)}/n_j \right], \tag{4.30}$$

which requires $I \times J \times K$ evaluations of a MNP function. The computational requirements are given by the expression of Section 2.4.2 with N replaced by $I \times J \times K$.

If all the variables can be considered normal, Eq. (4.30) simplifies because $P_{ij}(\boldsymbol{\theta})$ is a MNP choice function, and one can set $K = 1$ and $m_j^{(k)} = n_j$. The measured-attractiveness vector and covariance matrix are given by

$$\bar{\mathbf{U}}(\boldsymbol{\theta}, j) = \bar{\mathbf{A}}_j \lceil\ \boldsymbol{\theta} \rceil \tag{4.31a}$$

and

$$\boldsymbol{\Sigma}_U(\boldsymbol{\theta}, j) = \boldsymbol{\Sigma}_\xi(\boldsymbol{\theta}) + [\boldsymbol{\theta}]^{\mathrm{T}} \boldsymbol{\Sigma}_{A_j} [\boldsymbol{\theta}], \tag{4.31b}$$

where $\bar{\mathbf{A}}_j$ and $\boldsymbol{\Sigma}_{A_j}$ characterize the distribution of $\mathbf{A}$ in group j.

Since $P_{ij}(\boldsymbol{\theta})$ is a MNP function, Eq. (4.30) has the form of the pseudo-log-likelihood function of a choice-based sample [Eq. (2.7b)], which can be calibrated with a standard code and the specification in Eqs. (4.31).

As an example of estimation, we use the example introduced in Section 4.2.1. We have only one zone, one nonnormal variable, and three alternatives.

Let us assume that the specification of the model is

$$U_1 = \xi_1,$$
$$U_2 = 3 - \theta A_T - \theta R_T + \xi_2,$$
$$U_3 = 3.5 - \theta A_A - \theta R_A + AO + \xi_3.$$

We use only one unknown parameter, so the computations can easily be verified by hand.

The data consist of 3487 no trips, 1672 transit trips, and 4841 auto trips. Since these data coincide with the predictions in Section 4.3.2, the maximum-likelihood estimate $\hat{\theta}$ should be equal to six.

The calculations proceed as follows. Equations (4.31) yield

$$\bar{\mathbf{V}}(\theta, 1) = (0, 3 - 0.583\theta, 3.5 - 0.525\theta)$$

and

$$\boldsymbol{\Sigma}_U(\theta, 1) = \frac{1}{9600}\begin{bmatrix} 960 & 0 & 0 \\ 0 & 960 + 100\theta^2 & -10\theta^2 \\ 0 & -10\theta^2 & 960 + \theta^2 \end{bmatrix}.$$

This enables us to calculate $P_{i1}(\theta | AO)$ for $i = 1$, 2, and 3, for $AO = 0$ and -1000, and for different values of θ. Since $m_1^{(1)}/n_1 = 0.7$ and $m_1^{(2)}/n_1 = 0.3$, Eq. (4.30) yields

$$\begin{aligned}\log L(\theta) = {} & 3487 \log[0.7 P_{11}(\theta | AO = 0) + 0.3 P_{11}(\theta | AO = -1000)] \\ & + 1672 \log[0.7 P_{21}(\theta | AO = 0) + 0.3 P_{21}(\theta | AO = -1000)] \\ & + 4841 \log[0.7 P_{31}(\theta | AO = 0) + 0.3 P_{31}(\theta | AO = -1000)].\end{aligned}$$

As expected, $\log L(\theta)$ is maximized for $\hat{\theta} = 6$, and

$$\log L(\hat{\theta}) = -8278.07.$$

The reader can check that for $\theta = 5$, $\log L(\theta) = -10868.97$, for $\theta = 7$, $\log L(\theta) = -9728.41$, and that indeed $\hat{\theta} = 6$.

The statistical analysis of Chapter 3 can also be applied here since under similar regularity conditions it can be shown that the estimator $\hat{\boldsymbol{\Theta}}$ is asymptotically efficient and normal, and that properties (1)–(5) in Section 3.2.1 apply. It must be remembered however that because the variability of $\bar{\mathbf{A}}_j$ and $\boldsymbol{\Sigma}_{A_j}$ across the data is usually much smaller in Eqs. (4.31) than the variability of $\mathbf{A}$ with disaggregate data, it may be a problem to ensure that $\boldsymbol{\theta}$ is estimable and/or that the sample size (i.e., number of groups) for which the asymptotic approximations become valid is large enough. As a matter of fact, unless the variability of $\bar{\mathbf{A}}_j$ and $\boldsymbol{\Sigma}_{A_j}$ is large, the role of calibrating disaggregate models with aggregate data must be restricted to complementing the information extracted from disaggregate data sources; this can be done with the model-updating technique of Section 3.3. For this application estimability problems disappear since the combined estimator is no worse than the original one.

4.5.2 Calibration with Choice-Based Samples

The likelihood equation of a choice-based sample for a MNP model requires that $P_i(\boldsymbol{\theta})$ be calculated once for each alternative [see Eq. (2.7c)] in addition to the calculation of exactly N choice functions. If the number of classes K into which the population must be partitioned for prediction is small (as happens with the binary logit model and all MNP models with specifications that are linear in the parameters when the shortcut method is used), the computational effort that goes into calculating the second terms of Eq. (2.7c) is negligible, and as long as the distribution of $\mathbf{A}$ is known calibration by maximum likelihood of a model with a choice-based sample is just as fast as for a random sample.

4.6 Summary

The mechanical aspects of predicting with disaggregate demand models are explored in this chapter; the main issue is how to translate a figure of merit characterizing homogeneous groups of individuals into an aggregate figure of merit for heterogeneous groups. In Section 4.1 two common figures of merit and their elasticities are discussed; the first one is the choice probability function and the second one a measure of the benefits that accrue to the population from the existence of the choice set (Williams, 1977, Sheffi and Daganzo, 1978a, Ben-Akiva and Lerman, 1978); this measure is called the satisfaction. The discussion in that section centers about ways of calculating these figures of merit and their elasticities; and, in the case of the satisfaction, also about ensuring that it is uniquely defined.

General prediction techniques are explored in Section 4.2. The reader can find additional general discussions regarding the mechanics prediction in Koppelman (1974), which gives one of the first presentations of the problem, Koppelman (1976a), which contains a taxonomy of the available prediction methods at the time, and Reid (1978). The classification by $\mathbf{V}$ and $\boldsymbol{\Sigma}_\xi$ is discussed for the logit model by Reid (1978).

Section 4.3 discusses shortcut prediction techniques and is based on the work of Westin (1974), McFadden and Reid (1975), and Bouthelier and Daganzo (1979). The techniques discussed are based on the linearity of the measured-attractiveness functions on the attributes, and on a MVN approximation to the distribution of $\mathbf{A}$. Of historical interest mainly is a forerunner of these methods (Talvitie, 1973) which was based on the linearization of the choice function itself.

The next two sections are extensions of the prediction techniques to the computation of economic equilibrium (Section 4.4) and to some calibration problems (Section 4.5).

Section 4.4 considers exclusively equilibrium problems in which the price of an alternative depends only on the usage of the corresponding alternative. Although this paradigm suffices for many economics applications, there may be cases where the price of an alternative depends on the usage of several alternatives. This happens in transportation network studies where one often has a system of streets connecting the points of a study zone and the usage of the major street network (the traffic flows) can be visualized as the aggregation of the decisions of the people in the study area regarding whether or not to travel and what route to take. The alternatives of this problem are the routes, and the prices the travel time on each route. However, when routes overlap, the price of a route is affected by the usages of all the routes that overlap with it and Theorem 4.2 does not apply. In such a case it may be possible to use standard fixed-point algorithms, as Hasan and Talvitie (1977) and McFadden *et al.* (1977) did with Scarf's algorithm (Scarf, 1973), but problems still persist because the number of routes in a study zone is usually so large that the algorithms are not capable of handling them. An approach that shows a good deal of promise because it can handle the large problems that arise in the transportation field has been investigated by Sheffi (1978a); it is based on a traffic assignment algorithm developed by Daganzo (1977a,b).

Section 4.5 discusses ways to calibrate MNP models by the maximum-likelihood method when one has observations for groups of individuals (this part is based on the paper by Bouthelier and Daganzo, 1979) and when one has a choice-based data set.

Chapter 5 The Statistical Interpretation of Predictions

In most demand-forecasting applications, the parameter estimate, output of the calibration process, is entered in the choice and satisfaction functions to investigate how these figures of merit vary across both homogeneous and heterogeneous groups of individuals. However, if the parameter estimate $\hat{\boldsymbol{\theta}}$ is not close to the true parameter value, $\boldsymbol{\theta}_o$, the calculated figures of merit will not be close to their true values and the result of such analyses will not be meaningful. The question we investigate in this chapter is how inaccuracies in the estimation of $\boldsymbol{\theta}_o$ affect the values of the forecasted figures of merit for both homogeneous and heterogeneous groups of people. To do this we shall use some of the results of Chapter 3 since they give an idea of the likely magnitude of the difference between $\hat{\boldsymbol{\theta}}$ and $\boldsymbol{\theta}_o$.

Since within a random utility framework most of the relevant information concerning a choice situation and any one given individual is contained in the vector of perceived attractiveness, relevant figures of merit for individuals can usually be represented as functions of the perceived attractiveness vector $\tau(\mathbf{U})$. This will be the only kind of figure of merit considered in this chapter. Throughout this chapter, we shall also distinguish between the average value of a figure of merit across a very large homogeneous group of individuals (in agreement with the terminology introduced in Chapter 4, we will call this average a *figure of merit*) and the actual value of the figure of merit for a given individual, which we shall call an *individual figure of merit*. Note that, depending on the type of function selected, the value of an individual figure of merit may or may not be observable; for instance, the chosen alternative is an observable figure of merit but the actual satisfaction of an individual, $\tau(\mathbf{U}) = \max\{U_i\}$, is not.

A figure of merit corresponding to an individual figure of merit can always be expressed as a function of $\boldsymbol{\theta}$ and $\mathbf{a}$, $T(\boldsymbol{\theta}, \mathbf{a})$, since the distribution of $\mathbf{U}$ across the members of a homogeneous population group depends on $\boldsymbol{\theta}$ and $\mathbf{a}$. Consequently, figures of merit can always be predicted, whether or not the corresponding individual figure of merit is observable. In mathematical terms, the relationship between $\tau(\mathbf{U})$ and $T(\boldsymbol{\theta}, \mathbf{a})$ is

$$T(\boldsymbol{\theta}, \mathbf{a}) = E_U[\tau(\mathbf{U}) | \boldsymbol{\theta}, \mathbf{a}].$$

For example, if the individual figure of merit is $\max_i(U_i)$, the corresponding figure of merit is $S(\boldsymbol{\theta}, \mathbf{a})$ (this was the definition of the satisfaction function introduced in Chapter 4), and if the individual figure of merit is

$$\tau(\mathbf{U}) = \begin{cases} 1 & \text{if} \quad U_i > U_j \quad \forall j \neq i, \\ 0 & \text{otherwise,} \end{cases}$$

it is not difficult to show that the figure of merit is $P_i(\boldsymbol{\theta}, \mathbf{a})$.

Sections 5.1 and 5.2 in this chapter discuss the accuracy of predicting figures of merit when the true value of $\boldsymbol{\theta}$ is uncertain, and Section 5.3 extends the results to small groups of individuals. Section 5.4 briefly explores how to ascertain adequate sample size for the calibration process and how to translate the uncertainty in the forecasted distribution of the attribute vector into uncertainty of the predictions.

5.1 Confidence Intervals on the Mean: Binary Models

Since the parameter estimate $\hat{\boldsymbol{\theta}}$ can be regarded as an outcome of a random variable $\hat{\boldsymbol{\Theta}}$ that takes different values each time the sampling–calibration process is repeated, one can regard a figure of merit $T(\hat{\boldsymbol{\Theta}}, \mathbf{a})$, and its mean $T(\hat{\boldsymbol{\Theta}})$ across a heterogeneous group of individuals as random variables that take different values each time the sampling–calibration process is repeated. As discussed in Chapter 3, since for sufficiently large samples, $\hat{\boldsymbol{\Theta}}$ is MVN distributed with mean $\boldsymbol{\theta}_o$ (the true parameter value) and a covariance matrix $\boldsymbol{\Sigma}_\theta$ that is approximately given by $-[\nabla_\theta^2 \log L(\hat{\boldsymbol{\theta}})]^{-1}$, one can obtain the distribution of $T(\hat{\boldsymbol{\Theta}}, \mathbf{a})$ and $T(\hat{\boldsymbol{\Theta}})$ with statistical change of variable techniques. From that, confidence intervals for $T(\boldsymbol{\theta}_o, \mathbf{a})$ and $T(\boldsymbol{\theta}_o)$ can be developed.

5.1.1 Exact Results for Homogeneous Populations

Let us consider binary probit models whose choice functions can be expressed as

$$p_1 = \Phi(\boldsymbol{\theta}\mathbf{a}^{\mathrm{T}}), \tag{5.1a}$$

$$p_2 = \Phi(-\boldsymbol{\theta}\mathbf{a}^{\mathrm{T}}), \tag{5.1b}$$

that is, models in which the probit of the choice probabilities $\Phi^{-1}(p_i)$ are linear functions of $\boldsymbol{\theta}$. For notational simplicity let us represent throughout this section $\Phi(\hat{\boldsymbol{\Theta}}\mathbf{a}^{\mathrm{T}})$ by $\hat{P}_1$ and $\Phi(\boldsymbol{\theta}_o\mathbf{a}^{\mathrm{T}})$ by p_1.

Our objective is to develop a confidence interval for p_1. We start by finding a function of p_1 and the data ($\hat{\boldsymbol{\Theta}}$ and $\mathbf{a}$) whose distribution is known. Such a function, called a *pivotal quantity*, will enable us to obtain confidence intervals.

Since $\hat{\boldsymbol{\Theta}}$ is MVN distributed with mean $\boldsymbol{\theta}_o$ and covariance matrix $\boldsymbol{\Sigma}_\theta$, $\hat{\boldsymbol{\Theta}}\mathbf{a}^{\mathrm{T}}$ is normal with mean $\hat{\boldsymbol{\theta}}_o\mathbf{a}^{\mathrm{T}}$ and variance $\mathbf{a}\boldsymbol{\Sigma}_\theta\mathbf{a}^{\mathrm{T}}$. Furthermore, since $\boldsymbol{\theta}_0\mathbf{a}^{\mathrm{T}} = \Phi^{-1}(p_1)$, the random variable

$$[\hat{\boldsymbol{\theta}}\mathbf{a}^{\mathrm{T}} - \Phi^{-1}(p_1)]/(\mathbf{a}\boldsymbol{\Sigma}_\theta\mathbf{a}^{\mathrm{T}})^{1/2}$$

is a standard normal pivotal quantity for p_1. Letting η_β denote the 100β percentile of the standard normal distribution, we can write

$$\Pr\left\{-\eta_{(1+\alpha)/2} \leq \frac{\hat{\boldsymbol{\Theta}}\mathbf{a}^{\mathrm{T}} - \Phi^{-1}(p_1)}{(\mathbf{a}\boldsymbol{\Sigma}_\theta\mathbf{a}^{\mathrm{T}})^{1/2}} \leq \eta_{(1+\alpha)/2}\right\} = \alpha,$$

which can be rewritten as

$$\Pr\{-\hat{\boldsymbol{\Theta}}\mathbf{a}^{\mathrm{T}} - \eta_{(1+\alpha)/2}(\mathbf{a}\boldsymbol{\Sigma}_\theta\mathbf{a}^{\mathrm{T}})^{1/2} \leq -\Phi^{-1}(p_1) \leq -\hat{\boldsymbol{\Theta}}\mathbf{a}^{\mathrm{T}} + \eta_{(1+\alpha)/2}(\mathbf{a}\boldsymbol{\Sigma}_\theta\mathbf{a}^{\mathrm{T}})^{1/2}\} = \alpha$$

or

$$\Pr\{\hat{\boldsymbol{\Theta}}\mathbf{a}^{\mathrm{T}} - \eta_{(1+\alpha)/2}(\mathbf{a}\boldsymbol{\Sigma}_\theta\mathbf{a}^{\mathrm{T}})^{1/2} \leq \Phi^{-1}(p_1) \leq \hat{\boldsymbol{\Theta}}\mathbf{a}^{\mathrm{T}} + \eta_{(1+\alpha)/2}(\mathbf{a}\boldsymbol{\Sigma}_\theta\mathbf{y}^{\mathrm{T}})^{1/2}\} = \alpha.$$

But since $\Phi(\cdot)$ is a strictly increasing function, the above probabilistic statement can be modified to read

$$\Pr\{\Phi[\hat{\boldsymbol{\Theta}}\mathbf{a}^{\mathrm{T}} - \eta_{(1+\alpha)/2}(\mathbf{a}\boldsymbol{\Sigma}_\theta\mathbf{a}^{\mathrm{T}})^{1/2}] \leq p_1 \leq \Phi[\hat{\boldsymbol{\Theta}}\mathbf{a}^{\mathrm{T}} + \eta_{(1+\alpha)/2}(\mathbf{a}\boldsymbol{\Sigma}_\theta\mathbf{a}^{\mathrm{T}})^{1/2}]\} = \alpha.$$

A $100\alpha\%$ confidence interval for p_1 is thus

$$\{\Phi[\hat{\boldsymbol{\theta}}\mathbf{a}^{\mathrm{T}} - \eta_{(1+\alpha)/2}(\mathbf{a}\boldsymbol{\Sigma}_\theta\mathbf{a}^{\mathrm{T}})^{1/2}], \Phi[\hat{\boldsymbol{\theta}}\mathbf{a}^{\mathrm{T}} + \eta_{(1+\alpha)/2}(\mathbf{a}\boldsymbol{\Sigma}_\theta\mathbf{a}^{\mathrm{T}})^{1/2}]\}. \tag{5.2}$$

The reader can verify that replacing $\hat{\boldsymbol{\theta}}\mathbf{a}^{\mathrm{T}}$ by $-\hat{\boldsymbol{\theta}}\mathbf{a}^{\mathrm{T}}$ in Eq. (5.2) yields a $100\alpha\%$ confidence interval for p_2.

We now turn our attention to the satisfaction. If Eqs. (5.1) arise from a random utility probit model with a constant covariance matrix $\boldsymbol{\Sigma}_\xi$, such that $\mathrm{var}(\xi_1 - \xi_2) = (1, -1)\boldsymbol{\Sigma}_\xi\binom{1}{-1} = \sigma^2$, the measured-attractiveness functions $V_1(\boldsymbol{\theta}, \mathbf{a})$ and $V_2(\boldsymbol{\theta}, \mathbf{a})$ must satisfy

$$V_1(\boldsymbol{\theta}, \mathbf{a}) - V_2(\boldsymbol{\theta}, \mathbf{a}) = \boldsymbol{\theta}\mathbf{a}^{\mathrm{T}}\sigma;$$

this shows that the coefficient of an attribute in the measured-attractiveness function in which it appears must be σ times larger than the element of $\boldsymbol{\theta}$ associated with it. The relative satisfaction $S'(\boldsymbol{\theta}, \mathbf{a}) = S(\boldsymbol{\theta}, \mathbf{a}) - V_1(\boldsymbol{\theta}, \mathbf{a})$ is given by [see Eq. (4.7)]

$$\begin{aligned} S' &= V_2 - V_1 + (V_1 - V_2)\Phi[(V_1 - V_2)/\sigma] + \sigma\phi[(V_1 - V_2)/\sigma] \\ &= \boldsymbol{\theta}\mathbf{a}^{\mathrm{T}}\sigma[\Phi(\boldsymbol{\theta}\mathbf{a}^{\mathrm{T}}) - 1] + \sigma\phi(\boldsymbol{\theta}\mathbf{a}^{\mathrm{T}}) \\ &= \sigma[\phi(\boldsymbol{\theta}\mathbf{a}^{\mathrm{T}}) - \boldsymbol{\theta}\mathbf{a}^{\mathrm{T}}\Phi(-\boldsymbol{\theta}\mathbf{a}^{\mathrm{T}})] \\ &= \sigma[\phi(-\boldsymbol{\theta}\mathbf{a}^{\mathrm{T}}) - \boldsymbol{\theta}\mathbf{a}^{\mathrm{T}}\Phi(-\boldsymbol{\theta}\mathbf{a}^{\mathrm{T}})]. \end{aligned}$$

In order to express S' in units of a certain attribute a_j, the above expression must be divided by the coefficient of such an attribute in the measured-attractiveness vector, $\theta_j\sigma$, and since such a coefficient is proportional to σ, we know that σ will not appear in the new expression. For the rest of the discussion on binary models, we find it convenient to express S' in units of an attribute a_j for which θ_j is unity; that is,

$$S' = [\phi(-\boldsymbol{\theta}\mathbf{a}^{\mathrm{T}}) - \boldsymbol{\theta}\mathbf{a}^{\mathrm{T}}\Phi(-\boldsymbol{\theta}\mathbf{a}^{\mathrm{T}})]. \tag{5.3}$$

To transform the units of S' in Eq. (5.3) into those of attribute a_k, the right-hand side of Eq. (5.3) is simply divided by θ_k.

If we represent by $\hat{S}'$, $\hat{s}'$, and S' the expressions obtained by replacing, respectively, $\hat{\boldsymbol{\Theta}}$, $\hat{\boldsymbol{\theta}}$, and $\boldsymbol{\theta}_o$ in Eq. (5.3), a confidence interval for S' can be obtained in the same way as was done for p_1.

Let us first investigate the properties of the function

$$\psi(x) = \phi(x) + x\Phi(x), \qquad -\infty < x < \infty, \tag{5.4}$$

which we call the *standard probit satisfaction function*. Since, as the reader can check, $\psi(x) = \int_{-\infty}^{x} \Phi(w)\,dw$, the standard probit satisfaction function is positive, increasing $[d\psi(x)/dx = \Phi(x)]$, and ranges from zero to infinity. Therefore, one can define its inverse function $\psi^{-1}(\cdot)$, which goes from $-\infty$ to ∞ as its argument goes from 0 to ∞. The standard probit satisfaction function is tabulated in Table 5.1.

Since, as can be seen from Eq. (5.3), $S' = \psi(-\boldsymbol{\theta}_o\mathbf{a}^{\mathrm{T}})$, $\boldsymbol{\theta}_o\mathbf{a}^{\mathrm{T}} = -\psi^{-1}(S')$ and the random variable

$$[\hat{\boldsymbol{\Theta}}\mathbf{a}^{\mathrm{T}} + \psi^{-1}(S')]/(\mathbf{a}\boldsymbol{\Sigma}_\theta\mathbf{a}^{\mathrm{T}})^{1/2}$$

is a standard normal pivotal quantity for S'. The same algebraic manipulations used with p_1 yield the following $100\alpha\%$ confidence interval for S':

$$\{\psi[-\hat{\boldsymbol{\theta}}\mathbf{a}^{\mathrm{T}} - \eta_{(1+\alpha)/2}(\mathbf{a}\boldsymbol{\Sigma}_\theta\mathbf{a}^{\mathrm{T}})^{1/2}], \psi[-\hat{\boldsymbol{\theta}}\mathbf{a}^{\mathrm{T}} + \eta_{(1+\alpha)/2}(\mathbf{a}\boldsymbol{\Sigma}_\theta\mathbf{a}^{\mathrm{T}})^{1/2}]\}. \tag{5.5}$$

The values of $\psi(\cdot)$ can be read from Table 5.1.

Similar results can be derived for the binary logit model. If the model is

$$p_1 = \frac{\exp(\boldsymbol{\theta}_o\mathbf{a}^{\mathrm{T}})}{1 + \exp(\boldsymbol{\theta}_o\mathbf{a}^{\mathrm{T}})}, \qquad p_2 = \frac{1}{1 + \exp(\boldsymbol{\theta}_o\mathbf{a}^{\mathrm{T}})}, \tag{5.6}$$

Table 5.1

Tabulation of the Standard Probit Satisfaction Function $\psi(x)$

x	$\psi(x)$	x	$\psi(x)$	x	$\psi(x)$	x	$\psi(x)$
−3.9	0.0000	−1.9	0.0111	0.1	0.4509	2.1	2.1065
−3.8	0.0000	−1.8	0.0143	0.2	0.5069	2.2	2.2049
−3.7	0.0000	−1.7	0.0183	0.3	0.5668	2.3	2.3037
−3.6	0.0000	−1.6	0.0232	0.4	0.6304	2.4	2.4027
−3.5	0.0001	−1.5	0.0293	0.5	0.6978	2.5	2.5020
−3.4	0.0001	−1.4	0.0367	0.6	0.7687	2.6	2.6015
−3.3	0.0001	−1.3	0.0455	0.7	0.8429	2.7	2.7011
−3.2	0.0002	−1.2	0.0561	0.8	0.9202	2.8	2.8008
−3.1	0.0003	−1.1	0.0686	0.9	1.0004	2.9	2.9005
−3.0	0.0004	−1.0	0.0833	1.0	1.0833	3.0	3.0004
−2.9	0.0005	−0.9	0.1004	1.1	1.1686	3.1	3.1003
−2.8	0.0008	−0.8	0.1202	1.2	1.2561	3.2	3.2002
−2.7	0.0011	−0.7	0.1429	1.3	1.3455	3.3	3.3001
−2.6	0.0015	−0.6	0.1687	1.4	1.4367	3.4	3.4001
−2.5	0.0020	−0.5	0.1978	1.5	1.5293	3.5	3.5001
−2.4	0.0027	−0.4	0.2304	1.6	1.6232	3.6	3.6000
−2.3	0.0037	−0.3	0.2668	1.7	1.7183	3.7	3.7000
−2.2	0.0049	−0.2	0.3069	1.8	1.8143	3.8	3.8000
−2.1	0.0065	−0.1	0.3509	1.9	1.9111	3.9	3.9000
−2.0	0.0085	0.0	0.3989	2.0	2.0085		

If $x < -3.9$, $\psi(x) \approx 0$; if $x > 3.9$, $\psi(x) \approx x$.

the derivation of a $100\alpha\%$ confidence interval for p_1 parallels the one for the binary probit model. The final result is

$$\{1 + \exp[-\hat{\boldsymbol{\theta}}\mathbf{a}^{\mathrm{T}} \pm \eta_{(1+\alpha)/2}(\mathbf{a}\boldsymbol{\Sigma}_{\theta}\mathbf{a}^{\mathrm{T}})^{1/2}]\}^{-1}. \tag{5.7}$$

Since the relative satisfaction can be expressed as a function of the difference in measured attractiveness [see Eq. (4.19b)]:

$$S' = \log[1 + \exp(V_2 - V_1)]$$

and for the model in Eq. (5.6) $V_1 - V_2 = \boldsymbol{\theta}\mathbf{a}^{\mathrm{T}}$, we can write

$$S' = \log[1 + \exp(-\boldsymbol{\theta}_o\mathbf{a}^{\mathrm{T}})]$$

and

$$-\log[e^{S'} - 1] = \boldsymbol{\theta}_o\mathbf{a}^{\mathrm{T}}.$$

A standard normal pivotal quantity for S' is

$$(\hat{\boldsymbol{\Theta}}\mathbf{a}^{\mathrm{T}} + \log[e^{S'} - 1])/(\mathbf{a}\boldsymbol{\Sigma}_{\theta}\mathbf{a}^{\mathrm{T}})^{1/2},$$

and a 100α% confidence interval is

$$\log(1 + \exp\{-[\hat{\boldsymbol{\theta}}\mathbf{a}^{\mathrm{T}} \pm \eta_{(1+\alpha)/2}(\mathbf{a}\boldsymbol{\Sigma}_{\theta}\mathbf{a}^{\mathrm{T}})^{1/2}]\}). \tag{5.8}$$

The application of these formulas is illustrated below.

Example Consider the non–car-owner segment of the population in the example introduced in Section 4.2. Since the members of this subgroup of the population can choose only between alternative 1 (not to travel) and alternative 2 (travel by public transit), their choice process can be modeled by the binary probit model

$$U_1 = \xi_1, \qquad U_2 = 3 - 6a_{\mathrm{T}} - 6r_{\mathrm{T}} + \xi_2$$

with

$$\boldsymbol{\Sigma}_{\xi} = \begin{bmatrix} 0.1 & 0 \\ 0 & 0.1 \end{bmatrix}.$$

In the expression for U_2, a_{T} and r_{T} represent values (in hours) for the walking time to the transit station, and waiting and riding time, respectively.

The choice functions of the binary model can be expressed as

$$\begin{aligned} p_1 &= \Phi[(-3 + 6a_{\mathrm{T}} + 6r_{\mathrm{T}})/\sqrt{0.2}] \\ &= \Phi(-6.71 + 13.42a_{\mathrm{T}} + 13.42r_{\mathrm{T}}) \end{aligned} \tag{5.9}$$

and

$$p_2 = 1 - p_1,$$

which conform to the type of functions studied in this section.

Let us assume that the values of the coefficients used in Eq. (5.9) are not the true values but are estimates obtained from a data set, that is, Eq. (5.9) gives the *estimated* choice probability for a given value of the attribute vector

$$\hat{p}_1 = \Phi(\hat{\boldsymbol{\theta}}\mathbf{a}^{\mathrm{T}}),$$

where in our case $\hat{\boldsymbol{\theta}} = (-6.71, 13.42, 13.42)$ and $\mathbf{a} = (1, a_{\mathrm{T}}, r_{\mathrm{T}})$. Let us further assume that the aforementioned hypothetical calibration process yielded

$$\boldsymbol{\Sigma}_{\theta} \approx \begin{bmatrix} 0.02 & 0 & 0 \\ 0 & 0.04 & 0.02 \\ 0 & 0.02 & 0.06 \end{bmatrix},$$

and that we desire a confidence interval for p_1 for different values of $\mathbf{a}$.

Since in the original example r_{T} was fixed and was equal to 0.33 hr, we shall let only a_{T} vary; thus $\mathbf{a} = (1, a_{\mathrm{T}}, 0.33)$. The confidence interval is obtained by entering with $\hat{\boldsymbol{\theta}}$, $\mathbf{a}$, and $\boldsymbol{\Sigma}_{\theta}$ into Eq. (5.2). For instance, if $a_{\mathrm{T}} = 0.25$

(the access time from the center of the zone),

$$\boldsymbol{\theta}\mathbf{a}^{\mathrm{T}} = 1.12, \qquad \hat{p}_1 = \Phi(\hat{\boldsymbol{\theta}}\mathbf{a}^{\mathrm{T}}) = 0.87,$$

and

$$\mathbf{a}\boldsymbol{\Sigma}_{\theta}\mathbf{a}^{\mathrm{T}} = (1, 0.25, 0.33)\begin{bmatrix} 0.02 & 0 & 0 \\ 0 & 0.04 & 0.02 \\ 0 & 0.02 & 0.33 \end{bmatrix}\begin{bmatrix} 1 \\ 0.25 \\ 0.33 \end{bmatrix} = 0.0324.$$

If a 90% confidence is desired, $\alpha = 0.9$, $\eta_{0.95} = 1.65$, and Eq. (5.2) yields

$$[\Phi(0.82), \Phi(1.42)] = (0.79, 0.92).$$

The same calculations can be repeated for different values of a_{T}. Although in our example the results are only meaningful for values of a_{T} between 0 and 0.5, Fig. 5.1 depicts the results for the full range. It can be seen from the figure that the length of the confidence interval depends on the probability of choice, with both high and low choice probabilities yielding short confidence intervals. The reader should not be misled, however, because in most demand-forecasting applications, one is interested in the relative error that is committed in the estimation of p_1 and the relative error increases with decreasing choice probabilities. Figure 5.1 also displays the length of the confidence interval over the midpoint value as an indication of the relative error. From Eq. (5.2) it is actually possible to show that as $\hat{p}_1$ becomes small (i.e., $\hat{\boldsymbol{\theta}}\mathbf{a}^{\mathrm{T}} \to -\infty$)

$$\Phi[\hat{\boldsymbol{\theta}}\mathbf{a}^{\mathrm{T}} + \eta_{(1+\alpha)/2}(\mathbf{a}\boldsymbol{\Sigma}_{\theta}\mathbf{a}^{\mathrm{T}})^{1/2}]/\Phi[\hat{\boldsymbol{\theta}}\mathbf{a}^{\mathrm{T}} - \eta_{(1+\alpha)/2}(\mathbf{a}\boldsymbol{\Sigma}_{\theta}\mathbf{a}^{\mathrm{T}})^{1/2}] \to \infty$$

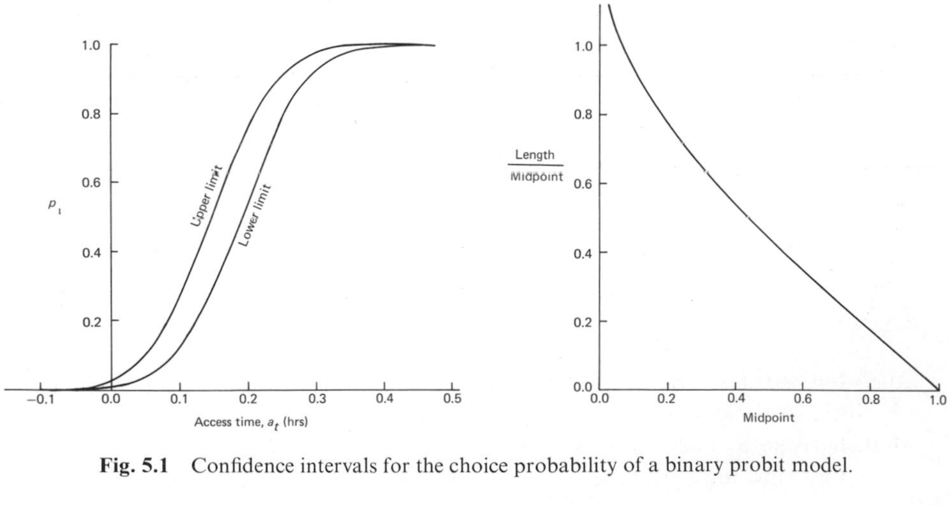

Fig. 5.1 Confidence intervals for the choice probability of a binary probit model.

and consequently

$$\text{length/midpoint} \approx 2.$$

This illustrates the inherent difficulty in estimating the choice probability function for alternatives with small choice probabilities. The result also holds for binary logit models.

A similar analysis can be done with the satisfaction. If $a_T = 0.25$, the confidence interval for S' is

$$[\psi(-1.42), \psi(-0.82)] = (0.035, 0.116).$$

An approximate confidence interval in hours of access travel time can be obtained dividing the values by $\hat{\boldsymbol{\theta}}_2$; it is

$$(0.0026, 0.0096) \quad \text{hr} \qquad \text{or} \qquad (0.16, 0.58) \quad \text{min.} \quad \blacksquare$$

5.1.2 Approximate Results for Heterogeneous Populations

We now show how to build approximate confidence intervals for the average of a figure of merit across a heterogeneous group of individuals. Let $T(\boldsymbol{\theta}_o)$ be the sought average value which can be expressed as

$$T(\boldsymbol{\theta}_o) = E_A[T(\boldsymbol{\theta}_o, \mathbf{A})].$$

$T(\boldsymbol{\theta}_o)$ may be taken to denote an average choice probability $P_i(\boldsymbol{\theta}_o)$, an average satisfaction $S(\boldsymbol{\theta}_o)$, or any other figure of merit. The expressions derived in connection with $T(\boldsymbol{\theta}_o)$ will apply to all of these. As in the previous section, we denote by T the true value $T(\boldsymbol{\theta}_o)$, by $\hat{t}$ the estimated value $T(\hat{\boldsymbol{\theta}})$, by $\hat{T}$ the random variable $T(\hat{\boldsymbol{\Theta}})$.

A procedure similar to the one in the previous section cannot be employed unless one can find a pivotal quantity for T. Since in the most general case the distribution of $\hat{T}$ does not seem to depend on $\boldsymbol{\theta}_o$ in a closed form, a pivotal quantity for T is difficult to obtain, and alternative confidence interval building methods have to be developed. We do that now.

Assume that the MNP model was calibrated on a large sample with the maximum-likelihood method and that, consequently, $\hat{\boldsymbol{\Theta}}$ is approximately MVN distributed with mean $\boldsymbol{\theta}_o$ and covariance matrix $\boldsymbol{\Sigma}_\theta$. Let us further assume that the sample size was so large that the entries of $\boldsymbol{\Sigma}_\theta$ are very small. A criterion to determine whether the entries of $\boldsymbol{\Sigma}_\theta$ are small enough is provided later.

Let us expand $T(\hat{\boldsymbol{\Theta}})$ in a Taylor series around $T(\boldsymbol{\theta}_o)$:

$$T(\hat{\boldsymbol{\Theta}}) = T(\boldsymbol{\theta}_o) + (\hat{\boldsymbol{\Theta}} - \boldsymbol{\theta}_o)[\nabla T(\boldsymbol{\theta}_o)]^{\mathrm{T}} + R_2(\hat{\boldsymbol{\Theta}}); \tag{5.10}$$

in this expression $R_2(\hat{\boldsymbol{\Theta}})$ is the remainder in the Lagrange form

$$R_2(\hat{\boldsymbol{\Theta}}) = \tfrac{1}{2}(\hat{\boldsymbol{\Theta}} - \boldsymbol{\theta}_o)\nabla^2 T(\boldsymbol{\Theta}')(\hat{\boldsymbol{\Theta}} - \boldsymbol{\theta}_o)^{\mathrm{T}}, \tag{5.11}$$

where

$$\boldsymbol{\Theta}' = \boldsymbol{\theta}_o + \eta(\hat{\boldsymbol{\Theta}} - \boldsymbol{\theta}_o) \qquad \text{for some} \quad 0 < \eta < 1.$$

The random variable $\hat{T} = T(\hat{\boldsymbol{\Theta}})$ is the sum of three components, the last of which can be neglected if we can be reasonably sure that the outcomes of $\hat{\boldsymbol{\Theta}}$ are sufficiently close to $\boldsymbol{\theta}_o$. This is so because $R_2(\hat{\boldsymbol{\Theta}})$ approaches zero as $(\hat{\boldsymbol{\Theta}} - \boldsymbol{\theta}_o) \to 0$ faster than the other components of Eq. (5.10).

The consistency property of maximum-likelihood estimators ensures that this will happen for sufficiently large sample sizes.

If we want to check whether $R_2(\hat{\boldsymbol{\Theta}})$ is likely to be small enough relative to $T(\boldsymbol{\theta}_o)$, we might like to verify whether

$$\Pr\{|R_2(\hat{\boldsymbol{\Theta}})|/|T(\boldsymbol{\theta}_o)| \le \delta\} \ge \alpha' \tag{5.12}$$

for some small relative error δ and high probability α'. Unfortunately, Eq. (5.12) is not easy to use because the distribution of $R_2(\hat{\boldsymbol{\Theta}})$ is unknown. Instead, we use the following inequality, which applies to nonnegative random variables such as $|R_2(\hat{\boldsymbol{\Theta}})|/|T(\boldsymbol{\theta}_o)|$ when a statement such as Eq. (5.12) does not hold:

$$E\{|R_2(\hat{\boldsymbol{\Theta}}|/|T(\hat{\boldsymbol{\theta}}_o)|\} \ge \delta(1 - \alpha').$$

Thus to verify Eq. (5.12), it suffices to verify whether

$$E\{|R_2(\hat{\boldsymbol{\Theta}})|\} \le \delta(1 - \alpha')|T(\boldsymbol{\theta}_o)|,$$

or, since this is usually an order-of-magnitude comparison for which great accuracy is not needed, whether

$$E\{|R_2(\hat{\boldsymbol{\Theta}})|\} \le \delta(1 - \alpha')|T(\hat{\boldsymbol{\theta}})|. \tag{5.13}$$

Furthermore, since great accuracy is not needed either in the evaluation of $E\{|R_2(\hat{\boldsymbol{\Theta}})|\}$, we can use

$$R_2(\hat{\boldsymbol{\Theta}}) \approx \tfrac{1}{2}(\hat{\boldsymbol{\Theta}} - \boldsymbol{\theta}_o)\nabla^2 T(\hat{\boldsymbol{\theta}})(\hat{\boldsymbol{\Theta}} - \boldsymbol{\theta}_o)^{\mathrm{T}} \tag{5.14}$$

in order to derive an approximate upper bound for $E\{|R_2(\hat{\boldsymbol{\Theta}})|\}$. Because $\nabla^2 T(\hat{\boldsymbol{\theta}})$ is a known symmetric matrix, it can be diagonalized as

$$\nabla^2 T(\hat{\boldsymbol{\theta}}) = \mathbf{C}\boldsymbol{\Lambda}\mathbf{C}^{\mathrm{T}} \qquad \mathbf{C}\mathbf{C}^{\mathrm{T}} = \mathbf{I},$$

where $\boldsymbol{\Lambda}$ is a diagonal matrix of eigenvalues. Letting λ denote the absolute value of the largest eigenvalue in absolute value, we see that if $\mathbf{x}$ is an arbitrary row vector of dimension r (r is the number of parameters),

$$\begin{aligned}|\mathbf{xC\Lambda C^T x^T}| &= |(\mathbf{xC})\mathbf{\Lambda}(\mathbf{xC})^{\mathrm{T}}| \\ &\le (\mathbf{xC})\begin{bmatrix} |\lambda_1| & 0 & \cdots \\ 0 & |\lambda_2| & \cdots \\ \vdots & \vdots & \ddots \end{bmatrix}(\mathbf{xC})^{\mathrm{T}} \\ &\le (\mathbf{xC})\lambda\mathbf{I}(\mathbf{xC})^{\mathrm{T}} = \lambda(\mathbf{xCC^T x^T}) = \lambda\mathbf{xx}^{\mathrm{T}}.\end{aligned}$$

Consequently

$$|R_2(\hat{\mathbf{\Theta}})| \le \tfrac{1}{2}\lambda(\hat{\mathbf{\Theta}} - \boldsymbol{\theta}_o)(\hat{\mathbf{\Theta}} - \boldsymbol{\theta}_o)^{\mathrm{T}}$$

and

$$E\{|R_2(\hat{\mathbf{\Theta}})|\} \le \frac{\lambda}{2} E\left[\sum_{i=1}^{r} (\hat{\Theta}_i - \theta_{oi})^2\right] = \frac{\lambda}{2}\sum_{i=1}^{r} \operatorname{var}(\hat{\Theta}_i) \approx \operatorname{tr}(\mathbf{\Sigma}_\theta)\frac{\lambda}{2},$$

where $\operatorname{tr}(\mathbf{\Sigma}_\theta)$ is the trace of $\mathbf{\Sigma}_\theta$ (the sum of the elements in the main diagonal). Equations (5.13) and (5.12) thus will be met if

$$\tfrac{1}{2}\lambda \operatorname{tr}(\mathbf{\Sigma}_\theta) \le \delta(1 - \alpha')|T(\hat{\boldsymbol{\theta}})|. \tag{5.15}$$

In words, it is reasonable to neglect $R_2(\hat{\mathbf{\Theta}})$ in Eq. (5.10) if the trace of $\mathbf{\Sigma}_\theta$ times the largest absolute eigenvalue of $\mathbf{\nabla}^2 T(\hat{\boldsymbol{\theta}})$ is much smaller (in absolute value) than $T(\hat{\boldsymbol{\theta}})$.

We now develop an approximate confidence interval for $T(\boldsymbol{\theta}_o)$ assuming that Eq. (5.12) holds. Since the remainder of Eq. (5.10) will exceed $\delta|T(\boldsymbol{\theta}_o)|$ only $100(1 - \alpha')\%$ of the time, we can write

$$\Pr\{T(\hat{\mathbf{\Theta}}) \in [T(\boldsymbol{\theta}_o) + (\hat{\mathbf{\Theta}} - \boldsymbol{\theta}_o)[\mathbf{\nabla}T(\boldsymbol{\theta}_o)]^{\mathrm{T}} \pm \delta|T(\boldsymbol{\theta}_o)|]\} \ge \alpha',$$

or using the abbreviation $T_l(\hat{\mathbf{\Theta}}, \boldsymbol{\theta}_o)$ instead of the linearization of $T(\hat{\mathbf{\Theta}})$ around $\boldsymbol{\theta}_o$, $T(\boldsymbol{\theta}_o) + (\hat{\mathbf{\Theta}} - \boldsymbol{\theta}_o)[\mathbf{\nabla}T(\boldsymbol{\theta}_o)]^{\mathrm{T}}$:

$$\Pr\{T_l(\hat{\mathbf{\Theta}}, \boldsymbol{\theta}_o) - \delta|T(\boldsymbol{\theta}_o)| \le T(\hat{\mathbf{\Theta}}) \le T_l(\hat{\mathbf{\Theta}}, \boldsymbol{\theta}_o) + \delta|T(\boldsymbol{\theta}_o)|\} \ge \alpha'.$$

The event in braces, which we call event 1, can be rewritten as

$$\{T(\hat{\mathbf{\Theta}}) - \delta|T(\boldsymbol{\theta}_o)| \le T_l(\hat{\mathbf{\Theta}}, \boldsymbol{\theta}_o) \le T(\hat{\mathbf{\Theta}}) + \delta|T(\boldsymbol{\theta}_o)|\}$$

Since $T_l(\hat{\mathbf{\Theta}}, \boldsymbol{\theta}_o)$ is a linear function of $\hat{\mathbf{\Theta}}$ it is normally distributed with mean $T(\boldsymbol{\theta}_o)$ and variance σ_l^2, given by

$$\sigma_l^2 = \mathbf{\nabla}T(\boldsymbol{\theta}_o)\mathbf{\Sigma}_\theta[\mathbf{\nabla}T(\boldsymbol{\theta}_o)]^{\mathrm{T}}.$$

Therefore the expression

$$\frac{[T_l(\hat{\mathbf{\Theta}}, \boldsymbol{\theta}_o) - T(\boldsymbol{\theta}_o)]}{\sigma_l}$$

is a standard normal random variable and the following event (event 2) occurs with probability α:

$$\{T_l(\hat{\boldsymbol{\Theta}}, \boldsymbol{\theta}_o) - \eta_{(1+\alpha)/2}\sigma_l \leq T(\boldsymbol{\theta}_o) \leq T_l(\hat{\boldsymbol{\Theta}}, \boldsymbol{\theta}_o) + \eta_{(1+\alpha)/2}\sigma_l\}.$$

If $T_l(\hat{\boldsymbol{\theta}}, \boldsymbol{\theta}_o)$ were known, event 2 would be a $100\alpha\%$ confidence interval for $T(\boldsymbol{\theta}_o)$, but since it is not, we use the information given by event 1 to build such a confidence interval.

From the basic laws of probability we know that events 1 and 2 must occur concurrently with a probability α'' such that

$$\alpha'' \geq \alpha + \alpha' - 1$$

(the reader can easily verify this from *Venn diagrams*). However, if events 1 and 2 occur, event 3

$$\{T(\hat{\boldsymbol{\Theta}}) - \eta_{(1+\alpha)/2}\sigma_l - \delta|T(\boldsymbol{\theta}_o)| \leq T(\boldsymbol{\theta}_o) \leq T(\hat{\boldsymbol{\Theta}}) + \eta_{(1+\alpha)/2}\sigma_l + \delta|T(\boldsymbol{\theta}_o)|\}$$

also occurs, and therefore must occur with at least probability $\alpha'' \geq \alpha + \alpha' - 1$.

If δ is below the accuracy level desired, the term $\delta|T(\boldsymbol{\theta}_o)|$ can be dropped from event 3 and we have

$$\Pr\{T(\boldsymbol{\theta}_o) \in [T(\hat{\boldsymbol{\Theta}}) \pm \eta_{(1+\alpha)/2}\sigma_l]\} \geq \alpha + \alpha' - 1.$$

Consequently the expression

$$[T(\hat{\boldsymbol{\theta}}) \pm \eta_{(1+\alpha)/2}\sigma_l] \tag{5.16}$$

is at least an $\alpha + \alpha' - 1$ confidence interval for $T(\boldsymbol{\theta}_o)$. As usual, since σ_l is a function of $\boldsymbol{\theta}_o$, we approximate it by

$$\sigma_l^2 \approx \boldsymbol{\nabla} T(\hat{\boldsymbol{\theta}})\boldsymbol{\Sigma}_\theta[\boldsymbol{\nabla} T(\hat{\boldsymbol{\theta}})]^{\mathrm{T}}. \tag{5.17a}$$

It should be noted that since $\alpha + \alpha' - 1 \leq \alpha'$, it is not possible to obtain a confidence interval with confidence level greater than α'; therefore we should like to select α' as close to one as possible. Equation (5.15), however, indicates that

$$\alpha' \leq 1 - (\lambda \operatorname{tr}(\boldsymbol{\Sigma}_\theta)/2\delta T(\hat{\boldsymbol{\theta}})) \tag{5.17b}$$

in order for Eq. (5.12) to apply; consequently, this is a practical limit on the confidence level we can put on Eq. (5.16). The above inequality, however, should not be taken too strictly since several conservative assumptions were made in developing it.

The general procedure to obtain a confidence interval is

Step 1 Calculate $T(\hat{\boldsymbol{\theta}})$, $\boldsymbol{\nabla} T(\hat{\boldsymbol{\theta}})$ and $\boldsymbol{\nabla}^2 T(\hat{\boldsymbol{\theta}})$ as outlined in Chapter 4.

Step 2 Check whether Eq. (5.15) can be satisfied for small δ and large α'.

Step 3 Evaluate Eq. (5.17a) and replace the result into Eq. (5.16) for a $100[\alpha - \{\lambda\,\mathrm{tr}(\mathbf{\Sigma}_\theta)/2\delta T(\hat{\boldsymbol{\theta}})\}]\%$ (or more) confidence interval on $T(\boldsymbol{\theta}_o)$.

Example Let us obtain a confidence interval for $P_1(\boldsymbol{\theta}_o)$ and the subgroup of the population of the example in Section 4.2 that does not own cars. As in Section 5.1, the model is

$$U_1 = \xi_1,$$
$$U_2 = \theta_1 - \theta_2 a_{\mathrm{T}} - \theta_3 r_{\mathrm{T}} + \xi_2,$$

with

$$\mathbf{\Sigma}_\xi = \begin{bmatrix} 0.1 & 0 \\ 0 & 0.1 \end{bmatrix}.$$

As was done in Section 4.3, we assume that the attributes of a choice maker randomly selected from the population of non–car-owners A_{T} and R_{T} are approximately MVN distributed. In our case $E(R_{\mathrm{T}}) = 0.33$, $E(A_{\mathrm{T}}) = 0.25$, $\mathrm{var}(R_{\mathrm{T}}) = 0$, $\mathrm{var}(A_{\mathrm{T}}) = \frac{1}{96}$, and $\mathrm{cov}(R_{\mathrm{T}}, A_r) = 0$. As discussed in Section 4.3, the perceived-attractiveness vector of a random individual is MVN distributed with mean $\bar{\mathbf{U}}$, and covariance matrix $\mathbf{\Sigma}_U$:

$$\bar{U}_1 = 0, \qquad \bar{U}_2 = \theta_1 - 0.25\theta_2 - 0.33\theta_3,$$

and

$$\mathbf{\Sigma}_U = \begin{bmatrix} 0.1 & 0 \\ 0 & 0.1 + \theta_2^2 \frac{1}{96} \end{bmatrix}.$$

Step 1 The choice probability $P_1(\boldsymbol{\theta})$ for such an individual is

$$P_1(\boldsymbol{\theta}) = \Pr\{U_1 > U_2\} = \Pr\{U_2 - U_1 < 0\} = \Phi\left\{\frac{-\theta_1 + 0.25\theta_2 + 0.33\theta_3}{(0.2 + \theta_2^2/96)^{1/2}}\right\}, \tag{5.18}$$

and if we assume that as in Section 5.1 the calibration process yielded[1]

$$\hat{\boldsymbol{\theta}} = (3, 6, 6)$$

and

$$\mathbf{\Sigma}_\theta \approx \begin{bmatrix} 0.005 & 0 & 0 \\ 0 & 0.01 & 0.005 \\ 0 & 0.005 & 0.015 \end{bmatrix},$$

[1] The $\hat{\boldsymbol{\theta}}$ vector differs from the one in Section 5.1 because in here the model is expressed in its random utility form.

we can find $P_1(\hat{\boldsymbol{\theta}})$ by substituting $\hat{\boldsymbol{\theta}}$ in Eq. (5.18):

$$P_1(\hat{\boldsymbol{\theta}}) = 0.737.$$

By evaluating $P_1(\hat{\boldsymbol{\theta}})$ in the neighborhood of $\hat{\boldsymbol{\theta}} = (3, 6, 6)$, we can evaluate $\nabla P_1(\hat{\boldsymbol{\theta}})$ and $\nabla^2 P_1(\hat{\boldsymbol{\theta}})$ numerically. Table 5.2 contains values of $P_1(\boldsymbol{\theta})$ for ten points, $\boldsymbol{\theta}_1$ to $\boldsymbol{\theta}_{10}$, in the neighborhood of $\hat{\boldsymbol{\theta}}$. With these values it is possible to approximate numerically the first and second derivatives of $P_1(\hat{\boldsymbol{\theta}})$. As an example, the reader can check that

$$\frac{\partial P_1(\hat{\boldsymbol{\theta}})}{\partial \theta_1} = \frac{P_1(\boldsymbol{\theta}_2) - P_1(\boldsymbol{\theta}_1)}{0.01} = -0.432$$

and

$$\frac{\partial^2 P_1(\hat{\boldsymbol{\theta}})}{\partial \theta_1\, \partial \theta_2} = \frac{P_1(\boldsymbol{\theta}_8) + P_1(\boldsymbol{\theta}_1) - P_1(\boldsymbol{\theta}_2) - P_1(\boldsymbol{\theta}_3)}{(0.01)(0.01)} = 0.118.$$

With the same method one finally obtains

$$\nabla P_1(\hat{\boldsymbol{\theta}}) \approx (-0.432, 0.085, 0.142)$$

and

$$\nabla^2 P_1(\hat{\boldsymbol{\theta}}) \approx \begin{bmatrix} -0.355 & 0.118 & 0.118 \\ 0.118 & -0.034 & -0.039 \\ 0.118 & -0.039 & -0.039 \end{bmatrix}.$$

Although for this particular problem it would have been possible to calculate the first and second derivatives of $P_1(\hat{\boldsymbol{\theta}})$ directly from Eq. (5.18), we preferred

Table 5.2

Ten Values of $P_1(\boldsymbol{\theta})$ in the Neighborhood of $\hat{\boldsymbol{\theta}}$

	$\boldsymbol{\theta}_k$			
number k	θ_1	θ_2	θ_3	$P_1(\boldsymbol{\theta}_k)$
1	3	6	6	0.7366349576
2	3.01	6	6	0.7323111345
3	3	6.01	6	0.7374850896
4	3	6	6.01	0.7380539532
5	3.02	6	6	0.7279518241
6	3	6.02	6	0.7383318445
7	3	6	6.02	0.7394690183
8	3.01	6.01	6	0.7331730410
9	3.01	6	6.01	0.7337419420
10	3	6.01	6.01	0.7389001971

to obtain them numerically since this can be done even in more complicated problems.

Step 2 Since according to the Gerschgorin theorem[2] the eigenvalues of $\nabla^2 P_1(\hat{\boldsymbol{\theta}})$ belong to the following intervals:

$$\lambda_1 \in [-0.355 \pm 0.236], \quad \lambda_2 \in [-0.034 \pm 0.157], \quad \lambda_3 \in [-0.039 \pm 0.157],$$

we know that $\lambda < 0.355 + 0.236 = 0.591$. Thereofre Eq. (5.15) will be satisfied if

$$0.591(\tfrac{1}{2})\,\mathrm{tr}(\boldsymbol{\Sigma}_\theta) \leq (1 - \alpha')\delta|P_1(\hat{\boldsymbol{\theta}})| = 0.737\delta(1 - \alpha').$$

Since $\mathrm{tr}(\boldsymbol{\Sigma}_\theta) = 0.03$, the left-hand side is 0.009; since this is much smaller than 0.737, it allows us to proceed.

Step 3 If $\delta = 0.1$, $\alpha' \leq 0.88$. Thus at the $\delta = 0.1$ accuracy level, the maximum level of significance is 0.88. An 80% (or higher) confidence interval can be obtained by setting $\alpha = 0.92$ since $\alpha + \alpha' - 1 = 0.8$.

We can now use Eqs. (5.17a) to obtain

$$\sigma_l - \sqrt{0.00143} = 0.038,$$

and an approximate 80% (or better) confidence interval is

$$(0.737 \pm 1.75 \times 0.038) \approx (0.67, 0.8). \quad ■$$

It should be remembered that the bounds used to develop Eq. (5.15) are not necessarily tight and that consequently on many occasions, it may be perfectly warranted to use the technique with values of α' larger than those allowed by Eq. (5.17b). In the cases for which this is not possible, the reader may wonder how one can cope with the problem. This is indeed a legitimate concern, which will be addressed in the next section for the general multinomial case.

5.2 Confidence Intervals on the Mean: Multinomial Models

5.2.1 *Analytic Confidence Intervals*

For multinomial logit models with specfications that are linear in the parameters ($\mathbf{V} = \boldsymbol{\theta}[\mathbf{a}]$, where $[\mathbf{a}]$ is an $r \times I$ matrix whose entries are either known constants or elements of the attribute vector $\mathbf{a}$) it is possible to derive

[2] This theorem was used in connection with the proof of Lemma 3.1 (see footnote 15 in Chapter 3).

a joint confidence region for the choice probabilities of a homogeneous population and for the ratio of the choice probabilities of any two alternatives.

Since

$$\log(p_i/p_j) = V_i(\boldsymbol{\theta}, \mathbf{a}) - V_j(\boldsymbol{\theta}, \mathbf{a}) = \boldsymbol{\theta}[\mathbf{a}]\boldsymbol{\delta}^{\mathrm{T}},$$

($\boldsymbol{\delta}^{\mathrm{T}}$ represents a column vector with zero entries except for $\delta_i = 1$ and $\delta_j = -1$) the random variable $\log(\hat{P}_i/\hat{P}_j)$ [as before P_i denotes $P_i(\hat{\boldsymbol{\Theta}}, \mathbf{a})$] is normally distributed with mean $\log(p_i/p_j)$ and variance

$$\sigma_p^2 = \boldsymbol{\delta}[\mathbf{a}]^{\mathrm{T}}\boldsymbol{\Sigma}_\theta[\mathbf{a}]\boldsymbol{\delta}^{\mathrm{T}}.$$

Thus

$$[\log(\hat{P}_i/\hat{P}_j) - \log(p_i/p_j)]/\sigma_p$$

is a standard normal pivotal quantity for p_i/p_j, and

$$\exp\{\log(\hat{p}_i/\hat{p}_j) \pm \eta_{(1+\alpha)/2}\sigma_p\}$$

or

$$[(\hat{p}_i/\hat{p}_j)\exp(\pm\eta_{(1+\alpha)/2}\sigma_p)] \tag{5.19}$$

is a $100\alpha\%$ confidence interval for p_i/p_j.

Analogously, letting

$$\boldsymbol{\Delta} = \left[\begin{array}{ccc|c} -1 & -1 & -1 & -1 \\ 1 & 0 & 0 & 0 \\ 0 & 1 & 0 & 0 \\ \hline 0 & 0 & 0 & 1 \end{array}\right]$$

be a $[I \times (I-1)]$ matrix, we can write

$$\log(\hat{\mathbf{P}}'/\hat{P}_1) = [\log(\hat{P}_2/\hat{P}_1), \ldots, (\hat{P}_I/\hat{P}_1)] = \mathbf{V}\boldsymbol{\Delta} = \hat{\boldsymbol{\Theta}}[\mathbf{a}]\boldsymbol{\Delta}.$$

Since $\log(\hat{\mathbf{P}}'/\hat{P}_1)$ is a linear function of $\hat{\boldsymbol{\Theta}}$, it is MVN distributed with mean $\log(\mathbf{p}'/p_1)$ and covariance matrix

$$\boldsymbol{\Sigma}_p = \boldsymbol{\Delta}^{\mathrm{T}}[\mathbf{a}]^{\mathrm{T}}\boldsymbol{\Sigma}_\theta[\mathbf{a}]\boldsymbol{\Delta}.$$

Thus, the quantity

$$[\log(\hat{\mathbf{P}}'/\hat{P}_1) - \log(\mathbf{p}'/p_1)]\boldsymbol{\Sigma}_p^{-1}[\log(\hat{\mathbf{P}}'/\hat{\mathbf{P}}_1) - \log(\mathbf{p}'/\mathbf{p}_1)]^{\mathrm{T}}$$

is a pivotal quantity that is χ^2 distributed with $I - 1$ degrees of freedom. The corresponding $100\alpha\%$ confidence region for $\log(\mathbf{p}'/\mathbf{p}_1)$ is

$$[\log(\hat{\mathbf{p}}'/\hat{p}_1) - \mathbf{x}]\boldsymbol{\Sigma}_p^{-1}[\log(\hat{\mathbf{p}}'/\hat{p}_1) - \mathbf{x}]^{\mathrm{T}} \leq \chi^2_{(I-1,\alpha)}, \tag{5.20}$$

which is an $[(I-1)$-dimensional$]$ ellipsoid centered at $\log(\hat{\mathbf{p}}'/\hat{p}_1)$. Equation (5.20) also defines a confidence region for $(p_1, \ldots, p_I)$ because for every value of $\mathbf{x} = \log(p_2/p_1, \ldots, p_I/p_i)$ there is one and only one probability vector.

Equation (5.20) can be generalized for MNP models with covariance matrix independent of $\boldsymbol{\theta}$ since according to Con ecture 3.1 and Fact 3.1 there is a one-to-one relationship between $(\mathbf{p}'/p_1)$ and the reduced-attractiveness vector $\mathbf{V}' = (V_2 - V_1, \ldots, V_I - V_1)$ (note that $\mathbf{p}'$ and p_1 are not the true values in this context). Letting $\mathbf{f}(\cdot)$ denote such a relationship,

$$\mathbf{V}' = \mathbf{f}(\mathbf{p}'/p_1),$$

the confidence region is

$$[\mathbf{f}(\hat{\mathbf{p}}'/\hat{p}_1) - \mathbf{f}(\mathbf{p}'/p_1)]\boldsymbol{\Sigma}_p^{-1}[\mathbf{f}(\hat{\mathbf{p}}'/\hat{p}_1) - \mathbf{f}(\mathbf{p}'/p_1)]^{\mathrm{T}} \leq \chi^2_{(I-1,\alpha)}. \qquad (5.21)$$

Equations (5.20) and (5.21) can be used for hypothesis testing quite handily in efforts to validate a given discrete choice model. Unforuntately, although possible, the function $\mathbf{f}(\cdot)$ is not so easy to evaluate for the MNP model.[3]

In cases for which one must consider a heterogeneous population or a model that is not linear in the parameters it is possible to use the large sample method of Section 5.1.2. As a matter of fact such a method can be exercised exactly as explained there since nowhere in the explanation did we use the fact that the models were binary.

5.2.2 Simulation Method for Smaller Samples

In cases for which the calibration sample size is sufficiently large to assume $\hat{\boldsymbol{\Theta}}$ is MVN$(\boldsymbol{\theta}_o, \boldsymbol{\Sigma}_\theta)$ but not large enough to permit use of the approximation method described in Section 5.1.2, it is useful to regard $\boldsymbol{\theta}_o$ and $T(\boldsymbol{\theta}_o)$ as random variables in a Bayesian sense and use simulation as a means to derive confidence intervals.

Imagine the set of all experiments that can possibly be performed to estimate a parameter vector of the same dimension as $\boldsymbol{\theta}_o$.

This set of experiment need not be restricted to one scientific discipline or one particular data set; it encompasses all possible circumstances. Consequently, the true values of the parameter vector will vary so much

[3] A possible evaluation method would consist of finding with a calibration code

$$\max_{\boldsymbol{\theta}} \sum_{i=1}^{I} p_i \log P_i(\boldsymbol{\theta}, \mathbf{a}),$$

where the specification of the model is set equal to

$$\boldsymbol{\Sigma}_\xi = \boldsymbol{\Sigma}_\xi(\mathbf{a}), \qquad V_1 = 0, \qquad V_i = \theta_i, \qquad i = 2, \ldots, I.$$

As was demonstrated in Chapter 3 the solution to this problem is values of θ_i for which $P_i(\boldsymbol{\theta}, \mathbf{a}) = p_i$; by construction, these values are the sought $V_i - V_1$ values.

across the set that its elements can be visualized as outcomes of a random variable $\boldsymbol{\Theta}_o$ having an almost-constant probability density function $f_{\theta_o}(\cdot)$ that takes on very small values. Bayesian statisticians call such distributions *diffuse* because the probability density is assumed to be diffused very homogeneously all over $\mathscr{R}^r$. The MVN distribution with covariance matrix given by $k\mathbf{I}$ (k large) is an example. Furthermore, if in the present case the researcher knows very little about the true value of the parameter $\boldsymbol{\theta}_o$, he can surely think of $\boldsymbol{\theta}_o$ as a random drawing from the above set. Since, as is shown below, the exact form of the distribution does not affect the results—only the fact that it is diffuse—this hypothesis is not particularly restrictive.

With this in mind we may endeavor to obtain the distribution of the also random $T(\boldsymbol{\theta}_o)$, conditional on the results of the calibration. If we succeed, the $100[(1-\alpha)/2]$ and $100[(1+\alpha)/2]$ percentile points of the resulting distribution will, by definition, bracket $T(\boldsymbol{\theta}_o)$ with probability α, and will therefore be a $100\alpha\%$ confidence interval for $T(\boldsymbol{\theta}_o)$. In other words a researcher who uses this technique to build many $100\alpha\%$ confidence intervals over his life span will have been right $100\alpha\%$ of the time. We proceed now to do that.

Since we know that the distribution of $\hat{\boldsymbol{\Theta}}$ conditional on $\boldsymbol{\Theta}_o = \boldsymbol{\theta}_o$ is MVN with mean $\boldsymbol{\theta}_o$ and covariance matrix $\boldsymbol{\Sigma}_\theta$, we can obtain the joint distribution of $\boldsymbol{\Theta}_o$ and $\hat{\boldsymbol{\Theta}}$:

$$\Pr\{\hat{\boldsymbol{\Theta}}_o \in (\hat{\boldsymbol{\theta}}, \hat{\boldsymbol{\theta}} + d\hat{\boldsymbol{\theta}}), \boldsymbol{\Theta}_o \in (\boldsymbol{\theta}_o, \boldsymbol{\theta}_o + d\boldsymbol{\theta}_o)\} = \phi(\hat{\boldsymbol{\theta}} \mid \boldsymbol{\theta}_o, \boldsymbol{\Sigma}_\theta) f_{\theta_o}(\boldsymbol{\theta}_o)\, d\hat{\boldsymbol{\theta}}\, d\boldsymbol{\theta}_o$$

and the conditional density of $\boldsymbol{\Theta}_o$ on $\hat{\boldsymbol{\theta}}$:

$$f_{\Theta_o}(\boldsymbol{\theta}_o \mid \hat{\boldsymbol{\theta}}) = \phi(\hat{\boldsymbol{\theta}} \mid \boldsymbol{\theta}_o, \boldsymbol{\Sigma}_\theta) f_{\Theta_o}(\boldsymbol{\theta}_o) \Big/ \int_{\boldsymbol{\theta}_o} \phi(\hat{\boldsymbol{\theta}} \mid \boldsymbol{\theta}_o, \boldsymbol{\Sigma}_\theta) f_{\Theta_o}(\boldsymbol{\theta}_o)\, d\boldsymbol{\theta}_o.$$

Since $f_{\Theta_o}(\cdot)$ is diffuse, it will take on practically the same value for all values of $\boldsymbol{\theta}_o$ for which $\phi(\hat{\boldsymbol{\theta}} \mid \boldsymbol{\theta}_o, \boldsymbol{\Sigma}_\theta)$ is substantially different from zero; thus $f_{\theta_o}(\boldsymbol{\theta}_o)$ can be replaced by $f_{\Theta_o}(\hat{\boldsymbol{\theta}})$ in the denominator and the numerator. Consequently the conditional density of $\boldsymbol{\Theta}_o$ on $\hat{\boldsymbol{\theta}}$ simplifies to

$$f_{\Theta_o}(\boldsymbol{\theta}_o \mid \hat{\boldsymbol{\theta}}) \approx \phi(\hat{\boldsymbol{\theta}} \mid \boldsymbol{\theta}_o, \boldsymbol{\Sigma}_\theta) = \phi(\boldsymbol{\theta}_o \mid \hat{\boldsymbol{\theta}}, \boldsymbol{\Sigma}_\theta),$$

indicating that $\boldsymbol{\Theta}_o$ is MVN distributed with mean $\hat{\boldsymbol{\theta}}$ and covariance $\boldsymbol{\Sigma}_\theta$.[4] The percentiles of $T(\boldsymbol{\Theta}_o)$, $T_{(1-\alpha)/2}$, and $T_{(1+\alpha)/2}$ can be obtained from the distribution of $\boldsymbol{\Theta}_o$ through the change of variable $T = T(\boldsymbol{\Theta}_o)$.

Unfortunately the change of variable $T(\boldsymbol{\Theta}_o)$ is complicated and $T_{(1-\alpha)/2}$ and $T_{(1+\alpha)/2}$ cannot be obtained in closed form from $\hat{\boldsymbol{\theta}}$ and $\boldsymbol{\Sigma}_\theta$ in the most general cases; however, the Monte Carlo simulation strategy described in

[4] This is a well-known result in Bayesian decision theory.

Section 2.2.2 can be used to develop approximate values for $T_{(1-\alpha)/2}$ and $T_{(1+\alpha)/2}$. This is done as follows:

Step 1 With the simulation method described in Section 2.2.2 sample K observations from a $\mathrm{MVN}(\hat{\boldsymbol{\theta}}, \boldsymbol{\Sigma}_\theta)$ distribution $\boldsymbol{\theta}_{(1)}, \ldots, \boldsymbol{\theta}_{(K)}$ and calculate $T_{(1)}, \ldots, T_{(K)}$, using the transformation $T_{(k)} = T(\boldsymbol{\theta}_{(k)})$.

Step 2 Plot the sample cumulative distribution function of T and use the percentiles of the sample, $\tilde{T}_{(1+\alpha)/2}$ and $\tilde{T}_{(1-\alpha)/2}$, for the confidence interval.

Since for large values of K the percentiles of the sample $\tilde{T}_\beta$ are approximately normally distributed with mean the true percentile T_β and variance

$$\mathrm{var}(\tilde{T}_\beta) = \beta(1-\beta)/K[f(T_\beta)]^2,$$

where $f_T(\cdot)$ is the density function of $T(\boldsymbol{\Theta}_o)$, the quantity

$$\varepsilon_T \approx \sqrt{\beta(1-\beta)/K}[1/f_T(T_\beta)]$$

gives an indication of the size of error likely to be encountered. If $f_T(\cdot)$ is normal with variance σ_T^2, the following are values of ε_T for different values of β:

β	0.5	0.25 and 0.75	0.9 and 0.1	0.95 and 0.05	0.99 and 0.01
ε_T	$\frac{1.253}{\sqrt{K}}\sigma_T$	$\frac{1.363}{\sqrt{K}}\sigma_T$	$\frac{1.709}{\sqrt{K}}\sigma_T$	$\frac{2.113}{\sqrt{K}}\sigma_T$	$\frac{3.733}{\sqrt{K}}\sigma_T$

The value of σ_T can be inferred from the sample standard deviation of $T_{(1)}, \ldots, T_{(k)}$. Note that according to this method confidence intervals for high values of α are more difficult to obtain since more observations are needed to obtain a similar precision.

To illustrate typical values of K needed, consider a 90% confidence interval that is to be determined with a typical error of no more than 0.05σ. This requires a value of K such that

$$1.709/\sqrt{K} = 0.05$$

and $K \geq (1.709/0.05)^2 \approx 1169$ observations.

Thus, in order to get a confidence interval, one may sometimes have to perform of up to 1000 predictions. In some other cases fewer predictions may be sufficient, but in all cases hand simulations seem out of the question. On the other hand, if the function $T(\boldsymbol{\theta})$ is computerized and does not take much computer time (this is in general true if one uses the shortcut prediction techniques described in Chapter 4), sampling $\boldsymbol{\theta}$ and calculating $T(\boldsymbol{\theta})$ a few hundred times is not a problem.

5.3 Prediction Intervals

5.3.1 Analytic Method

Let us assume that instead of seeking the value $T(\boldsymbol{\theta}_o)$ of a figure of merit for a given distribution of the attribute vector $F_A(\mathbf{a})$, we are interested in obtaining the actual accumulated value of the individual figures of merit, $\sum_{m=1}^{M} \tau(\mathbf{U}_{(m)})$ (M and $\mathbf{U}_{(m)}$ are, respectively, the number of individuals in the group and the perceived utility vector of the mth individual).

If the number of individuals in the group is very large, the weak law of large numbers ensures that the actual accumulated value of the individual figures of merit equals the value of the mean $T(\boldsymbol{\theta}_o)$ times M. Thus, in such a case a confidence interval for the accumulated value of the individual figure of merit, which we call a *prediction interval*, is given by M times the confidence interval for $T(\boldsymbol{\theta}_o)$ and the methods in the previous two sections can be applied. On the other hand, if M is small, the actual accumulated value cannot be predicted deterministically even if $T(\boldsymbol{\theta}_o)$ is known, and prediction intervals must be obtained in a different way.

Homogeneous Population Groups

Since for a user who is sampled at random from the population the distribution of $\mathbf{U}$ is known (provided $\mathbf{a}$ and $\boldsymbol{\theta}$ are known), it is possible to determine (at least conceptually) the distribution of τ for a person who is sampled at random from a homogeneous group with $\mathbf{A} = \mathbf{a}$.

Under those conditions the accumulated value of τ, τ_{ac}, is the sum of M independent and identically distributed variables, $\tau_{(m)} = \tau(\mathbf{U}_{(m)})$:

$$\tau_{\text{ac}} = \sum_{m=1}^{M} \tau_{(m)},$$

and for moderately large values of M (although not large enough to neglect the variability of τ_{ac}) the accumulated value must be normal with

$$E(\tau_{\text{ac}}) = ME_{\xi}[\tau(\mathbf{U})] = MT(\boldsymbol{\theta}_o, \mathbf{a}), \tag{5.22}$$

where as usual the expected value of the individual figure of merit is denoted by $T(\boldsymbol{\theta}, \mathbf{a})$. The second moment about the origin of $\tau_{(m)}$ can be obtained from the distribution of $\mathbf{U}$ (at least theoretically) and is, therefore, a function of $\boldsymbol{\theta}$ and $\mathbf{a}$ which we denote $\bar{\bar{T}}(\boldsymbol{\theta}, \mathbf{a})$. Therefore

$$\text{var}(\tau_{(m)}^2) = \bar{\bar{T}}(\boldsymbol{\theta}_o, \mathbf{a}) - [T(\boldsymbol{\theta}_o, \mathbf{a})]^2$$

and

$$\text{var}(\tau_{\text{ac}}) = M\{\bar{\bar{T}}(\boldsymbol{\theta}_o, \mathbf{a}) - [T(\boldsymbol{\theta}_o, \mathbf{a})]^2\}. \tag{5.23}$$

Let us see now how one can calculate $\text{var}(\tau_{ac})$ in some simple cases (see also Section 1.5).

If, for example, we are interested in the usage of the ith alternative, $\tau(\mathbf{U})$ should be defined as follows:

$$\tau = \begin{cases} 1 & \text{if } U_i = \max_{j=1,\ldots,I} (U_j), \\ 0 & \text{otherwise.} \end{cases}$$

Then $E(\tau_{(m)}) = T(\boldsymbol{\theta}_o, \mathbf{a}) = P_i(\boldsymbol{\theta}_o, \mathbf{a})$, and since $\tau^2 \equiv \tau, E(\tau_{(m)}^2) = E(\tau_{(m)}) = \overline{\overline{T}}(\boldsymbol{\theta}_o, \mathbf{a}) = P_i(\boldsymbol{\theta}_o, \mathbf{a})$. Equation (5.23) yields

$$\text{var}(\tau_{ac}) = M[P_i(\boldsymbol{\theta}_o, \mathbf{a})][1 - P_i(\boldsymbol{\theta}_o, \mathbf{a})].$$

If, on the other hand, $\tau(\mathbf{U}) = \max_i(U_i)$, we know that

$$E[\tau(\mathbf{U})] = S(\boldsymbol{\theta}_o, \mathbf{a}),$$

which is given by previously discussed formulas for both logit and probit models. It can also be shown that for the MNL model (see Section 1.3.1)

$$\text{var}[\tau(\mathbf{U})] = \text{var}(U_i) = \tfrac{1}{6}\pi^2$$

and that for the MNP model

$$\text{var}[\tau(\mathbf{U})] = \text{var}[\max(U_i)],$$

which can be approximated with the formulas of Section 2.2.3 (the result is exact for the binary case).

With expressions for Eqs. (5.22) and (5.23) readily available, one can obtain a prediction interval for τ_{ac}. Write

$$[\tau_{ac} - MT(\hat{\boldsymbol{\Theta}}, \mathbf{a})] = M[T(\boldsymbol{\theta}_o, \mathbf{a}) - T(\hat{\boldsymbol{\Theta}}, \mathbf{a})] + [\tau_{ac} - MT(\boldsymbol{\theta}_o, \mathbf{a})]. \tag{5.24}$$

The first term on the right-hand side, for sufficiently small values of $\boldsymbol{\Sigma}_\theta$, can be considered normal (see the linearization method in Section 5.1.2) with zero mean and variance

$$\sigma_{\text{I}}^2 = M^2 \,\text{var}[T(\hat{\boldsymbol{\Theta}}, \mathbf{a})] \simeq M^2[\boldsymbol{\nabla}_\theta T(\hat{\boldsymbol{\theta}}, \mathbf{a})]\boldsymbol{\Sigma}_\theta[\boldsymbol{\nabla}_\theta T(\hat{\boldsymbol{\theta}}, \mathbf{a})]^{\text{T}}. \tag{5.25}$$

Also, as just discussed, if M is sufficiently large the central limit theorem applies and the second term of Eq. (5.24) is also normal (τ_{ac} is the sum of M independent and identically distributed components). It also has zero mean and variance σ_{II}^2, which can be approximately expressed as a function of $\hat{\boldsymbol{\theta}}$ by entering with $\hat{\boldsymbol{\theta}}$ in Eq. (5.23).

Since the two right-hand-side terms of Eq. (5.24) can be considered independent (the first one arises from a calibration experiment and the second from the selection of a random group with M people) the left-hand side is normally distributed with zero mean and variance $(\sigma_{\text{I}}^2 + \sigma_{\text{II}}^2)$, and the random variable

$$(\tau_{ac} - MT(\hat{\mathbf{\Theta}}, \mathbf{a}))/(\sigma_{\mathrm{I}}^2 + \sigma_{\mathrm{II}}^2)^{1/2}$$

is a standard normal pivotal quantity for τ_{ac}. Therefore a 100α% prediction interval for τ_{ac} is

$$[MT(\hat{\boldsymbol{\theta}}, \mathbf{a}) \pm \eta_{(1+\alpha)/2}(\sigma_{\mathrm{I}}^2 + \sigma_{\mathrm{II}}^2)^{1/2}], \tag{5.26}$$

which solves the problem.

Note that by increasing the sample size of the calibration stage, σ_{I} is made smaller and one can reduce the length of the prediction interval; however, it is impossible to decrease the length beyond $2\eta_{(1+\alpha)/2}\sigma_{\mathrm{II}}$.

Example We return to the binary probit example of Section 5.1.1 in which the specification was

$$p_1 = \Phi(\boldsymbol{\theta}\mathbf{a}^{\mathrm{T}}), \qquad p_2 = 1 - p_1,$$

with $\hat{\boldsymbol{\theta}} = (-6.71, 13.42, 13.42)$ and $\mathbf{a} = (1, a_{\mathrm{T}}, r_{\mathrm{T}})$. Let us find a prediction interval for the usage of public transit (alternative 2) for $M = 100$ and $\mathbf{a} = (1, 0.25, 0.33)$ if

$$\mathbf{\Sigma}_\theta \approx \begin{bmatrix} 0.02 & 0 & 0 \\ 0 & 0.04 & 0.02 \\ 0 & 0.02 & 0.06 \end{bmatrix}.$$

Since in this case $\mathbf{\Sigma}_\theta$ is small enough (the reader can verify this) and M is within the range where the central limit theorem applies, Eq. (5.26) will be used.

We first calculate σ_{I}^2. For the usage of alternative 2 we have

$$\begin{aligned} \nabla_\theta P_2(\hat{\boldsymbol{\theta}}, \mathbf{a}) &= -\phi(\hat{\boldsymbol{\theta}}\mathbf{a}^{\mathrm{T}})\mathbf{a} \\ &= -\phi(1.12) \times (1, 0.25, 0.33) \\ &= (-0.213, -0.053, -0.071) \end{aligned}$$

and using Eq. (5.25), $\sigma_{\mathrm{I}}^2 = 100^2 \times 0.0014 = 14$.

We now calculate σ_{II}^2, assuming that $\boldsymbol{\theta}_o = \hat{\boldsymbol{\theta}}$. For the usage we have

$$\begin{aligned} \sigma_{\mathrm{II}}^2 = \mathrm{var}(\tau_{ac}) &= M[1 - P_2(\hat{\boldsymbol{\theta}}, \mathbf{a})][P_2(\hat{\boldsymbol{\theta}}, \mathbf{a})] \\ &= 100\Phi(1.12)[1 - \Phi(1.12)] \\ &= 100 \times 0.114 = 11.4. \end{aligned}$$

Since $P_2(\hat{\boldsymbol{\theta}}, \mathbf{a}) = \Phi(-\hat{\boldsymbol{\theta}}\mathbf{a}) = 0.13$, a 90% prediction interval is

$$(13 \pm \eta_{(1+\alpha)/2}\sqrt{11.4 + 14}) = (13 \pm 8.3) = (4.7, 21.3),$$

and we can expect between 4 and 22 out of the 100 randomly selected people to become users of alternative 2. ■

Heterogeneous groups

For heterogeneous groups of people the technique is identical. Instead of Eq. (5.24) we have

$$[\tau_{\mathrm{ac}} - MT(\hat{\mathbf{\Theta}})] = M[T(\boldsymbol{\theta})_o - T(\hat{\mathbf{\Theta}})] + [\tau_{\mathrm{ac}} - MT(\boldsymbol{\theta}_o)], \tag{5.27}$$

and in the same way it is possible to develop an approximate confidence interval based on the variances of the first and second terms of the right-hand side of Eq. (5.27). σ_{I}^2 is given by the right-hand side of Eq. (5.17a), premultiplied by M^2. The variance of the second term σ_{II}^2 depends on how the group of people that we consider was gathered. In most cases it is reasonable to assume that the M individuals are independent drawings from a subgroup of the population with known distribution of the attribute vector $F_A(\mathbf{a})$, and the variance of τ_{ac} is M times the variance of $\tau(\mathbf{U})$ for one such drawing. The variance of $\tau(\mathbf{U})$ can be calculated as follows: first evaluate

$$E[\tau(\mathbf{U})] = E_A\{E_U[\tau(\mathbf{U})|\mathbf{A}]\} = E_A[T(\boldsymbol{\theta}, \mathbf{A})] = T(\boldsymbol{\theta})$$

and

$$E[\tau(\mathbf{U})^2] = E_A\{E_U[\tau(\mathbf{U})^2|\mathbf{A}]\} = E_A[\bar{T}(\boldsymbol{\theta}, \mathbf{A})] = \bar{\bar{T}}(\boldsymbol{\theta}),$$

using a prediction method (cf. Chapter 4), and then set

$$\sigma_{\mathrm{II}}^2 = \mathrm{var}(\tau_{\mathrm{ac}}) \approx M[\bar{\bar{T}}(\hat{\boldsymbol{\theta}}) - T(\hat{\boldsymbol{\theta}})^2]. \tag{5.28}$$

Equation (5.26) with $T(\hat{\boldsymbol{\theta}}, \mathbf{a})$ replaced by $T(\hat{\boldsymbol{\theta}})$ then applies.

Note that when we predict usage, $\tau^2(\mathbf{U}) \equiv \tau(\mathbf{U})$; consequently $\bar{\bar{T}}(\hat{\boldsymbol{\theta}}) = T(\hat{\boldsymbol{\theta}}) = P_i(\hat{\boldsymbol{\theta}})$, and Eq. (5.28) is simply

$$\sigma_{\mathrm{II}}^2 = MP_i(\hat{\boldsymbol{\theta}})[1 - P_i(\hat{\boldsymbol{\theta}})].$$

For the satisfaction the technique involves predicting its second moment about the origin, $\bar{\bar{S}}(\hat{\boldsymbol{\theta}})$, but the process is identical to prediction of $S(\hat{\boldsymbol{\theta}})$; instead of averaging $S(\boldsymbol{\theta}, \mathbf{A})$ with the prediction methods of Chapter 4 we average $\bar{\bar{S}}(\boldsymbol{\theta}, \mathbf{A})$, which is given by

$$\bar{\bar{S}}(\boldsymbol{\theta}, \mathbf{A}) = S(\boldsymbol{\theta}, \mathbf{A})^2 + \tfrac{1}{6}\pi^2$$

for the MNL model or by the approximation formulas for the MNP model.

Example Let us find a prediction interval for the usage of alternative 2 in the example in Section 5.1.2. A group of $M = 100$ randomly selected individuals from the whole population of non–car owners is considered.

Since from the example there we found

$$P_1(\hat{\boldsymbol{\theta}}) = 0.737 \qquad \text{and} \qquad \nabla_\theta P_1(\hat{\boldsymbol{\theta}}) = (-0.432, 0.085, 0.142),$$

we automatically have

$$P_2(\hat{\boldsymbol{\theta}}) = 0.263 \qquad \text{and} \quad \nabla_\theta P_2(\hat{\boldsymbol{\theta}}) = (0.432, -0.085, -0.142).$$

Also from the example we know that $\sigma_l^2 = 0.00143$, and therefore

$$\sigma_{\mathrm{I}}^2 = 100^2 \times 0.00143 = 14.3.$$

σ_{II}^2 can be obtained with the expression that was derived above for the usage:

$$\sigma_{\mathrm{II}}^2 = 100(0.263)(0.737) = 19.3.$$

Thus $\sigma = 5.8$ and the approximate 90% prediction interval is

$$(26.3 \pm 1.645 \times 5.8) = (16.8, 35.8),$$

that is, we know that very likely between 16 and 36 people out of 100 randomly selected individuals would elect to use public transit. ■

5.3.2 *Simulation Method*

When either $\boldsymbol{\Sigma}_\theta$ is too large or M is too small to be able to approximate the two terms of Eq. (5.27) by normal distributions the problem is more involved; however, a simulation procedure similar to the one described to develop confidence intervals can be used.

If we regard $\boldsymbol{\theta}_o$ as the outcome of a random variable $\boldsymbol{\Theta}_o$ whose distribution conditional on $\hat{\boldsymbol{\theta}}$ and $\boldsymbol{\Sigma}_\theta$ is MVN($\hat{\boldsymbol{\theta}}, \boldsymbol{\Sigma}_\theta$), we can develop (at least conceptually) the distribution of $\tau(\mathbf{U})$ for a randomly selected individual, since the conditional distribution of $\mathbf{U}$ given $\boldsymbol{\theta}_o$ is known. Although developing the analytic cumulative distribution function of $\tau(\mathbf{U})$ is difficult, Monte Carlo simulation yields it readily. The procedure parallels an imaginary experiment in which, first, we would select a value of $\boldsymbol{\theta}_o$, and then sample a person from the population, observe $\mathbf{U}$ (this value would depend statistically on the value of $\boldsymbol{\theta}_o$ previously determined), and calculate $\tau(\mathbf{U})$.

After many repetitions it will be possible to estimate the percentile points of $\tau(\mathbf{U})$, which may then be used as prediction intervals. A $100\alpha\%$ prediction interval developed in such a way must, of course, be physically interpreted in the same way as the Bayesian confidence intervals developed in Section 5.2.2. The procedure to obtain an observation of $\tau(\mathbf{U})$ is as follows:

Step 1 Sample $\boldsymbol{\theta}_o$ from a MVN($\hat{\boldsymbol{\theta}}, \boldsymbol{\Sigma}_\theta$) distribution.

Step 2 Sample $\mathbf{a}$ from $F_A(\mathbf{a})$.

Step 3 Calculate $\mathbf{V}(\boldsymbol{\theta}_o, \mathbf{a})$ and $\boldsymbol{\Sigma}_\xi(\boldsymbol{\theta}_o, \mathbf{a})$ with the values obtained in Steps 1 and 2.

Step 4 Sample ξ from a $\text{MVN}[\mathbf{0}, \boldsymbol{\Sigma}_\xi(\boldsymbol{\theta}_o, \mathbf{a})]$ distribution and calculate $\tau(\mathbf{U}) = \tau(\mathbf{V} + \xi)$.

With a computer, obtaining $\tau(\mathbf{U})$ takes milliseconds, and it is not difficult to calculate $\tau(\mathbf{U})$ many times. If $M = 1$, the percentile points of $\tau(\mathbf{U})$ can be obtained by repeating the above procedure. If M is small, say $M < 20$ or 30, Steps 2–4 of the above procedure can be repeated M times to give M observations and a value of τ_{ac}. Repeated observations of τ_{ac} will yield the prediction interval. If M is large, but we still cannot obtain the prediction interval numerically because $\boldsymbol{\Sigma}_\theta$ is too large, it is not necessary to repeat Steps 2–4 M times since for a given value of $\boldsymbol{\theta}_o$ we know that τ_{ac} is normally distributed with mean $MT(\boldsymbol{\theta}_o)$ and variance $M[\bar{\bar{T}}(\boldsymbol{\theta}_o) - T(\boldsymbol{\theta}_o)^2]$. The procedure can thus be streamlined as follows:

Step 1 Sample $\boldsymbol{\theta}_o$ from a $\text{MVN}(\hat{\boldsymbol{\theta}}, \boldsymbol{\Sigma}_\theta)$ distribution.

Step 2 Use one of the methods in Chapter 4 to calculate $MT(\boldsymbol{\theta}_o)$ and $M[\bar{\bar{T}}(\boldsymbol{\theta}_o) - T(\boldsymbol{\theta}_o)^2]$.

Step 3 Sample τ_{ac} from a $N\{MT(\boldsymbol{\theta}_o), M[\bar{\bar{T}}(\boldsymbol{\theta}_o) - T(\boldsymbol{\theta}_o)^2]\}$ distribution.

The confidence intervals can be derived from the string of τ_{ac}s. Note that Step 2 of this process may be relatively time consuming (for several hundred repetitions) unless a shortcut prediction method is used. Also note that if M is very large, for any given $\boldsymbol{\theta}_o$, the standard deviation of τ_{ac} is very small and $\tau_{\text{ac}} \approx MT(\boldsymbol{\theta}_o)$. Thus, the simulation process requires neither Step 3 nor the calculation of $M[\bar{\bar{T}}(\boldsymbol{\theta}_o) - T(\boldsymbol{\theta}_o)^2]$. It coincides with the confidence-interval calculation method given in Section 5.2.2.

5.4 Other Considerations

5.4.1 *Uncertainty in the Distribution of the Attribute Vector*

When the distribution of $\mathbf{A}$ is estimated with an inaccurate method the errors introduced will be reflected in the final forecast just as the errors in the estimation of $\boldsymbol{\theta}_o$ affected the results of the forecasts. The techniques used to obtain confidence and prediction intervals when the value of $\boldsymbol{\theta}_o$ was uncertain can be extended easily to capture the uncertainty in the distribution of $\mathbf{A}$.

Let the true distribution of $\mathbf{A}$ be $F_A(\mathbf{a} | \zeta_o)$, where ζ_o is an unknown vector of parameters whose values must be forecasted inaccurately. For instance, with prediction methods where the distribution of **A** is approximated by the multivariate normal distribution, the vector ζ_o includes the true (unknown mean vector and covariance matrix of **A**, $\bar{\mathbf{A}}$, and $\boldsymbol{\Sigma}_A$. With this in mind, and treating ζ_o as an outcome of a random variable $\mathbf{Z}_o$, in the same sense as $\boldsymbol{\theta}_o$ was treated as an outcome of $\boldsymbol{\Theta}_o$, we can express our uncertainty in ζ_o by saying that $\mathbf{Z}_o$ is $F_Z(\mathbf{x})$ distributed, where the mean of $\mathbf{Z}_o$ is close to the forecasted value $\hat{\zeta}$ of ζ_o, and its variance indicates the degree of uncertainty placed on $\hat{\zeta}$.

The simulation process for prediction interval development is almost identical to the one in Section 5.3, except for Step 1, which is as follows:

Step 1 Sample $\boldsymbol{\theta}_o$ from a $\text{MVN}(\hat{\boldsymbol{\theta}}, \boldsymbol{\Sigma}_\theta)$ distribution, and sample ζ_o from $F_{Z_0}(\mathbf{x})$. Of course, ζ_o determines the distribution $F_A(\mathbf{a})$ of **A**. The rest of the process is analogous.

An analytic prediction-interval construction method can also be developed in this case if in addition to the conditions of Section 5.3.1 we can assume that $\hat{\zeta}$ is an observation from a MVN distribution with mean ζ_o and known covariance matrix $\boldsymbol{\Sigma}_\zeta$. The procedure involves linearizing

$$T(\boldsymbol{\theta} \mid \zeta) = \int_{\mathbf{a}} T(\boldsymbol{\theta}, \mathbf{a}) F_A(\mathbf{a} \mid \zeta)\, d\mathbf{a}$$

with respect to both $\boldsymbol{\theta}$ and ζ, and writing $[T(\hat{\boldsymbol{\Theta}} \mid \hat{\mathbf{Z}}) - T(\boldsymbol{\theta}_o \mid \zeta_o)]$ as a normal pivotal quantity with zero mean and known variance (function of $\boldsymbol{\Sigma}_\zeta$ and $\boldsymbol{\Sigma}_\theta$).

5.4.2 *Sample-Size Considerations*

In the discussion of Chapters 3 and 5 we saw, respectively, how it is possible to derive the distribution of $\hat{\boldsymbol{\Theta}}$ from the results of an estimation process, and the distribution of $T(\hat{\boldsymbol{\Theta}})$ and τ_{ac} from the distribution of $\hat{\boldsymbol{\Theta}}$. This is important because if, with these techniques, we find that not enough accuracy was obtained, it is possible to decide whether or not to collect more data. However, since in most instances such data re-collection is not desirable, an approximate sample-size selection guideline is suggested below.

A discrete choice model is not useful unless it can reproduce to a prespecified degree of accuracy the fractions of the population that select each alternative. Since it is reasonable to require that this be the case for the population from which the data were gathered, an a priori check to ensure this should be performed.

Let us assume that we use a random sampling mechanism to obtain a disaggregate data set from a given population, and that we estimate the fraction of the population that selects alternative i with the following two methods:

Method a Direct Estimation For each observation n, let $X_{(n)}$ be a random variable that is set equal to one if $c_{(n)} = i$ and to zero otherwise. Under these conditions, the maximum-likelihood estimator of p_i is

$$\hat{p}_i = \sum_{n=1}^{N} X_{(n)}/N.$$

Method b Indirect Estimation Assume known the distribution of the attribute vector $F_A(\mathbf{a})$; then, obtain a value for $\hat{\boldsymbol{\theta}}$ by calibrating a discrete choice model $P_i(\boldsymbol{\theta}, \mathbf{a})$ with the data, and estimate p_i with $P_i(\hat{\boldsymbol{\theta}})$.

We note that $p_i = E_A[P_i(\boldsymbol{\theta}_o, \mathbf{A})]$ [assuming that $P_i(\boldsymbol{\theta}_o, \mathbf{a})$ is a correct specification]; thus p_i is a function of $\boldsymbol{\theta}_o$ and the invariant property of maximum-likelihood estimators[5] suggests that

$$\hat{p}_i = E_A[P_i(\hat{\boldsymbol{\theta}}, \mathbf{A})] = P_i(\hat{\boldsymbol{\theta}}).$$

Consequently, if the specification of the choice model is correct, Methods a and b yield the same answer. This is important because the accuracy of $P_i(\hat{\boldsymbol{\theta}})$ can be analyzed from that of $\hat{p}_i$, which is easier to assess.

If N is large, $\hat{p}_i$ is approximately normal with mean p_i and variance $p_i(1 - p_i)/N$; therefore the relative error $\varepsilon = (\hat{p}_i - p_i)/p_i$ is also normal with zero mean and variance

$$\operatorname{var}(\varepsilon) = (1 - p_i)/Np_i.$$

Since the relative error will rarely exceed $1.5\sqrt{(1 - p_i)/Np_i}$ in absolute value, that expression can be used as a criterion to select N. To be fair, of course, one should select the alternative that is selected by the fewest people in the population since $1.5\sqrt{1 - p_i/Np_i}$ decreases with p_i.

The minimum number of observations is then given by

$$N \approx 2.2(1 - p_i)/p_i\varepsilon^2.$$

For instance, if we know that the approximate shares of three alternatives in the population we are about the sample from are approximately 0.2, 0.3, and 0.5, and we are satisfied with 20% accuracy,

$$N \approx \frac{2.2}{(0.2)^2}\frac{0.8}{0.2} = 220.$$

[5] The invariant property of the MLE estimators follows immediately from their definition. It is as follows: If $\boldsymbol{\theta}'_o$ has a one-to-one relationship with $\boldsymbol{\theta}_o$ $[\boldsymbol{\theta}'_o = \boldsymbol{\theta}'(\boldsymbol{\theta}_o)$ and $\boldsymbol{\theta}_o = \boldsymbol{\theta}(\boldsymbol{\theta}'_o)]$, $\hat{\boldsymbol{\theta}}' = \boldsymbol{\theta}'(\hat{\boldsymbol{\theta}})$. In our case and to be rigorous, we would have to prove that there exist $r - 1$ functions that define a one-to-one relationship between $\boldsymbol{\theta}_o$ and $P_i(\boldsymbol{\theta}_o)$.

Although this value will in most cases be a good preliminary indicator of the required number of observations, the final decision must be deferred until after calibration. This is important to remember because the expression does not strictly apply to non-random sampling strategies since the objective of these is to reduce the value of N by sampling from very different substrata of the population. Postcalibration analysis is also necessary because the ultimate role of the model is predicting a figure of merit other than p_i (otherwise we could have used method a, above, which does not require a choice model) and such a figure of merit usually will be more or less sensitive than p_i to errors in $\hat{\boldsymbol{\theta}}$.

5.5 Summary

In order for discrete choice models to be really useful it is necessary to find ways of assessing the accuracy of their predictions. Inaccuracies in the forecasts have three basic sources: specification errors, insufficient or poor data, and poor or erroneous prediction of the distribution of the attribute vector.

Specification errors as well as some of the consequences of deficiencies in the data are explored in Section 3.1, where it is suggested that the MNP model was quite robust in the presence of some of these phenomena. There it is shown how the problems could be handled and identified by manipulation of the specification of the covariance matrix of the disturbances and by proper interpretation of the results of calibration. Yet another type of specification–data problem is also identified in Section 3.4.3, where it was argued that unless one has the right type of data with the right specification one can hardly claim a discrete choice model to be behavioral and therefore transferrable and valid for policy analysis.

In the analysis of the present chapter the aforementioned problems were assumed solved, which left us with two remaining sources of inaccuracies: insufficient data and uncertain distribution of the attribute vector. As is traditional in the econometrics literature the uncertainty of the predictions is expressed by means of confidence and prediction intervals. Since not much effort has been devoted by researchers to this subject [only Koppelman (1976b), who discusses some aspects of the binary logit model, and Daganzo (1979a), who extended the results to discrete choice models, seem to have investigated the problem in the open literature] most of the material presented in this chapter follows standard econometric practice as far as prediction with nonlinear models is concerned.

The first three sections of the chapter cover errors in the estimation of $\boldsymbol{\theta}_o$ due to lack of data and how those errors propagate to the final prediction.

Sections 5.1 and 5.2 explore the subject for very large groups of people and for both binary and multinomial models; the logic there parallels the development of confidence intervals for points on the regression line of the standard linear model. Section 5.3 develops prediction intervals for small groups of individuals. Section 5.4 addresses two miscellaneous items; Section 5.4.1 shows how it is possible to handle the uncertainty in the distribution of the attribute vector; and Section 5.4.2 gives a simple rule of thumb to select an adequate sample size prior to calibration.

Since most of the material in this last chapter is rather rudimentary, it is reasonable to expect refinements to it to appear in the scientific literature in the near future. Of particular interest would be approximate shortcut confidence and prediction interval calculation methods when linearization of the figure of merit is not possible. It is also hoped that in the near future statistically optimal sampling strategies will be available.

Appendix A Some Properties and Definitions of Matrices, Determinants, and Quadratic Functions

Quadratic Function

1.1 A *quadratic function* is a second-degree polynomial of several variables $(x_1, \ldots, x_n)$. It can always be expressed in matrix notation as

$$y = R + \mathbf{x}\mathbf{P}^{\mathrm{T}} + \mathbf{x}\mathbf{Q}\mathbf{x}^{\mathrm{T}}, \tag{A.1}$$

where R is a scalar, $\mathbf{x}$ is a $1 \times n$ row vector of variables x_i, $\mathbf{P}$ is a $1 \times n$ row vector of constants p_i, and $\mathbf{Q}$ is a square $n \times n$ symmetric matrix of constants q_{ij}. This is easy to see, since for an arbitrary quadratic equation

$$y = a + \sum_{i=1} b_i x_i + \sum_{i=1} \sum_{j=1} c_{ij} x_i x_j \tag{A.2}$$

there are values of R, $\mathbf{P}$, and $\mathbf{Q}$ that reduce Eq. (A.1) to Eq. (A.2). They are $R = a$, $p_i = b_i$, $q_{ii} = c_{ii}$, and, for the off-diagonal elements of $\mathbf{Q}$, $q_{ij} = q_{ji} = (c_{ij} + c_{ji})/2$.

The First and Second Derivatives of a Quadratic Function

2.1 It can be seen by manipulation of (A.2) that

$$\nabla_x y = \mathbf{P} + 2\mathbf{x}\mathbf{Q} \qquad \text{and} \qquad \nabla_x^2 y = 2\mathbf{Q},$$

where $\nabla_x y$ and $\nabla_x^2 y$ represent, respectively, the gradient and Hessian of y.

2.2 If the matrix $\mathbf{Q}$ is not singular it is possible to find its inverse, and $\nabla_x y$ vanishes at one single point $\mathbf{x}^*$. It is found by setting

$$\mathbf{P} + 2\mathbf{x}^*\mathbf{Q} = \mathbf{0},$$

which post multiplied by $\frac{1}{2}\mathbf{Q}^{-1}$ yields $\mathbf{x}^* = -\frac{1}{2}\mathbf{P}\mathbf{Q}^{-1}$.

Quadratic Forms

3.1 A *quadratic form* is a homogeneous polynomial of second degree. It is a quadratic function with $R = 0$ and $\mathbf{P} = \mathbf{0}$, and can be expressed as

$$y = \mathbf{x}\mathbf{Q}\mathbf{x}^{\mathrm{T}},$$

where $\mathbf{Q}$ is symmetric.

3.2 A quadratic form and its associated matrix $\mathbf{Q}$ are said to be *positive* (*negative*) *definite* if y is strictly positive (negative) for all $\mathbf{x}$ different from the zero vector (e.g., $y = 3x_1^2 + x_2^2$ is a positive-definite quadratic form).

3.3 A quadratic form and its associated matrix $\mathbf{Q}$ are said to be *positive* (*negative*) *semidefinite* if y is nonnegative (nonpositive) for all $\mathbf{x}$ (e.g., $y = 3x_1^2 + 0x_2^2$ is a positive-semidefinite quadratic form).

Diagonalization of Symmetric Square Matrices

4.1 A symmetric square matrix $\mathbf{Q}$ with real elements can always be expressed as

$$\mathbf{Q} = \mathbf{L}\mathbf{\Lambda}\mathbf{L}^{\mathrm{T}}, \tag{A.3}$$

where $\mathbf{L}$ is an orthogonal matrix (i.e., a nonsingular matrix such that $\mathbf{L}\mathbf{L}^{\mathrm{T}} = \mathbf{I}$), and $\mathbf{\Lambda}$ is a diagonal matrix of real elements. The diagonal elements of $\mathbf{\Lambda}$ are called *eigenvalues* (or characteristic values).

4.2 The eigenvalues λ_i are given by the n roots of the so-called *characteristic equation*

$$|\mathbf{Q} - \lambda\mathbf{I}| = 0,$$

where the vertical bars represent the determinant of the enclosed quantity. The proof of these statements can be found in most introductory books on linear algebra.

Properties of Definite and Semidefinite Matrices

5.1 A symmetric $n \times n$ matrix $\mathbf{Q}$ is positive (negative) definite if and only if the eigenvalues are all positive (negative). This is easy to see because

$$y = \mathbf{x}\mathbf{Q}\mathbf{x}^{\mathrm{T}} = \mathbf{x}\mathbf{L}\mathbf{\Lambda}\mathbf{L}^{\mathrm{T}}\mathbf{x}^{\mathrm{T}} = (\mathbf{x}\mathbf{L})\mathbf{\Lambda}(\mathbf{x}\mathbf{L})^{\mathrm{T}} = \sum_{i=1}^{n} \lambda_i(\mathbf{x}\mathbf{L})_i^2,$$

and since if $\mathbf{x} \neq \mathbf{0}$, $\mathbf{x}\mathbf{L} \neq \mathbf{0}$ (otherwise $\mathbf{L}$ would be singular since one of its rows would be a linear combination of the others), y must necessarily have the sign of the eigenvalues λ_i.

5.2 A similar argument shows that a symmetric matrix is positive (negative) semidefinite if and only if the eigenvalues are nonnegative (nonpositive). Furthermore, if $\mathbf{B}$ is a nonsingular $n \times n$ square matrix, the transformation

$$\mathbf{Q}' = \mathbf{B}\mathbf{Q}\mathbf{B}^{\mathrm{T}}$$

does not alter the definiteness of $\mathbf{Q}$.

5.3 If a symmetric matrix $\mathbf{Q}$ is positive (negative) definite, it is nonsingular, and its inverse is positive (negative) definite with eigenvalues given by the reciprocals of those of $\mathbf{Q}$. This is easy to see since from Eq. (A.3) $|\mathbf{Q}| = \prod_{i=1}^{n} \lambda_i > 0$ (or <0 for negative definite $\mathbf{Q}$) and

$$\mathbf{Q}^{-1} = \mathbf{L}\mathbf{\Lambda}^{-1}\mathbf{L}^{\mathrm{T}}.$$

5.4 Since all the eigenvalues of a nonsingular matrix $\mathbf{Q}$ are different from zero (otherwise $|\mathbf{Q} - 0\mathbf{I}| = 0$ and $\mathbf{Q}$ would be singular), any symmetric nonsingular positive (negative) semidefinite matrix has strictly positive (negative) eigenvalues and must also be positive (negative) definite.

5.5 A symmetric matrix $\mathbf{Q}$ is positive definite if and only if it can be expressed as $\mathbf{Q} = \mathbf{T}\mathbf{T}^{\mathrm{T}}$, where $\mathbf{T}$ is a lower triangular matrix with diagonal elements given by the positive square root of the eigenvalues. This is equivalent to saying that $\mathbf{Q}$ can be expressed as

$$\mathbf{Q} = \mathbf{T}\mathbf{\Lambda}\mathbf{T}^{\mathrm{T}}, \tag{A.4}$$

where $\mathbf{T}$ is lower triangular with ones on the main diagonal. These two statements (as well as those in the next two paragraphs) are shown in most introductory books on matrices. Equation (A.4) is usually called the *Cholesky factorization* of a positive-definite matrix.

5.6 A symmetric $n \times n$ matrix $\mathbf{Q}$ is positive definite if and only if all the principal diagonal minors are strictly positive. That is, $\mathbf{Q}$ is positive definite if and only if

$$\begin{vmatrix} q_{11} & q_{12} & \cdots & q_{1i} \\ q_{21} & q_{22} & \cdots & q_{2i} \\ \vdots & \vdots & \ddots & \vdots \\ q_{i1} & q_{i2} & & q_{ii} \end{vmatrix} > 0, \qquad i = 1, 2, \ldots, n.$$

5.7 For negative-definite matrices the condition states that the principal diagonal minors should be positive if i is even, and negative if i is odd.

Maxima and Minima of Quadratic Functions

6.1 If $\mathbf{Q}$ is singular, the unique point $\mathbf{x}^*$ at which the gradient of the quadratic function defined by Eq. (A.1) vanishes is a local–global minimum (maximum) if and only if $\mathbf{Q}$ is positive (negative) definite. This is seen by verifying that for any point, $\mathbf{x} \neq \mathbf{x}^*$, the difference $y(\mathbf{x}) - y(\mathbf{x}^*)$ is always positive (negative):

$$\begin{aligned} y(\mathbf{x}) - y(\mathbf{x}^*) &= \mathbf{x}\mathbf{P}^{\mathrm{T}} - \mathbf{x}^*\mathbf{P}^{\mathrm{T}} + \mathbf{x}\mathbf{Q}\mathbf{x}^{\mathrm{T}} - \mathbf{x}^*\mathbf{Q}\mathbf{x}^{*\mathrm{T}} \\ &= -2\mathbf{x}\mathbf{Q}\mathbf{x}^{*\mathrm{T}} + 2\mathbf{x}^*\mathbf{Q}\mathbf{x}^{*\mathrm{T}} + \mathbf{x}\mathbf{Q}\mathbf{x}^{\mathrm{T}} - \mathbf{x}^*\mathbf{Q}\mathbf{x}^{*\mathrm{T}} \\ &= \mathbf{x}\mathbf{Q}\mathbf{x}^{\mathrm{T}} + \mathbf{x}^*\mathbf{Q}\mathbf{x}^{*\mathrm{T}} - 2\mathbf{x}\mathbf{Q}\mathbf{x}^{*\mathrm{T}} = (\mathbf{x} - \mathbf{x}^*)\mathbf{Q}(\mathbf{x} - \mathbf{x}^*)^{\mathrm{T}}, \end{aligned}$$

which if $\mathbf{x} \neq \mathbf{x}^*$ is positive (negative) if and only if $\mathbf{Q}$ is positive (negative) definite. In the above derivation we used the equality $\mathbf{P} = -2\mathbf{x}^*\mathbf{Q}$ from paragraph 2.2.

Appendix B — The Algebra of Expectations with Matrices

1.1 Throughout this appendix we study a vector-valued random variable $\mathbf{X} = (X_1, \ldots, X_n)$ and another random variable $\mathbf{Y} = (Y_1, \ldots, Y_l)$ that is related to $\mathbf{X}$ by a linear transformation

$$\mathbf{Y} = \mathbf{XA} + \mathbf{B}, \tag{B.1}$$

where $\mathbf{A}$ is an $n \times l$ matrix of constants a_{ij}, and $\mathbf{B}$ is a $1 \times l$ vector of constants b_i. Equation (B.1) can be written in expanded notation as

$$Y_i = \sum_{k=1}^{n} X_k a_{ki} + b_i, \qquad i = 1, \ldots, l. \tag{B.2}$$

1.2 If we denote the means of $\mathbf{X}$ and $\mathbf{Y}$ by $\mathbf{m}_x = [E(X_1), E(X_2), \ldots, E(X_n)]$ and $\mathbf{m}_y = [E(Y_1), \ldots, E(Y_l)]$, we can write

$$\mathbf{m}_y = \mathbf{m}_x\mathbf{A} + \mathbf{B}. \tag{B.3}$$

This can be seen by taking expectations on both sides of Eq. (B.2) and using the fact that the expectation of a linear function is the function of the expectations.

1.3 If we let $\sigma^2_{x,ij}$ denote the covariance of X_i and X_j and $\sigma^2_{y,ij}$ the covariance of Y_i and Y_j, we can develop a similar relationship between the covariances of $\mathbf{X}$ and $\mathbf{Y}$. Let us first arrange the covariances of the elements of X and Y in two square $n \times n$ and $l \times l$ matrices $\mathbf{\Sigma}_x = \{\sigma^2_{x,ij}\}$ and $\mathbf{\Sigma}_y = \{\sigma^2_{y,ij}\}$. These matrices are symmetric because the covariance of two random variables has the commutative property.

1.4 As is shown below, they are related by

$$\mathbf{\Sigma}_y = \mathbf{A}^{\mathrm{T}}\mathbf{\Sigma}_x\mathbf{A}. \tag{B.4}$$

The elements of $\mathbf{\Sigma}_y$ can be expressed as

$$\sigma^2_{y,ij} = E\{[Y_i - E(Y_i)][Y_j - E(Y_j)]\},$$

and, defining the expectation of a matrix as a matrix containing as elements the expectations of the elements of the original matrix, we can write

$$\mathbf{\Sigma}_y = E[(\mathbf{Y} - \mathbf{m}_y)^{\mathrm{T}}(\mathbf{Y} - \mathbf{m}_y)]. \tag{B.5}$$

Since by subtraction of Eq. (B.3) from Eq. (B.1)

$$(\mathbf{Y} - \mathbf{m}_y) = (\mathbf{X} - \mathbf{m}_x)\mathbf{A},$$

Eq. (B.5) can be rewritten as

$$\mathbf{\Sigma}_y = E\{[(\mathbf{X} - \mathbf{m}_x)\mathbf{A}]^{\mathrm{T}}(\mathbf{X} - \mathbf{m}_x)\mathbf{A}\} = E[\mathbf{A}^{\mathrm{T}}(\mathbf{X} - \mathbf{m}_x)^{\mathrm{T}}(\mathbf{X} - \mathbf{m}_x)A].$$

Furthermore, since the expectation of a linear function is a linear function of the expectations, we can bring $\mathbf{A}^{\mathrm{T}}$ and $\mathbf{A}$ outside of the expectation and have

$$\mathbf{\Sigma}_y = \mathbf{A}^{\mathrm{T}}E[(\mathbf{X} - \mathbf{m}_x)^{\mathrm{T}}(\mathbf{X} - \mathbf{m}_x)]\mathbf{A} = \mathbf{A}^{\mathrm{T}}\mathbf{\Sigma}_x\mathbf{A},$$

which coincides with Eq. (B.4).

1.5 Covariance matrices must be positive semidefinite. This is true because otherwise the diagonalization of a covariance matrix $\mathbf{\Sigma}_x$ (see Appendix A, paragraph 4.1)

$$\mathbf{\Sigma}_x = \mathbf{L\Lambda L}^{\mathrm{T}}$$

would yield a negative element in $\mathbf{\Lambda}$ (Appendix A, paragraph 5.2) and this would mean that at least one of the elements of the transformed random variable $\mathbf{XL}$, whose covariance matrix is $\mathbf{\Lambda}$ [this follows from Eq. (B.4)], would have a negative variance.

1.6 If a covariance matrix is singular, at least one of the elements of $\mathbf{\Lambda}$ is zero (from Appendix A, $|\mathbf{\Sigma}_x| = \prod_{i=1} \lambda_i$) and the variance of one of the elements of $\mathbf{XL}$ is zero. Consequently, that element is constant and there is a deterministic linear relationship between the elements of $\mathbf{X}$. In other words, the values of $\mathbf{X}$ that can occur are concentrated in a hyperplane of $\mathscr{R}^n$.

Appendix C Some Properties of the Multivariate Normal Distribution

The Standard Normal Distribution and the Logistic Curve

1.1 A continuous scalar random variable X is *standard normal distributed* if its density function is given by

$$\phi(x) = \frac{1}{\sqrt{2\pi}} \exp(-x^2/2), \qquad -\infty < x < \infty. \tag{C.1}$$

1.2 The cumulative distribution, which is called the *standard normal curve*,

$$\Phi(x) = \int_{-\infty}^{x} \frac{1}{\sqrt{2\pi}} \exp(-w^2/2)\, dw, \qquad -\infty < x < \infty, \tag{C.2}$$

is a monotonically increasing function going from zero to one as x goes from $-\infty$ to ∞.

1.3 A standard normal random variable has zero mean and unit variance. Table C.1 includes values of $-\log[\Phi(x)]$ from $x = -7.9$ to $x = 0$. For smaller values of x the approximation

$$-\log[(\Phi(x)] = x^2/2 + \ln|x| + 0.92, \qquad x \to -\infty, \tag{C.3}$$

yields an absolute error for $\log \Phi(x)$ smaller than 0.02 and a relative error smaller than 2% for $\Phi(x)$. For positive values of x we use $\Phi(x) = 1 - \Phi(-x)$.

1.4 A continuous random variable is *logistically distributed* with mean zero and unit standard deviation if its cumulative distribution function is

$$L(x) = \frac{\exp(x\pi/\sqrt{3})}{1 + \exp(x\pi/\sqrt{3})}, \qquad -\infty < x < \infty. \tag{C.4}$$

Table C.1

Standardized Normal and Logistic Cumulative Distribution Functions for $-8 < x \leq 0$[a]

	0.0	0.1	0.2	0.3	0.4	0.5	0.6	0.7	0.8	0.9
0	0.69315	0.77615	0.86574	0.96210	1.06543	1.17591	1.29370	1.41897	1.55185	1.69249
	0.69315	0.78794	0.89089	1.00178	1.12031	1.24606	1.37855	1.51724	1.66157	1.81095
1	1.84102	1.99756	2.16222	2.33510	2.51631	2.70594	2.90408	3.11080	3.32618	3.55028
	1.96483	2.12268	2.28401	2.44834	2.61528	2.78445	2.95553	3.12824	3.30233	3.47759
2	3.78319	4.02495	4.27562	4.53526	4.80392	5.08165	5.36848	5.66446	5.96963	6.28402
	3.65383	3.83091	4.00868	4.18704	4.36590	4.54517	4.72479	4.90470	5.08485	5.26520
3	6.60767	6.94062	7.28288	7.63450	7.99548	8.36587	8.74569	9.13495	9.53369	9.94191
	5.44572	5.62639	5.80717	5.98805	6.16901	6.35005	6.53114	6.71227	6.89345	7.07466
4	10.35963	10.78689	11.22369	11.67004	12.12598	12.59150	13.06662	13.55137	14.04574	14.54975
	7.25590	7.43717	7.79975	7.79975	8.16238	8.16238	8.34371	8.52506	8.70640	8.88775
5	15.06342	15.58675	16.11975	16.66244	17.21483	17.77691	18.34871	18.93023	19.52148	20.12246
	9.06911	9.25047	9.43184	9.61320	9.79457	9.97594	10.15731	10.33869	10.52006	10.70144
6	20.73319	21.35367	21.98391	22.62391	23.27368	23.93323	24.60257	25.28169	25.97060	26.66931
	10.88281	11.06419	11.24557	11.42695	11.60833	11.78970	11.97108	12.15246	12.33384	12.51522
7	27.37783	28.09616	28.8243	29.56226	30.31004	31.06765	31.83509	32.61237	33.39948	34.19644
	12.69660	12.87798	13.05936	13.24074	13.42212	13.60350	13.78488	13.96626	14.14764	14.32902

[a] The entries of this table give the negative of the logarithm of the standard normal cumulative distribution function (top of cell) and the negative of the logarithm of the logistic cumulative distribution function with zero mean and unit variance (bottom of cell). The table is valid only for negative arguments up to a maximum absolute value of 7.9. To read, take the absolute value of the argument and find the corresponding cell as indicated by the numbers at the margins.

1.5 Table C.1 also gives the values of $-\log L(x)$ from $x = -7.9$ to $x = 0$. For smaller values of x Eq. (C.4) is approximated well by

$$-\log[L(x)] = x/\sqrt{3}, \qquad x \to -\infty. \tag{C.5}$$

Note that Eq. (C.5) is linear in x but Eq. (C.4) is (approximately) quadratic. As with the standard normal curve for positive values of x we can use $L(x) = 1 - L(-x)$.

The Multivariate Normal Distribution

2.1 A vector-valued random variable $\mathbf{X} = (X_1, \ldots, X_n)$ is *multivariate normally* (MVN) *distributed* with mean $\mathbf{m} = (m_1, \ldots, m_n)$ and nonsingular covariance matrix

$$\boldsymbol{\Sigma} = \begin{bmatrix} \sigma_{11}^2 & \sigma_{12}^2 & \cdots & \sigma_{1n}^2 \\ \vdots & \vdots & \cdots & \vdots \\ \sigma_{n1}^2 & \sigma_{n2}^2 & \cdots & \sigma_{nn}^2 \end{bmatrix},$$

if its density function is

$$\phi(\mathbf{x}\,|\,\mathbf{m}, \boldsymbol{\Sigma}) = (2\pi|\boldsymbol{\Sigma}|)^{-n/2} \exp[-(\mathbf{x} - \mathbf{m})\boldsymbol{\Sigma}^{-1}(\mathbf{x} - \mathbf{m})^{\mathrm{T}}/2]. \tag{C.6}$$

2.2 A very important property of the MVN family is that it is closed under linear transformations. That is, if $\mathbf{Y} = (Y_1, \ldots, Y_l)$ is related to $\mathbf{X}$ by

$$\mathbf{Y} = \mathbf{XA} + \mathbf{B},$$

where $\mathbf{A}$ is an $n \times l$ matrix, and $\mathbf{B}$ a $1 \times l$ vector of constants, the vector $\mathbf{Y}$ is MVN distributed with mean vector and covariance matrix given by (see Appendix B, paragraphs 1.2 and 1.4)

$$\mathbf{m}_y = \mathbf{mA} + \mathbf{B} \tag{C.7}$$

and

$$\boldsymbol{\Sigma}_y = \mathbf{A}^{\mathrm{T}}\boldsymbol{\Sigma}\mathbf{A}. \tag{C.8}$$

If $l \leq n$ and rank $(\mathbf{A}) = l$, $\boldsymbol{\Sigma}_y$ may be nonsingular, and the density function of $\mathbf{Y}$ is

$$\phi_y(\mathbf{y}\,|\,\mathbf{m}_y, \boldsymbol{\Sigma}_y). \tag{C.9}$$

2.3 A consequence of this result is that the one-dimensional normal cumulative distribution function $\Phi(x\,|\,m, \sigma^2)$, with mean m and variance σ^2, is standardizable because it can be expressed as a function of the standard normal curve. If X is normal with mean m and variance σ^2, the linear transformation $Y = X/\sigma - m/\sigma$ yields a standard normal random variable.

Consequently

$$\Phi(x|m, \sigma^2) = \Pr\{X \leq x\} = \Pr\{Y\sigma + m \leq x\}$$
$$= \Pr\{Y \leq (x - m)/\sigma\} = \Phi((x - m)/\sigma)$$

and it is possible to determine $\Phi(x|m, \sigma^2)$ from Table C.1.

The Chi-Square Distribution

3.1 A scalar random variable Z_n, obtained from a set of n independent identically distributed normal random variables $X_1, \ldots, X_n$ by

$$Z_n = \sum_{i=1}^{n} X_i^2, \tag{C.10}$$

has a *chi-square distribution* with n degrees of freedom (abbreviated as $\chi^2_{(n)}$).

3.2 The probability density function of Z_n is

$$f_{Z_n}(x) = \frac{2^{-n/2}}{\Gamma(n/2)} x^{n/2-1} e^{-x/2},$$

where $\Gamma(\cdot)$ is the gamma function; its mean and variance are n and $2n$, respectively.

3.3 Unfortunately, the cumulative distribution function neither assumes a closed form nor is standardizable. Because of this, only the percentile points of Z_n can be given in a reasonable amount of space. Table C.2 contains the upper tail percentile points of $\chi^2_{(n)}$ for up to 50 degrees of freedom. For more degrees of freedom the 100α percentile of Z_n, $\chi^2_{(n,\alpha)}$, can be approximated by

$$\chi^2_{(n,\alpha)} \approx n\left[1 - \frac{2}{9n} + \eta_\alpha \sqrt{\frac{2}{9n}}\right]^3, \tag{C.11}$$

where η_α is the 100α percentile of a standard normal random variable.

The Distribution of Some Quadratic Forms

4.1 If $\mathbf{X} = (X_1, \ldots, X_n)$ is MVN distributed with mean $\mathbf{m}$ and a nonsingular covariance matrix $\mathbf{\Sigma}$, the scalar random variable Z_n, defined by the quadratic form

$$Z_n = (\mathbf{X} - \mathbf{m})\mathbf{\Sigma}^{-1}(\mathbf{X} - \mathbf{m})^{\mathrm{T}}, \tag{C.12}$$

is $\chi^2_{(n)}$ distributed.

This is easy to see because $\mathbf{\Sigma}$ is positive definite [it is positive semidefinite (Appendix B, paragraph 1.5) and nonsingular] and, consequently, so is

Table C.2

Percentile Points of the $\chi^2_{(n)}$ Distribution

n degrees of freedom	α 0.900	0.950	0.975	0.990	0.995	0.999
1	2.706	3.841	5.024	6.635	7.879	10.828
2	4.605	5.991	7.378	9.210	10.597	13.816
3	6.251	7.815	9.348	11.345	12.838	16.266
4	7.779	9.488	11.143	13.277	14.860	18.467
5	9.236	11.070	12.833	15.086	16.750	20.515
6	10.645	12.592	14.449	16.812	18.548	22.458
7	12.017	14.067	16.013	18.475	20.278	24.322
8	13.362	15.507	17.535	20.090	21.955	26.124
9	14.684	16.919	19.023	21.666	23.589	27.877
10	15.987	18.307	20.483	23.209	25.188	29.588
11	17.275	19.675	21.920	24.725	26.757	31.264
12	18.549	21.026	23.337	26.217	28.300	32.909
13	19.812	22.362	24.736	27.688	29.819	34.528
14	21.064	23.685	26.119	29.141	31.319	36.123
15	22.307	24.996	27.488	30.578	32.801	37.697
16	23.542	26.296	28.845	32.000	34.267	39.252
17	24.769	27.587	30.191	33.409	35.718	40.790
18	25.989	28.869	31.526	34.805	37.156	42.312
19	27.204	30.144	32.852	36.191	38.582	43.820
20	28.412	31.410	34.170	37.566	39.997	45.315
21	29.615	32.671	35.479	38.932	41.401	46.797
22	30.813	33.924	36.781	40.289	42.796	48.268
23	32.007	35.172	38.076	41.638	44.181	49.728
24	33.196	36.415	39.364	42.980	45.559	51.179
25	34.382	37.652	40.646	44.314	46.928	52.620
26	35.563	38.885	41.923	45.642	48.290	54.052
27	36.741	40.113	43.195	46.963	49.645	55.476
28	37.916	41.337	44.461	48.278	50.993	56.892
29	39.087	42.557	45.722	49.588	52.336	58.301
30	40.256	43.773	46.979	50.892	53.672	59.703
31	41.422	44.985	48.232	52.191	55.003	61.098
32	42.585	46.194	49.480	53.486	56.328	62.487
33	43.745	47.400	50.725	54.776	57.648	63.870
34	44.903	48.602	51.966	56.061	58.964	65.247
35	46.059	49.802	53.203	57.342	60.275	66.619
36	47.212	50.998	54.437	58.619	61.581	67.985
37	48.363	52.192	55.668	59.893	62.883	69.346
38	49.513	53.384	56.896	61.162	64.181	70.703
39	50.660	54.572	58.120	62.428	65.476	72.055
40	51.805	55.758	59.342	63.691	66.766	73.402

Table C.2 (*continued*)

n degrees of freedom	α 0.900	0.950	0.975	0.990	0.995	0.999
41	52.949	56.942	60.561	64.950	68.053	74.745
42	54.090	58.124	61.777	66.206	69.336	76.084
43	55.230	59.304	62.990	67.459	70.616	77.419
44	56.369	60.481	64.201	68.710	71.893	78.750
45	57.505	61.656	65.410	69.957	73.166	80.077
46	58.641	62.830	66.617	71.201	74.437	81.400
47	59.774	64.001	67.821	72.443	75.704	82.720
48	60.907	65.171	69.023	73.683	76.969	84.037
49	62.038	66.339	70.222	74.919	78.231	85.351
50	63.167	67.505	71.420	76.154	79.490	86.661

$\mathbf{\Sigma}^{-1}$ (see Appendix A, paragraphs 5.3 and 5.4). The Cholesky factorization of $\mathbf{\Sigma}^{-1}$ is

$$\mathbf{\Sigma}^{-1} = \mathbf{T}\mathbf{T}^{\mathrm{T}},$$

which enables us to express Eq. (C.12) as

$$Z_n = [(\mathbf{X} - \mathbf{m})\mathbf{T}][(\mathbf{X} - \mathbf{m})\mathbf{T}]^{\mathrm{T}}. \tag{C.13}$$

The variable $(\mathbf{X} - \mathbf{m})\mathbf{T}$ is a linear function of $\mathbf{X}$ and is therefore MVN distributed with mean

$$E[(\mathbf{X} - \mathbf{m})\mathbf{T}] = \mathbf{mT} - \mathbf{mT} = \mathbf{0},$$

and covariance matrix

$$\mathrm{cov}[(\mathbf{X} - \mathbf{m})\mathbf{T}] = \mathbf{T}^{\mathrm{T}}\mathbf{\Sigma}\mathbf{T} = \mathbf{T}^{\mathrm{T}}(\mathbf{T}\mathbf{T}^{\mathrm{T}})^{-1}\mathbf{T} = \mathbf{T}^{\mathrm{T}}(\mathbf{T}^{\mathrm{T}})^{-1}\mathbf{T}^{-1}\mathbf{T} = \mathbf{I}.$$

Since Z_n is the sum of the squares of the elements of $(\mathbf{X} - \mathbf{m})\mathbf{T}$ and these elements are independent standard normal variables Z_n is given by an expression like Eq. (C.10) and it is therefore $\chi^2_{(n)}$ distributed.

Appendix D Some Definitions and Properties of Convex and Concave Functions

Convex Sets and Convex (Concave) Functions

1.1 A set $\mathscr{H}$ of points in $\mathscr{R}^n$ is *convex* if for any pair of points $\mathbf{x}^{(1)}$ and $\mathbf{x}^{(2)}$ belonging to $\mathscr{H}$ and for any real number α between zero and one, $\mathbf{x}^{(1)} + (\mathbf{x}^{(2)} - \mathbf{x}^{(1)})\alpha$ also belongs to $\mathscr{H}$; in geometric terms the line segment joining two points of the set also belongs to the set. Note that $\mathscr{R}^n$ is convex.

1.2 A function $y = F(\mathbf{x})$ $[\mathbf{x} = (x_1, \ldots, x_n)]$ of several variables is *strictly convex* (*concave*) if the following "chord above (below) the curve" property holds:

$$\text{Convex} \quad F[\mathbf{x}^{(1)} + \alpha(\mathbf{x}^{(2)} - \mathbf{x}^{(1)})] < F(\mathbf{x}^{(1)}) + \alpha[F(\mathbf{x}^{(2)}) - F(\mathbf{x}^{(1)})], \quad \text{(D.1)}$$

$$\text{Concave} \quad F[\mathbf{x}^{(1)} + \alpha(\mathbf{x}^{(2)} - \mathbf{x}^{(1)})] > F(\mathbf{x}^{(1)}) + \alpha[F(\mathbf{x}^{(2)}) - F(\mathbf{x}^{(1)})], \quad \text{(D.2)}$$

for every $0 < \alpha < 1$ and any pairs of points $\mathbf{x}^{(1)} \neq \mathbf{x}^{(2)}$.

1.3 If the strict inequality signs are replaced by inequality or equality signs, we say that $F(\mathbf{x})$ is convex (concave).

1.4 It immediately follows from the definition that changing the sign of a (strictly) convex function results in a (strictly) concave function. The converse is also true.

Since this result enables us to transform any property of convex functions into a parallel property of concave functions, for the rest of this appendix we shall restrict our attention to convex functions.

1.5 If Eq. (D.1), or the equivalent definition in paragraph 1.3, holds only between pairs of points belonging to a convex set $\mathscr{H}$, we say that F($\mathbf{x}$) is convex, or strictly convex, in that convex set. Note that since $\mathscr{H}$ is convex, $[\mathbf{x}^{(1)} + \alpha(\mathbf{x}^{(2)} - \mathbf{x}^{(1)})] \in \mathscr{H}$.

Differential Properties of Convex Functions

A proof of the following three results can be found in Avriel (1976):

2.1 The Hessian matrix of a continuously twice-differentiable function $F(\mathbf{x})$ in an open convex set $\mathscr{H}$ is positive semidefinite in $\mathscr{H}$ if and only if $F(\mathbf{x})$ is convex in $\mathscr{H}$.

2.2 If the Hessian matrix of a continuously twice differentiable function $F(\mathbf{x})$ in an open convex set $\mathscr{H}$ is positive definite in $\mathscr{H}$, $F(\mathbf{x})$ is strictly convex in $\mathscr{H}$. The converse is not true, however, since there are strictly convex functions whose Hessian is not positive definite ($y = x^4$ is strictly concave in $\mathscr{R}$ but $d^2y/dx^2|_{x=0} = 0$).

2.3 A differentiable function $F(\mathbf{x})$ is convex in an open convex set $\mathscr{H}$ if and only if

$$F(\mathbf{x}^{(1)}) + \nabla_x F(\mathbf{x}^{(1)})(\mathbf{x}^{(2)} - \mathbf{x}^{(1)})^{\mathrm{T}} \leq F(\mathbf{x}^{(2)}) \tag{D.3}$$

for any two points $\mathbf{x}^{(2)} \neq \mathbf{x}^{(1)}$ belonging to the set $\mathscr{H}$.

The same result with a strict inequality sign holds for strictly convex functions. Note that for functions of one variable, Eq. (D.3) can be rewritten as

$$\frac{dF(x^{(1)})}{dx} \leq \frac{F(x^{(2)}) - F(x^{(1)})}{x^{(2)} - x^{(1)}}.$$

In other words a differentiable function of one variable is (strictly) convex in an open interval $\mathscr{H}$ if and only if its first derivative is (strictly) increasing in $\mathscr{H}$.

Unimodality of Convex Functions

3.1 A function that is convex in an open convex set $\mathscr{H}$ cannot have a local minimum in $\mathscr{H}$ that is not also global in $\mathscr{H}$. This is proven by contradiction. Let $\mathbf{x}^* \in \mathscr{H}$ be a local minimum of $F(\mathbf{x})$ and assume that the statement is false; then there is a point $\mathbf{x}^{(1)} \in \mathscr{H}$, different from $\mathbf{x}^*$, for which $F(\mathbf{x}^{(1)}) < F(\mathbf{x}^*)$; and because $\mathbf{x}^*$ is a local minimum belonging to the interior of $\mathscr{H}$, there is a point $\mathbf{x}^{(2)}$ defined as

$$\mathbf{x}^{(2)} = \mathbf{x}^* + \varepsilon(\mathbf{x}^{(1)} - \mathbf{x}^*)$$

that for some $0 < \varepsilon < 1$ satisfies $F(\mathbf{x}^{(2)}) \geq F(\mathbf{x}^*)$ and $\mathbf{x}^{(2)} \in \mathscr{H}$.

Since $F(\mathbf{x}^{(1)}) < F(\mathbf{x}^*) \leq F(\mathbf{x}^{(2)})$ with $\mathbf{x}^{(1)}, \mathbf{x}^{(2)} \in \mathscr{H}$, and

$$\mathbf{x}^{(2)} = \mathbf{x}^* + \varepsilon(\mathbf{x}^{(1)} - \mathbf{x}^*)$$

Eq. (D.1) (with a $\leq$ sign) cannot hold for extreme points $\mathbf{x}^*$ and $\mathbf{x}^{(1)}$ when $\alpha = \varepsilon$, and $F(\mathbf{x})$ could not be convex in $\mathscr{H}$.

3.2 A function that is strictly convex in an open convex set $\mathscr{H}$ has at most one local minimum $\mathbf{x}^*$ in $\mathscr{H}$. We prove this by contradiction too. Assume that $\mathbf{x}^{(1)} \in \mathscr{H}$ is another local minimum; then by paragraph 3.1, $F(\mathbf{x}^{(1)}) = F(\mathbf{x}^*)$, and since for a sufficiently small but positive ε

$$F[\mathbf{x}^{(1)} + \varepsilon(\mathbf{x}^* - \mathbf{x}^{(1)})] \geq F(\mathbf{x}^{(1)})$$

($\mathbf{x}^{(1)}$ is a local minimum), condition (D.1) cannot be met with $\mathbf{x}^{(2)} = \mathbf{x}^*$ and $\alpha = \varepsilon$.

3.3 The gradient of a differentiable strictly convex function $F(\mathbf{x})$, defined in an open convex set $\mathscr{H}$, vanishes at most once in $\mathscr{H}$ and it it does so, that point $\mathbf{x}^*$ is the unique local–global maximum of $F(\mathbf{x})$ in $\mathscr{H}$.

If the gradient vanishes at $\mathbf{x}^*$, paragraph 2.3 ensures that $\mathbf{x}^*$ is a local minimum, which by paragraph 3.2 is unique and by paragraph 3.1 global.

Other Properties of Convex Functions

4.1 If $F(\mathbf{x}) = [F_1(\mathbf{x}), \ldots, F_m(\mathbf{x})]$ is a set of convex functions defined in a convex set $\mathscr{H}$, a linear combination of $F(\mathbf{x})$ with nonnegative coefficients

$$G(\mathbf{x}) = \sum_{i=1}^{m} \beta_i F_i(\mathbf{x}), \qquad \beta_i \geq 0, \tag{D.4}$$

is also convex in $\mathscr{H}$. Furthermore, if one of the functions $F_i(\mathbf{x})$ with a positive coefficient $\beta_i > 0$ is strictly convex, $G(\mathbf{x})$ is strictly convex.

These results are easily verified by entering with $G(\mathbf{x})$ into the definition of convex and strictly convex functions given in paragraphs 1.2 and 1.3.

4.2 If $\mathbf{Y} = (Y_1, \ldots, Y_m)$ is a vector-valued random variable and $F(\mathbf{x}, \mathbf{y})$ is a (strictly) convex function of $\mathbf{x}$ for every value of $\mathbf{y}$, $G(\mathbf{x}) = E_Y[F(\mathbf{x}, \mathbf{Y})]$ is a (strictly) convex function of $\mathbf{x}$.

This is seen by writing

$$G(\mathbf{x}) = \int_{y_1} \cdots \int_{y_m} F(\mathbf{x}, \mathbf{y}) F_Y(\mathbf{y})\, d\mathbf{y},$$

where $F_Y(\mathbf{y})$ represents the mass–density function of $\mathbf{Y}$, and entering with this expression into the definition of (strictly) convex functions given in paragraphs 1.2 and 1.3.

4.3 If $F(\mathbf{x})$ is a convex function of $\mathbf{x} = (x_1, \ldots, x_n)$, $\mathbf{A}$ is an arbitrary $m \times n$ matrix, and $\mathbf{y}$ is an m-dimensional row vector, then $G(\mathbf{y}) = F(\mathbf{yA})$ is a convex function of $\mathbf{y}$.

As with paragraphs 4.1 and 4.2, this is proven by entering with $G(\mathbf{y})$ into the definition of convex function given in paragraph 1.2.

References

Abramowitz, M., and Stegun, I. A. (1965). "Handbook of Mathematical Functions with Formulas, Graphs and Mathematical Tables." Dover, New York.

Albright, R., Lerman, S., and Manski, C. (1977). Preliminary report prepared for the Federal Highway Administration. Reprinted in Bouthelier (1978).

Anderson, T. W. (1958). "An Introduction to Multivariate Analysis." Wiley, New York.

Andrews, R. D., and Langdon, M. G. (1976). An individual cost minimizing method for determining modal split between three travel modes, *Transp. Road Res. Lab.* (*U.K.*) *TRRL Rep.* **698**.

Atherton, T. J., and Ben-Akiva, M. E. (1976). Transferability and updating of disaggregate travel demand models, *Trans. Res. Rec.* **610**, 12–18.

Avriel, M. (1976). "Nonlinear Programming: Analysis and Methods." Prentice-Hall, Englewood Cliffs, New Jersey.

Beesley, M. E. (1965). The value of time spent in traveling: Some new evidence, *Economica* **32**, 174–185.

Beilner, H., and Jacobs, F. (1972). Probabilistic aspects of traffic assignment, *Proc. 5th Intern. Symp. on the Theory of Traffic Flow and Transportation, Berkeley, 1971* pp. 183–194.

Ben-Akiva, M., and Lerman, S. R. (1978). Disaggregate travel and mobility choice models and measures of accessibility, *Proc. 3rd Intern. Conf. on Behavioral Travel Modelling, Adelaide, Australia* (in press).

Berkman, J., Brownstone, D., Duncan, G. M., and McFadden, D. (1977). QUAIL 3.0 User's Manual, Working paper, Dept. of Economics, Univ. of California, Berkeley, California.

Berkson, J. (1944). Application of the logistic function to bio-assay, *J. Am. Stat. Assoc.* **39**, 357–365.

Berkson, J. (1953). A statistically precise and relatively simple method of estimating the bioassay with quantal response, based on the logistic function, *J. Am. Stat. Assoc.* **48**, 565–599.

Blumenfeld, D. E., and Weiss, G. H. (1970). On the robustness of certain assumptions in the merging delay problem, *Transp. Res.* **4**, 125–139.

Bouthelier, F. (1978). An efficient methodology to estimate and predict with multinomial probit models: Applications to transportation problems, Ph. D. dissertation, Dept. of Ocean Engineering, Massachusetts Institute of Technology, Cambridge, Massachusetts.

Bouthelier, F., and Daganzo, C. F. (1979). Aggregation with multinomial probit and calibration of disaggregate demand models with aggregate data: A new methodological approach, *Transp. Res. B* **1**, **13B**, 133–146.

Burns, L. D., Golob, T. F., and Nicolaidis, G. C. (1976). A theory of urban household's automobile ownership decision, *Transp. Res. Rec.* **569**, 56–75.

Clark, C. E. (1961). The greatest of a finite set of random variables, *Oper. Res.* **9**, 145–162.

Daganzo, C. F. (1977a). Network representation continuum approximations and a solution of the spatial aggregation problem of traffic assignment, Working Paper 7702, Stochastic Traffic Assignment Project, Dept. of Civil Engineering, Univ. of California, Berkeley, California *Transp. Res. B* (in press).

Daganzo, C. F. (1977b). An algorithm for the spatial aggregation problem of traffic assignment, Working Paper 7701, Stochastic Traffic Assignment Project, Dept. of Civil Engineering, Univ. of California, Berkeley. California *Transp. Res. B* (in press).

Daganzo, C. F. (1978a). A closed form random utility model with error terms of different variances, unpublished research notes.

Daganzo, C. F. (1978b). Estimation of gap acceptance values, unpublished research notes.

Daganzo, C. F. (1979a). The statistical interpretation of predictions with disaggregate demand models, *Transp. Sci.* **13**, 1–12.

Daganzo, C. F. (1979b). Some properties of the trinomial probit model, unpublished research notes.

Daganzo, C. F., and Schoenfeld, L. (1978). CHOMP User's Manual, ITS Research Report UCB-ITS-RR-78-7, Institute of Transportation Studies, Univ. of California, Berkeley, California.

Daganzo, C. F., and Sheffi, Y. (1977). On stochastic models of traffic assignment, *Transp. Sci.* **11**, 253–274.

Daganzo, C. F., Bouthelier, F., and Sheffi, Y. (1977a). An efficient approach to estimate and predict with multinomial probit models, *56th Meeting Transp. Res. Board* (unpublished)

Daganzo, C. F., Bouthelier, F., and Sheffi, Y. (1977b). Multinomial probit and qualitative choice: A computationally efficient algorithm, *Transp. Sci.* **11**, 338–358.

Dial, R. B. (1971). A probabilistic multipath traffic assignment model which obviates path enumeration, *Transp. Res.* **5**, 83–111.

Domencich, T. A., and McFadden, D. (1975). "Urban Travel demand: A Behavioral Analysis." American Elsevier, New York.

Feller, W. (1968). "An Introduction to Probability Theory and Its Applications," 3rd ed., Vol. I, Wiley, New York.

Feller, W. (1971). "An Introduction to Probability Theory and Its Applications," 2nd ed. Vol. II, Wiley, New York.

Finney, D. (1971). "Probit Analysis." Cambridge Univ. Press, Cambridge, England.

Fishman, G. S. (1973). "Concepts and Methods in Discrete Event Digital Simulation." Wiley, New York.

Fleet, C. R., and Robertson, S. R. (1968). Trip generation in the transportation planning process, *Highw. Res. Rec.* **240**, 11–31.

Florian, M., and Fox, B. (1976). On the probabilistic origin of Dial's multipath traffic assignment model, *Transp. Res.* **10**, 339–346.

Hasan, I., and Talvitie, A. (1977). An equilibrium mode-split model of work trips along a transportation corridor, *Proc. World Conf. Transp. Res. Rotterdam, Holland*, pp. 129–135.

Hauser, J. R. (1978). Testing the accuracy, usefulness, and significance of probabilitistic choice models: An information theoretic approach, *Oper. Res.* **26**, 406–421.

Hausman, J. A., and Wise, D. A. (1978). A conditional probit model for qualitative choice: Discrete decisions recognizing interdependence and heterogeneous preferences, *Econometrica* **46**, 403–426.

Koppelman, F. (1974). Prediction with disaggregate models: The aggregation issue, *Transp. Res. Rec.* **527**, 73–80.

Koppelman, F. (1976a). Guidelines for aggregate travel prediction using disaggregate choice models, *Transp. Res. Rec.* **610**, 19–29.

Koppelman, F. (1976b). Methodology for analyzing errors in prediction with disaggregate choice models, *Transp. Res. Rec.* **592**, 17–23.

Kostiniuk, L., and Kitamura, R. (1978). Second order approximation of the utility function for aggregated choice alternatives, *57th Meeting Transp. Res. Board* (unpublished).

Lerman, S. R. (1975). A disaggregate demand model of urban mobility decisions, Ph.D. dissertation, Dept. of Civil Engineering, Massachusetts Institute of Technology, Cambridge, Massachusetts.

Lerman, S. R., and Ben-Akiva, M. (1975). A disaggregate behavioral model of auto ownership, *Transp. Res. Rec.* **569**, 34–55.

Lerman, S. R., and Manski, C. (1977). An estimator for the multinomial probit model, *56th Meeting Transp. Res. Board* (unpublished).

Lerman, S. R., Manski, C. F., and Atherton, T. J. (1976). Non-random sampling in the calibration of disaggregate choice models, Rep. No. 6-3-0021, U.S. Dept. of Transportation, Federal Highway Administration, Office of Highway Planning. U.S. GPO, Washington, D. C.

Lisco, T. (1967). The value of commuter's travel time: A study in urban transportation, Ph.D. dissertation, Dept. of Economics, Univ. of Chicago, Chicago, Illinois.

Manheim, M. (1979). "Fundamentals of Transportation Systems Analysis," MIT Press, Cambridge, Massachusetts.

Manski, C. (1973). The analysis of qualitative choice, Ph.D. dissertation, Dept. of Economics, Massachusetts Institute of Technology, Cambridge, Massachusetts.

Manski, C., and Lerman, S. (1977). The estimation of choice probabilities from choice-based Samples, *Econometrica* **45**, 1977–1988.

Marschak, J. (1960). Binary choice constraints on random utility indicators, *First Stanford Symp. Math. Methods in the Social Sciences*, Stanford, California, 1959, pp. 312–329.

McCarthy, G. M. (1969). Multiple regression analysis of household trip generation—A critique, *Highw. Res. Rec.* **297**, 31–43.

McFadden, D. (1973). Conditional logit analysis of qualitative choice behavior, *in* "Frontiers of Econometrics" (P. Zarembka, ed.), pp. 105–142. Academic Press, New York.

McFadden, D. (1974). The measurement of urban travel demand, *J. Public Econ.* **3**, 303–328.

McFadden, D. (1977). Quantitative methods for analyzing travel behavior of individuals: Some recent developments, *Peoc. 3rd Int. Conf. on Behavioral Travel Modelling, Adelaide, Australia* (in press).

McFadden, D., and Reid, F. (1975). Aggregate travel demand forecasting from disaggregate behavioral models, *Transp. Res. Rec.* **534**, 24–37.

McFadden. D., Talvitie, A., Cosslett, S., Hasan, I., Johnson, M., Reid F. A., and Train, K. (1977). Equilibration of travel demand and system performance: An application in a transportation corridor, *in* "Demand Model Estimation and Validation," Chapter 8. Institute of Transportation Studies Special Report UCB-ITS-SR-77-9, Univ. of California, Berkeley, California.

Miller, A. J. (1972). Nine estimators of gap-acceptance parameters, *Proc. 5th Int. Symp. Theory of Traffic Flow and Transp. Berkeley, California, 1971*, pp. 215–235.

Nicolaidis, G. C., and Murawski, C. A. (1977). Analysis of preference for mixed-mode transit, *Traffic Q.* **31**, 471–496.

Quarmby, D. A. (1967). Choice of travel mode for the journey to work: Some findings, *J. Transp. Econo. Policy* **1**, 273–314.

Rao, C. R. (1965). "Linear Statistical Interference and Its applications." Wiley, New York.

Rassam, P., Ellis, R., and Bennett, J. (1971). The *N*-dimensional logit model: Development and application, *Highw. Res. Rec.* **369**, 135–147.
Reid, F. A. (1978). Aggregation methods and tests, Institute of Transportation Studies Rep. No. UCB-ITS-RR-78-6, Univ. of California, Berkeley, California.
Richards, M., and Ben-Akiva, M. (1975). "A Disaggregate Travel Demand Model." Saxon House, Westmead, England.
Scarf, A. (1973). "The Computation of Economic Equilibria," Cowles Foundation Monograph 24.
Schneider, M. (1973). Probability maximization in networks, *Proc. 1st Int. Conf. Transp. Res.*, pp. 748–755.
Sheffi, Y. (1978a). Transportation networks equilibrium with discrete choice models, Ph.D. dissertation, Dept. of Civil Engineering, Massachusetts Institute of Technology, Cambridge, Massachusetts.
Sheffi, Y. (1978b). Estimating choice probabilities among nested alternatives, *Transp. Res.* (to appear).
Sheffi, Y., and Daganzo, C. F. (1978a). Another paradox of traffic flow, *Transp. Res.* **12**, 43–46.
Sheffi, Y., and Daganzo, C. F. (1978b). A unified approach to transportation forecasting: Hypernetworks and supply–demand equilibrium with disaggregate demand models, *Transp. Res. Rec.* (to appear).
Stein, F. M. (1967). "Introduction to Matrices and Determinants." Wadsworth, Belmont, California.
Stopher, P. R. (1975). Goodness-of-fit measures for probabilistic travel demand models, *Transportation* **4**, 67–83.
Stopher, P. R., and Meyburg, A. H. (1975). Behavioral Travel-Demand Models. "Urban Transportation Modeling and Planning." Chapter 16, pp. 273–317. Lexington. Massachusetts.
Talvitie, A (1973). Aggregate travel demand analysis with disaggregate or aggregate travel demand models, *Proc. Transp. Res. Forum* **14**, 583–603.
Tardiff, T. J. (1976). A note on goodness-of-fit statistics for probit and logit models, *Transportation* **5**, 377–388.
Theil, H. (1967). "Economics and Information Theory." Rand-McNally, Chicago.
Theil, H. (1969). A multinomial extension of the linear logit model, *Int. Econ. Rev.* **10**, 251–259.
Theil, H. (1971). "Principles of Econometrics." Wiley, New York.
U.S. Dept. of Transportation, Federal Highway Administration, Urban Planning Division (1975). "Trip Generation Analysis." U.S. GPO, Washington, D. C.
Versace, J. (1971). A review of the severity index, *Proc. 15th Stapp Car Crash Conf.* pp. 771–796.
Von Falkenhausen, H. (1966). Traffic assignment by a stochastic model, *Proc. 4th Int. Conf. Oper. Res.* pp. 415–421.
Warner, S. L. (1962). "Stochastic Choice of Mode in Urban Travel: A Study in Binary Choice." Northwestern Univ. Press, Evanston, Illinois.
Westin, R. (1974), Predictions from binary choice models, *J. Econometrics* **2**, 1–16.
Wilks, S. (1962). "Mathematical statistics." Wiley, New York.
Williams H., (1977). On the formation of travel demand models and economic evaluation measures of user benefits, *Environ. Plann. A* **9**, 285–344.
Wilson, A. G. (1973). "Urban and Regional Models in Geography and Planning." Wiley, New York.

Index

D

ECONOMIC THEORY, ECONOMETRICS, AND MATHEMATICAL ECONOMICS

Consulting Editor: Karl Shell

UNIVERSITY OF PENNSYLVANIA
PHILADELPHIA, PENNSYLVANIA

Franklin M. Fisher and Karl Shell. **The Economic Theory of Price Indices: *Two Essays on the Effects of Taste, Quality, and Technological Change***

Luis Eugenio Di Marco (Ed.). **International Economics and Development: *Essays in Honor of Raúl Presbisch***

Erwin Klein. **Mathematical Methods in Theoretical Economics: *Topological and Vector Space Foundations of Equilibrium Analysis***

Paul Zarembka (Ed.). **Frontiers in Econometrics**

George Horwich and Paul A. Samuelson (Eds.). **Trade, Stability, and Macroeconomics: *Essays in Honor of Lloyd A. Metzler***

W. T. Ziemba and R. G. Vickson (Eds.). **Stochastic Optimization Models in Finance**

Steven A. Y. Lin (Ed.). **Theory and Measurement of Economic Externalities**

David Cass and Karl Shell (Eds.). **The Hamiltonian Approach to Dynamic Economics**

R. Shone. **Microeconomics: *A Modern Treatment***

C. W. J. Granger and Paul Newbold. **Forecasting Economic Time Series**

Michael Szenberg, John W. Lombardi, and Eric Y. Lee. **Welfare Effects of Trade Restrictions: *A Case Study of the U.S. Footwear Industry***

Haim Levy and Marshall Sarnat (Eds.). **Financial Decision Making under Uncertainty**

Yasuo Murata. **Mathematics for Stability and Optimization of Economic Systems**

Alan S. Blinder and Philip Friedman (Eds.). **Natural Resources, Uncertainty, and General Equilibrium Systems: *Essays in Memory of Rafael Lusky***

Jerry S. Kelly. **Arrow Impossibility Theorems**

Peter Diamond and Michael Rothschild (Eds.). **Uncertainty in Economics: *Readings and Exercises***

Fritz Machlup. **Methodology of Economics and Other Social Sciences**

Robert H. Frank and Richard T. Freeman. **Distributional Consequences of Direct Foreign Investment**

Elhanan Helpman and Assaf Razin. **A Theory of International Trade Under Uncertainty**

Edmund S. Phelps. **Studies in Macroeconomic Theory, Volume 1:** ***Employment and Inflation.***

Marc Nerlove, David M. Grether, and José L. Carvalho. **Analysis of Economic Time Series:** ***A Synthesis***

Thomas J. Sargent. **Macroeconomic Theory**

Jerry Green and José Alexander Scheinkman (Eds.). **General Equilibrium, Growth, and Trade:** ***Essays in honor of Lionel McKenzie***

Michael J. Boskin (Ed.). **Economics and Human Welfare:** ***Essays in Honor of Tibor Scitovsky***

Carlos Daganzo. **Multinomial Probit:** ***The Theory and Its Application to Demand Forecasting***

in preparation

L. R. Klein, M. Nerlove and S. C. Tsiang (Eds.). **Quantitative Economics and Development:** ***Essays in Memory of T. C. Liu***

Giorgio P. Szengö. **Bank Asset Management:** ***A Portfolio-Theoretic Approach***